Exploring the Use of Metaverse in Business and Education

Jeetesh Kumar
Taylor's University, Malaysia

Manpreet Arora
Central University of Himachal Pradesh, India

Gül Erkol Bayram
Sinop University, Turkey

A volume in the Advances in
Social Networking and Online
Communities (ASNOC) Book Series

Published in the United States of America by
   IGI Global
   Information Science Reference (an imprint of IGI Global)
   701 E. Chocolate Avenue
   Hershey PA, USA 17033
   Tel: 717-533-8845
   Fax: 717-533-8661
   E-mail: cust@igi-global.com
   Web site: http://www.igi-global.com

Library of Congress Cataloging-in-Publication Data

CIP PENDING

Exploring the Use of Metaverse in Business and Education
 Jeetesh Kumar, Manpreet Arora, Gül Erkol Bayram
   2024 Information Science Reference

ISBN: 9798369358689 (h/c)
ISBN: 9798369358696 (s/c)
eISBN: 9798369358702

British Cataloguing in Publication Data
A Cataloguing in Publication record for this book is available from the British Library.

All work contributed to this book is new, previously-unpublished material.
The views expressed in this book are those of the authors, but not necessarily of the publisher.

For electronic access to this publication, please contact: eresources@igi-global.com.

Table of Contents

Detailed Table of Contents

Esra Anış, Department of Tourism Management, Adnan Menderes
University, Turkey
Ülker Çolakoğlu, Department of Tourism Management, Adnan
Menderes University, Turkey

This chapter of the book invites readers to step into a new world named "Metaverse" that transcends digital boundaries. Originating from the pages of a science fiction novel in 1992, the term has evolved from a mere concept into a transformative force affecting diverse sectors such as entertainment, business, and tourism. While it's a newer term for most people, it has an extensive history in games and movies. Moreover, the metaverse seems to be the next disruptive technology that will impact the tourists, hospitality, and travel industry in the following years by delivering immersive experiences in both physical and virtual worlds.

Kritika, Independent Researcher, India

The rapidly evolving technological space in 21st century traces to the development of novelty of the metaverse, a term first coined in 1992 by Neal Stephenson. Metaverse is defined as a 3D virtual cyberspace blending the physical and digital world, facilitated by the convergence between the internet and web technologies and extended reality (XR). The chapter aims to highlight the importance of metaverse by dividing into several sections dealing with introduction, history, pillars from the perspective of tech, socio-cultural, ethical, and environmental aspects, visionaries like Meta, Google, etc., learning environment, challenges, and future trends.

Chapter 3

Manjit Kour, Chandigarh University, India
Kavita Rani, Chandigarh University, India

This research explores the moral ramifications of the metaverse, a virtual environment where users can create and communicate. As consumers spend more time in the digital environment, worries about privacy and data security become more pressing, bringing up issues of data exploitation and cyberspace bullying. The study emphasises how virtual currencies and assets unintentionally create social inequalities and calls for ethical frameworks to guarantee equity. Issues with identity and representation in the metaverse, including those with authorization, authenticity, and identity theft, are discussed along with the mental health effects of extended virtual immersion. The study concludes by urging a responsible approach to the metaverse's evolution and highlighting the significance of comprehending and resolving ethical issues in order to put user welfare and ethical considerations first in the rapidly changing digital landscape.

Chapter 4

Muhammad Usman Tariq, Abu Dhabi University, UAE & University of
Glasgow, Glasgow, UK

Incorporating the Metaverse into trade and business represents a paradigm change, changing conventional tactics, and encouraging creative solutions. The Metaverse's revolutionary effects on branding, marketing, and e-commerce are examined in this abstract. It explores the development of virtual worlds, leading to the creation of the Metaverse and its pivotal role in modern trade. E-commerce experiences a tremendous shift in this virtual world, where virtual storefronts, immersive experiences, and 3D product displays boost sales and improve user engagement. Businesses looking to develop distinctive brand experiences have possibilities and problems as marketing and branding strategies adjust to virtual locations. Real-world case studies from the retail, entertainment, and hospitality sectors demonstrate successful Metaverse integration. These case studies provide insights into applications and consequences. Virtual commodities, digital real estate, and innovative monetization strategies are redefining the economic environment and affecting conventional revenue-generating strategies.

    Vaishali Dhiman, Central University of Himachal Pradesh, India
    Manpreet Arora, Central University of Himachal Pradesh, India

Entrepreneurs are gradually discovering the metaverse's immense potential as it evolves into a virtual environment in which users interact with digital domains and one another. This study aims to explain the tangled patterns of research, collaborations, and thematic trends at the nexus of the metaverse and entrepreneurial activities. Using Scopus database collection, this bibliometric analysis investigates the intellectual landscape of the metaverse and its ties with the entrepreneurial sector from 2005 to 2023. The key findings show that there has been a large increase in publications after 2020, indicating an increased interest in the metaverse's impact on entrepreneurship. Collaboration and the variety of documents demonstrate a thriving worldwide research community. Thematic maps depict interwoven themes, emphasizing key topics like big data, block chain, artificial intelligence, and virtual reality, as well as niche areas like human learning. This research contributes to a better understanding of the metaverse and its implications for entrepreneurship.

    Soni Rathi, Chandigarh University, India
    Praveen Kumar, Chandigarh University, India

In recent years, the term "HR analytics" and metaverse in HR have become prominent and have progressively been used in organisations as a systematic approach. Some organisations that have adopted the use of metaverse and analytics in their HR departments have been extremely successful. The current chapter strives to attain some objectives; namely, explore the meaning of HR analytics, its importance and benefits, the kinds of HR analytics, the meaning of metaverse, and the role of HR analytics and metaverse in employee engagement and employee turnover. This chapter will include a theoretical analysis to attain the mentioned objectives. The goal is to provide a holistic picture and discuss some aspects like definitions, importance, benefits, types, etc., under HR analytics and the aspects (meaning, role, and benefits).of the metaverse. The use of HR analytics and metaverse have reformed the performance of workforce and escalated efficiency in business, reforming the quality of recruitment, talent management, employee productivity, employee engagement, and diminishing employee turnover.

The analysis suggests that the application of the sustainability concept underpinning the framework of resilient branding (FRB) has a significant impact on business in contemporary markets, which is supported by the authors' prior narrative, examination, and systematic reflections. The study's practical application is to combine sustainable marketing to improve performance with the psychological capital theory, which emphasizes fostering optimism and personality where the system dynamic model for resilient branding and sigmoid action resilience of brand equity by Heise is used for better results. Future research should consider the suggested theories as worthwhile topics.

The advent of Industry 5.0 presents new challenges for the design of human communities that have the capacity to be both ecologically and economically sustainable. Industry 5.0 is characterized by its focus on human-centric business, as opposed to Industry 4.0, which prioritizes manufacturing and technology. Machine learning technologies have several applications and play a crucial role in both Industry 4.0 and 5.0. This chapter argues that for Industry 5.0 to really prioritize human needs, it is imperative that humans possess the ability to create, advance, and oversee reliable and morally sound artificial intelligence systems. To tackle this issue, the authors have established an AI ethical framework that aims to offer guidance on the ethical usage of AI in daily activities. The current study is based on the authors' previous research and is being further refined as part of continuing research to validate the proposed framework.

Chapter 9

Metaverse is a virtual environment where we interact with each other and the world around us. Metaverse integrates the physical environment with the digital environment. In this study, the author explored the extent to which different metaverse technologies have been disclosed in sustainability reports and integrated reports. For this, specific Indian companies have been selected from the Nifty 100 index that have made 'metaverse technologies'-related disclosures in these reports. Further, the sustainability reports of these companies have been extracted to analyse the content to see the extent to which metaverse technologies have been reported by major Indian industries. The study also attempts to highlight important internet of things (IoT), artificial intelligence (AI), and virtual reality (VR) technologies-based platforms, initiatives and projects initiated by Indian industries to improve their productivity and operational efficiency and ensure safety at the workplace.

The metaverse combines with reality and creates an alternate universe. The availability of technological advances enables us to perform new tasks or efficiently complete ordinary duties. The "metaverse," or extended reality, opens up fresh opportunities for fascinating telepathy as well as has the potential to simplify routine tasks. As much as these technologies assist us in this work, education, healthcare, consumption, and pleasure, they also pose several challenges. The chapter tackles the questions of why and when customers will accept an entirely integrated area for a variety of operations, such as buying things and making purchases of Banking services. Examining the potential of Metaverse banking, this study looks into interesting avenues for future development that will influence how financial environments change in virtual spaces. The research anticipates a financial transformation with a focus on Blockchain, virtual assets, smart contracts, decentralized finance (DeFi), and immersive technology.

Chapter 11

Nitika Sharma, Chitkara University, Punjab, India
Sridhar Manohar, Chitkara University, Punjab, India

The problem of intellectual property and legality in NFTs has gotten little attention thus far and requires additional research because of the increasingly digital nature of financial investments and the rapid growth of technology. Because NFTs are dynamic and ever-evolving and have an array of outcomes and impacts on digital ownership, technology, law, and various other aspects of society—both positive and negative—this chapter aims to examine NFTs in the context of the metaverse. The implications for digital intellectual property rights law will play a major role in this chapter. Research is required since previous studies have not sufficiently covered the rights of ownership of NFTs through digital intellectual property.

Chapter 12

Emre Yaşar, Isparta University of Applied Sciences, Turkey
Erge Tür, Istanbul Esenyurt University, Turkey
Eda Yayla, Bitlis Eren University, Turkey
Nesrin Aydın Alakuş, Suleyman Demirel University, Turkey

The primary objective of this study is to discern the role of the metaverse, specifically within travel agencies, and to unveil potential future trends in this context. Through an empirical approach, the research aims to contribute valuable insights into the practical implications and applications of the metaverse within travel agencies, shedding light on its evolving significance in the tourism sector. In general, it is seen that the opinions of travel agency employees about Metaverse are positive. As a result of the analysis, it was determined that Metaverse can make positive contributions to travel agency activities. It is also seen that the use of Metaverse may vary according to the profiles of the customers, but it is possible to provide a positive experience to the customers in general.

Chapter 13

Md. Tariqul Islam, Taylor's University, Malaysia
Jeetesh Kumar, Taylor's University, Malaysia
Siti Rahayu Hussin, Universiti Putra Malaysia, Malaysia
Foong Yee Wong, Universiti Putra Malaysia, Malaysia

A travel vlog is short for a travel video blog, which includes footage of the vlogger exploring different places, trying local foods, engaging in different activities, and interacting with the local culture. It plays a significant role in tourism by influencing and inspiring potential travellers. It is a powerful tool for promoting destinations, influencing travel decisions, and fostering a global community of adventure-seekers. Travel vlogs are commonly shared on video-sharing platforms such as YouTube and social media. This chapter delves into the evolutionary journey of travel vlogs, examining their roots in traditional word-of-mouth communication and their progression through electronic word-of-mouth (e-WoM), online consumer reviews (OCRs), and travel blogs. The chapter envisions the potential of virtual reality (VR) to redefine how travel stories are told and foster a deeper connection between creators and viewers. Finally, this study highlights the significance of travel vlogs in the tourism industry.

Chapter 14

Sridevi Nair, School of Business and Management, CHRIST University, India
Tanvi Tare, Incture Technologies, India

The Metaverse has been gaining importance, with businesses looking to adopt the same for processes ranging from onboarding to customer experience. The current study has been conducted to evaluate the impact of learner characteristics on motivation to participate in metaverse-based training programs across various organizations. Based on literature and theory, two main characteristics were identified: attitude towards the metaverse and experience with the technology. Data for the study was collected using a structured questionnaire and 103 responses were collected from employees belonging to various organizations in India. The analysis and interpretation of the data was done using statistical techniques through the tool of SPSS. The study found out that both the learner characteristics have a strong positive relationship with each other, and attitude towards metaverse has a stronger relationship with learner motivation than the experience of use. The findings suggest organizations focus more on the manner in which they should introduce metaverse at the workplaces and need to keep the employee attitude towards any kind of change; more of a technological change in mind when they are strategizing to implement metaverse-based training programs.

Chapter 15

Kadir Uludag, Shanghai Jiao Tong University Mental Health Center, China

The coronavirus pandemic has had a significant impact on academic settings, disrupting normal routines and limiting social interactions among students. In response to this challenge, educational systems have implemented temporary measures to improve the quality of education and communication in online learning environments.

While online learning communities have gained popularity, they often lack the immersive aspects provided by virtual reality (VR) and augmented reality (AR), resulting in decreased motivation and engagement compared to traditional classroom settings facilitated by web applications. This chapter aimed to explore how virtual academic environments, incorporating augmented reality elements, could improve educational outcomes by fostering social learning gains. By leveraging augmented reality features, virtual academic environments, including the Metaverse, have the potential to enhance academic productivity during situations like the coronavirus pandemic or future outbreaks by facilitating improved social interaction.

Preface

In the ever-evolving landscape of technology and human interaction, the metaverse concept has emerged as a focal point of exploration and innovation. As editors of this comprehensive reference book, *Exploring the Use of Metaverse in Business and Education*, we are thrilled to present a collection that delves deep into the multifaceted realm of the metaverse, examining its significance, applications, and implications across various domains.

In today's interconnected world, the metaverse stands at the intersection of virtual reality, augmented reality, artificial intelligence, and blockchain technologies. It offers immersive experiences and interconnects virtual realms that transcend traditional boundaries, shaping how we communicate, entertain, work, and learn. The COVID-19 pandemic has accelerated the adoption of digital solutions, further underscoring the metaverse's relevance in facilitating remote work, education, and social interaction.

This book is a testament to the growing importance of academic research in understanding and harnessing the potential of the metaverse. From exploring foundational technologies to investigating real-world applications, the contributions within these pages offer valuable insights into the metaverse's development and impact. Through interdisciplinary collaboration, researchers pave the way for innovation, set standards, and address ethical and technical challenges associated with this emerging technology.

We have structured this book to provide a comprehensive overview into four distinct parts. Part 1 introduces readers to the concept of the metaverse, tracing its historical evolution and examining current trends and future potential. Part 2 focuses on academic research, highlighting pioneering studies in metaverse development, human-computer interaction, security, and privacy. Part 3 explores industry applications and impacts, including the metaverse's role in business, education, society, and the economy. Finally, Part 4 offers insights into future directions and challenges, paving the way for further exploration and discourse.

Our goal in compiling this book is threefold: to attract the latest research contributions, to establish this publication as a significant resource within the field, and to stimulate growing interest among researchers, academicians, and practitioners. We believe that this book will serve as a valuable reference for academics, students, professionals, and policymakers seeking to navigate the complexities of the metaverse and its implications for the future.

We extend our gratitude to all the contributors who have shared their expertise and insights, helping to shape this compilation into a comprehensive resource. We hope that readers find this book both informative and inspiring as they embark on their journey into the fascinating world of the metaverse.

Chapter 1: Introduction to the Metaverse: Stepping Into the New World Beyond Digital Boundaries

Authors Esra Anis and Ülker Çolakoglu, both from Tourism Faculties in Turkey, invite readers to embark on a journey into the fascinating world of the metaverse. This chapter serves as a gateway into a concept that transcends digital boundaries, tracing its evolution from science fiction to its potential disruption in sectors like entertainment, business, and tourism.

Chapter 2: Embarking on Digital Frontiers of Metaverse

Ms. Kritika, representing the International Association of Engineers and WiCys India Affiliate, takes readers on a journey through the rapid evolution of the metaverse. The chapter defines the metaverse as a 3D virtual cyberspace blending physical and digital worlds, offering insights into its importance and future trends from various perspectives.

Chapter 3: Ethical Dilemmas in the Metaverse

Manjit Kour and Kavita Rani, both from Chandigarh University, India, delve into the moral complexities of the metaverse. This research explores concerns surrounding privacy, data security, and social inequalities exacerbated by virtual currencies and assets, advocating for ethical frameworks to ensure equity and user welfare.

Chapter 4: Metaverse in Business and Commerce

Muhammad Tariq from Abu Dhabi University, United Arab Emirates, explores the transformative impact of the metaverse on trade and business. Through real-world case studies, readers gain insights into how the metaverse revolutionizes branding, marketing, and e-commerce, reshaping conventional revenue-generating strategies.

Chapter 5: Current State of Metaverse in Entrepreneurial Ecosystem: A Retrospective Analysis of its Evolving Landscape

Vaishali Dhiman and Manpreet Arora, both from Central University of Himachal Pradesh, India, uncover evolving trends in metaverse research and entrepreneurship. Using bibliometric analysis, readers explore thematic trends and collaborations, contributing to a deeper understanding of the metaverse's implications for entrepreneurship.

Chapter 6: Role of Human Resource (HR) Analytics and Metaverse in Employee Engagement and Turnover Intention

Soni Rathi from Chandigarh University, India, examines the significance of HR Analytics and the metaverse in enhancing employee engagement and reducing turnover. Through theoretical analysis, readers gain insights into how these technologies reform workforce performance and talent management, improving business efficiency.

Chapter 7: The Resilient Brand Management Framework as a Responsive Business Strategy in the Industry 4.0 Era

Authors ASIK JAMADER, Santanu Dasgupta, and Govind Baibhaw from various institutions in India, explore the application of sustainability concepts in resilient brand management. They advocate for integrating sustainable marketing practices with psychological capital theory, fostering optimism and personality to improve business performance.

Chapter 8: Sustainable Development of Industry 5.0 and its Application of Metaverse Practices

Saumendra Das, Nayan Deep Kanwal, Udaya Patro, Tapaswini Panda, and N Saibabu from various institutions in India and Malaysia, delve into the challenges and opportunities of Industry 5.0. They propose an AI Ethical framework to ensure the responsible development and management of AI technologies in Industry 5.0, aiming to foster ethical AI applications in everyday life.

Chapter 9: Sustainability Reporting in the Metaverse: A Multi-Sectoral Analysis

Sunaina Rathore and Manpreet Arora from Central University of Himachal Pradesh, India, explores sustainability reporting in the metaverse. Through an analysis of Indian companies' disclosures related to metaverse technologies, readers gain insights into how these technologies foster sustainability across multiple sectors, impacting corporate reporting practices.

Chapter 10: Metaverse Banking 2.0: Future Trends and Challenges in Metaverse Banking Strategies

Saurabh Bhattacharya and Babita Singla from Chitkara Business School, Chitkara University, Punjab, India, explore the potential of Metaverse Banking. They anticipate a transformative financial landscape, examining future trends and challenges in banking strategies within virtual spaces, inviting readers to navigate the complexities of Metaverse Banking.

Chapter 11: Unlocking the Metaverse and Navigating Legal Implications in the NFT Landscape

Nitika Sharma and Sridhar Manohar from Chitkara University, Punjab, India, delve into the legal implications of NFTs within the metaverse. Through an exploration of digital intellectual property rights, readers gain insights into the dynamic impact of NFTs on technology, jurisprudence, and societal facets, underscoring the need for comprehensive legal frameworks.

Chapter 12: The Role and Future of Metaverse in Travel Agencies

Authors Emre Yasar, Erge Tür, Eda Yayla, and Nesrin Aydin Alakus from various universities in Turkey, examine the role and future trends of the metaverse within travel agencies. Through empirical insights, readers explore the potential contributions of the metaverse to travel agency activities, highlighting its positive impact on customer experiences within the tourism sector.

Chapter 13: Embarking on Virtual Journeys: The Evolutionary Dynamics of Travel Vlogs and the Integration of Virtual Reality

Md. Tariqul Islam, Jeetesh Kumar, Siti Rahayu Hussin, and Foong Yee Wong from various universities in Malaysia, explore the evolution of travel vlogs and the integration of virtual reality (VR). Readers gain insights into the role of travel vlogs in promoting destinations and fostering global communities of adventure-seekers, envisioning VR's potential to enhance travel storytelling within the tourism industry.

Chapter 14: Enhancing Instructional Effectiveness Using the Metaverse: An Empirical Analysis of the Role of Attitude and Experience of Participants

Sridevi Nair from Christ University, India, and Tanvi Tare from Incture Technologies, India, evaluate the impact of learner characteristics on motivation in metaverse-based training programs. Through empirical analysis, readers gain insights into the relationship between learner attitude, experience, and motivation, offering implications for instructional effectiveness in workplace settings.

Chapter 15: Use of Virtual Academic Environments During Coronavirus Epidemic

Author Kadir Uludag from Shanghai Jiao Tong University Mental Health Center, China, explores the use of virtual academic environments during the coronavirus epidemic. By examining augmented reality elements, readers discover how virtual environments can improve social interaction and engagement in educational settings, offering insights into leveraging technology for enhanced educational experiences during crises.

In concluding this edited reference book, "Exploring the Use of Metaverse in Business and Education," we reflect on our esteemed contributors' rich tapestry of insights and perspectives. Throughout its pages, this book has served as a portal into the transformative potential of the metaverse across various domains, from business and commerce to education and society.

As editors, we are deeply gratified by the diverse array of topics covered within this compilation, each shedding light on different facets of the metaverse's evolution and impact. Our contributors have provided a comprehensive overview of this burgeoning field, from the foundational technologies shaping virtual environments to the ethical considerations guiding their development.

One of the most striking aspects of this book is its interdisciplinary nature. Through collaborations across academia and industry, researchers have come together to explore the multifaceted dimensions of the metaverse, bridging gaps between theory and practice. This collaborative spirit underscores the collective effort required to navigate the complexities of emerging technologies and their implications for society.

As we look to the future, the metaverse will continue to play a pivotal role in shaping our digital landscape. Its potential to revolutionise how we work, learn, socialise, and conduct business is undeniable, offering opportunities and challenges for stakeholders across the globe.

We hope that this book serves as a valuable resource for academics, students, professionals, and policymakers seeking to deepen their understanding of the metaverse and its implications. The insights shared within these pages inspire further research, innovation, and dialogue, guiding us toward a future where the metaverse enriches lives and enhances human experiences.

In closing, we extend our heartfelt thanks to all the contributors who have shared their expertise and perspectives, as well as to our readers for their interest and engagement. We sincerely hope this book sparks curiosity, fosters collaboration, and contributes to the ongoing discourse surrounding the metaverse and its transformative potential.

Editors:

Jeetesh Kumar
Taylor's University, Malaysia

Manpreet Arora
Central University of Himachal Pradesh, India

Gül Erkol Bayram
Sinop University, Turkey

Chapter 1
Introduction to the Metaverse:
Stepping Into the New World Beyond Digital Boundaries

Esra Anış

https://orcid.org/0000-0002-6970-3180

Department of Tourism Management, Adnan Menderes University, Turkey

Ülker Çolakoğlu

Department of Tourism Management, Adnan Menderes University, Turkey

ABSTRACT

This chapter of the book invites readers to step into a new world named "Metaverse" that transcends digital boundaries. Originating from the pages of a science fiction novel in 1992, the term has evolved from a mere concept into a transformative force affecting diverse sectors such as entertainment, business, and tourism. While it's a newer term for most people, it has an extensive history in games and movies. Moreover, the metaverse seems to be the next disruptive technology that will impact the tourists, hospitality, and travel industry in the following years by delivering immersive experiences in both physical and virtual worlds.

INTRODUCTION

With the rapid advancement of technology in today's world, people's ability to switch between digital environments is also increasing. At the beginning of these developments is a term known as "Metaverse," that people often hear but cannot fully explore. Metaverse invites people to step into this new world that transcends digital boundaries. It encourages people to explore an area they may have heard of

DOI: 10.4018/979-8-3693-5868-9.ch001

but don't fully understand. This chapter aims to shed light on the intriguing world of the metaverse and encourages people to not only hear about it but also embark on a journey of discovery and understanding.

STEPPING INTO THE METAVERSE

In 2021, Mark Zuckerberg (the Chief Executive Officer of Facebook) informed the company's rebranding as "Meta." Zuckerberg asserted that the future landscape of the internet resides in the metaverse, a virtual world where individuals will engage in diverse activities such as living, working, shopping, and entertainment. However, the term's origin was first coined by science fiction author Neal Stephenson in 1992. In Neal Stephenson's science fiction novel "Snow Crash.", characters use digital avatars, similar to today, to explore the online world with goggles and "earphones." The central figure in the narrative, Hiro Protagonist, serves as a hacker and pizza delivery driver, with much of the story revolving around his endeavors to thwart a computer virus responsible for inducing real-world brain damage in metaverse users (Geraghty et al., 2022; Huddleston, 2021; Stephenson, 1992).

The Metaverse has an impact on various industries, including gaming, film, television, real estate, business, and tourism. This captivating realm has been prominently featured in numerous science fiction films, portraying narratives within this innovative reality where virtual and tangible experiences coexist. For example, notable cinema and television series that reflect the Metaverse include "Minority Report" (2002), "The Thirteenth Floor" (1999), "Ready Player One" (2018), "Free Guy" (2020), "Avatar" (2009), "Her" (2013), "The Matrix" (1999), "Lucy" (2014), as well as television series such as "Black Mirror" (2011-2019), "Person of Interest" (2011-2016), "Love Death + Robots" (2019-...), among others (Özyalvaç, 2023).

Following the rebranding of his company as Meta, Facebook CEO Mark Zuckerberg outlined a vision for an embodied internet, bringing the metaverse to the forefront. After this announcement, several technology companies have initiated metaverse projects, including notable entities such as video game franchises Fortnite and Roblox and technology giants Nvidia and Microsoft. Furthermore, digital asset investor Tokens.com purchased a virtual parcel of land in the Metaverse platform and Decentral for $2.4 million in crypto currency for this acquisition (Forbes, 2022).

Similar to Meta Platforms led by Zuckerberg, other companies are planning their metaverse strategies nowadays. Notably, significant players in the metaverse market, including Tencent Holdings, Nvidia Corporation, Microsoft Corporation, Byte Dance, Epic Games, Net Ease, Roblox Corporation, Nextech AR Solutions Corporation, Unity Technologies, The Sandbox, Lilith Games, Active Theory, and Decentraland, have made substantial investments in this emerging domain. According to a Grand View Research report, metaverse market investments will be worth $678.8 Billion by 2030. The metaverse market is also growing due to the ongoing adoption of Extended Reality (XR) technologies to enhance user experiences across diverse platforms. Furthermore, the growing demand for the Metaverse to purchase digital assets using crypto currencies is anticipated to drive the market significantly. The development and dissemination of Virtual Reality (VR), Augmented Reality (AR), and Mixed Reality (MR) devices are expected to propel market growth in the coming years (Bloomberg, 2023).

Historical Roots: From Snow Crash to Modern Realities

While the term metaverse is relatively new to many people, it holds a substantial history in Neal Stephenson's (1992) novel "Snow Crash" and after in video games. The first of these, in 1995, was CyberTown, an online community featuring three-dimensional (3D) chat rooms and virtual life gameplay. After, it laid the foundation for video games focused on virtual worlds and community building, such as Second Life (2003), Roblox (2006), and Minecraft (2011). These video games begin with each user creating an avatar that is a digital representation of their body and personality before immersing themselves in the virtual world and connecting with other users. Users access these diverse virtual platforms through game consoles, personal computers, VR headsets, and other devices. Some games try to combine virtual and physical worlds. Games like Ingress, Pokémon Go, and Harry Potter: Wizards Unite leverage smartphone features such as the camera, clock, gyroscope, and GPS to overlay the game environment onto the player's real-world surroundings, operating a mixed reality experience (Geraghty et al., 2022).

The metaverse isn't just about video games anymore; it has expanded into social experiences like musical performances and sporting events. For example, TikTok and music artist The Weekend hosted a live, interactive, and immersive concert in August 2020 that attracted more than 275,000 concurrent viewers (TikTok., 2020). Moreover, Fortnite, an online video game, has successfully organized numerous concerts within its virtual world. Rapper Travis Scott's concert reached 12.3 million concurrent users and 27.7 million unique users. Similarly, a concert by singer Ariana Grande in Fortnite allowed attendees to enjoy the experience while participating in mini-games such as racing and target practice (Nishijima, 2021). Even one of the most watched events on live television (the Super Bowl) joined the metaverse during the Super Bowl LVI when Miller Lite collaborated with the Decentraland (a three-dimensional virtual world browser-based platform) to host a virtual event (Chaturvedi, 2022; Geraghty et al., 2022).

The term "metaverse" is a composite of the Greek prefix "Meta" and the English word "universe." In Greek, "Meta" is commonly employed as a prefix denoting

Figure 1. Video: Life inside the metaverse (you can see the video by scanning the QR code)
Source: YouTube (2024a). https://www.youtube.com/watch?v=ZptPoWfH2nA

"after" or "beyond," a usage that transcends into the English language (Xrtoday, 2021; Çolakoğlu et al., 2023). The term was first coined by Neal Stephenson's science fiction novel, Snow Crash (Stephenson, 1992). Conceptually, it refers to the convergence of digital and physical universes, enabling users to seamlessly transition between them for purposes such as work, exploration of interests, education and training, healthcare, and social interaction (see Figure 1). It is still largely conceptual and not executed. Even in the field of gaming alone, there is clear proof of mainstream adoption by players. Scholars from different disciplines work closely together to define the structure of the metaverse, organize it, and visualize its future. Present iterations of the metaverse empower users to create their own avatars and explore other resources on digital platforms (Dwivedi et al., 2022, 2023; Koohang et al., 2023; Buhalis et al., 2023a).

The characteristics of Stephensons' metaverse are exemplified by its 3D nature, which serves as a metaphor for the real world. Moreover, accessible to users employing goggles akin to contemporary VR headsets, the metaverse offers a first-person perspective and endows users with partially customizable virtual avatars (Çolakoğlu et al., 2023; Xrtoday, 2021). Also, the metaverse exhibits features such as there are no limits or boundaries; there is no singular authority in control; it is always active and can't turned off; it has a functional economy similar to the real world; it provides an immersive sensory experience and, people can make real social connections (Metamandrill, 2023).

The metaverse constitutes a realm wherein real-time, multi-sensory social interactions can provide customers and businesses with more profound experiences

Figure 2. Layers of the metaverse
Source: Radoff (2021).

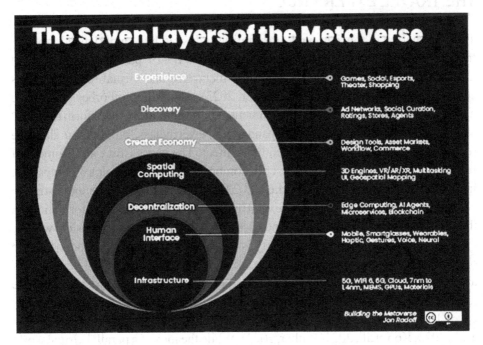

compared to traditional two-dimensional computer-mediated environments. Social interaction encompasses a multifaceted phenomenon, involving multiple dimensions of nonverbal and verbal behavior, numerous participants, dynamic contexts, and often technological mediation (Rather, 2023; De Jaegher et al., 2010). Gripping technologies within virtual worlds are designed to promote interactions and fulfill consumers' needs socially (Rather, 2023; Oh et al., 2023).

Jon Radoff, the author of the "Building the Metaverse" blog, has proposed a conceptual framework consisting of seven layers for the metaverse (see Figure 2). The first layer involves an experience of dematerialized reality, followed by the second layer, which focuses on the discovery and exploration of a vast and living world. The third layer emphasizes an economy where creators can thrive, while the fourth layer introduces spatial computing that blurs the boundaries between the real and virtual worlds. The fifth layer is characterized by a decentralized experience with interoperable components, followed by the sixth layer, which encompasses human interfaces allowing for direct interaction. The final layer is an infrastructure that creates a larger virtual network and interfaces (Metamandrill, 2023; Radoff, 2021).

TOURISM AND HOSPITALITY: REDEFINING THE TRAVEL EXPERIENCE

The international tourism and hospitality industry has experienced notable transformations, influenced not only by the COVID-19 pandemic globally but also by disruptive technologies such as the metaverse and virtual reality (Buhalis et al., 2023b; Shaheer et al., 2022; Rather, 2023). According to Forbes (2022), the metaverse, the futuristic digital environment, has the potential to transform the travel and hospitality industry hit by the pandemic. Nevertheless, building an alternate reality world will be a difficult accomplishment. The successful establishment of the metaverse necessitates robust collaborations among technology companies, innovators, and policymakers. Forbes (2022) predicts that it will be interesting to observe in the coming years to what extent the metaverse catalyzes transformations in the travel industry and blurs the boundaries between the digital and physical worlds.

The tourism and hospitality industry is attracting increasing attention to the role of the metaverse (Revfine, 2023a; Rather, 2023) as it enhances social interactions, a sense of presence, engagement, and emotions by encouraging tourists to promote tourism-based services and activities across a wide range of geographical locations beyond physical boundaries, especially during or after the COVID 19 pandemic (Cifci et al., 2023; Koo et al., 2022; Rather, 2023). While the idea of a parallel virtual world has been seriously mentioned for two decades, humanity's collective experiences with COVID-19 pandemic-related lockdowns, social distancing necessities, and the resulting feelings of disconnection and isolation have accelerated the collective imagination around creating an alternate reality. During this reality, people will act together and have shared experiences with others, especially potentially thousands or more people over some time at any given time. The metaverse could be a world where people could travel unrestricted whenever and wherever needed. It is a world where all kinds of experiences become possible and accessible (Gursoy et al., 2022: 3). Metatourism offers tourists the opportunity to experience different virtual destinations in an immersive way without leaving their current location or facing significant costs. This situation represents an important advantage in creating even partial equality in tourism (Demir, 2022: 546).

According to Buhalis et al. (2023a), the metaverse will become the next disruptive technology that will impact society in the forthcoming years by providing immersive experiences in both virtual and physical environments. Despite its current conceptual nature, the Metaverse combines the digital and physical universes, enabling users to seamlessly transition between them. Digital immersion opens avenues for temporal exploration, allowing users to virtually experience historical encounters, space explorations, or perilous natural events like volcanic eruptions. Users can explore immersive environments for work, learning, pursuing their interests, transactions,

Figure 3. The Ariva Wonderland NFT Metaverse (you can see the picture and video by scanning the QR code)
Source: *PortalCripto (2022) and YouTube (2024b).*

and socializing with others. This phenomenon is already conspicuous within gaming ecosystems, where players effectively engage with it. While still in the experimental phase, it is anticipated to bring about a revolution in the management and marketing of travel and tourism. The metaverse enhances destination awareness, positioning, and branding and facilitates coordination and management through digital twins. It presents opportunities to enhance trip planning, interaction, and participation, effectively influencing consumer behavior. The anticipation is that virtually visiting destinations will serve as motivation for actual travel rather than replacing it.

The reshaping of tourism by the metaverse appears to be feasible today. Thanks to VR and AR technologies, people will soon be able to travel almost from the comfort of their homes or experience sights and sounds they thought impossible. For instance, the Ariva Wonderland NFT Metaverse game (see Figure 3) is the latest technology offering virtual tours to real locations (such as the Pyramids, Eiffel Tower, Statue of Liberty, etc.). Includes travel, interaction, business, earnings, property, time travel and more. The Ariva Wonderland NFT Metaverse provides users with a fully immersive second-life experience, allowing them to travel, work, watch theater performances, take the stage, visit museums, interact with other users, go to the cinema, organize meetings and even get married in the Metaverse, and much more. The Ariva Wonderland NFT Metaverse, consisting of 7 galaxies and 7 craters, has a total of 49 land parcels connected to the continent across 160,000 different space areas. Ariva is a platform aiming to improve the inefficiencies of the current tourism industry by offering a new-generation, blockchain-focused ecosystem for blockchain tourism and the travel sector. Ariva hopes to revolutionize the global industry by incorporating the latest products and services into its ecosystem (PortalCripto, 2022).

Moreover, the metaverse holds the potential to revolutionize the digital universes and generate new prospects within the hospitality industry. Addressing the ever-evolving expectations of guests stands out as one of the hospitality sector's foremost challenges. There is a heightened demand for optimized guest expectations, encompassing seamless booking procedures, distinctive stay offerings, and valuable package deals. Given the tech-savvy nature of many contemporary travelers, the metaverse can reshape the hospitality industry and redefine the guest experience. The guest experience initiates with the research phase for accommodation, and if the metaverse is embraced, it can elevate the hotel booking process to a more advanced level. Customers can access information about their room reservations, including details such as room size, price, and features, and also with the metaverse, as they do now. However, with the integration of the metaverse, travelers can also immerse themselves in virtual three-dimensional hotel tours. Before check-in, individuals can transform into digital avatars, navigating the hotel property virtually. A three-dimensional walkthrough offers travelers an immersive, firsthand experience of hotel rooms, decor, and amenities, surpassing the capabilities of static prints or pictures. Such a tour provides guests with a tangible sense of confidence in their hotel decision-making process and has the potential to boost direct booking and conversion rates. In the realm of hotel management, guest satisfaction is the ultimate benchmark for success. Therefore, utilizing the metaverse to offer an interactive hotel room experience or an authentic local and cultural immersion can be a decisive advantage for hoteliers. This elevated level of service not only positions hoteliers ahead of competitors but also empowers guests with greater control over their upcoming travel experiences (Forbes, 2022).

The hospitality industry has many exciting opportunities, and businesses are gradually becoming aware of this reality. Restaurants, in particular, wield the ability to attract potential customers by offering immersive cooking experiences to incentivize reservations. Similarly, businesses in the guest accommodation sector can provide virtual tours and metaverse meetings. Within the tourism industry, various hospitality brands leverage the metaverse and NFTs for marketing and investment purposes. Examples include Hilton, Marriott Hotels, Mövenpick Hotel, Millennium Hotels, New Frontier, Coachella, Vueling, Seoul, Rendezverse, Qatar Airways, Emirates, Budweiser, Stella Artois, Domino's Pizza, CitizenM, Oveit, Lucky Block Casino, RendezVerse, Wendy's, Chipotle, Pinktada, and more (Revfine, 2023a; 2023b). In the future, tourists will increasingly choose metaverse tourism and hospitality experiences, services, and products as today (Buhalis et al., 2023b; Rather, 2023; Gursoy et al., 2022).

CONCLUSION

Last but not least, the metaverse is characterized as a seamless fusion of our physical and digital lives, creating a unified, virtual community where we can work, play, relax, transact, and socialize (Rather, 2023; Moy and Gadgil, 2022). The metaverse represents the next stage in the evolution of the internet, emphasizing the integration of both physical and digital experiences. To some users, the metaverse serves as an online realm designed to digitally replicate the real world. Conversely, for others, it signifies a shift in their interaction with the world through technologies such as three-dimensional computing, augmented reality (AR), virtual reality (VR), and blockchain. This shift aims to create novel immersive virtual experiences with the potential to overlay digital information onto our physical world. Furthermore, the metaverse can function as a space for leisure and recreation, providing an escape from the real world, or as a virtual domain where individuals can conduct their life's work (Geraghty et al., 2022). Therefore, it is seen that the metaverse provides a plethora of anticipation and remarkable opportunities for imagination and innovation to tourism customers as well as businesses. The combination of both virtual and physical worlds facilitates tourists to work seamlessly and generates huge challenges and opportunities for tourism destinations, hospitality businesses, and economic progress (Buhalis et al., 2023a; Rather et al., 2023). Although the metaverse is still in its initial stages, it is evolving as a disruptive/emerging future trend affecting the competitiveness of tourist destinations/sites and hospitality brands/firms (Rather, 2023).

In the future, prospective travelers may engage in virtual tours of destinations through the use of the Metaverse before making travel and accommodation arrangements, potentially replacing the need for physical travel for economic, business, and other considerations. The Metaverse technology also has the potential to substitute traditional tour guides, providing enhanced experiences at various attractions. This innovation could create a new business line in the hospitality and tourism industry. Both tourists and the tourism sector may face a dilemma, torn between the desire to immerse themselves in the virtual world and experience the physical world or embracing the Metaverse. To conclude, the Metaverse promises immersive travel experiences that transcend the limitations of traditional tourism, providing a glimpse into destinations through goggles or VR headsets for virtual exploration.

REFERENCES

Bloomberg. (2023). Metaverse Market Size Worth $678.8 Billion by 2030: Grand View Research, Inc. Bloomberg. https://www.bloomberg.com/press-releases/2022-03-09/metaverse-market-size-worth-678-8-billion-by-2030-grand-view-research-inc

Buhalis, D., Leung, D., & Lin, M. (2023a). Metaverse as a disruptive technology revolutionising tourism management and marketing. *Tourism Management, 97*(1), 1–11. doi:10.1016/j.tourman.2023.104724

Buhalis, D., Lin, M. S., & Leung, D. (2023b). Metaverse as a driver for customer experience and value co-creation: Implications for hospitality and tourism management and marketing. *International Journal of Contemporary Hospitality Management.* doi:10.1108/IJCHM-05-2022-0631

Chaturvedi, O. (2022). *Miller lite super bowl commercial running in the metaverse.* Techstory. https://techstory.in/miller-lite-super-bowl-commercial-running-in-the-metaverse/

Cifci, I., Rather, R., Taspinar, O., & Altunel, G. (2023). Demystifying destination attachment, self-congruity and revisiting intention in dark tourism destinations through the gender-based lens. *Tourism Recreation Research*, 1–17. doi:10.1080/02508281.2023.2190280

Çolakoğlu, Ü., Anış, E., Esen, Ö. and Tuncay, C.S. (2023). The evaluation of tourists' virtual reality experiences in the transition process to Metaverse. *Journal of Hospitality and Tourism Insights.* doi:10.1108/JHTI-09-2022-0426

De Jaegher, H., Di Paolo, E., & Gallagher, S. (2010). Can social interaction constitute social cognition? *Trends in Cognitive Sciences, 14*(10), 441–447. https://doi.org/.06.009 doi:10.1016/j.tics.2010

Demir, Ç. (2022). A Review on the Effects of Metaverse Technology on the Future of the Hotel Sector. *Journal of Tourism and Gastronomy Studies, 10*(1), 542–555.

Dwivedi, Y., Hughes, L., Wang, Y., Alalwan, A. A., Ahn, S., Balakrishnan, J., Barta, S., Belk, R., Buhalis, D., Dutot, V., Felix, R., Filieri, R., Flavi'an, C., Gustafsson, A., Hinsch, C., Hollensen, S., Jain, V., Kim, J., Krishen, A., & Wirtz, J. (2023). How metaverse will change the future of marketing: Implications for Research and Practice. *Psychology and Marketing.* doi:10.1002/mar.21767

Dwivedi, Y. K., Hughes, L., Wang, Y., Alalwan, A. A., Ahn, S. J., Balakrishnan, J., & Wirtz, J. (2022). Metaverse marketing: How the metaverse will shape the future of consumer research and practice. *Psychology and Marketing.* doi:10.1002/mar.21767

Forbes. (2022). Will The Metaverse Revolutionize The Hospitality Industry? *Forbes.* https://www.forbes.com/sites/forbestechcouncil/2022/01/10/will-the-metaverse-revolutionize-the-hospitality-industry/?sh=307cca4a25e7 (accessed 4 December 2023).

Geraghty, L., Lee, T., Glickman, J., & Rainwater, B. (2022). *Cities and the metaverse.* National League of Cities, Centre for City Solutions. https://www.nlc.org/wp-content/uploads/2022/04/CS-Cities-and-the-Metaverse_v4-Final-1.pdf

Gursoy, D., Malodia, S., & Dhir, A. (2022). The metaverse in the hospitality and tourism industry: An overview of current trends and future research directions. *Journal of Hospitality Marketing & Management*, 22(5), 1–8. doi:10.1080/19368623.2022.2072504

Huddleston, T., Jr. (2021). *This 29 year old book predicted the 'metaverse' and some of Facebook's plans are eerily similar.* CNBC. https://www.cnbc.com/2021/11/03/how-the-1992-sci-fi-novel-snow-crash-predicted-facebooks-metaverse.html

Koo, C., Kwon, J., Chung, N., & Kim, J. (2022). Metaverse tourism: Conceptual framework and research propositions. *Current Issues in Tourism.* doi:10.1080/13683500.2022.2122781

Koohang, A., Nord, J., Ooi, K., Tan, G., Al-Emran, M., Aw, E., Baabdullah, A., Buhalis, D., Cham, T., Dennis, C., Dutot, V., Dwivedi, Y., Hughes, L., Mogaji, E., Pandey, N., Phau, I., Raman, R., Sharma, A., Sigala, M., & Wong, L. (2023). Shaping the metaverse into reality: multidisciplinary perspectives on opportunities, challenges, and future research. *Journal of Computer Information Systems*, 63. https://www.academia.edu/94457087/

Metamandrill. (2023). *Metaverse Guide; Understanding The Basics Will Open Up a New World.* Meta Man Drill. https://metamandrill.com/metaverse/ (accessed 4 December 2023).

Moy, C., & Gadgil, A. (2022). *Opportunities in the metaverse: How businesses can explore the metaverse and navigate the hype vs reality.* JPMorgan.

Nishijima, I. (2021). Ariana Grande x Fortnite Rift Tour: the apogee of pop culture or just the beginning? *Medium.* https://medium.com/headlineasia/ariana-grande-x-fortnite-rift-tour-the-apogee-of-pop-culture-or-just-the-beginning-5052584f8d63 (accessed 2 February 2024).

Oh, H. J., Kim, J., Chang, J. J., Park, N., & Lee, S. (2023). Social benefits of living in the metaverse: The relationships among social presence, supportive interaction, social selfefficacy, and feelings of loneliness. *Computers in Human Behavior, 139*, 107498. https://doi.org/. 107498 doi:10.1016/j.chb.2022

Özyalvaç, B. (2023). İzlemeniz Gereken En İyi Metaverse Temalı Film ve Diziler. *Oggusto.* https://www.oggusto.com/teknoloji/en-iyi-metaverse-filmleri

PortalCripto. (2022). *Ariva Wonderland NFT Metaverse: Oyun ve VR Deneyimi Nedir?* Portal Cripto. https://portalcripto.com.br/tr/ariva-harikalar-diyar%C4%B1-nft-metaverse-oyunu-ve-rv-deneyimi-nedir/

Radoff, J. (2021). The Metaverse Value-Chain. *Medium.* https://medium.com/building-the-metaverse/the-metaverse-value-chain-afcf9e09e3a7.

Rather, R., Hollebeek, L. D., Loureiro, S. M. C., Khan, I., & Hasan, R. (2023). Exploring tourists' virtual reality-based brand engagement: A uses-and-gratifications perspective. *Journal of Travel Research.* doi:10.1177/00472875231166598

Rather, R. A. (2023). Metaverse marketing and consumer research: Theoretical framework and future research agenda in tourism and hospitality industry. *Tourism Recreation Research*, 1–9. Advance online publication. doi:10.1080/02508281.2023.2216525

Revfine. (2023a). *Metaverse Tourism: Overview, Benefits, Examples and More.* Revfine. https://www.revfine.com/metaverse-tourism/ (accessed 4 December 2023).

Revfine. (2023b). *Metaverse and the Hospitality Industry; The No. 1 Information Guide!* Revfine. https://www.revfine.com/metaverse-hospitality/

Shaheer, I., Nayak, N., & Polus, R. (2022). Challenges and opportunities for sacred journeys: A media representation of the impact of COVID-19. *Tourism Recreation Research*, 1–7. doi:10.1080/02508281.2022.2100195

Stephenson, N. (1992). *Snow crash.* Bantam Books.

TikTok. (2020). The Weeknd experience, an innovative TikTok live stream, draws over 2 million unique viewers. *The Weeknd Experience.*

Xrtoday. (2021). Unpacking meta: where did the word Metaverse come from? *XR Today.* https://www.xrtoday.com/virtual-reality/unpacking-meta-where-did-the-word-metaverse-come-from/ (accessed 4 December 2023).

YouTube. (2024a). *Life inside the Metaverse.* [Video]. Youtube. https://www.youtube.com/watch?v=ZptPoWfH2nA

YouTube. (2024b). *Ariva Wonderland Teaser #3.* [Video]. Youtube. https://www.youtube.com/watch?v=APa3Ka_3gTs

Chapter 2
Embarking on the Digital Frontiers of Metaverse

Kritika
🆔 https://orcid.org/0000-0002-1186-6032
Independent Researcher, India

ABSTRACT

The rapidly evolving technological space in 21st century traces to the development of novelty of the metaverse, a term first coined in 1992 by Neal Stephenson. Metaverse is defined as a 3D virtual cyberspace blending the physical and digital world, facilitated by the convergence between the internet and web technologies and extended reality (XR). The chapter aims to highlight the importance of metaverse by dividing into several sections dealing with introduction, history, pillars from the perspective of tech, socio-cultural, ethical, and environmental aspects, visionaries like Meta, Google, etc., learning environment, challenges, and future trends.

INTRODUCTION TO METAVERSE

The chapter delves into the various section associated with metaverse. The initial part consists of introduction and historical underpinnings. The second section deals with pillars of the metaverse from the perspective of technological, sociocultural, ethical and environmental aspects. The third section deals with various tech titans who gave rise to the concept of metaverse like meta, google etc. The fourth section deals with virtual learning environments and training and skill development requirement. The fifth section delves into the challenges faced in metaverse and lastly the upcoming future trends.

DOI: 10.4018/979-8-3693-5868-9.ch002

The evolution of technology at an astounding pace has continuously shaped and reshaped the way humans interact with the world around them. The term "Metaverse", coined by Neal Stephenson in his 1992 science fiction novel "Snow Crash" is a post-reality universe, incessant and tenacious (Mystakidis, 2022) multiuser environment which has permeated our cultural discourse, echoing through the conversations in technology circles, business boardrooms, and even casual discussions among individuals eager to comprehend the unfolding digital revolution where meta meaning beyond or transcending and universe meaning a particular sphere of activity or experience. The terminology is a convergence of virtual reality, augmented reality and other immersive technologies like blockchain for creating a seamless and interconnected digital world. The metaverse is the next gen technological transformation with the conceptualization of Digital Twin (Gadekallu et al., 2022) that accredit the implausible operation and administering of machines or vehicles with improvised visualization and harmonization to turn to one's advantage in both industrial and military sectors. The scholars had defined the term from the different perspectives (Zhao et al., 2022). Lee et al. defined metaverse as a 3D virtual cyberspace blending the physical and digital world, facilitated by the convergence between the Internet and Web technologies and <u>Extended Reality</u> (XR) (Lee et al., 2021). Duan et al. also categorized the related technologies of metaverse into three levels: infrastructure, interaction and ecosystem (Duan et al., 2021).

The metaverse characterised by several key elements (Park & Kim, 2022) that distinguishes from traditional online spaces. Firstly, it is captivating, providing users with a sense of presence and interaction in a computer-generated environment achieved through virtual reality (VR) and augmented reality (AR) technologies, enabling users to navigate and interact with the digital world in an additional and intuitive manner. Secondly, it is tenacious and dynamic where the interactions maintains a continuous existence, evolving and changing in real-time allowing for the creation of a persistent digital identity for users and transcending individual sessions. Thirdly, its congruency, allowing different worlds and platforms to be interconnected for a seamless transfer of assets, information and experiences across multiple domains fostering a sense of fluidity and continuity in virtual spaces.

The phrase "Metaverse," which has recently come to represent the future of immersive experiences and digital interaction (Park & Kim, 2022), has its roots in the long history of technological advancement, revealing the connections between innovations in technology, innovative ideas, and changes in society. From the inception of computer networks to the incoming of blockchain, virtual reality, augmented reality and artificial intelligence, the historical tour seeks to clarify the complex interactions that have risen the term to the forefront of modern discussion.

Historical Underpinnings

Earlier Virtual Spaces and Computer Networks

The inception of computer networks, particularly the establishment of ARPANET in the late 1960s (Hauben, 2007), is where the Metaverse got its start. The internet that we live in today was made possible by this innovative network that was created for military communication. Earlier, ARPANET allowed for text-based communication alone, raising the possibility of virtual interaction. With the growth of computer networks came the desire to administer virtual environments for cooperative interaction with Bulletin Board Systems (BBS) and Multi-User Dungeons (MUDs) (Dieterle, 2009) becoming popular in the 1970s and 1980s. Users could interact, converse, and even participate in basic shared virtual settings in these forerunners, despite their limitations, prepared the ground for the amalgamation of social reciprocity into cyberspaces.

The Idea of Cyberspace and Cyberpunk Literature

The cyberpunk literary style science fiction (Csicsery-Ronay, 1988) provided ideas for the Metaverse's intellectual underpinnings. The word "cyberspace" first appeared in William Gibson's ground breaking novel "Neuromancer" (1984), which described a virtual world in which users may traverse a worldwide network, sparking the speculation that the internet would develop into a spatial, tactile sensation by showing us a digital world that existed outside of reality. With its investigations of the human-machine interface and apocalyptic views, cyberpunk literature was a visionary for the immersive digital realms that laid the foundation for the integration of virtual and physical realities.

Online Gaming and Virtual Worlds

The examples of simulated universe and online gaming platforms that let players enter virtual worlds and communicate with other users using a shared virtual environment called Habitat, created by Lucasfilm Games in the 1980s, make avatars and interact with one another showed promise for long-lasting user generated virtual environments.

Massively Multiplayer Online Role-Playing Games (MMORPGs), like EverQuest and Ultima Online, became popular in the 1990s and 2000s along with offering immersive experiences (Cheok et al., 2004), and various social and economic facets that would eventually be essential to establish communities and common stories developing complex infrastructures that allows users to produce, possess and exchange items muddling the interlinkages between digital and real entities.

Developments in Augmented and Virtual Reality

Technological advancements in virtual and augmented reality have been the driving force behind the evolution. Although the first VR and AR trials took place in the 1960s, these technologies didn't really start to take off until the late 20th and early 21st centuries. With the augmentation of sophisticated VR headsets to users, the technology gained prominence in the 1990s with the firms like Oculus VR and HTC but exorbitant costs and technological constraints hindered wider implementation. Virtual reality is a technique that enables real-time manipulation and exploration of computer-generated 2D or 3D multimedia sensory environments (El Miedany & El Miedany, 2019). Virtual reality environment is an artificial or real-world environment represented by a computer that may be engaged with by outside parties, enabling immersion-based, first-hand active learning. Augmented reality is a non-captivating virtual reality system that works on the principle of augmenting reality in one way or the other to give users access to additional information about their circumambient (El Miedany & El Miedany, 2019).

Digital Ownership and Blockchain

The advent of blockchain (Swan, 2015) technology was a major factor in the evolution of metaverse with decentralised and secure characteristics of blockchain technology solving important concerns about digital possession, trust, and transparency. Traditional ideas of virtual assets were called into question by the concept of electronic scarcity, which was embodied by cryptocurrencies such as Bitcoin. The advent of non-fungible tokens (NFTs) (Wilson et al., 2022) on blockchain systems, especially Ethereum, transformed the concept of digital ownership in virtual environments creating digital art and virtual real estate, few of the unique digital assets that could be established, traded, and verified via NFTs, a move towards substantial digital rights.

Visionary Leadership

Thought leaders from a variety of professions have contributed innovatively and with visionary thinking to the establishment of the Metaverse as a transformational digital frontier with evolvement of technological discoveries and cultural influence foresee the possibilities of interlinked virtual worlds also shaping the destiny of the terminology.

Science fiction writer Neal Stephenson first used the word "Metaverse" in his 1992 book "Snow Crash," which described a virtual reality environment in which avatars communicate with digital components. Technologists and creatives were inspired by his investigation of digital identities, virtual economics, and societal ramifications, which established the foundation for further talks and advancements in the subject.

The CEO and co-founder of Meta, Mark Zuckerberg, is spearheading the inception of the Metaverse, which he sees as the next generation of the internet, the business making investments in haptic feedback, artificial intelligence, and virtual and augmented reality.

Virtual world and Metaverse implementation were pioneered by Philip Rosedale, the creator of Second Life and the founder of Linden Lab, to showcase the potentiality of virtual worlds for creativity, business, and socialisation, launched High Fidelity, a company that develops open-source software for virtual reality settings.

Tim Sweeney, founder and CEO of Epic Games, has transformed Fortnite into a social platform and the first successful embodiment of the Metaverse, hosts in-game concerts, events, and collaborations with global brands, allowing users to create, interact, and engage in diverse experiences.

The blockchain technology that powers the Metaverse has been greatly impacted by Ethereum co-founder Vitalik Buterin. By selling digital art as NFTs, cryptocurrency activists like Beeple have become well-known, questioning conventional ideas of ownership and dissemination and highlighting the impact of blockchain technology and cryptocurrencies on the Metaverse's economic environment.

The fusion of technological advancement and human ingenuity combining blockchain, virtual reality, augmented reality, and artificial intelligence pushes the limits of what is virtual or real, physical or digital traversing the unexplored region. The interoperability standards altering the perception of society that puts into question the conceptualisation of reality, property and interpersonal relationships, contingent upon tackling obstacles, promoting diversity and maintaining moral principles.

PILLARS OF METAVERSE

The complexity of metaverse delves into the foundations from variety of fields. The section delves deep into the various aspects of metaverse from the purview of technology, socioculture, ethical and environmental aspects.

Technological Aspect

Virtual Reality

The state of the art technology and a game changer, virtual reality (VR), submerges viewers in a computer-generated world, simulating reality and appealing to numerous senses in terms of how we work, study, play and communicate which

17

can be accomplished by utilising specialised hardware and software for an exciting engaging experience. The various hardware components such as VR headsets, input devices like motion controllers, gloves, or haptic feedback suits, and external sensors or cameras provide a 3D environment with high-resolution displays, while input devices track movements and gestures and sensory trackers use the position and orientation enabling them to interact with the virtual world. VR software encompasses applications, simulations, and content that define the virtual experience. It is used in gaming, education, healthcare, and simulations for immersive learning. VR content creation involves developing 3D environments and experiences, ranging from virtual tours to imagined landscapes in entertainment, art, and architecture. VR applications span various industries.

Augmented Reality

The use of virtual items and digital data overlayed on top of the physical world, augmented reality (AR) technology allows users a seamless integration of computer-generated content supplementing the physical world with applications in wide range of sectors including manufacturing, gaming, healthcare etc. It works by using sensors and cameras to encapsulate the real-world environment and superimpose computer-generated images or information onto the user's view with the use of smartphones, tablets, AR glasses, and specialized devices with possess powerful processors for processing data, allowing real-time analysis and rendering of digital content.

Haptic Feedback

Haptic feedback, or haptics (Xu, 2023), is a technology that uses physical stimuli to simulate tactile experiences, such as vibrations on a game controller or a smartphone screen to enhance user interaction and immerse in various industries, including gaming, virtual reality, healthcare, and automotive systems by developing an exoskeleton structure for virtual reality highly penetrating the cost and size of the device. It is a method used to simulate the sense of touch using various mechanisms, involving vibrations and force feedback for resistive forces against the user inputs, tactile feedback, and motion feedback for creating pressure points on surface providing a sense of movement. Haptic feedback technology faces challenges such as precision and realism, power consumption, standardization across devices and platforms, and seamless integration with other sensory technologies. Advancements aim to provide nuanced sensations and mimic real-world touch complexity. Power consumption is crucial for portable devices like smartphones and wearables. Standardization ensures consistent user experience across devices and platforms.

Artificial Intelligence

The integration of artificial intelligence (AI), a key component is causing a revolutionary evolution in the domain of metaverse, a communal virtual shared environment that integrates elements of social media, online gaming, augmented reality, virtual reality, and many more by improving the experience by impacting user interactions, content production, personalisation, security, and virtual environments' general performance. AI-driven intelligent avatars and virtual assistants are at the forefront of the metaverse experience, allowing users to interact in a natural and dynamic manner while Natural Language Processing (NLP) plays a crucial role in communication, enabling AI systems to understand and respond to human language, fostering more realistic and context-aware interactions including the generation of 3D models, landscapes, and entire virtual worlds, and allowing smart systems to adjust lighting, weather conditions, and other elements in real-time. However, ethical considerations and responsible AI governance while revolutionizing the metaverse are crucial for creating a secure, inclusive, and diverse metaverse which has the potential to redefine the connection, collaboration and experience of the digital realm.

Eye Tracking

Eye tracking technology (Clay et al., 2019), which records eye movements, is revolutionizing the metaverse by enhancing user experiences, interactivity, content creation, and analytics. It captures the user's gaze, directing attention, and adds a layer of natural interaction to virtual environments, demonstrating its immense potential. Eye tracking technology uses specialized sensors and cameras to monitor a user's eye movements, providing insights into their attention and engagement levels, using this information to enhance the metaverse experience, interactivity, immersion, and realism making it more user friendly. It also contributes to more realistic virtual environments by dynamically adjusting the depth of field based on the user's gaze, optimizing computational resources, reducing computational load on peripheral areas and allowing for higher-quality graphics and smoother experiences in resource-intensive applications.

It is a platform to gather insights into user preferences and interests, allowing for personalized content, advertisements, and recommendations inferring emotional states based on eye movements and expressions, enhancing communication and social interaction. It is valuable in training and simulation scenarios, such as medical training simulations, where it captures where a user is looking during a procedure enhancing the effectiveness of training modules and contributes to skill development and proficiency in various fields. Eye tracking data also generates valuable analytics and user insights, allowing developers to improve content design, user interfaces, and overall user experience, contributing to the ongoing refinement of the metaverse environment.

Blockchain

Blockchain technology is revolutionizing the metaverse, a digital space where users interact, create, and transact in virtual environments, providing transparency, trust, and new possibilities to the ecosystem, establishes ownership of virtual assets through non-fungible tokens (NFTs). It enables the establishment of decentralized identity systems, allowing users to have a single, secure digital identity that is portable across different environments enhancing user experiences and privacy concerns.

Cryptocurrency, often in the form of blockchain-based tokens, facilitates secure and transparent transactions allowing peer to peer trading and selling of virtual goods while smart contracts for automated transactions eliminate intermediaries and reduce fraud risk, bringing efficiency, transparency, and programmability to economic interactions.

Sociocultural Aspect

User Generated Content

User-Generated Content (UGC), a broad term is revolutionising the way we establish, dispense, and consume content on the internet (Duan et al., 2022), and has emerged as a key component of the digital environment which includes everything from social networking platforms to cooperative initiatives. The advent of user-generated content has revolutionized the way people express themselves innovatively with non-professional users establishing and sharing content like text, images, videos, and reviews, allowing users to share their thoughts, experiences, and creativity with a global audience. This democratization of creativity has led to the exploration of hidden talents, niche communities, and innovative storytelling forms. It is inherently social, fostering community building and engagement, with online communities centered around shared interests and hobbies while becoming a vehicle for amplifying diverse voices.

Inclusivity and Diversity

The metaverse, a virtual space for interaction and communication, holds immense potentiality for refurbishing our digital world. However, prioritizing inclusivity and diversity is crucial to imbibe a welcoming and representative environment where inclusivity respects individual differences, and diversity encompasses unique characteristics like race, ethnicity, gender, sexual orientation, and abilities. The current landscape in the digital realm has historically perpetuated inequalities, with certain groups underrepresented or marginalized, hindering the potential for a truly inclusive world. The challenges encountered in achieving the targets of inclusivity and diversity includes lack of diverse representation, unequal access to technology, and perpetuation of stereotypes and biases. To address these concerns, there is a need for inclusion of diverse avatars and identities to uniquely express themselves by avoiding reinforcing traditional stereotypes, active representation in design and development with accessible technology for promotion of equitable and just technological advancements to all, inclusive community standards, and education and awareness programs enforced through moderation and reporting mechanisms.

Education and Learning

A transformative paradigm shift in education, offering immersive, engaging, and inclusive learning experiences has its key advantages in inclusion of enhanced immersive learning environments, personalized learning paths, global collaboration, interactive 3D learning resources, inclusive learning environments, career readiness through simulations, and continuous lifelong learning. Global collaboration and connectivity as a possibility of virtual classrooms and collaborative spaces foster a sense of global community, promoting cross-cultural understanding and preparing students for a connected world with interactive 3D learning resources, such as 3D models, interactive simulations, and virtual experiments making learning tangible.

Contrary to the benefits of the neo world technologies, there also exists challenges which include addressing concerns about screen time and its negative impacts on physical and mental well-being. Successful integration requires collaboration between educators, policymakers, and technology developers to develop standards, guidelines, and ethical frameworks for responsible and effective use of metaverse technologies in educational settings.

Ethical Aspect

Digital Rights and Privacy Concerns

A virtual universe where digital and physical realities intersect, digital rights and privacy concerns become a crucial aspect. Key areas include promoting freedom of expression, ensuring equitable access to information, combating digital censorship, and ensuring digital inclusion with the need to balance, to curb hate speech and misinformation while promoting open and transparent communication channels along with addressing potential disparities to prevent digital divide and ensuring equitable access to the benefits in metaverse is an essentiality.

Intellectual Property Protection

The rapidly evolving digital space, poses significant challenges and opportunities for intellectual property protection (Kalyvaki, 2023) with the key areas, namely, virtual assets, digital art and design, and brand identity. The importance of recognizing and legalizing ownership and rights associated with these assets, balancing artistic expression with intellectual property rights, and protecting brand identity and trademarks to prevent unauthorized use or infringement along with the strategies to foster a respectful virtual environment, allowing brand owners to assert control over their virtual representations is critical in realm of metaverse. Obstacles in the Protection of Intellectual Property include:

Dispersion and Possession, addressing the problems that traditional IP ownership models have due to the decentralised nature of metaverse platforms, investigating distributed ledger and blockchain technology for transparent, unchangeable ownership verification.

Content Created by Users, navigating the metaverse's user-generated content difficulties and creating policies for the usage of third-party intellectual property (IP) in user works, putting in place mechanisms that strike a balance between user creativity and original work protection.

Transplatform Compatibility, taking into account how virtual assets and content work with one another on various metaverse systems and creating guidelines to guarantee uniformity in IP protection strategies across all virtual spaces.

The strategies for Intellectual Property Protection, includes the use of blockchain and smart contracts for transparent ownership records, automation of royalty payments and licensing agreements, digital watermarking and tracking technologies, collaboration with metaverse platform providers, and clear terms of service that aim to streamline IP transactions, prevent unauthorized use, and ensure the protection of virtual assets.

Governance

Strong governance procedures are essential as the metaverse grows and becomes more integrated into our virtual and real-world lives. The intricacies of metaverse governance, including topics like user behaviour, content control, monetary systems, and the development of inclusive and dynamic virtual communities (Fernandez & Hui, 2022) are its vitalities. Important Elements of Metaverse Governance are as follows:

Community Standards and User Behaviour, establishing unambiguous standards for user behaviour such as prohibitions on hate speech, harassment, and other wrongdoing by creating community guidelines that support a welcoming and constructive online community mode.

Moderation of Content, putting in place efficient content moderation procedures to deal with offensive or dangerous content while striking a balance between the dedication to free speech and a range of opinions and the necessity of moderation.

Regulation of the Virtual Economy, establishing laws governing virtual commodities, virtual property, and virtual currencies along with ensuring the fairness and transparency of financial transactions as well as eliminating fraud.

Protections for Identity and Privacy, putting in place safeguards to preserve user privacy and identities along with developing policies for the ethical gathering and use of user information.

The exploration of decentralized governance models, such as blockchain and DAOs (Goldberg & Schär, 2023), to distribute decision-making power among participants, ensuring transparency and accountability, and inception of tokenomics where tokens are introduced to incentivize positive behavior and participation in the processes. Various cross-platform collaboration and standards are promoting interoperability between platforms and developing common governance principles. The need for international collaboration is facilitated to address global challenges related to governance in metaverse, and alliances and partnerships are formed to share best practices. Legal and regulatory frameworks are being developed, to address unique challenges and define legal responsibilities for platform operators and users. Enforcement mechanisms are implemented, including penalties for violations and dispute resolution mechanisms, collaborating with legal entities to ensure the rule of law within virtual spaces.

Environmental Sustainability

Green Metaverse Networking

The idea of "green metaverse networking" (Zhang et al., 2023) aims to maximise the energy efficiency of each network component for long-term sustainable growth which seeks to address worries over the sustainability and energy usage of the technologies, including extended reality, blockchain, digital twins, and artificial intelligence. It seeks to enhance sustainable development in the Metaverse, minimise its negative effects on the environment, and maximise energy efficiency in order to create a more sustainable and ecologically friendly Metaverse which intends to lower the energy consumption of energy-intensive technologies like digital twins, artificial intelligence, blockchain, and extended reality, reduces the environmental effect and carbon footprint.

Several challenges (Zhang et al., 2023) faced include redefining Quality of Experience (QoE) through large-scale user studies, assessing its sustainability index, balancing system performance-energy consumption, designing new incentive schemes for green technology adoption, and ensuring system-level design. The shift towards human-centered design in communication systems requires redefining QoE through large-scale user studies. Assessing the overall sustainability is challenging due to the involvement of numerous technologies and stakeholders. Balancing system performance and energy consumption is crucial, as sacrificing performance can reduce energy consumption and carbon footprint.

Carbon Footprint

As the global market evolves, it is likely to lead to high carbon emissions accounting for nearly 0.5% of global emissions (Liu et al., 2023) and in order to quantify carbon emissions, it is correlated with the carbon intensity of electricity generation, which decreases due to an increasing share of clean energy. Estimating the correspondence, carbon emissions could reach as high as 115.30 Mt by 2030 and to achieve carbon neutrality, global CO_2 emissions should be reduced to 23.63 Gt by 2030.

TECH TITANS AND METAVERSE VISIONARIES

Of late, the idea of the metaverse, a communal virtual environment where people may communicate, fraternize, and build—has attracted a lot of interest, the broadening of the which has been aided and abetted by a number of tech behemoths.

Meta

Mark Zuckerberg, the CEO of Meta, formerly known as Facebook, is spearheading the metaverse campaign, emphasising the company's shift from a social media to a metaverse business. A major VR firm, Oculus VR bought by Meta in 2014, demonstrated the business's early fascination with immersive technology. Horizon Workrooms, which is a virtual reality conference platform for remote collaboration, is one of Meta's primary metaverse initiatives through which users may exchange data in a simulated three-dimensional environment, participate in virtual meetings, and communicate with co-workers via avatars along with AR glasses that combine the digital and real worlds.

Google

The Internet behemoth Google, well known search engine tool is incorporating virtual reality (VR) and augmented reality (AR) into everyday life demonstrating the interactions via handheld gadgets via ARCore and Daydream. With Google Cardboard, the company first unveiled VR gear. Later, turned its attention to augmented reality (AR), launching initiatives like Google Glass and AR mobile apps. Google's investment in immersive computing emphasises the confluence of virtual and physical realities, in line with the metaverse's guiding principles.

Microsoft

Microsoft is linchpin on integrating mixed reality technologies into the metaverse, with its HoloLens headset bridging the gap between physical and digital worlds, allowing the users to interact with holograms overlayed in the real world while offering unique opportunities for enterprise and consumer applications. Its adherence to mixed reality extends beyond hardware, including the Windows Mixed Reality platform, which provides developers with tools to create immersive experiences. Azure cloud services also play a crucial role in providing scalable infrastructure for virtual worlds, simulations, and collaborative platforms. The acquisition of Bethesda Softworks expedites to strengthen its position in the gaming and virtual reality landscape.

Tencent

Tencent, a Chinese conglomerate, plays a pivotal role in gaming and virtual reality global scenario with platforms like WeChat, it is well positioned to embark on its journey in metaverse reality. With the introduction of games like Honor of Kings and Fortnite lays unassailable stress on virtual environments and online multiplayer experiences where players can interact, compete, and socialize, forming the building blocks of the metaverse. The exploration of how blockchain technology and non-fungible tokens (NFTs) might be used in the metaverse to mould its future is varied, as seen by its involvement in the creation of virtual ecosystems and the incorporation of distributed ledger technologies.

Apple

Apple's investments in augmented reality, ARKit, and potential AR glasses market entry are indicating a keen interest in immersive technologies. The company's emphasis on user experience and ecosystem of devices could position it as a formidable force in the metaverse.

Amazon

Amazon, a global e-commerce giant, is exploring the virtual commerce opportunities with a vision to enable users to shop in virtual stores and interact with products in immersive ways aligning with the organisation's commitment to innovation and customer centric experiences.

The focus on immersive technologies, virtual worlds, and augmented reality along with a focus on user experience and virtual economies, form the foundation of the metaverse. An intricate and multifaceted concept, is set to evolve through collaborative efforts and cross-industry partnerships that will establish a transformative era by fading the boundaries between physical and digital worlds.

METAVERSAL LEARNING AND LABOUR

Virtual Learning Environment

Virtual learning environments (VLEs) (Rashid et al., 2021) have significantly transformed the educational landscape, enabling individuals to access, engage, and acquire knowledge through digital platforms, often facilitated by advanced technologies and the internet. Key components of VLEs that integrate various tools and resources to deliver the instructional content and collaboration exploring multifaceted aspects include online courses, multimedia content, discussion forums, assessment modules, and communication tools. Virtual learning environments' benefits include:

Flexibility and Accessibility: Virtual Learning Environments (VLEs) enable learners to access educational opportunities and materials from any place by removing geographical constraints. People may pursue learning at their own leisure and speed because to this improved accessibility, which also promotes diversity.

Interactive and Engaging information: The comprehension and engagement of educational information are improved by the use of multimedia components like movies, simulations, and interactive tests. Personalised and effective learning are achieved by VLEs through the use of these dynamic tools that accommodate a variety of learning styles.

Collaborative Learning Possibilities: Real-time communication tools, discussion boards, and group projects are some of the ways that virtual learning environments support collaborative activity. Interaction between students and teachers promotes a feeling a community and collaborative learning opportunities.

Real-Time Response and Assessment: Assignments and assessments can receive instant feedback with the help of assessment modules in virtual learning environments along with assisting students in understanding their development, allowing mentors to modify their pedagogical approaches in order to meet the requirements of individual students.

Cost-effectiveness: The cut in traditional educational costs correlating to physical facilities, printed materials, and travel expenditures increases the accessibility, affordability and scalability of high-quality education, particularly in settings with limited resources.

Virtual learning environments (VLEs) confront a number of difficulties, such as those related to technology, low student motivation and engagement, poor instructional material, data security and privacy, and inadequate professional development for teachers where students still struggle to obtain dependable connections to the internet and digital devices, which results in gaps in their access to educational possibilities. Leveraging face-face contact and physical classroom surroundings may have an influence on motivation and participation levels, careful design and execution are necessary to maintain learner engagement with high-quality instructional materials and pedagogical strategies are essential. Since VLEs gather and store sensitive student data, data security and privacy are particularly essential. Lastly, to fully utilise the endless opportunities of digital tools and platforms, teacher professional development programmes must be suitable.

A revolutionary force in the world of education, virtual learning environments provide never-before-seen levels of accessibility, engagement, and individualised instruction. There are still issues like the need for teacher preparation and technology limitations, but overall, VLEs have a good influence on international education. Future prospects for blockchain credentialing, the integration of augmented and virtual reality, and the continuous development of cutting-edge educational strategies are bright as long as technology keeps moving forward. Virtual educational environments have the power to transform education by embracing new trends and resolving obstacles to give students dynamic, inclusive, and productive learning experiences in the digital age.

Remote Work and Collaboration

The rise of digital technologies and global workforce connectivity has led to a significant shift in work, with remote work becoming a mainstream phenomenon. Technological advancements, particularly internet connectivity, collaboration tools, and cloud computing, have made remote work a viable option for employers and employees since the time of COVID-19 pandemic (Wheatley et al., 2021) in 2020 that forced organizations worldwide to adopt remote work models to ensure business continuity and employee safety.

The benefits offered to individuals, includes flexibility, improved work-life balance, reduced commuting stress, diverse talent acquisition, and increased autonomy and empowerment leveraging employees to structure their workdays according to their preferences promoting a healthier work-life balance. The elimination of daily commutes allows for better management of personal responsibilities and productivity during peak focus periods saving time and energy which can be redirected towards work, personal development or leisure for overall enhancement.

Organisations that adopt remote work models can save a lot of money since they can save expenses related to office space, utilities, and maintenance (Wheatley et al., 2021). Better financial efficiency results from this. Because they are not surrounded by office distractions and may customise their work settings, remote workers have claimed higher levels of productivity. As companies that value flexibility and work-life balance draw top talent, providing remote work choices also improves employee happiness and retention. Remote work models also help organisations become more resilient to unplanned interruptions, which puts them in a better position to continue operating during trying times.

Maintaining a strong corporate culture, bridging work-life borders, and communication obstacles are just a few of the difficulties (Prasad et al., 2023) that come with working remotely impacted by the problems of hardware access and internet connectivity. Face-to-face engagement is necessary to avoid misunderstandings, context loss, and feelings of isolation. It can be difficult to draw boundaries between one's personal and professional lives, which can result in burnout, overworking, and trouble "switching off." Organisations also need to take care of security and technological issues, such choosing the right tools for cooperation and protecting sensitive data.

Using cutting-edge platforms for document sharing, virtual meetings, and real-time communication like as Slack, Microsoft Teams, and Zoom is essential to effective remote collaboration. Maintaining team cohesiveness and avoiding misunderstandings need open lines of communication. Team cohesiveness is maintained and problems are quickly resolved when there are frequent virtual check-ins and meetings. Happy hours, cooperative projects, and online games are examples of virtual team-building exercises that may mimic in-person interactions. Employers should put employee well-being first by offering flexible work hours, mental health help, and a good work-life balance. Taking care of well-being issues improves performance and work satisfaction. Offering continual training and development opportunities enables staff members to keep abreast of market developments and make valuable contributions to remote collaboration. All things considered, these tactics assist businesses in cultivating a happy workplace and enhancing distant cooperation.

Training and Skill Development

The digital realm where virtual and augmented realities intersect, is revolutionizing training and skill development, offering a dynamic and immersive platform for training and skill enhancement, from virtual classrooms to simulated work environments allowing students to engage with content in three-dimensional, interactive ways for richer and more memorable learning experience. It also offers opportunities for professional development and upskilling, through virtual workshops, training sessions, and simulations enabling individuals to acquire new competencies and stay up to date in their respective fields reinforcing their understanding through hands on experience.

Through the use of immersive settings like virtual reality and augmented reality, metaverse-based training establishes dynamic learning spaces along with providing a varied and cooperative learning environment that improve knowledge retention and offer a genuine experience with AI algorithms analysing student data to customise content, pace, and evaluations, enabling personalised learning paths maximising the efficacy of training programmes. Global cooperation is yet another benefit which enables students from all over the world to work together on projects and exchange ideas, providing real time feedback and enhancing the learning process by enabling learners to adapt and develop in real time.

UNCHARTED WATERS: CHALLENGES IN THE EVOLUTION OF METAVERSE

The massively evolving networked virtual environment with a great deal of potential for human interaction, socialisation, and creativity faces several technological obstacles in the way of realising this digital paradise (Al-Ghaili et al., 2022; Uddin et al., 2023).

Limitations on Bandwidth and Connectivity

The requirement for reliable and fast internet access is one of the core issues facing the metaverse as virtual reality (VR) and augmented reality (AR) experiences are immersive, requiring humongous amounts of bandwidth in order to disperse large volumes of data in an efficient manner preventing lag, latency, and decreased overall performance caused due to improper internet connectivity, impeding the immersive experience and preventing a significant segment of the populace from engaging.

Cross-Platform Harmoniousness

The multiplatform ecosystem that encompasses a range of devices, operating systems, and applications does not provide flawless cross-platform interoperability. Completing a seamless transition between VR headsets, AR glasses, cell phones, and additional gadgets without compromising on the immersive experience consumers receive from each demands complex technological solutions and industry-wide standardisation.

Security and Privacy Issues With Data

Users create enormous volumes of data when they interact with the metaverse, including behavioural patterns, user preferences, and personal information arising the need to safeguard this sensitive data from unauthorised access, data breaches, and cyber attacks by using decentralised techniques like blockchain to mitigate the risks.

Creation and Quality of Content

It is a complex task to guarantee a wide variety of materials to develop and construct virtual worlds, 3D models, and interactive features, content producers want tools that are both powerful and intuitive calls for a robust content ecosystem essential to streamline the information creation process while upholding high standards of quality.

Latency and Interactions in Real Time

A smooth and engaging metaverse experience for applications like online gaming, virtual meetings, and team work depends an achieving minimal latency in real-time interactions. Efficient protocols and technologies are necessary to synchronise user actions, motions, and replies across remote servers and devices.

Infrastructure for Servers and Scalability

One of the biggest technological challenges today is ensuring that server infrastructure that can scale to support such a large user base which can possibly be aided through distributed computing methods, cloud computing, and edge computing.

Standards and Interoperability

The challenge of establishing standards for interoperability that allow for smooth communication and interaction between various components in a colossal network of platforms, apps and technological advances in order to avoid fragmentation and improve the user experiences across different virtual environments and apps.

Technological obstacles including restricted connection, the development of avatars, and data privacy must be overcome in order for the industry, standardisation organisations, and technology firms to improve working efficiency and build a unified digital space. The power to completely change the way we work, live, and interact in the digital age by tackling these issues and ushering in a neo era of virtual experiences that seamlessly integrate with the real world is the need of the hour.

METAVERSE ODYSSEY: NAVIGATING THE FUTURE TRENDS OF VIRTUAL WORLDS

The metaverse, a digital frontier is the interconnection of virtual spaces with unique characteristics and rules, allowing users to seamlessly navigate diverse digital realms. where virtual and physical realities intertwine, is undergoing rapid evolution that promises to reshape how we interact, work, and play. Emerging trends in the metaverse include the rise of the multiverse, decentralization and blockchain integration, AI-driven realism, social metaverse, extended reality convergence, digital economies and jobs, sustainability, and education revolution.

Interoperability becomes key, fostering a dynamic ecosystem where experiences can transcend individual virtual worlds. Decentralization on the other hand, is driving this trend, as blockchain technology, powered by non-fungible tokens (NFTs), enables true ownership of virtual assets, from digital real estate to in-game items. This transforms the economics of the metaverse and empowers users with a sense of ownership and authenticity.

AI-driven realism is redefining digital interaction by enabling more sophisticated social interactions with the help of blending AI algorithms with user centric behavior, creating more immersive and personalized experiences that includes intelligent NPCs in gaming and lifelike avatars with natural language processing capabilities.

Extended reality (XR) convergence, a transformation by merging virtual reality (VR), augmented reality (AR), and mixed reality (MR) into a unified experience, opening up new possibilities for education, entertainment, and productivity is redefining work and commerce, with virtual real estate, digital goods, and services becoming commodities with real-world value (Sunny, 2023).

Sustainability is a pressing concern, with green computing practices, energy-efficient servers, and eco-friendly virtual architectures gaining attention. The metaverse industry is increasingly aware of the need to balance technological innovation with environmental responsibility, paving the way for a greener digital future.

Education is poised to revolutionize by providing immersive and interactive learning experiences through virtual classrooms, educational simulations, and collaborative projects while integrating AI-driven tutoring, virtual field trips, and skill-building exercises to build a dynamic and personalized learning environment.

Ethical considerations and digital citizenship are also crucial as the metaverse expands, with challenges such as data privacy, digital identity, and virtual addiction requiring establishment of digital citizenship norms and guidelines.

The intention to build a feeling of community by creating a warm, approachable environment for individuals from all walks of life through decentralisation, sophisticated AI emancipation and ethical considerations, the metaverse is becoming a more dynamic and linked place. With this shift, portals to previously unimaginable possibilities and experiences will open up in a digital world where fantasy and reality collide. The metaverse's promise in the digital era is demonstrated by the efforts being made to create a metaverse that is inclusive, ethical, and sustainable.

REFERENCES

Al-Ghaili, A. M., Kasim, H., Al-Hada, N. M., Hassan, Z., Othman, M., Hussain, T. J., & Shayea, I. (2022). A review of metaverse's definitions, architecture, applications, challenges, issues, solutions, and future trends. *IEEE Access : Practical Innovations, Open Solutions*, *10*, 125835–125866. doi:10.1109/ACCESS.2022.3225638

Cheok, A. D., Hwee, G. K., Wei, L., Teo, J., Lee, T. S., Farbiz, F., & Ping, L. S. (2004). Connecting the real world and virtual world through gaming. In *Building the Information Society: IFIP 18th World Computer Congress Topical Sessions 22–27 August 2004 Toulouse, France* (pp. 45-50). Springer US. 10.1007/978-1-4020-8157-6_7

Clay, V., König, P., & Koenig, S. (2019). Eye tracking in virtual reality. *Journal of Eye Movement Research*, *12*(1). doi:10.16910/jemr.12.1.3 PMID:33828721

Csicsery-Ronay, I. (1988). Cyberpunk and neuromanticism. *Mississippi Review*, *16*(2/3), 266–278.

Dieterle, E. (2009). Multi-user virtual environments for teaching and learning. In *Encyclopedia of Multimedia Technology and Networking* (2nd ed., pp. 1033–1041). IGI Global. doi:10.4018/978-1-60566-014-1.ch139

Duan, H., Huang, Y., Zhao, Y., Huang, Z., & Cai, W. (2022, August). User-generated content and editors in video games: Survey and vision. In 2022 IEEE conference on games (CoG) (pp. 536-543). IEEE.

Duan, H., Li, J., Fan, S., Lin, Z., Wu, X., & Cai, W. (2021, October). Metaverse for social good: A university campus prototype. In *Proceedings of the 29th ACM international conference on multimedia* (pp. 153-161). ACM. 10.1145/3474085.3479238

El Miedany, Y., & El Miedany, Y. (2019). Virtual reality and augmented reality. *Rheumatology teaching: the art and science of medical education*, 403-427.

Fernandez, C. B., & Hui, P. (2022, July). Life, the metaverse and everything: An overview of privacy, ethics, and governance in metaverse. In *2022 IEEE 42nd International Conference on Distributed Computing Systems Workshops (ICDCSW)* (pp. 272-277). IEEE.

Gadekallu, T. R., Huynh-The, T., Wang, W., Yenduri, G., Ranaweera, P., Pham, Q. V., & Liyanage, M. (2022). Blockchain for the metaverse: A review. *arXiv preprint arXiv:2203.09738*.

Goldberg, M., & Schär, F. (2023). Metaverse governance: An empirical analysis of voting within Decentralized Autonomous Organizations. *Journal of Business Research*, *160*, 113764. doi:10.1016/j.jbusres.2023.113764

Hauben, M. (2007). History of ARPANET. *Site de l'Instituto Superior de Engenharia do Porto*, *17*, 1–20.

Kalyvaki, M. (2023). Navigating the Metaverse Business and Legal Challenges: Intellectual Property, Privacy, and Jurisdiction. *Journal of Metaverse*, *3*(1), 87–92. doi:10.57019/jmv.1238344

Lee, L. H., Braud, T., Zhou, P., Wang, L., Xu, D., Lin, Z., & Hui, P. (2021). All one needs to know about metaverse: A complete survey on technological singularity, virtual ecosystem, and research agenda. *arXiv preprint arXiv:2110.05352*.

Liu, F., Pei, Q., Chen, S., Yuan, Y., Wang, L., & Muhlhauser, M. (2023). When the Metaverse Meets Carbon Neutrality: Ongoing Efforts and Directions. *arXiv preprint arXiv:2301.10235*.

Mystakidis, S. (2022). Metaverse. *Encyclopedia*, *2*(1), 486–497. doi:10.3390/encyclopedia2010031

Park, S. M., & Kim, Y. G. (2022). A metaverse: Taxonomy, components, applications, and open challenges. *IEEE Access : Practical Innovations, Open Solutions*, *10*, 4209–4251. doi:10.1109/ACCESS.2021.3140175

Prasad, K. D. V., Vaidya, R., & Rani, R. (2023). Remote working and occupational stress: Effects on IT-enabled industry employees in Hyderabad Metro, India. *Frontiers in Psychology*, *14*, 998. doi:10.3389/fpsyg.2023.1069402 PMID:37063549

Rashid, A. H. A., Shukor, N. A., Tasir, Z., & Na, K. S. (2021). Teachers' Perceptions and Readiness toward the Implementation of Virtual Learning Environment. *International Journal of Evaluation and Research in Education*, *10*(1), 209–214. doi:10.11591/ijere.v10i1.21014

Sunny, B. (2023). An Analysis of Future Prospects of Metaverse. In *How the Metaverse Will Reshape Business and Sustainability* (pp. 17–25). Springer Nature Singapore. doi:10.1007/978-981-99-5126-0_3

Swan, M. (2015). *Blockchain: Blueprint for a new economy*. O'Reilly Media, Inc.

Uddin, M., Manickam, S., Ullah, H., Obaidat, M., & Dandoush, A. (2023). Unveiling the Metaverse: Exploring Emerging Trends, Multifaceted Perspectives, and Future Challenges. *IEEE Access : Practical Innovations, Open Solutions*, *11*, 87087–87103. doi:10.1109/ACCESS.2023.3281303

Wheatley, D., Hardill, I., & Buglass, S. (Eds.). (2021). *Handbook of research on remote work and worker well-being in the post-COVID-19 era*. IGI Global. doi:10.4018/978-1-7998-6754-8

Wilson, K. B., Karg, A., & Ghaderi, H. (2022). Prospecting non-fungible tokens in the digital economy: Stakeholders and ecosystem, risk and opportunity. *Business Horizons*, *65*(5), 657–670. doi:10.1016/j.bushor.2021.10.007

Xu, T. (2023). *What is Haptic Feedback?* Built In. builtin.com/hardware/haptic-technology

Zhang, S., Lim, W. Y. B., Ng, W. C., Xiong, Z., Niyato, D., Shen, X. S., & Miao, C. (2023). Towards green metaverse networking: Technologies, advancements and future directions. *IEEE Network*, *37*(5), 223–232. doi:10.1109/MNET.130.2200510

Zhao, Y., Jiang, J., Chen, Y., Liu, R., Yang, Y., Xue, X., & Chen, S. (2022). Metaverse: Perspectives from graphics, interactions and visualization. *Visual Informatics*, *6*(1), 56–67. doi:10.1016/j.visinf.2022.03.002

Chapter 3
Ethical Dilemmas in the Metaverse

Manjit Kour
ⓘ https://orcid.org/0000-0003-1043-3187
Chandigarh University, India

Kavita Rani
Chandigarh University, India

ABSTRACT

This research explores the moral ramifications of the metaverse, a virtual environment where users can create and communicate. As consumers spend more time in the digital environment, worries about privacy and data security become more pressing, bringing up issues of data exploitation and cyberspace bullying. The study emphasises how virtual currencies and assets unintentionally create social inequalities and calls for ethical frameworks to guarantee equity. Issues with identity and representation in the metaverse, including those with authorization, authenticity, and identity theft, are discussed along with the mental health effects of extended virtual immersion. The study concludes by urging a responsible approach to the metaverse's evolution and highlighting the significance of comprehending and resolving ethical issues in order to put user welfare and ethical considerations first in the rapidly changing digital landscape.

INTRODUCTION

Metaverse is the buzz word in both business and academia. Businesses are getting aware about the significance of metaverse (Kour & Rani, 2023). Although there isn't yet a consensus on what constitutes a metaverse, its development would require

DOI: 10.4018/979-8-3693-5868-9.ch003

the simultaneous development and integration of several supporting infrastructures, including 5G, virtual reality, holographic technology, and sophisticated graphic and data processors (Ball, 2020). Ball (2020) has made an effort to list the essential elements of a metaverse. A fully-fledged economy, unprecedented interoperability—that is, the capacity for users to transport their avatars and things from one location in the metaverse to another, regardless of who controls that location—and a span spanning both the physical and virtual worlds are among its requirements. Crucially, the metaverse will be governed by numerous entities rather than just one corporation; in other words, it will function as a "embodied internet"(Ball, 2020).

A new era with significant ethical consequences has begun with the emergence of the metaverse, a linked virtual reality realm where users can create, communicate, and exchange. This study examines the many ethical conundrums that arise in the metaverse by examining the relationship between morality, technology, and human behaviour. The study starts by looking at privacy and data security concerns because users are spending more and more time in a digital world where personal data is both widely available and easily compromised. The study looks into the possibility of user data exploitation, cyberspace bullying, and other emerging issues for metaverse.

The metaverse's impact on society and economy is another important issue that is being examined. As virtual economies grow, concerns about digital property rights, wealth distribution, and the possibility of economic inequality in this new digital frontier surface (Kour & Sharma, 2023). This study investigates how virtual currencies, assets, and platforms may unintentionally deepen social divides, calling for a reassessment of ethical frameworks to guarantee equity and inclusivity. The chapter also discusses the moral dilemmas posed by identity and representation in the metaverse. Authenticity, permission, and the possibility of identity theft or misuse are all questioned by the capacity to build and modify digital personas. It looks into the ethical issues surrounding the development and management of virtual identities as well as the psychological implications of prolonged immersion in virtual settings. The metaverse's governance and regulatory concerns are included in the ethical dimension. The lack of a generally recognised regulatory framework creates questions regarding responsibility, content regulation, and the avoidance of malevolent activity as this digital environment crosses traditional boundaries. The study evaluates the part played by international organisations, governments, and players in the metaverse in developing moral standards that strike a balance between user protection and innovation.

To sum up, this chapter offers a thorough analysis of the moral conundrums raised by the metaverse. By tackling concerns related to privacy, identification, socioeconomic impact, and governance, it hopes to add to the current conversation about the responsible advancement and application of this game-changing technology. Understanding and addressing these ethical issues will be essential to forming a

Figure 1. Privacy and data security concerns

digital environment where people's welfare and ethical concerns are given top priority as the metaverse develops.

Privacy and Data Security Concerns

Privacy and data security concerns are the major issues which needs to be sorted for providing safe and secure metaverse environment. Some major privacy and security concerns (Fig.1) are discussed in this section.

Data safety. In the metaverse, the user's alter ego, the avatar, creates a range of data: private information (voice, video, and message content), trade secrets of the corporation for professional use, and the personal information needed to keep services running. There is always security threat of data in the metaverse. Content and private information stored in virtual environments, metaverse platforms, and service systems could be falsified and leaked. An attacker may build a phoney avatar and use it for harmful purposes, or if a person is on the platform, their avatar's data, including video and voice recordings, could be compromised. The security features and management rules of the current system are insufficient to protect the virtual environment of the metaverse from cybercrime and cyberattacks; therefore, it has to be upgraded to better suit the demands of the metaverse. For example, it may be essential to implement more exact authentication, a dynamic data access control policy, or pseudonymize personal data. To lessen the effects of unauthorised access, sensitive data should also be encrypted and stored securely.

Privacy. Compared to traditional systems, metaverse systems have the ability to gather substantially more sensitive data, which can seriously compromise user privacy. As we know, HMDs with cameras always-on can capture footage in private areas, while every discussion is recorded by metaverse headsets with live microphones . Moreover, eye tracking technology has the ability to capture the user's gaze (Fineman & Lewis, 2018). As is the case with data security countermeasures, sensitive data needs to be more tightly safeguarded by encryption, dynamic access control, fine-grained authentication, and pseudonymization in order to prevent privacy issues. Furthermore, privacy obligations should be made clear and privacy plans for personal information gathered by metaverse platform providers should be devised. Falchuk et al. (2018) addressed privacy issues in the metaverse and offered recommendations, especially concerning avatars and other elements that contribute to the metaverse's constant evolution. They emphasised how important it is to protect user privacy and provided a number of alternatives, such as physically invisible avatars, teleportable avatars, and several cloned avatars that could identify patterns in user behaviour and behave similarly.

Software security. Above all, it is critical to strengthen the security of the metaverse platform itself. The metaverse is vulnerable to a variety of security risks, just like current software systems are (e.g., virus, ransomware, unpatched software, unsecured system architecture). In addition, there's a chance that children will see violent or pornographic content. For instance, hackers targeted Roblox, a metaverse that serves as an example. Robux is a virtual money used in the game that hackers sought after infecting the Roblox system with ransomware. Hackers also made offensive photos and racial statements visible, as well as causing video game characters to act indecently. Also, the application of augmented reality (AR) in real-world settings like industry and medical presents opportunity for malevolent attackers to compromise safety and human life. (Fineman & Lewis, 2018).

Hardware (device) security. Certain gadgets (such as VR headsets, HMDs, and Internet of Things devices) can be used to govern content access and offer authentication (Rogers et al., 2015; Schneegass et al., 2016). They could enable users to bypass the required authentication and authorization processes without needing to enter a username and password. Biometric data, such movement monitoring, may also be linked to devices. Therefore, if malicious attackers use security flaws in metaverse devices to hijack the administrator or user rights of the devices, they can compromise the central management server in metaverse systems, steal specific device information (like gaze information, metaverse activities, etc.), or remotely control the connected devices. Any device used with the metaverse platform must therefore be secured. At the absolute least, the devices need to follow strict security safeguards and receive patch updates. Additionally, because of the high CPU load and possible decrease in device performance, it is recommended to use a separate secure chip instead of the software module in the device when implementing security features.

Network security. Network connections—that is, connections made from the user's device to the metaverse platform—and connections made between avatars are typically not encrypted on metaverse platforms. Sniffing and spoofing attacks on the metaverse platform allow attackers to intercept messages or sensitive data. Consequently, a safe and effective cryptography technique must be used to encrypt network connections, contingent on the data and the metaverse context. Another major worry is availability, since security breaches like distributed denial of service (DDoS) or network outages would have a greater detrimental effect on metaverse services than they would on asynchronous online services. A business continuity and disaster recovery strategy should be in place if a system is essential to a business operation, as a DDoS attack, for example, could have unanticipated effects on a metaverse system.

Impact on Society and Economy

Individuals can converse and act in ways that would not be conceivable in the offline world thanks to avatars, which enable users to distance themselves from who they truly are and behave in ways that their users would never do in real life (Franks, 2011). Avatars' purported anonymity in the metaverse and their ability to empower real-life individuals may encourage the arbitrary use of power to further individual interests at the expense of the community as a whole. People might have their belongings taken away from them with no method to get them back, which could cause social unrest (Locke, 2003). Society has laws in place to deal with conduct that deviates from social norms for this reason. People would have to give up their autonomy to punish others on their own in exchange for society's promise to protect their other rights. merely when the rule of law is implemented equitably to all people and not merely to further the interests of a chosen few will society be able to establish stability (Locke, 2003). There is therefore a case to be made for the equivalent protection of an avatar's rights in the metaverse.

The metaverse presents new threats to people and society in addition to excitement and potential (The Conversation, 2022). There is a growing number of recorded incidences of harassment, sexual abuse, bullying, hate speech, racism, unregulated gambling, and many sorts of aberrant activities in the metaverse. In the metaverse, for example, the BBC News researcher reportedly saw grooming, racial comments, sexual content, and a threat of rape while assuming the identity of a 13-year-old girl. A British lady claimed in a December 2021 blog post that she had experienced verbal and sexual harassment from three to four male avatars in the sixty seconds after signing up for the virtual game Horizon Worlds, which was created by Meta (previously known as Facebook). There are various reasons why aberrant behaviours are frequent in the metaverse. Deviant behaviour appears to be largely caused by online disinhibition, a psychological condition in which people feel more at ease and inclined to participate in specific activities in an online setting (Cheung et al., 2021). The person who harassed her avatar sexually allegedly told the undercover reporter at the New York Times, "I don't know what to tell you." I'll do whatever I want because it's the metaverse.

Defamation

As previously mentioned, the metaverse would eliminate all restrictions on the right to free speech. However, as social media platforms demonstrate, this has the unintended consequence of giving people—also referred to as "internet trolls"—unrestricted access to post needless and false statements about other people or entities, damaging their reputation and goodwill in the process. Since the relationship between "the avatar and the user [...] is akin to that between a non-living business entity and a sole shareholder, where the entity is essentially an alter ego of the controller, an action [for defamation] may be sustainable on that basis," it is appropriate to draw a veil in such a situation (Chin, 2007). Based on it, a defamation lawsuit might be viable (Chin, 2007). It would be reasonable to accept the idea that avatars are just like a company's "alter ego" if we accept the theory that they are only conduits for people to engage in their activities in the metaverse and do not possess a distinct consciousness.

Moral Dilemmas

Governments, businesses, and individuals all prioritise sustainability (Whittaker et al., 2021). Divergent perspectives exist about the role that the metaverse plays in promoting sustainability. One the one hand, it is claimed that the metaverse will reduce carbon emissions by minimising travel by air, rail, and private vehicle for in-person meetings and sightseeing. In addition, by removing travel and other associated resource use, it would increase job productivity. From another angle, the metaverse will require high computational power and fast broadband speed in addition to the growing use of NFTs and user base. Power demand will rise as a result, mostly from non-renewable sources. Future researchers may undertake a cost-benefit analysis (CBA) and examine this matter from the perspectives of pricing and information management. How decision-makers, environmentalists, and information technology (IT) specialists comprehend and evaluate this intricate problem is another factor.

Identity Theft

Identity holds much greater significance in the metaverse. For instance, in account takeover, an individual may use another person's avatar to impersonate that person (Haihan Duan et al., 2021). In essence, this would place the genuine person at risk for liability in addition to reputational damage. These issues are exacerbated by bad actors' increased sense of impunity, as they believe they can get away with anything by using the metaverse's anonymity. One possible way to hold an avatar accountable for their acts in the metaverse is to register, or incorporate, their avatar.

Governance and Regulatory Concerns

Governance is necessary to run the metaverse and accomplish the safety objective. It should guarantee that decision-making powers, accountability, and incentives that promote appropriate behaviour are in place. The entire software ecosystem needs to be updated and maintained, which requires metaverse governance. The security and privacy flaws in the underlying technology may be carried over into the metaverse (Wang et al., 2022). Such vulnerabilities and breaches could jeopardise the entire metaverse, hence regular upgrades and modifications are required. Governance concerns in the metaverse include those pertaining to national laws, policies, consent and accountability, and private rulemaking, as well as the applicability of the rule of law (de Zwart & Lindsay, 2010).

It is crucial to ask if the laws and norms of the virtual world will apply to the digital one, as well as how national laws will be reflected in the metaverse. Will different domains have comparable rules and governance? The metaverse will be influenced by national laws and policies, at the very least, as the figure below illustrates. It's conceivable that the metaverse will alter over time as new groups join it, expectations shift, and novel concepts and experiences emerge. The administration of the metaverse will change along with it. Governance should guarantee the proper operation of the metaverse and the safety of community members from villains. Government rules must be followed; they cannot be avoided. Financial transactions in the metaverse will be governed by a wide range of laws, including those pertaining to consumer protection, cybersecurity, privacy, and money laundering. In the metaverse, it is simple to spy on, track, and log information about people. This surveillance extends beyond their purchasing habits and involves tracking their multiple identities, how they spend their time, and even when they are working. It is possible to monitor biometric data, like heart rate, gaze, and gait, which can provide a variety of personal details about a user's psychology (Renaud, Rouleau, Granger, Barsetti, & Bouchard, 2002). The governance pertaining to these kinds of data may differ in complexity. While many places focus their value propositions on utilising or even selling data, other spaces base their business models on protecting users' privacy.

Intellectual Property Rights

Property law stipulates that there are two owners in the "real" world when it comes to intellectual property rights, specifically when buying an artwork. First, the physical artwork itself can be used to determine ownership. Second, depending on the conditions of the transaction, the buyer might or might not be the owner of the artwork's intellectual property. However, exactly what form of ownership is involved in a digital art transaction? One could argue that in the metaverse, "ownership" is essentially just a licence or service provision. True ownership in these situations still belongs to the owner. This could imply, for instance, that the buyer cannot sell the item without the original owner's consent (Cheong,2022). With people and businesses shelling out huge sums of money to buy a "property" in the metaverse, virtual real estate has also turned into an NFT. One may claim that the metaverse is a place where land law principles can be applied. One challenge might be determining if trespassers on private property in the metaverse would be covered by laws in the actual world. If someone in the real world decided to take out a mortgage on their virtual home, laws would also need to change. In order to safeguard their users, platforms and services would have to incorporate both contractual safeguards like the terms of use and technological defences. Thus, the question becomes how companies and individuals should safeguard their copyright as the metaverse grows. Mason Rothschild, a digital artist, produced "MetaBirkins," which were NFT replicas of Hermes' well-known Birkin purses, as one instance. Then, Hermes wrote a cease-and-desist letter to Rothschild (Garno, 2022). Content owners and licensors must assess the necessary scope of monitoring such platforms and enforcing their rights, as the metaverse presents new avenues for intellectual property theft.

CONCLUSION

Despite a lot of research being done on metaverse technology, security and privacy in the metaverse have not gotten much focus. The metaverse, like social media platforms, presents significant privacy and security challenges. Hackers can collect biometrics—like voice inflections and facial expressions—as well as user behavior—like interactions and purchases—from other metaverse users in real-time. These data can then be used to identify the user. We must consider cybersecurity and privacy issues since the metaverse is interwoven with the cyber (or digital) world. Only then can we provide users with the necessary services in a safe and efficient manner. Cybersecurity and privacy should provide a range of measures, approaches, and solutions to ensure that people and systems are protected from a variety of risks and vulnerabilities (Zhang et al., 2022). It should be required to provide privacy and security in the metaverse. These are fundamental and necessary components that, in a metaverse setting, need to be continuously observed during the entire service process. That is, privacy and security should be considered and controlled through maintenance from the time of first deployment until decommissioning.

REFERENCES

Alspach, K. (2022). *Why the fate of the metaverse could hang on its security*. Venture Beat. https:// venturebeat.com/2022/01/26/why-the-fate-of-the-metaverse-could-hang-on-its-security/

Ball, M. (2020). *The Metaverse: What It Is, Where to Find it, Who Will Build It, and Fortnite*. MatthewBall.vc.

Bonifacic, I. (2021) 'Project Cambria' is a high-end VR headset designed for Facebook's metaverse. *Tech Crunch*. https://techcrunch.com/2021/10/28/project-cambria-is-a-high-end-vr-headset-designed-for-facebooks-metaverse/

Casey, P., Baggili, I., & Yarramreddy, A. (2021). Immersive virtual reality attacks and the human joystick. *IEEE Transactions on Dependable and Secure Computing*, *18*(2), 550–562. doi:10.1109/TDSC.2019.2907942

Cheong, B. C. (2022). Avatars in the metaverse: Potential legal issues and remedies. *International Cybersecurity Law Review*, *3*(2), 467–494. doi:10.1365/s43439-022-00056-9

Cheung, C. M., Wong, R. Y. M., & Chan, T. K. H. (2021). Online disinhibition: Conceptualization, measurement, and implications for online deviant behavior. *Industrial Management & Data Systems*, *121*(1), 48–64. doi:10.1108/IMDS-08-2020-0509

Chin, B. (2007). Regulating Your Second Life: Defamation in Virtual Worlds. *Brooklyn Law Review, 72*(4) 1303, 1334.

Creamer Media Engineering News. (2022) Meta safety Meta security. *Creamer Media Engineering News*. https:// www.engineeringnews.co.za/article/meta-safety-meta-security-metaverse-2022–02- 07.

Damar, M. (2021). Metaverse shape of your life for future: A bibliometric snapshot. *Journal of Metaverse*, *1*(1), 1–8.

de Zwart, M., & Lindsay, D. (2010). Governance and the global metaverse. In *Emerging Practices in Cyberculture and Social Networking* (pp. 63–82). Brill. doi:10.1163/9789042030831_005

Duan, H. (2021). Metaverse for Social Good: A University Campus Prototype. In *Proceedings of the 29th ACM International Conference on Multimedia*. ACM. <10.1145/3474085.3479238

Dwivedi, Hughes, L., Baabdullah, A. M., Ribeiro-Navarrete, S., Giannakis, M., Al-Debei, M. M., Dennehy, D., Metri, B., Buhalis, D., Cheung, C. M. K., Conboy, K., Doyle, R., Dubey, R., Dutot, V., Felix, R., Goyal, D. P., Gustafsson, A., Hinsch, C., Jebabli, I., & Wamba, S. F. (2022). Metaverse beyond the hype: Multidisciplinary perspectives on emerging challenges, opportunities, and agenda for research, practice and policy. *International Journal of Information Management*, *66*, 66. doi:10.1016/j.ijinfomgt.2022.102542

Falchuk, B., Loeb, S., & Neff, R. (2018). The social metaverse: Battle for privacy. *IEEE Technology and Society Magazine*, *37*(2), 52–61. doi:10.1109/MTS.2018.2826060

Fineman, B., & Lewis, N. (2018). *Securing Your Reality: Addressing Security and Privacy in Virtual and Augmented Reality Applications*. Educause. https://er.educause.edu/articles/ 2018/5/securing-your-reality-addressing-security-and-privacy-in-virtual-and-augmented-reality-applications

Franks, M. (2011). Unwilling Avatars: Idealism and Discrimination in Cyberspace. *Columbia Journal of Gender and Law, 20*(2), 224, 232.

Frenkel, S., & Browning, K. (2021). The Metaverse's Dark Side: Here Come Harassment and Assaults. *New York Times*. https://www.nytimes.com/2021/12/30/technology/metaverse-harassment-assaults.html

Ghosh, D. (2018). How GDPR will transform digital marketing. *Harvard Business Review Digital Articles*, 2–4.

Hunter, T. (2022) Surveillance will follow us into 'the metaverse,' and our bodies could be its new data source. *Washington Post*. https://www.washingtonpost.com/technology/ 2022/01/13/privacy-vr-metaverse/

ISACA. (2014). *Generating value from big data analytics* [White paper]. Information Systems Audit and Control Association. http://www.isaca.org/Knowledge-Center/Research/ResearchDeliverables/Pages/Generating-Value-From-Big-Data-Analytics.aspx.

Kour, M., & Rani, K. (2023). Challenges and Opportunities to the Media and Entertainment Industry in Metaverse. In M. Gupta, K. Shalender, B. Singla, & N. Singh (Eds.), *Applications of Neuromarketing in the Metaverse* (pp. 88–102). IGI Global. doi:10.4018/978-1-6684-8150-9.ch007

Kour, M., & Sharma, N. (2023). Security Issues in e-Banking. *2nd International Conference on Applied Artificial Intelligence and Computing (ICAAIC)*, Salem, India. 10.1109/ICAAIC56838.2023.10140397

Kshetri, N. (2021). *Cybersecurity management: An organizational and strategic approach.* The University of Toronto Press. doi:10.3138/9781487531249

Lau, P. L. (2022). The metaverse: three Legal issues we need to Address. *The Conversation.* https://theconversation.com/the-metaverse-three-legal-issues-we-need-to-a ddress-175891

Lee, L.-H., Braud, T., Zhou, P., Wang, L., Xu, D., Lin, Z., & Hui, P. (2021a). All one needs to know about metaverse: A complete survey on technological singularity, virtual ecosystem, and research agenda. *arXiv, 2110*, 05352. https://doi.org//arXiv.2110.05352 doi:10.48550

Locke, J. (2003). In I. Shapiro (Ed.), *Two Treatises of Government and A Letter Concerning Toleration* (pp. 107, 154–156). Yale University Press.

Merre, R. (2022). *Security Will Make Or Break The Metaverse.* NASDAQ. https://www.nasdaq.com/articles/security-will-make-or-break-the-metaverse

Nichols, S. (2022) Metaverse rollout brings new security risks, challenges. *Tech Target.*

Renaud, P., Rouleau, J. L., Granger, L., Barsetti, I., & Bouchard, S. (2002). Measuring sexual preferences in virtual reality: A pilot study. *Cyberpsychology & Behavior, 5*(1), 1–9. doi:10.1089/109493102753685836 PMID:11990970

Robertson, A. (2022). Meta is adding a 'personal boundary' to VR avatars to stop harassment. *The Verge.* https://www.theverge.com/2022/2/4/22917722/meta-horizon-worlds-venues-metaverse-harassment-groping-personal-boundary-feature

Rogers, C. E., Witt, A. W., Solomon, A. D., & Venkatasubramanian, K. K. (2015). An approach for user identification for head-mounted displays. *Proceedings of the 2015 ACM International Symposium on Wearable Computers*, (pp. 143–146). ACM. 10.1145/2802083.2808391

Schneegass, S., Oualil, Y., & Bulling, A. (2016). SkullConduct: Biometric user identification on eyewear computers using bone conduction through the skull. *Proceedings of the 2016 CHI Conference on Human Factors in Computing Systems*, (pp. 1379–1384). ACM. 10.1145/2858036.2858152

The Conversation. (2022). The metaverse offers a future full of potential – for terrorists and extremists, too. *The Conversation*. https://theconversation.com/the-metaverse-offers-a-future-full-of-potential-for-terrorists-and-extremists-too-173622.

The Verge. (2021). Mark in the Metaverse. *The Verge*. https://www. theverge. com/22588022/mark-zuckerberg-facebook-ceo-metaverse-interview

Vellante, D. (2022). Cybersecurity, blockchain and NFTs meet the metaverse. *Silicon Angle*. https://siliconangle.com/2022/01/17/cybersecurity-blockchain-nfts-meet-metaverse/

Wang, Y., Su, Z., Zhang, N., Liu, D., Xing, R., Luan, T.H., & Shen, X.J. a p a. (2022). A Survey on Metaverse: Fundamentals. *Security and Privacy*.

Whittaker, L., Mulcahy, R., & Russell-Bennett, R. (2021). 'Go with the flow' for gamification and sustainability marketing. *International Journal of Information Management*, *61*, 102305. doi:10.1016/j.ijinfomgt.2020.102305

Zhang, L.-J. (2022). MRA: Metaverse Reference Architecture. In B. Tekinerdogan, Y. Wang, & L. J. Zhang (Eds.), *Internet of Things - ICIOT 2021* (Vol. 12993, pp. 102–120). Springer International Publishing AG. doi:10.1007/978-3-030-96068-1_8

Chapter 4
Metaverse in Business and Commerce

Muhammad Usman Tariq

(iD) https://orcid.org/0000-0002-7605-3040

Abu Dhabi University, UAE & University of Glasgow, Glasgow, UK

ABSTRACT

Incorporating the Metaverse into trade and business represents a paradigm change, changing conventional tactics, and encouraging creative solutions. The Metaverse's revolutionary effects on branding, marketing, and e-commerce are examined in this abstract. It explores the development of virtual worlds, leading to the creation of the Metaverse and its pivotal role in modern trade. E-commerce experiences a tremendous shift in this virtual world, where virtual storefronts, immersive experiences, and 3D product displays boost sales and improve user engagement. Businesses looking to develop distinctive brand experiences have possibilities and problems as marketing and branding strategies adjust to virtual locations. Real-world case studies from the retail, entertainment, and hospitality sectors demonstrate successful Metaverse integration. These case studies provide insights into applications and consequences. Virtual commodities, digital real estate, and innovative monetization strategies are redefining the economic environment and affecting conventional revenue-generating strategies.

INTRODUCTION

The term "Metaverse" has recently gained significant attention as a complex and multifaceted concept with profound implications for human interaction and business. Coined by Neal Stephenson in his 1992 science fiction novel "Snow Crash," the Metaverse has evolved from a speculative idea to a distinct and transformative force

DOI: 10.4018/979-8-3693-5868-9.ch004

in technology and commerce (Stephenson, 1992). Advancements in technology have transformed the Metaverse from a mere conceptual space into a dynamic digital universe encompassing virtual and augmented reality, blockchain technology, artificial intelligence, and the 3D web.

This section aims to delve into the intricacies of the Metaverse, particularly exploring its definition, evolutionary trajectory, and overall significance in the landscape of business and commerce. Through a comprehensive review of relevant literature and scholarly works, this section seeks to provide a thorough understanding of the Metaverse, its origins, and the implications it holds for businesses in the contemporary digital era.

Definition of the Metaverse

At its core, the Metaverse refers to a collective virtual shared space that integrates elements of online entertainment, gaming, augmented reality, and virtual reality to create an immersive digital environment. It represents a convergence of various technologies that enable users to interact with each other and computer-generated environments in real time. Key components include virtual reality (VR), augmented reality (AR), blockchain technology, and artificial intelligence (AI) (Damer, 1997; Cai et al., 2020).

While the concept of the Metaverse originated in science fiction, it has transcended its imaginary roots to become a tangible and rapidly developing phenomenon. As Stephenson (1992) envisioned a digital realm where users could interact through avatars, contemporary definitions encompass a broader spectrum, acknowledging the integration of technologies that facilitate seamless, immersive, and interconnected digital experiences (Stephenson, 1992; Castronova, 2005).Comprehending the nuances of the Metaverse requires an examination of its technological foundations and the diverse ways in which it manifests in the digital landscape. This section aims to unravel the complexities of the Metaverse, drawing upon foundational works and contemporary research to provide a nuanced and updated definition.

Evolution of the Metaverse Concept

The evolution of the Metaverse concept is a fascinating journey that traces its roots from science fiction fantasies to the cutting-edge technological landscape of the present day. Stephenson's (1992) depiction of a virtual reality space in "Snow Crash" laid the conceptual groundwork, inspiring subsequent generations of technologists and visionaries. Over the years, advancements in computing power, internet infrastructure, and immersive technologies have propelled the Metaverse from speculative fiction to a tangible and evolving reality (Stephenson, 1992; Damer, 1997).

The trajectory of the Metaverse's development involves the convergence of various technological streams. Virtual reality, initially a niche interest, gained momentum with the advent of accessible VR headsets, creating immersive digital environments. Augmented reality, fueled by the proliferation of smartphones, expanded the possibilities of blending digital and physical realities (Milgram & Kishino, 1994; Azuma et al., 2001).

Furthermore, integrating blockchain technology brought unprecedented opportunities for secure and decentralized digital interactions within the Metaverse (Swan, 2015). Artificial intelligence, with its ability to enhance user experiences, personalization, and predictive analytics, has become a cornerstone in shaping the dynamic nature of the Metaverse (Cai et al., 2020).

This section provides a comprehensive overview of the Metaverse's transformative journey, highlighting key milestones, technological breakthroughs, and the convergence of various elements that have contributed to its contemporary conceptualization.

Significance of the Metaverse in Business and Trade

The Metaverse has emerged as a transformative force with significant implications for business and commerce. Its relevance lies in its potential to revolutionize traditional business models, redefine consumer relationships, and create innovative avenues for economic activities. As businesses increasingly recognize the valuable opportunities the Metaverse presents, strategic considerations and proactive engagement are crucial for those seeking to harness its true potential (Castronova, 2005).

One of the primary impact areas is e-commerce, where the Metaverse provides a platform for virtual marketplaces and immersive shopping experiences. Virtual real estate, another facet of the Metaverse, offers unique opportunities for property development and investment, shaping an intelligent economic landscape (Wan, 2019). The social nature of the Metaverse enables businesses to cultivate virtual communities, enhancing customer engagement and brand loyalty (Hsu et al., 2018).

Moreover, the Metaverse serves as a business training ground, offering simulation environments for employee training, skill development, and collaborative problem-solving (Rosenberg, 2019). The potential applications are diverse, from virtual conferences and expos to team-building activities conducted in immersive digital spaces.

This section aims to elucidate the multi-layered significance of the Metaverse in the realm of business and commerce, drawing on empirical studies, industry reports, and scholarly insights to provide a thorough understanding of the transformative potential it holds for the business landscape (Tariq, 2024).

Historical Context

The genuine development of the Metaverse traces its origins from speculative ideas in science fiction to the dynamic and rapidly progressing technological landscape of the present day. This section aims to provide an in-depth analysis of the historical context of the Metaverse, encompassing the concept's origins, key technological milestones that paved the way, and the early applications of this innovative idea in business.

Genesis of the Metaverse Concept

The genesis of the Metaverse concept can be traced back to Neal Stephenson's seminal 1992 science fiction novel, "Snow Crash." In this groundbreaking narrative, Stephenson introduced a virtual reality space where users, represented by avatars, could interact with one another and navigate a digital landscape. The term "Metaverse" was coined within the pages of this influential work, laying the foundation for subsequent explorations and real-world manifestations (Stephenson, 1992).

Stephenson's visionary depiction inspired a generation of technologists and scholars, shaping the discourse around virtual worlds and digital realms. The idea of a shared, immersive space where individuals could transcend physical boundaries captured the imagination of researchers and developers, paving the way for the exploration of technologies that could bring the Metaverse from fiction to reality (Damer, 1997).

As we delve into the origins of the Metaverse concept, it is crucial to acknowledge the speculative nature of these early conceptualizations and their significant impact on the subsequent development of immersive digital environments.

Technological Milestones Leading to the Metaverse

Significant technological milestones mark the journey from the conceptualization of the Metaverse to its realization. These milestones, each contributing to the intricate tapestry of the Metaverse, highlight the evolution of various technologies that collectively define this expansive digital space. Virtual reality (VR) emerged as a fundamental element, with early explorations dating back to the 1960s. The development of immersive VR headsets and computer-generated environments in the late 20th century laid the groundwork for creating immersive digital spaces (Milgram & Kishino, 1994). The 1990s witnessed the commercialization of VR technologies, making them more accessible to the general public.

Augmented reality (AR), another essential component of the Metaverse, gained prominence with the proliferation of smartphones in the early 21st century. The ability to overlay digital information onto the physical world opened additional possibilities for blending digital and real-world experiences (Azuma et al., 2001). Blockchain technology, introduced with the advent of Bitcoin in 2009, added a layer of security and decentralization to the Metaverse. The transparent and tamper-resistant nature of blockchain facilitated secure transactions and ownership of assets within digital environments (Swan, 2015). Artificial intelligence (AI) has become increasingly critical to the Metaverse, enhancing user experiences through intelligent algorithms, natural language processing, and predictive analytics (Cai et al., 2020). These technological advancements propelled the Metaverse from conceptual theory to a tangible and evolving digital reality (Tariq, 2024).

Early Applications of the Metaverse in Business

The early applications of the Metaverse in the business landscape reflect the exploratory phase of integrating this innovative concept into real-world scenarios. While the Metaverse was initially associated with entertainment and gaming, its true potential in business quickly became apparent. Virtual real estate emerged as a notable application, with businesses and individuals investing in digital spaces within the Metaverse. This paved the way for innovative property development and virtual commerce, creating an intelligent economic landscape (Wan, 2019). E-commerce platforms began experimenting with virtual marketplaces, offering users immersive and interactive shopping experiences. Brands explored the potential of creating virtual storefronts and engaging customers within the Metaverse, showcasing products and services dynamically and visually appealingly (Tariq, 2024).

The early 21st century witnessed the integration of the Metaverse into corporate training and development programs. Companies utilized virtual environments for employee training, simulation exercises, and collaborative workspaces, providing a glimpse into the diverse applications of the Metaverse beyond entertainment (Rosenberg, 2019).

As we explore the early applications of the Metaverse in business, it is essential to recognize the experimental nature of these initiatives and the lessons learned that have shaped the subsequent evolution of Metaverse applications in the corporate world.

Key Components of the Metaverse

The Metaverse encapsulates a complex amalgamation of various technologies, each playing a crucial role in shaping the immersive and interconnected digital universe. This section provides a detailed assessment of the key components that constitute the Metaverse, exploring the intricacies of Virtual Reality (VR) and Augmented

Reality (AR), Blockchain Technology, Artificial Intelligence (AI), and 3D Web with Spatial Computing.

Virtual Reality (VR) and Augmented Reality (AR)

Virtual Reality (VR) and Augmented Reality (AR) stand as primary elements of the Metaverse, offering users immersive and interactive experiences that bridge the gap between the digital and physical worlds. Using specialised hardware such as VR headsets, VR establishes synthetic environments that users can navigate and interact with. On the other hand, AR overlays digital information in the real-world environment, enhancing the user's perception of reality.

The development of VR can be traced back to early experiments in the 1960s, gaining significant momentum with the commercialisation of VR headsets in the late twentieth century. Innovations like Oculus Rift and HTC Vive brought immersive VR experiences to a broader audience, facilitating the creation of digital spaces within the Metaverse (Milgram & Kishino, 1994).

AR, propelled by the ubiquity of smartphones, became more accessible in the early 21st century. Applications like Pokémon GO demonstrated the potential of blending digital content with the physical world, showcasing the versatility of AR in creating interactive and location-based experiences (Azuma et al., 2001). Together, VR and AR provide the foundation for the spatial and sensory aspects of the Metaverse, enabling users to engage with digital content in a dynamic and immersive manner.

Blockchain Technology

Blockchain technology has emerged as a crucial component of the Metaverse, addressing fundamental issues related to security, ownership, and decentralised transactions within digital environments. Beginning with the introduction of Bitcoin in 2009, blockchain is a decentralised and distributed ledger that records transactions across a network of computers, ensuring transparency, permanence, and security. In the context of the Metaverse, blockchain serves as the backbone for secure and verifiable ownership of digital assets. Non-fungible tokens (NFTs), built on blockchain technology, enable creating and transferring unique digital assets within the Metaverse. Whether virtual real estate, digital art, or in-game items, blockchain ensures authenticity and provenance, empowering users with genuine ownership (Swan, 2015).

The decentralised nature of blockchain also mitigates the risk of central points of failure and enhances security, fostering trust within the Metaverse. Smart contracts, self-executing contracts with coded terms, further streamline transactions and interactions within digital environments.As the Metaverse continues evolving, blockchain technology remains instrumental in shaping the economic and social dynamics of this interconnected digital space.

Artificial Intelligence (AI)

Artificial Intelligence (AI) plays a transformative role in the Metaverse, enhancing user experiences, personalisation, and the overall intelligence of digital environments. AI algorithms power a range of functionalities within the Metaverse, including natural language processing, computer vision, and machine learning.

In user interactions, AI enables the creation of responsive and intelligent virtual entities, often called NPCs (Non-Player Characters) or virtual assistants. These entities can mimic human-like behaviour, respond to user input, learn from interactions, and adapt to user preferences over time (Cai et al., 2020).

Moreover, AI contributes to content curation and recommendation systems within the Metaverse. By analysing user behaviour and preferences, AI algorithms can tailor content recommendations, creating a personalised and engaging digital experience for each user.

Integrating AI in the Metaverse extends beyond user interactions, including dynamic content generation, procedural world-building, and predictive analytics. As the Metaverse continues to expand, the role of AI in shaping intelligent and responsive digital environments becomes increasingly prominent.

3D Web and Spatial Computing

3D Web and Spatial Computing are integral components that contribute to the visual and interactive aspects of the Metaverse, allowing users to navigate and interact within immersive digital spaces. The concept of 3D Web involves representing digital information in three-dimensional space, creating a more realistic and engaging user experience.

Spatial Computing, on the other hand, focuses on the interaction between humans and computers within a spatial environment. This includes technologies like gesture recognition, spatial mapping, and haptic feedback, enabling users to interact with digital content in a way that simulates real-world interactions.

In the Metaverse, 3D Web and Spatial Computing work to create dynamic and interactive digital environments. Users can explore virtual landscapes, interact with objects, and engage in spatially aware interactions with other users. This immersive spatial experience is crucial for replicating real-world interactions within the digital realm, providing a sense of presence and depth to the Metaverse (Damer, 1997). As technological advancements continue to enhance the capabilities of 3D Web and

Spatial Computing, the Metaverse evolves into a more sophisticated and realistic digital space, offering users unprecedented levels of immersion and interactivity.

Business Opportunities in the Metaverse

The advent of the Metaverse has ushered in a new era of business opportunities, transcending traditional models and providing a dynamic digital landscape for innovation and growth. This section explores key avenues through which businesses can harness the potential of the Metaverse, focusing on E-commerce and Virtual Marketplaces, Virtual Land and Property Development, Social Connections and Networking, and Training and Simulation for Organizations.

E-Commerce and Virtual Marketplaces

E-commerce within the Metaverse signifies a paradigm shift in consumer engagement with products and services. Virtual marketplaces, embedded in immersive digital environments, redefine the shopping experience. Users can explore dynamic virtual storefronts, interact with products in 3D space, and make purchases using virtual currencies or secure blockchain transactions. Businesses can create visually appealing and interactive digital stores in this virtual retail landscape. Brands can leverage the immersive nature of the Metaverse to showcase products through virtual try-ons, interactive demonstrations, and social shopping experiences. Integrating artificial intelligence-driven personalization algorithms ensures personalized product recommendations, enhancing customer engagement and satisfaction (Wan, 2019). The Metaverse redefines the boundaries of traditional E-commerce, offering businesses a unique platform to captivate consumers through innovative and personalized experiences.

Virtual Land and Property Development

Virtual land has emerged as a lucrative frontier within the Metaverse, mirroring the physical real estate market dynamics. Blockchain technology, particularly non-fungible tokens (NFTs), facilitates secure ownership and transfer of virtual properties. Investors and businesses engage in virtual property development, enhancing the aesthetics and functionalities of their digital assets. Blockchain's role in creating unique and verifiable digital assets ensures the value and ownership of virtual land, buildings, and other assets. This has allowed businesses to outline a digital presence, host events, and create branded spaces within the Metaverse (Swan, 2015). As the virtual real estate market continues to evolve, businesses can explore novel approaches to branding and engagement, creating innovative experiences that extend beyond traditional online platforms.

Social Connections and Networking

The social fabric of the Metaverse provides a fertile ground for businesses to connect with consumers in unprecedented ways. Social interactions and networking within the Metaverse extend beyond conventional online platforms, enabling users to communicate, collaborate, and build communities in a shared digital space. Businesses can establish a presence within these social spaces, hosting virtual events, product launches, and interactive brand experiences. Immersive environments facilitate engagement, allowing users to interact with brands and each other. Social interactions within the Metaverse span virtual conferences, trade shows, and collaborative workspaces, offering businesses innovative avenues for networking and relationship-building.

Intelligent entities powered by AI-driven chatbots and virtual assistants enhance social interactions by simulating human-like conversations. These entities provide customer support and personalized recommendations and facilitate seamless communication within the virtual social landscape (Hsu et al., 2018). The Metaverse is a dynamic arena where businesses can redefine their social presence and establish meaningful connections with a global audience.

Training and Simulation for Organizations

The Metaverse presents a unique platform for organizations to revolutionize training and simulation methods. Virtual environments offer realistic and immersive training scenarios, enabling employees to gain hands-on experience in a risk-free digital space.

Businesses can leverage the Metaverse for various training purposes, from onboarding programs to specialized skill development. Programmatic experiences facilitate the training of complex tasks, situational training, and collaborative problem-solving exercises. This immersive training approach proves particularly valuable in industries like healthcare, aviation, and manufacturing, where hands-on experience is crucial (Rosenberg, 2019).

The integration of AI further enhances training and simulation modules. AI algorithms analyze user performance, provide real-time feedback, and dynamically adjust the difficulty level of simulations based on individual learning progress (Cai et al., 2020).

In the evolving landscape of the Metaverse, businesses can redefine employee training, fostering a culture of continuous learning and development.

Challenges and Risks in the Metaverse

The rapid evolution of the Metaverse introduces a myriad of challenges and risks that demand careful consideration. This section delves into the intricacies surrounding privacy and security concerns, regulatory and ethical considerations, accessibility and inclusivity issues, and technological barriers, shedding light on the obstacles that must be addressed to ensure the responsible development and widespread adoption of the Metaverse.

Privacy and Security Concerns

Privacy and security concerns take centre stage among the challenges in the Metaverse, as the immersive and interconnected nature of this digital space raises significant issues related to user data security and cyber threats. The collection and utilization of vast amounts of personal information within the Metaverse raise concerns about user privacy, data ownership, and the potential for unauthorized access. The extensive tracking of user behaviour, interactions, and preferences within the Metaverse poses data breaches and misuse risks. As virtual environments become more sophisticated, the potential for malicious actors to exploit vulnerabilities and compromise sensitive user data grows (Dinh et al., 2018).

Addressing privacy and security concerns requires a robust framework incorporating encryption protocols, decentralized identity management, and stringent access controls. Implementing blockchain technology plays a pivotal role in enhancing the security of user data within the Metaverse, ensuring transparent and tamper-resistant transactions (Dinh et al., 2018).

Regulatory and Ethical Considerations

The Metaverse's borderless and decentralized nature presents challenges concerning regulatory oversight and ethical considerations. The lack of a centralized legal framework governing activities within the Metaverse raises questions about jurisdiction, intellectual property rights, and accountability for virtual actions.

Regulatory frameworks must adapt to address issues like virtual property ownership, virtual currency transactions, and virtual asset trading. The absence of standardized rules may lead to legal ambiguities, potentially hindering the growth of businesses operating within the Metaverse (Garlick, 2017).

Ethical considerations encompass a range of issues, from the ethical use of AI algorithms in virtual environments to the prevention of virtual harassment and the protection of vulnerable users. Striking a balance between innovation and the ethical implications of Metaverse activities is crucial for creating a sustainable and responsible digital ecosystem.

Accessibility and Inclusivity Challenges

While the Metaverse holds promise for immersive experiences, it also introduces challenges related to accessibility and inclusivity. Ensuring that the Metaverse is accessible to users of diverse abilities, including those with disabilities, is critical. Virtual environments may unintentionally exclude individuals with visual, auditory, or motor impairments, limiting their ability to participate fully in digital experiences (Gulliver et al., 2020).

Inclusivity issues also extend to economic factors, as not all individuals may have access to the hardware or high-speed internet connections required for optimal participation in the Metaverse. This digital divide raises concerns about establishing an environment that is not only technologically accessible but also economically equitable.

Addressing accessibility and inclusivity challenges in the Metaverse involves implementing universal design principles, incorporating features such as voice commands and haptic feedback, and actively involving users with diverse abilities in virtual environments' design and testing phases (Gulliver et al., 2020).

Technological Barriers

The development and widespread adoption of the Metaverse encounter technological barriers that must be overcome to realize its full potential. Issues such as network latency, bandwidth constraints, and hardware requirements can hinder the seamless integration of immersive technologies and compromise the user experience within the Metaverse (Damer, 1997). The interoperability of various technologies, including VR headsets, AR devices, and AI-driven applications, poses a challenge for creating a robust and interconnected Metaverse. Standardization efforts are essential to ensure compatibility and a smooth transition between different virtual environments (Damer, 1997).

Moreover, the scalability of the Metaverse infrastructure needs to be considered to accommodate the growing user base and the increasing complexity of virtual experiences.

Technological advancements, including 5G networks and edge computing, significantly address these scalability challenges (Azuma et al., 2001).

The seamless integration of the Metaverse into business operations marks a significant journey for organisations leveraging the potential of this immersive digital realm. Examining instances where enterprises have adeptly navigated challenges and reaped benefits from Metaverse integration provides valuable insights into effective strategies and outcomes.

Case Study One: Virtual Land Development

An exemplary success story lies in the strategic utilisation of the Metaverse for virtual land development. A pioneering real estate company harnessed the decentralised nature of the Metaverse, employing blockchain technology to establish secure ownership and transfer of virtual properties through non-fungible tokens (NFTs) (Swan, 2015). By embracing the concept of digital ownership and creating a unique virtual experience for users, the company attracted a global audience interested in investing in the Metaverse's virtual land and properties.

The outcome of this case underscores the importance of aligning with the intrinsic features of the Metaverse, such as decentralised ownership facilitated by blockchain. Additionally, incorporating interactive and engaging experiences within the virtual land contributed to the thriving Metaverse business model (Swan, 2015).

Case Study Two: Immersive E-Commerce Platforms

In the retail sector, innovative companies have successfully integrated the Metaverse into their e-commerce strategies, creating immersive and interactive platforms. These platforms enable users to explore virtual stores, interact with products in 3D space, and even try virtual versions of clothing items or accessories. A notable fashion brand achieved remarkable success by launching a virtual store within a Metaverse environment, providing users with a unique and engaging shopping experience (Wan, 2019).

The key takeaway from this case is the essential incorporation of Metaverse capabilities to enhance traditional e-commerce models. By embracing the immersive nature of the Metaverse, companies can create a dynamic and visually appealing shopping experience, fostering customer engagement and loyalty (Wan, 2019).

Lessons Learned From Unsuccessful Endeavors

While successes abound, the Metaverse has witnessed its share of failed attempts at integration, offering valuable lessons for businesses navigating this evolving landscape. Examining instances where endeavours fell short sheds light on pitfalls and challenges that require careful consideration.

Case Study One: Inadequate User Onboarding and Education

A notable failure in Metaverse integration occurred when a tech startup aimed to introduce a virtual collaboration platform for remote teams. Despite having a robust technological foundation, the company should have noticed the importance of comprehensive user onboarding and education. Users needed help to adapt to the new virtual environment, leading to disengagement and, ultimately, the abandonment of the platform.

This case highlights the significance of user experience and education when introducing Metaverse solutions. Effective onboarding processes, clear communication of functionalities, and ongoing support are crucial for ensuring user adoption and success in the Metaverse (Rosenberg, 2019).

Case Study Two: Lack of Cross-Platform Compatibility

A gaming company's attempt to create a Metaverse-like experience faced challenges due to a lack of cross-platform compatibility. Users experienced difficulties transitioning between different virtual environments, limiting the seamless integration promised by the concept of the Metaverse. This failure highlighted the importance of standardisation and interoperability for a robust and user-friendly Metaverse experience (Damer, 1997).

The key takeaway from this case is the need for extensive collaboration and standardisation efforts. For the Metaverse to realise its potential, companies must prioritise compatibility between various virtual platforms to create a truly interconnected digital space (Damer, 1997).

Emerging Business Models in the Metaverse

As the Metaverse continues to evolve, novel and innovative business models are emerging, shaping how organisations operate and engage with customers in this immersive digital space. Examining these emerging business models provides insights into how organisations leverage the Metaverse for growth and sustainability (Tariq, 2024).

Case Study One: Virtual Events and Experiences

A media and entertainment company successfully transitioned live events to the Metaverse, creating virtual conferences, concerts, and immersive experiences.

By leveraging the capabilities of virtual reality and interactive technologies, the company maintained engagement with its audience and expanded its global reach. Virtual ticket sales, virtual merchandise, and partnerships with virtual venue owners contributed to a new sustainable revenue stream (Raimi et al. 2022).

This case illustrates the potential for businesses to monetise virtual events and experiences within the Metaverse. The ability to offer unique and engaging digital content opens up revenue-generating opportunities beyond traditional models, showcasing the adaptability of businesses in embracing the Metaverse (Hsu et al., 2018).

Case Study Two: Metaverse as a Service (MaaS)

A tech startup introduced a Metaverse-as-a-Service (MaaS) platform, providing companies with the infrastructure and tools to establish and customise their virtual environments. This platform offers a turnkey solution for organisations looking to establish a digital presence in the Metaverse without the complexities of developing their immersive technologies. By offering a scalable and accessible MaaS platform, the startup has rapidly enabled businesses to integrate the Metaverse into their operations.

This case highlights the emergence of service-oriented business models, where companies provide Metaverse-related solutions as a service. MaaS models democratise access to the Metaverse, allowing a broader range of businesses to participate in the digital transformation (Cai et al., 2020).

Future Outlook of the Metaverse

The trajectory of the Metaverse is poised for dynamic growth, driven by anticipated technological advancements, the widespread integration of the Metaverse in business, and the potential for disruptive innovations. This section explores the directions that shape the future of the Metaverse, providing insights into the developments that are likely to unfold.

Anticipated Technological Progressions

The future of the Metaverse is intricately linked to advancements in key technologies that underpin its immersive and interconnected nature. Virtual Reality (VR) and Augmented Reality (AR) are prominent areas of expected progress. As hardware becomes more sophisticated and affordable, VR and AR experiences are projected to reach new levels, providing users with increasingly realistic and immersive digital environments (Liang et al., 2020).

Integrating Artificial Intelligence (AI) is another crucial advancement with transformative potential for the Metaverse. AI algorithms will likely play a more prominent role in creating intelligent and responsive virtual entities, enhancing user interactions and personalising digital experiences. The ability of AI to analyse user behaviour and adapt to virtual environments in real-time contributes to a more dynamic and engaging Metaverse (Cai et al., 2020).

Blockchain technology, with its role in establishing secure ownership and facilitating decentralised transactions, is expected to continue shaping the economic aspects of the Metaverse. Using blockchain for virtual asset ownership, digital currencies, and secure transactions ensures transparency and trust, laying the groundwork for digital economy growth within the Metaverse (Swan, 2015).

The integration of 5G networks is also expected to impact Metaverse significantly, addressing current limitations associated with network latency and bandwidth constraints. Improved connectivity will provide a more seamless and responsive user experience, unlocking additional possibilities for real-time interactions and collaborative activities within the Metaverse (Azuma et al., 2001).

Growth and Expansion of the Metaverse in Business

The Metaverse is poised to become an integral part of the business landscape, with sustained growth and expansion across various sectors. One of the notable avenues of growth lies in the continued integration of the Metaverse into e-commerce and retail. Companies increasingly recognise the potential of immersive virtual shopping experiences, where customers can explore products in three-dimensional spaces and engage in social interactions. The Metaverse offers a unique platform for businesses to differentiate themselves and capture the attention of a digitally savvy consumer base (Wan, 2019).

Virtual real estate, as a burgeoning market within the Metaverse, is expected to grow significantly. The concept of digital land ownership and development, facilitated by blockchain technology, opens up opportunities for companies to establish a virtual presence, host events, and create branded spaces. This digital real estate market will likely expand as businesses explore innovative ways of utilising virtual properties for marketing, engagement, and collaboration (Swan, 2015).

The Metaverse's potential in education and training is expected to grow, with organisations recognising the effectiveness of immersive simulations and virtual environments for employee development. From onboarding programs to specialised skill training, the Metaverse provides a platform for realistic and hands-on learning experiences. This adoption is expected to extend beyond traditional industries, influencing the future of corporate training and skill development (Rosenberg, 2019).

Additionally, the rise of virtual events and conferences within the Metaverse is reshaping the business landscape. As organisations seek alternatives to traditional gatherings, the Metaverse offers a scalable and accessible platform for hosting events, connecting with global audiences, and creating unique and interactive experiences. The growth of virtual events is poised to redefine how businesses approach networking, marketing, and collaboration in a digital-first era (Hsu et al., 2018).

Anticipated Disruptions and Innovations

The future of the Metaverse is also characterised by the potential for disruptions and innovations that could reshape industries and societal interactions. One disruptive force is the emergence of decentralised autonomous organisations (DAOs) within the Metaverse. These entities, facilitated by blockchain technology, operate without centralised control and enable collective decision-making by participants. The concept of decentralised governance can disrupt traditional organisational structures and redefine how businesses operate within the Metaverse (Casey, 2018).

Advancements in AI-driven virtual entities and avatars are expected to bring new dimensions to social interactions within the Metaverse. Advanced AI algorithms will enable virtual entities to mimic human-like behaviour, understand natural language, and respond intelligently to user interactions. This development opens possibilities for realistic and engaging social experiences, challenging the boundaries between human and artificial intelligence within the digital realm (Cai et al., 2020).

Integrating Metaverse technologies with the Internet of Things (IoT) will create a more interconnected and immersive digital environment. Smart devices within the Metaverse can interact with each other and virtual spaces, enhancing the overall user experience. From smart homes to interconnected virtual cities, the convergence of Metaverse and IoT technologies can revolutionise how individuals interact with their digital surroundings (Dinh et al., 2018).

Additionally, the Metaverse is expected to witness advancements in decentralised finance (DeFi) applications. Using blockchain for financial transactions within the Metaverse allows for secure and transparent decentralised financial services. From virtual banking to decentralised marketplaces, these innovations could disrupt traditional financial models and redefine economic transactions within the digital space (Swan, 2015).

Strategies for Organizations to Enter the Metaverse

Embarking on the journey into the Metaverse necessitates a strategic approach to harness the immersive potential of this digital realm. Organizations can consider the following strategies to adeptly navigate and capitalize on the opportunities presented by the Metaverse.

1.   User-Driven Content Creation:

Prioritizing user-centric content creation is essential for businesses aiming to tailor virtual experiences to the preferences and expectations of their target audience. This involves identifying unique aspects of the Metaverse where user engagement thrives on interactive and immersive content. Businesses can enhance their Metaverse presence by investing in compelling narratives and interactive elements to establish a meaningful connection with users (Wan, 2019).

2.   Integration of Virtual and Physical Experiences:

To seamlessly integrate the Metaverse into their operations, organizations can explore methods of connecting virtual and physical experiences. This may involve developing hybrid experiences that allow users to effortlessly transition between the digital and physical worlds. For instance, a retail brand could provide virtual try-on experiences for products that customers can subsequently purchase in physical stores. This strategy aligns with evolving consumer expectations for a seamless integration of online and offline interactions (Liang et al., 2020).

3.   Utilization of Blockchain for Digital Assets:

Embracing blockchain technology is crucial for organizations entering the Metaverse, especially in areas where digital ownership and transactions play a significant role. By utilizing blockchain for the creation of non-fungible tokens (NFTs) and secure digital asset management, organizations can establish clear ownership within virtual environments. This not only enhances the authenticity of virtual goods but also aligns with the decentralized nature of the Metaverse (Swan, 2015).

4.   Engagement in Virtual Commerce (V-commerce):

Organizations can explore the potential of virtual commerce (V-commerce) by establishing virtual storefronts and marketplaces within the Metaverse. Leveraging the growing trend of social shopping in virtual spaces, businesses can design immersive shopping experiences featuring interactive product displays and virtual showcases. This strategy is particularly relevant for retail and e-commerce entities seeking to expand their reach and engage with informed consumers in innovative ways (Wan, 2019).

5.   Augmentation with Augmented Reality (AR):

Augmented Reality (AR) can play a crucial role in enhancing user experiences within the Metaverse. Organizations can explore the integration of AR elements that overlay digital information onto the physical environment, creating a seamless blend of the real world and virtual content. Whether used for advertising, navigation, or interactive storytelling, AR enhancements contribute to a more dynamic and engaging Metaverse experience for users (Liang et al., 2020).

Regulatory Frameworks and Guidelines

As organizations immerse themselves in the Metaverse, adherence to regulatory frameworks and guidelines becomes critical to ensure ethical practices, user privacy, and legal compliance. The following recommendations form key considerations for organizations navigating the evolving regulatory landscape of the Metaverse (Raimi et al. 2022).

1.   Proactive Engagement with Regulatory Authorities:

Businesses should adopt a proactive approach by engaging with the relevant regulatory authorities. Actively participating in discussions, providing data, and staying informed about emerging regulations contribute to the establishment of fair and effective guidelines. By fostering open communication, organizations can contribute to shaping regulations that balance innovation with user protection (Garlick, 2017).

2.   Transparent Data Security and Privacy Policies:

To address privacy concerns within the Metaverse, organizations must articulate clear privacy policies and robust data security measures. Compliance with privacy regulations is ensured by clearly outlining data collection practices, user rights, and security protocols in user agreements. Organizations should prioritize the protection of user data and communicate their commitment to maintaining secure virtual environments (Dinh et al., 2018).

3.   Age Verification Mechanisms and Child Protection:

Given the potential presence of underage users in the Metaverse, organizations should implement effective age verification mechanisms. Adhering to age restrictions and incorporating age verification processes is crucial for child protection and compliance with regulations governing the online presence of minors. This action ensures a safe and age-appropriate virtual environment (Garlick, 2017).

4.   Adaptation to Cross-Border Regulatory Challenges:

The borderless nature of the Metaverse presents cross-border regulatory challenges. Organizations must adapt to varying legal requirements in different jurisdictions. This may involve collaborating with legal experts to navigate global regulatory frameworks and ensure compliance with diverse legal standards. A nuanced understanding of global regulatory variations is essential for organizations operating in the international Metaverse landscape (Garlick, 2017).

5.   Advocacy for Ethical Industry Standards:

Organizations can actively advocate for the establishment of ethical industry standards within the Metaverse. This includes collaborating with industry peers, participating in industry associations, and contributing to initiatives focused on responsible practices. By advocating for user protection, ethical content creation, and fair business policies, organizations contribute to the development of a sustainable and trustworthy Metaverse environment (Garlick, 2017).

Metaverse Development Through Partnerships and Collaboration

Partnerships and collaboration are crucial to the development of the Metaverse. In order to encourage growth and innovation within the Metaverse, strategic alliances, shared resources, and collaborative initiatives can be beneficial to businesses. The following recommendations form effective strategies for organizations to engage in cooperative endeavors.

1.   Forging Alliances with Tech Innovators:

To stay at the forefront of Metaverse development, organizations should forge alliances with technology innovators. Collaborating with companies specializing in Virtual Reality (VR), Augmented Reality (AR), Artificial Intelligence (AI), and blockchain can bring cutting-edge technologies to Metaverse projects. Such collaborations foster innovation, enhance technological capabilities, and position organizations as leaders in the evolving digital landscape (Cai et al., 2020).

2.   Engaging in Cross-Industry Collaborations:

   Cross-industry collaborations present opportunities for organizations to explore innovative uses of the Metaverse. Partnering with companies outside their traditional domains allows organizations to leverage diverse expertise and perspectives. For example, collaboration between a healthcare provider and a gaming company could result in the development of therapeutic VR experiences. Cross-industry collaborations open avenues for novel applications and solutions within the Metaverse (Hsu, Chang, and Lee, 2018).

3.   Participation in Open-Source Initiatives:

   Embracing open-source initiatives within the Metaverse community promotes collaboration and shared development. By participating in open-source projects, organizations contribute to a collaborative environment where knowledge and resources are shared. This fosters innovation and accelerates the development of common standards and protocols within the Metaverse. Businesses can actively engage in open-source communities to help advance Metaverse technologies collectively (Cai et al., 2020).

4.   Collaborations for Research and Development (R&D):

   Organizations can fuel innovation by investing in Research and Development (R&D) partnerships. Collaborating with academic institutions, research organizations, and tech startups provides access to emerging technologies and creative ideas. According to Hsu, Chang, & Lee (2018), R&D partnerships contribute to the development of Metaverse capabilities, ensuring that businesses maintain a competitive edge and remain at the forefront of technological advancements.

5.   Exploration of Strategic Partnerships for Market Expansion:

   To expand their market reach within the Metaverse, organizations should explore strategic alliances. Forming partnerships with content creators, influencers, and established Metaverse platforms facilitates broader visibility and audience engagement. Strategic alliances enable organizations to leverage existing Metaverse ecosystems, reaching a wider audience and establishing a presence within vibrant digital communities (Hsu, Chang, and Lee, 2018).

CONCLUSION

The exploration of the Metaverse's impact on business and commerce has uncovered a landscape rich with opportunities, challenges, and transformative potential. This conclusion provides a comprehensive summary of key findings and expresses final perspectives on the evolving role of the Metaverse in shaping the future of business.

Recap of Key Discoveries

Throughout this research paper, a thorough assessment of the Metaverse in the context of business and commerce has yielded several key discoveries. The definition of the Metaverse has evolved beyond a mere virtual reality to a multi-layered digital realm encompassing augmented reality, blockchain, artificial intelligence, and spatial computing. The historical context of the Metaverse reveals its roots in science fiction, gradually evolving through technological milestones and finding early applications in business.

The diverse applications of the Metaverse demonstrate its significance to commerce and business. From immersive e-commerce experiences and virtual land development to social interactions, networking, and training simulations, the Metaverse offers a versatile platform for businesses to innovate and engage with their audiences. The key components of the Metaverse, including augmented reality, blockchain, artificial intelligence, and spatial computing, play crucial roles in shaping its capabilities and potential applications.

Business opportunities within the Metaverse span various sectors, including e-commerce and virtual marketplaces, land and property development, social interactions, and training simulations. These potential opportunities signify a paradigm shift in how businesses connect with customers, manage assets, and conduct training and collaborative activities.

However, the Metaverse also poses challenges and risks, including privacy and security concerns, regulatory and ethical considerations, accessibility issues, and technological barriers. Navigating these challenges is essential for businesses aiming to establish a foothold in this dynamic digital space.

Examining case studies, encompassing both successful integrations and lessons learned from unsuccessful endeavors, provides valuable insights into the strategies and pitfalls encountered by businesses venturing into the Metaverse. The future outlook of the Metaverse anticipates technological advancements, growth in business applications, and potential disruptions and innovations that could reshape industries

Final Contemplations on the Role of the Metaverse in Business and Trade

As we conclude this exploration, it is evident that the Metaverse is not merely a technological trend but a transformative force with extensive implications for business and commerce. It is more than just a technological platform for virtual interactions; the Metaverse is becoming a digital frontier where businesses can redefine customer experiences, explore new revenue streams, and transform industry norms.

The immersive and interconnected nature of the Metaverse offers businesses unprecedented opportunities to engage meaningfully with their audience. E-commerce and virtual marketplaces within the Metaverse provide a dynamic space for personalized shopping experiences, while virtual land development enables businesses to establish a distinctive presence and host interactive events.

Social interactions and networking in the Metaverse are not mere extensions of traditional online platforms but represent a paradigm shift in how individuals connect and collaborate in digital spaces. Businesses can leverage these social elements to build communities, foster brand loyalty, and engage with consumers on a deeper level.

The role of the Metaverse in training and simulation for businesses extends beyond conventional methods. Immersive and realistic training environments offer employees hands-on experiences, contributing to skill development and knowledge retention. Virtual training within the Metaverse has the potential to revolutionize corporate learning and development strategies.

Despite the contributions and potential opportunities, businesses must navigate a landscape rife with challenges. Privacy and security concerns, regulatory considerations, accessibility issues, and technological barriers demand careful attention. Successfully integrating the Metaverse into business operations requires a strategic approach, proactive engagement with regulatory frameworks, and a commitment to addressing ethical considerations.

In conclusion, the role of the Metaverse in business and commerce is a dynamic journey characterized by innovation, transformation, and collaboration. Businesses that embrace the Metaverse not only position themselves at the forefront of technological advancement but also contribute to shaping the digital future. As we move forward, the evolving Metaverse presents an exciting canvas for businesses to redefine their narratives, connect with audiences in intelligent ways, and explore the uncharted territories of this digital frontier.

REFERENCES

Ali, S., Abdullah, Armand, T. P. T., Athar, A., Hussain, A., Ali, M., Yaseen, M., Joo, M.-I., & Kim, H.-C. (2023). Metaverse in healthcare integrated with explainable ai and blockchain: Enabling immersiveness, ensuring trust, and providing patient data security. *Sensors (Basel)*, *23*(2), 565. doi:10.3390/s23020565 PMID:36679361

Allam, Z., Sharifi, A., Bibri, S. E., Jones, D. S., & Krogstie, J. (2022). The metaverse as a virtual form of smart cities: Opportunities and challenges for environmental, economic, and social sustainability in urban futures. *Smart Cities*, *5*(3), 771–801. doi:10.3390/smartcities5030040

Basil, W. (2022). *The" metaverse." The arrival of the future of 3D research, learning, life & commerce.* Research Gate.

Bibri, S. E. (2022). The social shaping of the metaverse as an alternative to the imaginaries of data-driven smart Cities: A study in science, technology, and society. *Smart Cities*, *5*(3), 832–874. doi:10.3390/smartcities5030043

Cagnina, M. R., & Poian, M. (2008). How to compete in the metaverse: the business models in Second Life. *U of Udine Economics Working Paper*, (01-2007).

Chen, Z., Wu, J., Gan, W., & Qi, Z. (2022, December). Metaverse security and privacy: An overview. In *2022 IEEE International Conference on Big Data (Big Data)* (pp. 2950-2959). IEEE. 10.1109/BigData55660.2022.10021112

Chu, N. H., Hoang, D. T., Nguyen, D. N., Phan, K. T., Dutkiewicz, E., Niyato, D., & Shu, T. (2023). Metaslicing: A novel resource allocation framework for metaverse. *IEEE Transactions on Mobile Computing*.

De Felice, F., De Luca, C., Di Chiara, S., & Petrillo, A. (2023). Physical and digital worlds: Implications and opportunities of the metaverse. *Procedia Computer Science*, *217*, 1744–1754. doi:10.1016/j.procs.2022.12.374

Enache, M. C. (2022). Metaverse Opportunities for Businesses. *Annals of the University Dunarea de Jos of Galati: Fascicle: I, Economics & Applied Informatics*, *28*(1).

Gao, H., Chong, A. Y. L., & Bao, H. (2023). Metaverse: Literature Review, Synthesis and Future Research Agenda. *Journal of Computer Information Systems*, 1–21. doi:10.1080/08874417.2023.2233455

Guo, H., & Gao, W. (2022). Metaverse-powered experiential situational English-teaching design: An emotion-based analysis method. *Frontiers in Psychology*, *13*, 859159. doi:10.3389/fpsyg.2022.859159 PMID:35401297

Hopkins, E. (2022). Virtual Commerce in a Decentralized Blockchain-based Metaverse: Immersive Technologies, Computer Vision Algorithms, and Retail Business Analytics. *Linguistic and Philosophical Investigations*, (21), 203–218.

Hwang, G. J., & Chien, S. Y. (2022). Definition, roles, and potential research issues of the metaverse in education: An artificial intelligence perspective. *Computers and Education: Artificial Intelligence*, 3, 100082. doi:10.1016/j.caeai.2022.100082

Ismail, L., Niyato, D., Sun, S., Kim, D. I., Erol-Kantarci, M., & Miao, C. (2022, October). Semantic information market for the Metaverse: An auction based approach. In *2022 IEEE Future Networks World Forum (FNWF)* (pp. 628-633). IEEE.

Jeong, H., Yi, Y., & Kim, D. (2022). An innovative e-commerce platform incorporating metaverse to live commerce. *International Journal of Innovative Computing, Information, & Control*, *18*(1), 221–229.

Nguyen, L. T., Duc, D. T. V., Dang, T. Q., & Nguyen, D. P. (2023). Metaverse Banking Service: Are We Ready to Adopt? A Deep Learning-Based Dual-Stage SEM-ANN Analysis. *Human Behavior and Emerging Technologies*, *2023*, 2023. doi:10.1155/2023/6617371

Parcu, P. L., Rossi, M. A., Innocenti, N., & Carrozza, C. (2023). How real will the metaverse be? Exploring the spatial impact of virtual worlds. *European Planning Studies*, *31*(7), 1–23. doi:10.1080/09654313.2023.2221323

Periyasami, S., & Periyasamy, A. P. (2022). Metaverse as future promising platform business model: Case study on fashion value chain. *Businesses*, *2*(4), 527–545. doi:10.3390/businesses2040033

Popescu, G. H., Valaskova, K., & Horak, J. (2022). Augmented reality shopping experiences, retail business analytics, and machine vision algorithms in the virtual economy of the metaverse. *Journal of Self-Governance and Management Economics*, *10*(2), 67–81.

Raimi, L., Kah, J. M., & Tariq, M. U. (2022). The Discourse of Blue Economy Definitions, Measurements, and Theories: Implications for Strengthening Academic Research and Industry Practice. In L. Raimi & J. Kah (Eds.), *Implications for Entrepreneurship and Enterprise Development in the Blue Economy* (pp. 1–17). IGI Global. doi:10.4018/978-1-6684-3393-5.ch001

Raimi, L., Tariq, M. U., & Kah, J. M. (2022). Diversity, Equity, and Inclusion as the Future Workplace Ethics: Theoretical Review. In L. Raimi & J. Kah (Eds.), *Mainstreaming Diversity, Equity, and Inclusion as Future Workplace Ethics* (pp. 1–27). IGI Global. doi:10.4018/978-1-6684-3657-8.ch001

Rathore, B. (2017). Virtual Consumerism: An Exploration of E-Commerce in the Metaverse. *International Journal of New Media Studies: International Peer Reviewed Scholarly Indexed Journal, 4*(2), 61–69. doi:10.58972/eiprmj.v4i2y17.109

Sami, H., Hammoud, A., Arafeh, M., Wazzeh, M., Arisdakessian, S., Chahoud, M., & Guizani, M. (2023). The Metaverse: Survey, Trends, Novel Pipeline Ecosystem & Future Directions. *arXiv preprint arXiv:2304.09240.*

Sharifi, A., Khavarian-Garmsir, A. R., Allam, Z., & Asadzadeh, A. (2023). Progress and prospects in planning: A bibliometric review of literature in Urban Studies and Regional and Urban Planning, 1956–2022. *Progress in Planning, 173*, 100740. doi:10.1016/j.progress.2023.100740

Sun, J., Gan, W., Chao, H. C., & Yu, P. S. (2022). Metaverse: Survey, applications, security, and opportunities. *arXiv preprint arXiv:2210.07990.*

Sunny, B. (2023). An Analysis of Future Prospects of Metaverse. In *How the Metaverse Will Reshape Business and Sustainability* (pp. 17–25). Springer Nature Singapore. doi:10.1007/978-981-99-5126-0_3

Tariq, M. U. (2024). Equity and Inclusion in Learning Ecosystems. In F. Al Husseiny & A. Munna (Eds.), *Preparing Students for the Future Educational Paradigm* (pp. 155–176). IGI Global., doi:10.4018/979-8-3693-1536-1.ch007

Tariq, M. U. (2024). Revolutionizing Health Data Management With Blockchain Technology: Enhancing Security and Efficiency in a Digital Era. In M. Garcia & R. de Almeida (Eds.), *Emerging Technologies for Health Literacy and Medical Practice* (pp. 153–175). IGI Global., doi:10.4018/979-8-3693-1214-8.ch008

Toraman, Y., & Geçit, B. B. (2023). User acceptance of metaverse: an analysis for e-commerce in the framework of technology acceptance model (TAM). *Sosyoekonomi, 31*(5).

Truong, V. T., Le, L. B., & Niyato, D. (2023). Blockchain meets metaverse and digital asset management: A comprehensive survey. *IEEE Access : Practical Innovations, Open Solutions, 11*, 26258–26288. doi:10.1109/ACCESS.2023.3257029

Xu, M., Ng, W. C., Lim, W. Y. B., Kang, J., Xiong, Z., Niyato, D., & Miao, C. (2022). A full dive into realizing the edge-enabled metaverse: Visions, enabling technologies, and challenges. *IEEE Communications Surveys & Tutorials.*5), 85-104.

Yawised, K., Apasrawirote, D., & Boonparn, C. (2022). From traditional business shifted towards transformation: The emerging business opportunities and challenges in 'Metaverse' era. *Incbaa, 2022*, 162–175.

Yu, J. E. (2022). Exploration of educational possibilities by four metaverse types in physical education. *Technologies*, *10*(5), 104. doi:10.3390/technologies10050104

Zhang, J., Zong, M., & Li, W. (2022). A truthful mechanism for multibase station resource allocation in metaverse digital twin framework. *Processes (Basel, Switzerland)*, *10*(12), 2601. doi:10.3390/pr10122601

Chapter 5
Current State of Metaverse in Entrepreneurial Ecosystem:
A Retrospective Analysis of Its Evolving Landscape

Vaishali Dhiman
Central University of Himachal Pradesh, India

Manpreet Arora
(iD) https://orcid.org/0000-0002-4939-1992
Central University of Himachal Pradesh, India

ABSTRACT

Entrepreneurs are gradually discovering the metaverse's immense potential as it evolves into a virtual environment in which users interact with digital domains and one another. This study aims to explain the tangled patterns of research, collaborations, and thematic trends at the nexus of the metaverse and entrepreneurial activities. Using Scopus database collection, this bibliometric analysis investigates the intellectual landscape of the metaverse and its ties with the entrepreneurial sector from 2005 to 2023. The key findings show that there has been a large increase in publications after 2020, indicating an increased interest in the metaverse's impact on entrepreneurship. Collaboration and the variety of documents demonstrate a thriving worldwide research community. Thematic maps depict interwoven themes, emphasizing key topics like big data, block chain, artificial intelligence, and virtual reality, as well as niche areas like human learning. This research contributes to a better understanding of the metaverse and its implications for entrepreneurship.

DOI: 10.4018/979-8-3693-5868-9.ch005

INTRODUCTION

The metaverse, which was previously only a science fiction notion, has quickly evolved into a vibrant and expanding ecosystem in the startup scene or entrepreneurial world. The metaverse has shown great promise for new economic initiatives and technological innovations (Allam et al., 2022; Yaqoob et al., 2023). Thereby the visionaries and the entrepreneurs have quickly grabbed this opportunity by examining the metaverse's development within the entrepreneurial ecosystem from its early stages to its present status as a complex digital domain. From the metaverse's development, it is clear that it has gone far beyond virtual game environments and it has developed quickly from a theoretical idea to a thriving ecosystem for entrepreneurs (Weking et al., 2023; Yemenici, 2022). Although the idea of the metaverse has been around for a while, but with the COVID-19 pandemic, it attracted a lot of attention and undergone significant shifts. During the COVID-19 pandemic, people suffered and looked for alternate means to interact, work, and socialize while maintaining social distancing mechanisms, and this led to an acceleration of the acceptance and development of virtual technology and virtual world (Arora & Sharma, 2023). The course of metaverse has been greatly influenced by entrepreneurs who have taken advantage of opportunities for business ventures and scientific breakthroughs. Entrepreneurs have been essential in expanding the uses of the metaverse, which has had a significant impact on a variety of industries, from commerce and education to entertainment and social interactions. The incorporation of advanced technologies, such virtual reality and blockchain, has helped to further popularise the metaverse and given entrepreneurs new opportunities to rethink ownership models, user experiences, and economic paradigms (Calandra et al., 2023). Furthermore, both established companies and up-and-coming entrepreneurs are interested in the metaverse because of its ability to cross boundaries and promote innovative social dynamics and collaboration. Entrepreneurs operating in this virtual world have to traverse a landscape that is constantly changing, much as the experiences it offers, from regulatory concerns to the need for improved privacy and security measures. The metaverse is still a dynamic place where entrepreneurs negotiate changing environments while addressing privacy and regulatory concerns, despite certain obstacles.

Understanding the Term "Metaverse"

The term "metaverse," which is wide and constantly changing, generally refers to a group virtual shared environment that is enabled by the internet and allows users to communicate with each other and a computer-generated environment (Dionisio et al., 2013; Sparkes, 2021). It is frequently explained as a shared virtual environment for collectives that arises from the fusion of virtual and actual reality. Users have access to a variety of activities in the metaverse, including gaming, socializing, working, studying, and even conducting business. The digital universe is dynamic and interconnected, with the goal of expanding upon and replicating elements of the real world in a virtual setting. Virtual reality, augmented reality, 3D technology, and social interaction are essential elements of the metaverse, which combines these elements to create an advanced and diverse digital environment (Arora & Sharma, 2022; Arora et al., 2023). This term has grown in popularity as technological developments carry us closer to a digital future that is more integrated and interconnected. It is a dynamic environment where people from all over the world may connect and collaborate, not only for fun but also for the work and business.

Metaverse in Entrepreneurial World

An individuals who has an idea and see opportunities to act upon that idea and develop something innovative for the current market are considered entrepreneurs (Arora & Sharma, 2021; Arora et al., 2023; Dhiman & Arora, 2024). Entrepreneurs are the pioneers in the metaverse, setting new trails and creating interesting things. The metaverse has become a disruptive force in the realm of entrepreneurship, offering a wide range of digital opportunities to entrepreneurs. Within this vast virtual environment, entrepreneurs are essential designers of novel experiences who have guts to challenge the established business models or current entrepreneurial environment (Enache, 2022). These entrepreneurs are paving new paths in the metaverse for trade, social engagement, and entertainment beyond just making virtual games. They are creating a new type of digital economy by imagining and creating virtual real estate where users may purchase, sell, and exchange digital assets. In the world of entrepreneurship, the metaverse is starting to change things up and present entrepreneurs with new and intriguing prospects. The metaverse has become a game-changing space for entrepreneurship where visionaries and inventors reshape the possibilities available in the digital realm. In the boundless world of the digital future, the metaverse has evolved into a canvas for entrepreneurial innovation, where concepts bloom and conventional corporate boundaries are reinterpreted. The metaverse, which offers a glimpse of a future where the lines between the physical and virtual worlds blur and offer countless opportunities for exploration, cooperation, and creative entrepreneurship, is becoming more and more popular as technology develops (Kraus et al., 2022; Arora et al., 2016). It is essentially a digital frontier that keeps reshaping and redefining how we engage and interact with the always changing internet.

Here are some examples of renowned entrepreneurs (in the entrepreneurial ecosystem) who are gradually discovering the enormous potential of metaverse;

- **Mark Zuckerberg**: Under Zuckerberg's direction, Meta Platforms, Inc.—formerly Facebook—has made significant investments in the creation of the metaverse. Their goal is to build a virtual world that combines many digital activities such as gaming, entertainment, work, and social connections.
- **Elon Musk:** The SpaceX and Tesla CEO has shown interest in virtual reality and the metaverse fields of study. Musk has recognised the promise of virtual worlds and their influence on numerous businesses, even though his main focus is still on space exploration, electric cars, and other revolutionary ventures.
- **Philip Rosedale:** The creator of Second Life, has been working on High Fidelity, a virtual reality platform that aims to create a decentralized metaverse where users can create, interact, and transact in virtual spaces. High Fidelity is focused on enabling user-generated content and immersive social experience.

The objective of this retrospective analysis is to present a thorough account of the metaverse's journey within the entrepreneurial ecosystem. By highlighting significant intellectual structures, major themes, patterns and clusters as well as promising future prospects that have molded the entrepreneurial environment in the metaverse. Considering the objective, this study will address few research questions by conducting quantitative analysis of scholarly publications published in this knowledge domain.

a) What is the publication pattern, potential countries who publish in this knowledge domain?
b) What are the main conceptual structures and themes of research within the said discipline?

The research questions were analyzed with the help of network visualization and intellectual structures. The organization of chapter as follows: Section 2 provide brief insights about literature of the field. In Section 3 authors has discussed the methodology section of the paper. Section 4 present results and their respective interpretation and finally Section 5 provide conclusion of the study.

LITERATURE REVIEW

The Metaverse's popularity as a research topic has grown due to its ability to build immersive environments that bring individuals closer to different realities. It is determined that the subject has attracted academic attention, not only because of its impact on emerging technology knowledge, but also because of its significance in the growth of digital ecosystems (George-Reyes et al., 2023). Jacobides et al., (2023) stated that the metaverse is a collection of technologies that provide shared digital experiences through immersive virtual worlds or decentralized markets. Metaverse is seen as a collection of overlapping and partly competing ecosystems. Author discovered that incumbent enterprises hurried to embrace the metaverse in the expectation of avoiding disruption and preserving their competitive position, which resulted in over-investment. Overall, their research sheds the new light on the dynamics of innovation and technology hypes, as well as the problems involved in establishing and coordinating ecosystems. Yemenici (2022) mentioned that for individuals who aspire to be entrepreneurs in the Metaverse, the business potential, amenities, and obstacles of Metaverse are to be well evaluated first. The duet of entrepreneurship and metaverse has potential to offers many business opportunity to aspiring founders. The concepts of virtual world and virtual reality, which are the indications of the fast evolving digital age, are gaining prominence. The metaverse technology are appears to be the future central focus for online social interactions (Kraus et al., 2022). Handoko et al., (2023) mentioned that the development of the digital world is a current emergence in the era of the fourth industrial revolution. Virtual reality and augmented reality are two of the most recent technologies that have created a new technology known as the metaverse. The Metaverse is a virtual environment where people can communicate online. Many businesses have invested in the metaverse as it has grown. They acquire land and construct buildings and other infrastructure all across the metaverse. AI system-based organizations can expand automated services by leveraging data-driven technology and process innovation capabilities. Fintechs powered by AI and IoT enable immersive and collaborative financial transactions, purchases, and investments via payment tokens and metaverse wallets, while also managing financial data, infrastructure, and value exchange across shared interactive virtual 3D and simulated digital worlds (Andronie et al., 2023). Non-fungible token (NFT) goods are useful in industrial settings. They have rapidly gained relevance in the realm of blockchain mixed with metaverse in recent years. As many industries began to use NFTs creatively to raise new business innovation chances in entrepreneurship, the concept of NFTs rapidly evolved. According to authors findings, the most appealing NFT product types are collectible digital works and creative artworks characteristics (Wu et al., 2023).

The metaverse is predicted to be a trillion-dollar market within the next decade, changing the nature of entrepreneurship. However, research on the metaverse has its prospects and limitations, as well as the nature of entrepreneurship, is limited. This study establishes a paradigm for investigating metaverse-enabled entrepreneurship, including supply and demand enablers, as well as technological and social enablers. In the study authors have demonstrated how the metaverse provides transformative routes, such as purely virtual, physical to virtual, virtual to physical, and hybrid, and shapes offerings, initiatives, and processes. Authors have also examined the consequences for entrepreneurship research and map out a future research agenda so that research can lead and inform practice (Weking et al., 2023). Calandra et al. (2023) expressed that the metaverse encourages the creation of new entrepreneurial initiatives based on theoretical concepts such as gamification, co-design, and digital twins. Simultaneously, building new business models using technology might open up new avenues for entrepreneurship. The metaverse can help digital entrepreneurs by reinforcing the importance of technology as a tool for developing new business models. By using new opportunities, the metaverse can help digital entrepreneurs to expand beyond their primary business. Gupta et al,. (2023) stated that the metaverse opens up an entirely new world of opportunity for young entrepreneurs to capitalize on this new digital arena. However, because the metaverse is still in its early stages of growth, it is necessary to build new norms and policies for the advancement of sustainable entrepreneurship practices in the metaverse.

METHODOLOGY

This study has adopted bibliometric methodology to analyze the scholarly publications data on metaverse and entrepreneurship that was downloaded from Scopus database. The study has presented a keyword analysis through network structure and thematic map to examine the intellectual structure. These methods guide the present, emerging and future prospects of the said field. The network structure has been displayed by using VOSviewer and thematic map presented by using bibliometrix package of R software. The search was performed on 5th December, 2023 by searching key terms "metaverse" AND "entrepreneurial world" or "business world" OR "startup ecosystem" OR "innovation". Before applying filters a total set of 309 items were appeared in Scopus search and after filtration 235 items was extracted as a dataset. The search string used is: TITLE-ABS-KEY ("metaverse" AND "entrepreneurial world" OR "business world" OR "startup ecosystem" OR "innovation")

Data Collection Process

Here, Figure 1 depicts the current research's data extraction and filtering method. Scopus is a well-known database for scholarly publications; it contain and stores a vast amount of information about authors, publications, journals, books, countries that publish research all over the world (Dhiman & Arora, 2024). This is why the authors chose SCOPUS as a data collection tool. The keyterms "metaverse" AND "entrepreneurial world" OR "business world" OR "startup ecosystem" OR "innovation" were searched, and a group of 309 items appeared as the first result.

Figure 1. Process of data collection
Source: *Created by author*

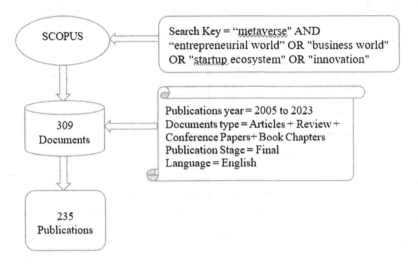

The results were then narrowed down using filters such as document type – articles, reviews, book chapters, and conference papers, publication stage – final and documents written other than English language were excluded from the dataset. Following cleaning, a final group of 235 papers has used to perform the analysis.

RESULTS AND INTERPRETATIONS

Table 1 describe the main statistical information about the data, which we have consider for further analysis. The data provides a complete snapshot of scholarly activities within that time period of 2005 to 2023. The academic world appears to be prolific, with 174 sources including various journals, books and conference proceedings contributing to a total of 235 documents. There was a 33.02% of yearly growth rate of indicates that there was a significant high increase in research production during last years. Because the concept has gained much more important after the COVID due to its virtual nature, where management through physical setting became difficult.

The large number of references (10,207) demonstrates the depth of interaction with existing material, demonstrating a rigorous and well-informed approach to study. Additionally, the 1,762 keywords used demonstrate diversity, highlighting the multidisciplinary nature of the investigations. With an average of 3.23 co-authors per document suggests the high collaboration among authors, emphasizing the importance

Table 1. Brief description about the data

Main Information of Data	
Timespan	2005:2025
Sources (Journals, Books, Conferences, etc.)	174
Documents	235
Annual Growth Rate (%)	33.02
Authors	702
Keywords	1762
References	10207
Authors Collaboration	
Single-Authored docs	53
Co-Authors per doc	3.23
Type of Documents	
Articles	83
Review	23
Book Chapter	46
Conference Paper	83

Source: Created by author and analyzed in RStudio

of teamwork and shared expertise in knowledge creation and development. The wide range of document forms, which includes articles, reviews, book chapters, and conference papers, demonstrates a comprehensive strategy to distributing research findings. Overall, this statistical analysis presents a vivid image of a vibrant and collaborative scholarly community that is actively contributing to the progress of knowledge across the fields.

4.1 Publications Pattern

Figure 2 presents the publication's patterns in the metaverse along with entrepreneurship, indicating a distinct trajectory between 2005 to 2023. The first few years, such as 2005 and 2009, witnessed a very few number of publications, indicating a slow investigation of the concept. A gap in publications until 2019 was witnessed, could imply that a period with inadequate scholarly attention to the convergence of metaverse and entrepreneurship. The noteworthy resurgence following 2020, with a single publication that year, indicates a renewed interest in the topic during and after the pandemic where connecting physically became challenging and

Figure 2. Production of Documents by Year
Source: *Scopus database*

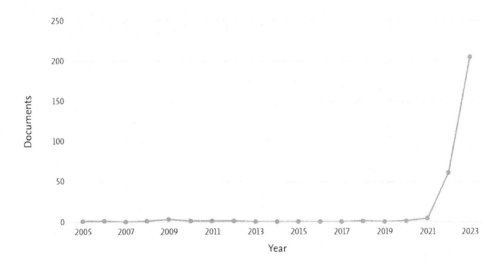

virtual platform become necessity to connect communicate and run the activities due to which metaverse concept gained the importance.

However, the major spike in number of publications arrived in 2021, with a considerable increase to 61 publications. This unexpected increase could be related to scholars' rising interest in understanding of the Metaverse as a transformative environment for entrepreneurial endeavours, encouraging them to investigate its possible ramifications and applications. The peak in 2022, with 205 articles, suggests a significant increase in scholarly activity, which could be attributed to technology breakthroughs, increasing corporate engagement, or a greater understanding of the entrepreneurial opportunities available in the Metaverse. This trend highlights the changing nature of research interests in response to emerging technological landscapes, with 2023 continuing the momentum with 205 publications, indicating sustained scholarly enthusiasm and a deeper exploration of the dynamic relationship between the Metaverse and Entrepreneurship.

Potential Countries Publishing in Knowledge Domain

Figure 3 shows the major contributions from a variety of countries reinforce the clear trends in metaverse and entrepreneurship studies. India emerges as the most prolific contributor, with the most articles. This could be attributed to India's growing interest and participation in innovative technology, as well as its thriving entrepreneurial ecosystem. China closely follows, showing the country's aggressive

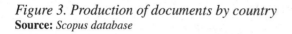

Figure 3. Production of documents by country
Source: *Scopus database*

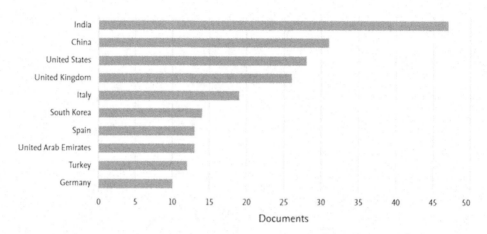

approach to technical innovation and its expanding role as a worldwide leader in the digital sphere. The United States and the United Kingdom, both recognized for their entrepreneurial ecosystems, secure their positions as important contributors, highlighting the global relevance of Metaverse-related entrepreneurship. The increase in research output corresponds to these countries' concentration on technology developments and commercial innovation, creating an atmosphere appropriate to the examination of novel concepts such as the Metaverse in an entrepreneurial context.

Conceptual Structures and Themes

Conceptual structures are used to identify specialized, developed, and evolving themes (Dhiman & Arora, 2023), which require organizing and understanding the underlying concepts in a particular field. Figure 4 presents the thematic map, which depicts two unique time slices, 2005 to 2020 and 2021 to 2023, provides useful insights into the changing environment of research in the metaverse along with entrepreneurship field. The key terms "mixed reality", "virtual reality", and "augmented reality" were ingeniously woven with the overarching concept of "metaverse" on the other side of the slice i.e. 2021-23. This interaction encourages a more in-depth and integrated investigation of these immersive technologies within the larger context of the metaverse. Furthermore, there was a theme shift with interconnecting waves containing "blockchain", "avatar" and "sustainability". This development could point to an increasing emphasis on sustainable practices within the metaverse, possibly driven by a greater awareness of environmental repercussions and the need for responsible development in the context of blockchain and avatar

Figure 4. Thematic evolution in knowledge domain
Source: *RStudio*

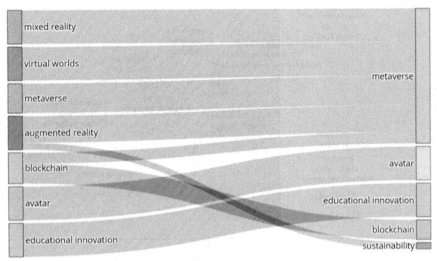

technologies. The inclusion of sustainability in the thematic map corresponds to broader global trends underlining ethical and environmentally conscientious issues in technical breakthroughs.

Figure 5 shows the major, core and evolving themes of the said discipline. Following figure of thematic map describes a dynamic and interconnected landscape of research themes within the metaverse and entrepreneurship domains, indicating a subtle evolution over time. The motor themes, includes key terms "big data", "block chain", "social networking", "e-learning", "engineering education", "health care", "augmented reality", and "immersive experiences", are at the core of the thematic map. These major themes represent the underlying foundations that shape the convergence of metaverse field. Health care, big data, and block chain show the importance of technology in addressing complicated problems, whereas social networking and e-learning highlight the impact on human connections, education and entrepreneurial avenues. Augmented reality and immersive experiences add to the Metaverse's revolutionary potential in a variety of industries. The specialized theme are "human learning", "digital innovation", "virtual power plants", and "energy trading", these themes indicate targeted areas of inquiry within the larger context, suggesting a deeper grasp of certain elements connected to human, learning, and the application of digital technology in energy-related fields. The emerging themes, which include "learning things", "Internet of Things" (IoT), "digital technologies",

Figure 5. Thematic map
Source: *RStudio*

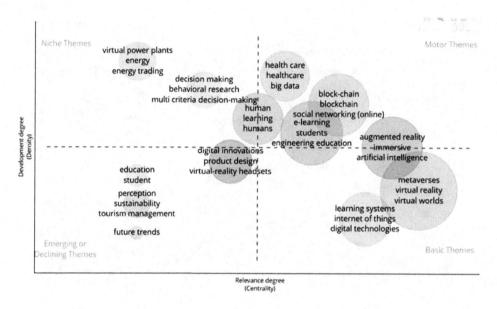

"artificial intelligence", "virtual reality", and "metaverse". These evolving themes point to a gradual change in study emphasis towards emerging technologies and their consequences for learning, networking, and immersive experiences.

CONCLUSION

The exploration of metaverse within the field of entrepreneurship has evolved greatly between 2005 and 2023. The observed trends indicate a vital stage in research, as evidenced by the spike of publications after 2020 and the significant increase in 2022 and 2023. This time period demonstrates a heightened understanding of the metaverse's revolutionary potential, with scholars focused on its applications in diverse fields. Thematic map analysis indicate a dynamic landscape characterized by numerous themes and an expanding scholarly interest in the convergence of technology, entrepreneurship, business, and societal problems. The increase of publications, collaborative activities, and the incorporation of developing issues like as artificial intelligence and metaverse itself highlight the expanding importance of these disciplines. Key central themes like big data, block chain and social networking, as well as minor themes like human learning and energy trading, demonstrate the complex character of study in this domain. As the Metaverse continues to draw attention, these findings contribute to a comprehensive knowledge of the business opportunities and challenges posed by this disruptive technology landscape.

The collaborative traits of the research, as seen by the large number of co-authored documents and contributions from various nations, highlights the worldwide importance and joint effort in understanding and exploiting the potential of the metaverse for entrepreneurial endeavors. The presence of keywords "mixed reality", "virtual reality", and "augmented reality" "metaverse" suggests a thorough analysis of diverse reality-altering technologies over time, demonstrating deep grasp of their applicability in entrepreneurial endeavours. This focus may represent that the scholars increasingly recognize the metaverse as a crucial and transformative issue in the area of entrepreneurship. The prominence of the keyword "metaverse" reflecting a greater emphasis on investigating business potential and difficulties inside the metaverse particularly. In nutshell, the metaverse and entrepreneurship study landscape has expanded dynamically, displaying a thorough investigation of immersive technology, societal implications, and creative commercial applications. The growing emphasis on sustainability, digital technology, and learning emphasizes scholars' approach to comprehending the complexity of this new topic. This research can makes a substantial contribution to constructing the metaverse narrative, giving vital insights for entrepreneurs, politicians, and scholars navigating the obstacles and opportunities in this transformational domain.

REFERENCES

Allam, Z., Sharifi, A., Bibri, S. E., Jones, D. S., & Krogstie, J. (2022). The metaverse as a virtual form of smart cities: Opportunities and challenges for environmental, economic, and social sustainability in urban futures. *Smart Cities, 5*(3), 771–801. doi:10.3390/smartcities5030040

Andronie, M., Iatagan, M., Uță, C., Hurloiu, I., Dijmărescu, A., & Dijmărescu, I. (2023). Big data management algorithms in artificial Internet of Things-based fintech. *Oeconomia Copernicana, 14*(3), 769–793. doi:10.24136/oc.2023.023

Arora, M. (2016). Creative dimensions of entrepreneurship: A key to business innovation. *Pacific Business Review International, 1*(1), 255–259.

Arora, M., Dhiman, V., & Sharma, R. L. (2023). Exploring the dimensions of spirituality, wellness and value creation amidst Himalayan regions promoting entrepreneurship and sustainability. *Journal of Tourismology, 9*(2), 86–96.

Arora, M., Kumar, J., & Valeri, M. (2023). Crises and Resilience in the Age of Digitalization: Perspectivations of Past, Present and Future for Tourism Industry. In Tourism Innovation in the Digital Era (pp. 57-74). Emerald Publishing Limited.

Arora, M., & Sharma, R. L. (2021). Repurposing the Role of Entrepreneurs in the Havoc of COVID-19. In Entrepreneurship and Big Data (pp. 229-250). CRC Press. doi:10.1201/9781003097945-16

Arora, M., & Sharma, R. L. (2022). Integrating Gig Economy and Social Media Platforms as a Business Strategy in the Era of Digitalization. In *Integrated Business Models in the Digital Age: Principles and Practices of Technology Empowered Strategies* (pp. 67–86). Springer International Publishing. doi:10.1007/978-3-030-97877-8_3

Arora, M., & Sharma, R. L. (2023). Artificial intelligence and big data: Ontological and communicative perspectives in multi-sectoral scenarios of modern businesses. *Foresight, 25*(1), 126–143. doi:10.1108/FS-10-2021-0216

Calandra, D., Oppioli, M., Sadraei, R., Jafari-Sadeghi, V., & Biancone, P. P. (2023). Metaverse meets digital entrepreneurship: A practitioner-based qualitative synthesis. *International Journal of Entrepreneurial Behaviour & Research.*

Calandra, D., Oppioli, M., Sadraei, R., Jafari-Sadeghi, V., & Biancone, P. P. (2023). Metaverse meets digital entrepreneurship: A practitioner-based qualitative synthesis. *International Journal of Entrepreneurial Behaviour & Research.*

Dhiman, V., & Arora, M. (2023). *How foresight has evolved since 1999? Understanding its themes, scope and focus. Foresight.* EarlyCite. doi:10.1108/FS-01-2023-0001

Dhiman, V., & Arora, M. (2024). *Exploring the linkage between business incubation and entrepreneurship: understanding trends, themes and future research agenda. LBS Journal of Management & Research.* EarlyCite. doi:10.1108/LBSJMR-06-2023-0021

Dionisio, J. D. N., Iii, W. G. B., & Gilbert, R. (2013). 3D virtual worlds and the metaverse: Current status and future possibilities. *ACM Computing Surveys, 45*(3), 1–38. doi:10.1145/2480741.2480751

Enache, M. C. (2022). Metaverse Opportunities for Businesses. *Annals of the University Dunarea de Jos of Galati: Fascicle: I, Economics & Applied Informatics, 28*(1).

George-Reyes, C. E., Ramírez-Montoya, M. S., & López-Caudana, E. O. (2023). Imbrication of the Metaverse in the complexity of education 4.0: Approach from an analysis of the literature. Pixel-Bit. *Revista de Medios y Educación, 66*, 199–237. doi:10.12795/pixelbit.97337

Gupta, B. B., Gaurav, A., Albeshri, A. A., & Alsalman, D. (2023). New paradigms of sustainable entrepreneurship in metaverse: A micro-level perspective. *The International Entrepreneurship and Management Journal, 19*(3), 1–17. doi:10.1007/s11365-023-00875-0

Handoko, B. L., Lindawati, A. S. L., Sarjono, H., & Mustapha, M. (2023). Innovation Diffusion and Technology Acceptance Model in Predicting Auditor Acceptance of Metaverse Technology. *Journal of System and Management Sciences, 13*(5), 443–456.

Jacobides, M. G., Candelon, F., Krayer, L., Round, K., & Chen, W. (2023). Building synthetic worlds: Lessons from the excessive infatuation and oversold disillusionment with the metaverse. *Industry and Innovation*, 1–25.

Kraus, S., Kanbach, D. K., Krysta, P. M., Steinhoff, M. M., & Tomini, N. (2022). Facebook and the creation of the metaverse: Radical business model innovation or incremental transformation? *International Journal of Entrepreneurial Behaviour & Research, 28*(9), 52–77. doi:10.1108/IJEBR-12-2021-0984

Sparkes, M. (2021). *What is a metaverse*. Research Gate.

Weking, J., Desouza, K. C., Fielt, E., & Kowalkiewicz, M. (2023). Metaverse-enabled entrepreneurship. *Journal of Business Venturing Insights, 19*, e00375. doi:10.1016/j.jbvi.2023.e00375

Weking, J., Desouza, K. C., Fielt, E., & Kowalkiewicz, M. (2023). Metaverse-enabled entrepreneurship. *Journal of Business Venturing Insights, 19*, e00375. doi:10.1016/j.jbvi.2023.e00375

Wu, C. H., Liu, C. Y., & Weng, T. S. (2023). Critical Factors and Trends in NFT Technology Innovations. *Sustainability (Basel), 15*(9), 7573. doi:10.3390/su15097573

Yaqoob, I., Salah, K., Jayaraman, R., & Omar, M. (2023). Metaverse applications in smart cities: Enabling technologies, opportunities, challenges, and future directions. *Internet of Things : Engineering Cyber Physical Human Systems, 23*, 100884. doi:10.1016/j.iot.2023.100884

Yemenici, A. D. (2022). Entrepreneurship in the world of metaverse: Virtual or real? *Journal of Metaverse, 2*(2), 71–82. doi:10.57019/jmv.1126135

Chapter 6
Role of Human Resource (HR) Analytics and Metaverse in Employee Engagement and Turnover Intention

Soni Rathi

iD https://orcid.org/0000-0002-2997-8622
Chandigarh University, India

Praveen Kumar
Chandigarh University, India

ABSTRACT

In recent years, the term "HR analytics" and metaverse in HR have become prominent and have progressively been used in organisations as a systematic approach. Some organisations that have adopted the use of metaverse and analytics in their HR departments have been extremely successful. The current chapter strives to attain some objectives; namely, explore the meaning of HR analytics, its importance and benefits, the kinds of HR analytics, the meaning of metaverse, and the role of HR analytics and metaverse in employee engagement and employee turnover. This chapter will include a theoretical analysis to attain the mentioned objectives. The goal is to provide a holistic picture and discuss some aspects like definitions, importance, benefits, types, etc., under HR analytics and the aspects (meaning, role, and benefits).of the metaverse. The use of HR analytics and metaverse have reformed the performance of workforce and escalated efficiency in business, reforming the quality of recruitment, talent management, employee productivity, employee engagement, and diminishing employee turnover.

DOI: 10.4018/979-8-3693-5868-9.ch006

INTRODUCTION

The dynamic role of human resources (HR) has lately been taken over by Human resource management (HRM). HR departments are no longer considered a subset of a company generated solely for the reason of recruiting and terminating staff members (Nishii, Lepak and Schneider, 2008). Human resources, an organisation's most valuable asset, have the tendency to offer competitive advantages over time. The field of HRA has been around for a while, but its popularity has only recently grown. Workforce, talent, human capital and people analytics are other terms for HR analytics (Tursunbayeva, Lauro and Pagliari, 2018), which is used interchangeably by academics and the business world. The link amid analytics and human resource management is obvious, although human resource management is late in joining the data analytics trend (Sharma and Sharma, 2017). HR analytics is the result of unifying and merging human resource metrics and business analysis in general.

HR enters the metaverse, and it has an essential role in aiding the combination of virtual environments into Human resource (HR) practices. This includes overseeing virtual reality in recruitment and remote onboarding processes, developing virtual training and development programs, and fostering a sense of virtual community and employee engagement. The purpose of HRA is to improve decisions about people to enhance individual performance and/or organisational performance by applying a methodology and integrated process (Bassi, 2011). The key goals of this article is to identify the meaning of HR Analytics, benefits & types of HR Analytics, what is the role of HR Analytics in employee engagement & employee turnover intention?, what is metaverse and the role of HR in metaverse?

A brief overview of HR analytics is presented in this article, along with its importance, types, various latest definitions from existing sources and strive to put them altogether in an efficient manner. The study consists of four sections. The first is the introduction, the second describes the HR Analytics, additionally, the third section is devoted to the HR analytics roles in employee engagement & employee turnover intention, and the fourth section has included what is Metaverse? and what is the role of HR in Metaverse? The conclusion, limitations, and future direction are also mentioned eventually in this chapter.

What Is Human Resource Analytics?

"HR Analytics is a proactive and systematic process for ethically gathering, analyzing, communicating and using evidence-based HR research and Analytical insights to help organisations achieve their strategic objectives" (Falletta and Combs 2021). Inspite of the significant interest in people/talent analytics (Boudreau and Casio, 2017; Falletta, 2014; Huselid, 2018), there is an error in the meaning and capabilities of talent analytics. Both locally and globally, it has become a major issue. Analytical models can be developed to boost employee retention by identifying what employees like and dislike. It also supports supervisors in determining whether or not to compete with an equivalent enrollment offer from other organizations, schedule tailored incentive programmes, or determine the ideal time for disclosing promotions or raises. The use of HRA is growing with the availability of increasing amounts of data. Because of the rising awareness of personnel management and the way to revenues, data like this will assist to fulfil any demands that might take place (Bassi, 2011). With the aim to make better use of human capital more effectively, HRA will aid in anticipating worker actions (Schneider, 2006). HR Analytics aids in assembling, interpretation, and evaluating of HR data. It also offer latest and reliable data as well as enhanced future options. Further, it aids in rendering solutions to organisational obstacles and aligns HR strategy. Human Resource analytics works on various levels, both tactical and functional because it offers an approach for coordinating team goals with corporate goals.

Proceeding further in this chapter, HRA is often refereed to by other terms like workforce and people analytics since they are interchangeable with HR/talent analytics (Heuvel and Bondarouk, 2017). Analytics, in general, refers to *"the use of analysis, data and systematic reasoning to make decisions"* (Davenport, Harris and Morison, (2010). According to Jones (2014), Human resource managers discover human resource analytics as a tool which gives them the data they need for making decisions which may assist them to struggle with high levels of employee turnover, enhance the proficiency of fresh employees, and anticipate organisational efficiency and achievement. Ranjan and Basak (2013) mentioned the HR analytics as *"the scope and approach to HRA should be determined based on contextual factors such as objective, internal readiness, investment appetite, and target time frame to achieve the objective"*. There are several goals of HR Analytics (Ben-Gal, 2018) namely: to assembling and maintaining data in a useful manner to anticipating both immediate and distant patterns of personnel demands and supply throughout distinct places of work, to aid worldwide corporations/firms to give verdicts regarding the optimal attainment, to generate and keep of human capital, to render with respect to effectively managing workforce for achieving organisational goals swiftly and significantly and to positively influence the successful implementation of an organisation's strategies.

Based on a MIT and IBM survey, organisations with high HRA experienced 8% higher sales growth, 24% higher profitability, and 58% higher average sales per human resource. Almost 22% of respondents said that using data to improve recruitment turnaround time helped their organisations protect excellent recruits, and over 55% stated that an effective HR data analytics assists in retaining excellent recruits. The are some of the popular global trends of HR analytics:

- By 2027, the global HR analytics market is expected to grow by 14.2 percent annually to reach US$6.29 billion.
- Due to COVID-19, global labor markets have swung dramatically, and 55% of Americans plan to seek new employment within the next year.
- Data analytics professionals and HR analytics solution vendors are expected to have more job opportunities as machine learning (ML) & artificial intelligence (AI) increase in HR analytics across millions of organisations worldwide.
- Prior to the pandemic, 73% of HR pros said people analytics would be a major priority for the company in the next five years, according to LinkedIn's 2020 Global Talent Trends Report. A path to more widespread adoption of emerging technologies and tools has recently begun to emerge, such as the integration of Glint with Microsoft Viva.

Meanings or Definitions of Human resource Analytics

The application of personnel analytics has a high possibility of escalation in the future (Fernandez and Gallardo-Gallardo (2021). Interestingly, there are some definitions of HR or people or workforce analytics mentioned below (Huselid, 2018; Tursunbayeva, Lauro and Pagliari, 2018; McIver, Lengnick-Hall and Lengnick- Hall, 2018; Mondare, Douthitt and Carson, 2011). HRA can be examined as a systematic approach from an organisational perspective. As previously stated, it is a new domain of study for academic review, and the authors' professional backgrounds are reflected in these definitions.

Importance and Significance of HR Analytics

The main target of personnel analytics is to improve the organisation's durability over time by making brilliant and intellectual decisions about workforce after the evaluation of accumulated data in a substantive way using analytical techniques to reform corporate efficiency and success. According to Kale, Aher and Anute, 2022; Reddy and Lakshmikeerthi (2017); Kiran, Sharma, and Brijmohan (2018); Bhattacharyya (2017); Reena, Ansari,and Jayakrishnan (2019); Fred and Kinange (2015); Kirtane (2015), significance of HR Analytics are given below:

- Reform the workforce's output and return on investment.
- Render the chance to evaluate how employees contribute to the company and determines how well they can fulfil their career expectations.
- Identify the need for human resources and how to fill the open positions.

Figure 1. Human resource analytics
(Source: Choudhury and Barman, 2016)

- Establish a link between the use of human resources and strategic and financial objectives to improve organisational performance.
- Planning for human resources is aided by HR analytics. ·
- Future HR trends and patterns can be predicted in a number of different ways (turnover, absenteeism, etc.).
- Aids in identifying the flawed procedures that end up being the main reason for attrition, which helps in keeping and keeping high-performing employees.
- Unearths the antecedents that lead to greater workforce contentment and productivity.
- Identifies high-value employees who may be leaving and ascertains the root causes of employee attrition.
- It aids in forecasting employee needs and skill sets in order to meet organisational goals.
- Develops efficient education, development and training programmes.

Table 1. Definitions and meanings

Sno	Definitions/meanings	Authors
1.	*"HR Analytics is not only understood as a tool where statistical methods are applied and the focus is on key figures, but as a systematic approach".*	FallettaiandiCombs,i(2021)
2.	*"HR Analytics could be used to measure investments in reskilling, which will deliver the right competencies to support a new revenue model, using data-driven insights to modify the training offering as sales results emerge".*	Lalwani, 2021
3.	*"HR Analytics specifically deals with the metrics of the HR function, such as time to hire, training expense per employee, and time until promotion".*	Lalwani, 2021
4.	*"Workforce Analytics is an all-encompassing term referring specifically to employees of an organization. It includes on-site employees, remote employees, gig workers, freelancers, consultants, and any other individuals working in various capacities in an organization".*	Lalwani, 2021
5.	*"People Analytics, though comfortably used as a synonym for HR Analytics, is technically applicable to "people" in general. It can encompass any group of individuals even outside the organization. For instance, the term "people Analytics" may be applied to Analytics about the customers of an organization and not necessarily only employees".*	Lalwani, 2021
6.	*"HR Analytics is a methodology that uses statistical tools and techniques to unify and evaluate employees quantitative and qualitative data that helps in bringing out meaningful insights to develop better future decision making".*	Tomar and Gaur, (2020)
7.	*"HR Analytics is an experimental approach that uses software and method based on HR metrics to provide reliable and justifiable human capital results impact effectively and efficiently".*	Tomar and Gaur, (2020)
8.	*"HR Analytics is a data-driven framework that understands and evaluates the relationship between workforce problems and employee's performance by driving new insights through existing insights".*	Tomar and Gaur, (2020)
9.	*"HR Analytics is HRM innovation enabled by companies to analyses HR data, processes, human capital statically for making data-driven decision making and ignoring the process of gut feeling".*	Tomar and Gaur, (2020)
10.	*"Workforce Analytics refers to the processes involved with understanding, quantifying, managing and improving the role of talent in the execution of strategy and the creation of value. It includes not only a focus on metrics (e.g. what do we need to measure about our workforce?), but also Analytics (e.g. how do we manage and improve the metrics we deem to be critical for business success)".*	Huselid, (2018)
11.	*"People Analytics is an area of HRM practice, research and innovation concerned with the use of information technologies, descriptive and predictive data Analytics and visualization tools for generating actionable insights about workforce dynamics, human capital and individual and team performance that can be used strategically to optimize organizational effectiveness, efficiency and outcomes and improve employee experience".*	Tursunbayeva,iLauroiandi, Pagliari,i(2018)
12.	*"HRA as a communication device that paints a cohesive and actionable picture of the current situation and the future outcomes".*	Reddy and Lakshmikeerthi (2017)
13.	*"HR Analytics has unfortunately become synonymous with anything related to numbers, data collection and measurement in the context of HR".*	LevensoniandiFink,i(2017)
14.	*"HR Analytics means different things to different people. For some, HR Analytics simply refers to descriptive HR metrics while for others it means sophisticated predictive modeling procedures".*	Bassi, (2011)
15.	*"HR Analytics is a systematic procedure to comprehend the influence of HR practices and policies on organizational performance. Statistical techniques and experimental approaches can be used to tease out the causal relationship between particular HR practices and such performance metrics as customer satisfaction, sales per employee and, of course, the profitability of particular business activities".*	Lawler, Levenson, and Boudreau, (2004)

- Evaluates the data using different HR metrics.
- It aids in showing the outcomes and how they were achieved.
- Aids supervisors or employers in implementing pragmatic choices.
- Estimates the financial influence on staffing policies.
- Determines who fits into the organisation's culture through evaluations of job responsibility, engagement of staff members, dedication among workers, and so on.
- Based on data on staff efficiency, academic record, discipline background, and so on, it offers helpful information for personnel to estimate which employees can be up-skilled to become experts.
- The profession of staffing practice and its specialist gain more credibility.
- It aids in achieving better organisational achievements through excellent choices, particularly in recruiting talents.
- Personnel managers tend to be involved in tactical discussions since they are able to measure their several impacts on corporate results.
- The personnel departments can be held accountable for influencing the bottom-line the same way business leaders are held accountable.
- It aids in the unbiased staffing of the most promising skilled workers for particular roles.
- Greater ability to justify human capital investments.
- It helps in highlighting essential performance of personnels which might have a significant impact on the success of an organisation.

Types of HR Analytics

The goal of human resource Analytics is to improve critical talent by collecting and analyzing talent data. It is primarily utilised to make decisions based on data that is accessible, anticipate turnover of staff, and discover more talented workers. It can additionally used for predicting which abilities should be became more proficient. Human resources analytics can be referred people analytics. It allows the organisation to assess the effect of human resources metrics on the overall efficiency of the organisations while making data-driven decisions. Human resource analytics is a data-driven method of analysis with an emphasis on more effective HR administration. It operates with the goal of making a particular organisation which is more capable instead of other organisations around it. The distinct kinds of HR Analytics used by HR departments to aid the workplace such as descriptive, diagnostic, predictive and prescriptive analytics.

1.   Descriptive Analytics

Figure 2. Descriptive analytics
Source: (Singh, Singh and Singh, 2022)

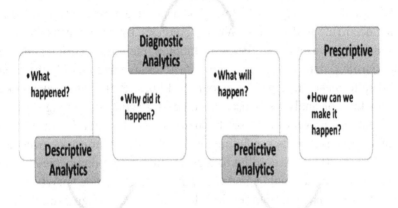

The most fundamental type of analytics is descriptive analytics, also referred to as observing and reporting. According to Kale, Aher, and Anute (2022) "descriptive analytics" is the procedure of gathering and reporting data regarding what occurred previously. What happened is depicted in this analysis? Human resource analytics that are descriptive in nature indicate and explain the associations as well as past and present data structures. (Reddy and Lakshmikeerthi, 2017). It generally gathers all of the accessible archival data, presents it to make a reasonable aspect and helps in determining future actions (Kale, Aher and Anute, 2022). The descriptive analytics is used, for example, to compare the turnover rates between two departments and to evaluate the average number of paid off days for human resources.

2.   Diagnostic Analytics

Diagnostic analytics attempts to identify the main reasons of issues effectively. This analysis depicts why did it happen? Identifying the issues is essential for resolving the issue. It relies on a number of methods which comprises data drilling and data mining. Business organisations must comprehend the reason why problems occurs and find solutions of them (Kale, Aher and Anute, 2022). For example, Hr managers use diagnostic analytics to find out why employees are missing work more often. It also aids to reform the employees' engagement because highly engaged employees tend to be the most productive. According to 2019 report a shoe retailer Clarks discovered that employee engagement can increase the performance of an organisation by 0.4 percent for every 1% improvement.

3.   Predictive Analytics

With predictive analytics, organisations predict future occurrences by using archival data activity. Analyzing historical data aids in determining the likelihood of something occurring in the future. What is predicted by this analysis will occur? It is obtained using a variety of statistical techniques, including artificial intelligence, machine learning, data modelling, and data mining, which use both recent and archival data to make anticipations about the future (Reddy and Lakshmikeerthi, 2017). This kind of analytics is used to forecast whether upcoming projects will succeed or fail. Employers can lessen the likelihood of failure and thus increase the growth of an organisation by predicting the likelihood of a future occurrence (Kale, Aher and Anute, 2022). According to reports, automobile companies can predict when employees will take unplanned vacations using predictive analytics. By using absence forecasts, managers can reschedule shifts and/or assign extra workers.

4.   Prescriptive Analytics

Prescriptive analytics is associated with making recommendations for subsequent actions based on predictive analytics predictions. This analysis depicts How can we make it happen? This analytics can go further by anticipating and explaining options for decision-making as well as personnel optimised performance. It is implemented to analyse complicated data in order to anticipate final results, deliver alternatives to decisions, and highlight another commercial effects (Reddy and Lakshmikeerthi, 2017). The recommendations pitched by this analytics have been founded on analysis of data which makes them less erratic. This entails that performing statistical modelling in identifying the optimal strategy to follow around prospective achievement. It includes generating suggested measures in order to comprehend results. Organisations utilise this kind of analytics to make tactical choices (Kale, Aher and Anute, 2022). For instance, if a person watches shoe review videos frequently on YouTube, the platform's algorithm is likely to analyze that data and suggest similar content that the person may enjoy.

Stages/Procedure of Human Resource Analytics

Human resource Analytics consists of 5 stages (Jain and Nagar, 2015; Boakye and Lamptey, 2020) which are given below:

1.   Defining Objectives of HR Analytics

Figure 3. HR-Related objectives
Source: (Jain and Nagar, 2015)

Source:(Jain and Nagar, 2015)

To be able to implement human resource analytics with regard to managerial operational objectives, HR professionals first need to identify the topmost critical objectives. An objective might be, for example, to find out the elements that lead to improved efficiency among staff members, to determine the percentage of staff leaving for the upcoming year, to assess how satisfied staff members are, to assess the consequences of occupational risks on staff productivity, and so on.

2.   Gather data

It is crucial that HR professionals collect data relevant to the variables of HR-related objectives once they have identified what HR-related objectives they wish to accomplish. A variety of methods of data collection are available to HR professionals, including questionnaires, interviews, discussions, observations, and electronic platforms (HRIMS). This data collection can be internal or external such as employee tenure, passive data from employees right from recruitment stage, data on high and low performers, HR program evaluation, employee training records and so on.

3.   Evaluation of HR Metrics

The following phase is in determining the human resources metrics which an organisation intends to employ for taking decisions according to the data gathered for the goals that have been identified. In simple terms, this entails identifying dimensions for evaluating employees antecedents. For instance, employee job satisfaction index, rate of employee turnover, and etc. It consequently becomes critical to gather and transform relevant data from workers that is established, preserved, and distributed to ensure consistency and accessibility. The structure and nature of the data both are equally significant. Human resource managers must also make sure that the data for evaluation is of excellent quality and suitable for evaluations.

4.   Data Analysis

To gain meaningful information from the data, it is necessary to conduct highly developed statistical analyses. Making effective human assets decisions requires a strong logical foundation in HR departments. In order to determine if workplace hazards have a significant negative effect on employee performance, a regression analysis must be conducted. It is stated that workplace hazards influence workforce performance significantly and negatively when the result of the variance is negative and significant. Moreover, to determine the staff departures level, split the total number of staff members who quit the company over a particular period of time by the total number of staff members who remained.

5.   Decision making stage

Data analysis and the extraction of meaningful information are the first steps to making informed decisions. In most cases, this requires altering existing human resource practices and processes in order to achieve organisational goals or creating new HR policies, procedures, and processes. To prevent workplace hazards, workforce must modify existing rules and regulations or develop new ones after finding that workplace hazards have a significant negative impact on employee performance.

Employee Engagement

Managing staff/personnel at a workplace can be made easier through human resource analytics. The technique is used to store related information about staff profiles, such as experience, skill set, academic skills, etc. A variety of metrics are used to provide data that helps the HR department with the recruitment process. HR analytics assesses the explanation for the increment and decrement in the number of resignations of workers. This keeps the evidence of staff or work contentment, commitment within the workplace, and other relevant information (Tomar and Gaur, 2020). Employee engagement is highly desirable and an affective-motivational element because an highly engaged employees means innovative employees (Gawke, Gorgievski and

Bakker 2017; Orth and Volmer, 2017) and because of it they have positive attitude toward job. It also leads to lower absenteeism and intent to quit (Schaufeli and Bakker, 2004; Saks, 2006). Many researchers have defined employee engagement in terms of a person's psychological and cognitive affiliation (Baumruk, 2004; Shaw, 2005; Richman, 2006). It is additionally referred to as "discretionary effort" demonstrated by individuals in their positions of employment. (Frank, Finnegan and Taylor, 2004). This emphasises on "psychological availability, safety, and meaningfulness" in carrying out official assigned duties (Bhatnagar, 2007; Bhatnagar, 2009).

HR Analytics may assist organisations to keep their staff members engaged while enhancing their performance. When organisations have data of excellent quality, the skills to interpret and the tactical ability to make decisions, they should use value-added HR analytics (Minbaeva,2018). In contrast, it was difficult for Human Resources departments to have value-added human resource analytics due to low technological devices, poor data interpretation capability, fewer resources, and an absence of quality data (Anderson, 2017). Engaged employees are not necessarily happy or satisfied employees. There is a lack of understanding and proper representation of this term in reports. organisations and their employees form a relationship described by this term. It's important to determine how passionate employees are about their work based on their dedication to the organisation's goals. Engagement tends to improve retention, performance, and productivity, and high performers go above and beyond their responsibilities (KUDOS, 2021). Engagement levels among employees began to decline in 2021 for the first time in a decade. Based on a examination of over 57,000 part-time and full-time employees, employee engagement dipped in the second half of 2021 from 36 to 34 (in percent), as employee disengagement escalated from 14 to 16 (in percent) (WNDYR, 2022). Teams must constantly report and monitor employee satisfaction in in order to handle it effectively. There are a few measures of job satisfaction, including the employee engagement score, the proportion of engaged workers, employee satisfaction with benefits and pay, hiring process retention rate, and overall satisfaction scores (HCMI, 2022).

Role of HR Analytics in Employee Engagement

A more data-driven, methodical approach to monitoring and boost employee participation is made possible by HR analytics. After its implementation, the HR department do not have to rely on hunches or dubious survey findings. HR analytics gives verifiable proof of how workers interact with the modern workforce of the company. HR analytics, which functions as a modern information system, assists in the regular collection and evaluation of data regarding the firm's personnel. Based on HR analytics, it is possible to assess employee engagement, organisational effectiveness, managerial decision excellence, and other aspects of human resource management (Tikhonov, 2020). Although achieving work engagement is regarded as a strategic goal, doing so blindly is frequently ineffective. Therefore, measurement and motivation are the two key components of HR analytics and employee engagement. Measuring engagement is difficult because it is a feeling. In order to understand how well employees are engaged, HR departments can use employee engagement surveys with the aid of HR analytics. Human resources and finance leaders can use this information to evaluate current workforce conditions and develop plans to improve employee engagement, satisfaction, and retention. They can also get a snapshot of employee opinions of their work, managers, coworkers, and the company as a whole.

Additionally, HR analytics inspires workers and provides them with objective information and feedback according to their behaviors and outputs within the organisation. Employees gain a better understanding of their strengths and weaknesses, as well as practical advice on how to improve (WNDYR, 2022). Employees who are highly engaged are devoted, concentrated, enthusiastic, and committed to both individual and organisational growth. HR managers can assess the impact of employee engagement on the organisation's financial performance by gathering data on employee performance and financial performance data. This assists the manager in determining how engaged the employees are at work, as well as assisting the HR department in developing better employee engagement and performance management policies in the future. At work, there is higher productivity, more innovation, better performance, higher commitment, and higher productivity when there is a high degree of participation of employees. It is believed that organisations perform much better and are more productive when their employees are more engaged which also lead to job satisfaction (Jain and Jain, 2020).

For instance, in April 2020, ASDA, a supermarket chain in the U.K., selected workday, an enterprise cloud application platform for human resources and finance, to improve its human resource experience and provide assistance to the global workforce with the help of workday absence management, workday benefits, workday compensation, workday learning and workday prism analytics. As a result of adopting these solutions, companies are able to improve employee engagement, alleviate employee on-boarding, and improve the productivity of their personnel. Organisations place a strong emphasis on how employee performance affects business performance, and they do this by offering health benefits as well that encourage employees to do hard work and take care of their families' medical needs. To draw in and maintain employees, a compensation package must include health benefits. It is believed by them that by taking care of workers, businesses will perform better because happier workers produce better work (Gates, 2002).

Turnover Intention

Turnover intention is the quantity or proportion of workers who quit their jobs and are replaced by new hires (Hom, Lee, Shaw, and Hausknecht 2017). In other words, to the movement of workers across organisational boundaries. Even though businesses invest so heavily in their workforce through hiring, training, development, and retention, it is regarded as a major managerial decisions. Expenses involved with turnover can be significant and these expenditure include those related to recruiting and selecting new employees, paying for their training, and replacing lost human resources. These expenses are generally challenging to quantify but can be significant (de Oliveira, Cavazotte, & Alan Dunzer, 2019). HR staff will definitely look at a wide range of data to get an accurate picture of turnover since it is influenced by many different factors. That is why it is pivotal for HR leaders to adopt a vigorous data-driven practice to aid organisations in spotting, engaging, and encouraging high performers (HCMI, 2022).

Role of HR Analytics in Turnover Intention

Analytics and efforts to increase retention to lower turnover are two ways that human resources assist businesses in saving time and money. Retaining staff members reduces cost overruns, increases profitability, recruitment of fresh talents increases expenses for training, and it additionally requires a period of time to get used to a new worker to the needs of the organisation, skilled staff members tend to be appointed from outside sources but that becomes expensive and that is why HR analytics are important for HR strategy planners (Jain and Jain, 2020). The first step in reforming retention is to highlight the areas of the organisation with high turnover rates or less sustained employment (Patil, 2021). HR analytics serve a purpose in determining who is the top performer within the company and which employees have the potential to lead, along with prioritising human resource retention by predicting turnover early (Harris, Craig and Light, 2011). Some of the the organisations have begun utilising predictive analytics to reduce turnover and enhance retention of their productive personnel, based on the effective implementation of machine learning algorithms. For example, the (former) senior vice president of HR at Google argued that statistics were used to fully automate their job interview questions based on their candidates' profiles and actually use employee data to predict turnover (Vahlen, 2016).

HR managers can gain a better understanding of the causes of high turnover among staff members by using HR analytics. For instance, HR managers may look into why employees left their jobs and discover the most common reasons behind it such as low pay and mismatch between the job role & the candidate hired which made him/her leave the organisation. According to HR analytics, there are some other reasons why staff members leave their jobs such as issues with particular managers or management staff, compensation that is not in line with local market compensation for in-person roles, industry-specific remuneration for virtual or hybrid jobs, equivalent positions in other firms, lack of opportunities for growth and learning, lack of promotions, and an unequal distribution of payouts (Marson, 2022). HR executives can investigate these problems and possibly develop strategies to address them, pay close attention to management practices, or discover methods for helping staff members advance their careers.

What is Metaverse?

Metaverse is defined as a *"virtual reality-based environment that allows users to interact with digital representations of the physical world"*. It has gained significant attention in recent years (Suhird, 2023). The metaverse has also emerged as a topic of interest in the field of human resource management (HRM). It combines various cutting-edge technologies, including artificial intelligence (AI), virtual reality (Wu et. al, 2023), augmented reality (Koohand et.al, 2023), robotics, and, blockchain (Huynh-The et. al, 2023). This convergence of technologies opens new avenues for delivering high-quality services in all aspects of our lives. The Metaverse has the potential to revolutionize diverse domains, such as education, entertainment, communication, commerce, and social interactions (Daneshfar et. al, 2023). It can completely reshape the way we learn, engage in entertainment, connect with others, conduct business, and interact in society. It allows people to connect in a virtual world that is almost as realistic as the physical world, but with endless opportunities for imagination, discovery, and experimentation (Knox, 2022).

The speedy progress of technology has significantly influenced the way of organizations, including how they manage their human resources. Human resource management (HRM), as a critical function in organizations, has constantly evolved to keep pace with technological advancements. One of the recent technological advancements that have gained significant attention is the metaverse, a virtual reality based on environment that allows users to interact with digital representations of the physical world. From recruitment to training, employee engagement to diversity and inclusion, the metaverse offers unique opportunities for HRM professionals to enhance their practices and improve organizational outcomes (Suhird, 2023).

HR in the Metaverse: Virtual Reality for Enhanced Employee Engagement

HR and the metaverse go hand in hand, and there is no doubt that HR practices can be effectively implemented in a virtual environment. HR departments can take back brand culture and engage with team members again in the metaverse. The next evolution in communication, the metaverse is changing the way teams work, which changes how HR teams maintain remote company culture, support team member productivity and satisfaction, and manage human resource processes (Suhird, 2023). More than digital space for distributing and consuming content, the metaverse allows intentionally designed experiences. The metaverse comprises evolving augmented and virtual reality, artificial intelligence, blockchain, and 5G networks coming together in 3D environments. Additionally, it can offer virtual networking opportunities, allowing employees to connect and build relationships in virtual conferences or events. The metaverse has a significant impact on HR by transforming the way employees work, collaborate, and engage with their organizations (Suhird, 2023). For instance, virtual reality HR can enable immersive training experiences, allowing employees to learn new skills in simulated environments. Simultaneously, augmented reality HR can enhance remote collaboration by overlaying digital information onto the physical workspace. This technology facilitates real-time communication and problem-solving among team members, even when physically separated.

The metaverse offers opportunities to enhance employee engagement through virtual team-building activities and social events. Virtual team-building activities can be organized in the metaverse, allowing employees to connect and collaborate in a virtual environment. For example, employees can participate in virtual team-building games, escape rooms, or collaborative problem-solving activities. These activities can foster teamwork, communication, and trust among employees, even if they are geographically dispersed (Suhird, 2023). Social events, such as virtual happy hours, holiday parties, or networking events, can also be organized in the metaverse. These events provide employees with opportunities to socialize, bond, and build relationships with their colleagues in a virtual setting.

Metaverse: Virtual Reality for Turnover Intention

HR managers continue to be concerned about the high cost associated with employee turnover in terms of lost productivity, diminishing business performance, and damage to company culture and brand reputation. The cost of turnover also has significant bottom-line impacts on companies. Recognizing the value of the immersive nature of VR for improving employee retention, HR departments are using the technology to support remote and hybrid work, deliver more effective learning and development, and facilitate collaboration and team building that can make or break the employee experience. By 2026, it has been predicted by Upwork that, fully remote workers will represent 27.7 percent of the workforce, and partially remote workers will represent 20.4 percent.

The trend in remote and hybrid work aligns with today's employee desire for flexibility in where they work. Employers that do not offer this flexibility deal with their turnover rates which continue to rise. According to the survey conducted in Good Firms revealed that 70 percent of HR managers reported lack of flexibility of work as the most cited reason for resignations (Fleischmann, 2023).

Virtual reality facilitates remote team-building exercises to help employees feel more connected and engaged. Remote conferences, retreats, and social gatherings and events via VR technology are relationship builders effective in developing successful teams. For companies today, the employee experience is central to reducing turnover. VR, a vital component of the metaverse, can play a crucial role in strategies designed to enhance employee experience, build employee engagement, and boost retention.

Benefits of Using the Metaverse in HR

There are several benefits of using metaverse in human resource which are mentioned below:

- The metaverse, the next evolution in communication, is changing the way the team works, which changes how you maintain the brand culture, support team member productivity and satisfaction, and manage human resources processes.
- More team members prefer working remotely rather than in a physical office environment. Digital-first and hybrid work environments are increasingly becoming the norm rather than the exception.
- Improve team morale, decrease turnover, maintain brand culture and make immersive experience.
- Attract top talent with the virtual platform.
- Provide new hires with a space to complete all onboarding activities. Onboard new team members in an interactive, self-guided learning space with digital assets to get them more easily integrated, comfortable and productive.
- Create unique training virtual spaces designed to give team members what they need when they need it. For instance, New hire training, Product training, Team training, and Manage human resources processes.
- Take care of your human resource needs in the metaverse such as Host meetings and events, Integrate assets into the architecture of the space (e.g., HR resources room), Accounts management (benefits/payroll), Health and wellness events, and Social, cultural or holiday events (e.g. virtual Halloween parties, virtual Christmas parties, etc.)
- Provide analytics to measure the effectiveness of HR efforts.

- Duplicate a physical corporate office space or create something totally new with Metaverse such as a board room, virtual corporate events spaces, team rooms, and office spaces for individual team members.
- Create a metaverse workplace that connects the team, revitalizes the culture, and keeps the people happy.
- Transform the HR practices and embrace the future of work with Metaverse, the leading virtual platform for HR in the metaverse.

CONCLUSION, LIMITATIONS, AND FUTURE DIRECTIONS

Human Resource analytics and metaverse in HR have become an essential topic in organisations nationally as well as internationally. It gives HR department the opportunity to serve as an essential component of the organisation. The purpose of current chapter was to attain five objectives namely investigate the meaning of human resources (HR) analytics, what is HR Analytics and its importance, kinds of HR Analytics and the role of HR Analytics in employee engagement & employee turnover. In the current review, we briefly discussed the meaning, significance, process, types of HR Analytics, the role of HR analytics on employee engagement & turnover intention, and the meaning of Metaverse and the role metaverse in HR.

The integration of people analytics in human resource engagement and employee retention improves organisational performance. HR analytics must be implemented in every organisation in order to make sound business decisions (Kiran, Sujitha, Estherita and Vasantha, 2023). Corporations may employ the most effective human resources software with analytics to make strategic decisions based upon data in order to enhance productivity among workers, attain a higher retention rate, and develop better human resources procedures. Organisations must address burnout through targeted interventions (eg, explaining the job accurately while recruiting), determine if managers with more training have lower attrition on their teams, retain talent by offering a flexible work schedule, provide work from home option and allow them to balance care giving duties with work. According to human resources, people analytics are undoubtedly being used by employers as a means of developing and maintaining an edge over competitors because they improve staff morale, minimize quitting intent, reform hiring procedures, reform manpower planning, identify attrition and its causes, find the best talent, improve staff effectiveness, and switch personnel into a strong ally.

Moreover, the metaverse presents exciting opportunities for HRM professionals to enhance their practices and improve organizational outcomes. From recruitment and training to diversity and inclusion and global collaboration, the metaverse can offer innovative ways to engage, educate, and empower employees. However, it is crucial to approach the use of the metaverse in HRM with caution, considering the potential challenges and ethical considerations. HRM professionals need to stay informed, proactive, and responsible in their use of the metaverse to ensure that it aligns with the values, goals, and needs of their organizations and employees. As the metaverse continues to evolve, HRM professionals need to stay abreast of the latest developments, research, and best practices in leveraging this technology for HRM purposes. By carefully considering the opportunities and challenges of using them metaverse in HR, organizations can unlock its potential to transform HRM practices and create a more engaging, inclusive, and collaborative work environment for their employees. One of the main limitations of the current study is that it is entirely based on theoretical concept and reviews. This has been recommended that future researchers need to focus on HR analytics & metaverse, and strive to investigate empirically the role of HR analytics and metaverse in employee engagement and turnover intention.

Declaration of Conflicts of Interests

The authors declared no potential conflicts of interest.

Funding Disclosure

This research received no specific grant from any funding agency.

REFERENCES

Andersen, M. K. (2017). Human capital analytics: The winding road. *Journal of organisational Effectiveness. People and Performance*, 4(2), 133–136.

Bassi, L. (2011). Raging debates in HR analytics. *People Strategy*, 34(2), 14–18.

Baumruk, R. (2004). The missing link: The role of employee engagement in business success. *Workspan*, 47, 48–52.

Ben-Gal, C. H. (2019). An ROI-based review of HR analytics: Practical implementation tools. *Personnel Review*.

Bhatnagar, J. (2007). Talent management strategy of employee engagement of Indian ITES employees: Key to retention. *Employee Relations*, 29(6), 640–663. doi:10.1108/01425450710826122

Bhatnagar, J. (2009). Exploring psychological contract and employee engagement In India. In Budhwar, P.S. and Bhatnagar, J (Eds.) The changing face of people management in India. London: Routledge: Taylor and Francis doi:10.4324/9780203884867.pt4

Bhattacharyya, D. K. (2017). *HR Analytics: Understanding Theories and Applications.* SAGE Publications.

Boakye, A., & Lamptey, A. Y. (2020). The Rise of HR Analytics: Exploring Its Implications from a Developing Country Perspective. *Journal of Human Resource Management*, 8(3), 181–189. doi:10.11648/j.jhrm.20200803.19

Boudreau, J., & Cascio, W. (2017). Human capital analytics: Why are we not there? *J Organ Eff*, 4(2), 119–126. doi:10.1108/JOEPP-03-2017-0021

Choudhury, H. A., & Barman, A. (2016). Human Resource Analytics-Discovering Research Issues Posited in its Milleu in India organisation. *Discovering Research Issues in Applications of HRA in India*, (5-2016), 1-19.

Daneshfar, F., & Jamshidi, M. B. (2023). An octonion-based nonlinear echo state network for speech emotion recognition in Metaverse. *Neural Networks*, *163*, 108–121. doi:10.1016/j.neunet.2023.03.026 PMID:37030275

Davenport, T. H., Harris, J. G., & Morison, R. (2010). *Analytics at Work: Smarter Decisions, Better Results.* Harvard Business School Press.

de Oliveira, L. B., Cavazotte, F., & Alan Dunzer, R. (2019). The interactive effects of organisational and leadership career management support on job satisfaction and turnover intention. *International Journal of Human Resource Management*, 30(10), 1583–1603. doi:10.1080/09585192.2017.1298650

Falletta, S. V. (2014). In search of HR intelligence: Evidence-based HR Analytics practices in high performing companies. *People Strategy*, 36(4), 28–37.

Falletta, S. V., & Combs, W. L. (2021). The HR analytics cycle: A seven-step process for building evidence-based and ethical HR analytics capabilities. *Journal of Work-Applied Management*, 13(1), 51–68. doi:10.1108/JWAM-03-2020-0020

Fernandez, V., & Gallardo-Gallardo, E. (2021). Tackling the HR digitalization challenge: Key factors and barriers to HR analytics adoption. *Competitiveness Review*, 31(1), 162–187. doi:10.1108/CR-12-2019-0163

Frank, F. D., Finnegan, R. P., & Taylor, C. R. (2004). The race for talent: Retaining and engaging workers in the 21st century. *Human Resource Planning*, 27(3), 12–25.

Fred, M.O. & Kinange U.M. (2015). *Overview of HR Analytics to maximize Human capital investment*. Research Gate.

Gates, S. (2002). *Value at work: The risks and opportunities of human capital measurement and reporting*. Conference Board.

Gawke, J. C., Gorgievski, M. J., & Bakker, A. B. (2017). Employee intrapreneurship and work engagement: A latent change score approach. *Journal of Vocational Behavior, 100*, 88–100. doi:10.1016/j.jvb.2017.03.002

Harris, J. G., Craig, E., & Light, D. A. (2011). Talent and analytics: New approaches, higher ROI. *The Journal of Business Strategy, 32*(6), 4–13. doi:10.1108/02756661111180087

HCMI. (2022). Employee Engagement Analytics: How to Engage and Retain Talent. HCMI. https://www.hcmi.co/post/employee-engagement-analytics-how-to-engage-and-retain-talent.

Heuvel, S., & Bondarouk, T. (2017). The rise (and fall?) of HR Analyticss: A study into the future application, value, structure, and system support. *Journal of organisational Effectiveness. People and Performance, 4*(2), 127–148.

Hom, P. W., Lee, T. W., Shaw, J. D., & Hausknecht, J. P. (2017). One hundred years of employee turnover theory and research. *The Journal of Applied Psychology, 102*(3), 530–545. doi:10.1037/apl0000103 PMID:28125259

Huselid, M. A. (2018). The science and practice of workforce analytics: Introduction to the HRM special issue. *Human Resource Management, 57*(3), 679–684. doi:10.1002/hrm.21916

Huynh-The, T., Gadekallu, T. R., Wang, W., Yenduri, G., Ranaweera, P., Pham, Q. V., da Costa, D. B., & Liyanage, M. (2023). Blockchain for the metaverse: A Review. *Future Generation Computer Systems, 143*, 401–419. doi:10.1016/j.future.2023.02.008

Jain, A., & Nagar, N. (2015). An Emerging Trend in Human Resource Management. *SS International Journal of Economics and Management, 5*(1), 1–10.

Jones, K. (2014). Conquering HR Analyticss: Do you need a rocket scientist or a crystal ball? *Workforce Solutions Review, 5*(1), 43–44.

Kale, H., Aher, D., & Anute, A. (2022). HR Analytics and its Impact on organisations Performance. [IJRAR]. *International Journal of Research and Analytical Reviews, 9*(3), 619–630.

Kiran, K. S., Sharma, N., & Brijmohan, D. R. (2018). HR analytics: Transactional to transformational HR approach. *International Journal of Advance & Innovative Research, 5*(3), 1–11.

Kiran, P. V. S., Sujitha, S., Estherita, A. S., & Vasantha, S. (2023). Effect Of Hr Analytics, Human Capital Management on Organisational Performance. *Journal for Educators. Teachers and Trainers, 14*(2), 117–129.

Kirtane, A. (2015). Corporate sustainable HR Analytical practices. *Journal of Management & Administration Tomorrow, 4*(1), 33–40.

Knox, J. (2022). The metaverse, or the serious business of tech frontiers. *Postdigital Science and Education, 4*(2), 207–215. doi:10.1007/s42438-022-00300-9

Koohang, A., Nord, J. H., Ooi, K. B., Tan, G. W. H., Al-Emran, M., Aw, E. C. X., Baabdullah, A. M., Buhalis, D., Cham, T.-H., Dennis, C., Dutot, V., Dwivedi, Y. K., Hughes, L., Mogaji, E., Pandey, N., Phau, I., Raman, R., Sharma, A., Sigala, M., & Wong, L. W. (2023). Shaping the metaverse into reality: A holistic multidisciplinary understanding of opportunities, challenges, and avenues for future investigation. *Journal of Computer Information Systems, 63*(3), 735–765. doi:10.1080/0887441 7.2023.2165197

Kudos. (2021). *What You Need to Know About HR Analytics and Engagement.* Kudos. https://www.kudos.com/blog/hr-analytics-and-employee-enga gement-what-you-need-to-know.

Lalwani, P. (2021). *What Is HR Analytics? Definition, Importance, Key Metrics, Data Requirements, and Implementation.* Spice Works. https://www.spicew orks.com/hr/hr-analytics/articles/what-is-hr-analytics/

Lawler, E. E., Levenson, A., & Boudreau, J. W. (2004). HR Metrics and Analytics: Use and Impact. *Human Resource Planning, 27*, 27–35.

Levenson, A., & Fink, A. (2017). Human capital analytics: Too much data and analysis, not enough models and business insights. *J Organ Eff, 4*(2), 145–156. doi:10.1108/JOEPP-03-2017-0029

Marson, J. (2022). *6 ways people analytics can help HR improve retention.* Tech Target. https://www.techtarget.com/searchhrsoftware/tip/Ways-people- analytics-can-help- HR-improve-retention.

McIver, D., Lengnick-Hall, M. L., & Lengnick- Hall, C. A. (2018). A strategic approach to workforce analytics: integrating science and agility. *Bus Horiz, 61*(3), 397–407.

Minbaeva, D. (2018). Building credible human capital analytics for organisational competitive advantage. *Human Resource Management*, *57*(3), 701–713. doi:10.1002/hrm.21848

Mondare, S., Douthitt, S., & Carson, M. (2011). Maximizing the impact and effectiveness of HR Analytics to drive business outcomes. *People Strategy*, *34*, 20–27.

Nishii, L. H., Lepak, D. P., & Schneider, B. (2008). Employee attributions of the "why" of HR practices: Their effects on employee attitudes and behaviors, and customer satisfaction. *Personnel Psychology*, *61*(3), 503–545. doi:10.1111/j.1744-6570.2008.00121.x

Orth, M., & Volmer, J. (2017). Daily within-person effects of job autonomy and work engagement on innovative behaviour: The cross-level moderating role of creative self-efficacy. *European Journal of Work and Organizational Psychology*, *26*(4), 601–612. doi:10.1080/1359432X.2017.1332042

Patil, R. (2021). *How HR Analytics Can Help Improve Employee Performance*. Spice Works. https://www.spiceworks.com/hr/hr-analytics/guest-article/how-hr-analytics-can-help-improve-employee-performance/

Ranjan, R., & Basak, A. (2013). *Creating Value through Analytics in HR. Role of Third-party services*. Everest Global.

Reddy, P. R., & Lakshmikeerthi, P. (2017). HR Analyticss' - An Effective Evidence Based HRM Tool. *International Journal of Business and Management Invention*, *6*(7), 23–34.

Reena, R., Ansari, M. M. K., & Jayakrishnan, S. S. (2019). Emerging trends in human resource analytics in upcoming decade. *International Journal of Engineering Applied Sciences and Technology*, *4*(8), 260–264. doi:10.33564/IJEAST.2019.v04i08.045

Richman, A. (2006). Everyone wants an engaged workforce how can you create it? *Workspan*, *49*, 36–39.

Saks, A. M. (2006). Antecedents and consequences of employee engagement. *Journal of Managerial Psychology*, *21*(7), 600–619. doi:10.1108/02683940610690169

Schaufeli, W. B., Bakker, A. B., & Salanova, M. (2006). The measurement of work engagement with a short questionnaire: A cross-national study. *Educational and Psychological Measurement*, *66*(4), 701–716. doi:10.1177/0013164405282471

Schneider, C. (2006). The new human-capital metrics: A sophisticated crop of measurement tools could take the guesswork out of human resources management. *CFO Magazine*, 1-5.

Sharma, A., & Sharma, T. (2017). HR Analytics and Performance appraisal system: A Conceptual framework for employee performance improvement. *Management Research Review*, *40*(6), 684–697. doi:10.1108/MRR-04-2016-0084

Sharma, A., & Sharma, T. (2017). HR analytics and performance appraisal system: A conceptual framework for employee performance improvement. *Management Research Review*, *40*(6), 684–697. doi:10.1108/MRR-04-2016-0084

Shaw, K. (2005). An engagement strategy process for communicators. *Strategic Communication Management*, *9*(3), 26–29.

Singh, A., Singh, H., & Singh, A. (2022). People Analytics: Augmenting Horizon from Predictive Analytics to Prescriptive Analytics. In P. M. Jeyanthi, T. Choudhury, D. Hack-Polay, T. P. Singh, & S. Abujar (Eds.), *Decision Intelligence Analytics and the Implementation of Strategic Business Management. EAI/Springer Innovations in Communication and Computing*. Springer. doi:10.1007/978-3-030-82763-2_13

Soumyasanto, S. (2016). *Caring about Analytics for HR*. Data Science Central. http://www.datasciencecentral.com/profiles/blogs/caring-about-analytics-for-hr

Tikhonov, A. I. (2020). Maim objectives of Russian companies, solved by HR-analytics. *Journal of Natural and Humanitarian Studies*, *28*(2), 262–266.

Tomar, S., & Gaur, M. (2020). HR analytics in Business: Role, Opportunities, and Challenges of Using It. *Journal of Xi'an University of Architecture & Technology*, *xii*(vii), 1299–1306.

Tursunbayeva, A., Di Lauro, S., & Pagliari, C. (2018). People analytics—A scoping review of conceptual boundaries and value propositions. *International Journal of Information Management*, *43*, 224–247. doi:10.1016/j.ijinfomgt.2018.08.002

Vahlen, F. V. (2016). *Work Rules!: Wie Google die Art und Weise, wie wir leben und arbeiten*. Verändert.

Wu, D., Yang, Z., Zhang, P., Wang, R., Yang, B., & Ma, X. (2023). Virtual-Reality Inter-Promotion Technology for Metaverse: A Survey. *IEEE Internet of Things Journal*, *10*(18), 15788–15809. doi:10.1109/JIOT.2023.3265848

ADDITIONAL READING

Fernandez, V., & Gallardo-Gallardo, E. (2021). Tackling the HR digitalization challenge: Key factors and barriers to HR analytics adoption. *Competitiveness Review*, *31*(1), 162–187. doi:10.1108/CR-12-2019-0163

Jose, G., PM, N., & Kuriakose, V. (. (2024). HRM practices and employee engagement: Role of personal resources-a study among nurses. *International Journal of Productivity and Performance Management, 73*(1), 1–17. doi:10.1108/IJPPM-04-2021-0212

Marler, J. H., & Boudreau, J. W. (2017). An evidence-based review of HR Analytics. *International Journal of Human Resource Management, 28*(1), 3–26. doi:10.1080/09585192.2016.1244699

Naidu, K. V., & Reddy, P. KV, R. K. Interplay of Artificial Intelligence and the Metaverse in HR. In *The Business of the Metaverse* (pp. 178–198). Productivity Press.

Raj, A. (2024). Artificial Intelligence: A Comprehensive Overview on An Integration of Computer Aided Design and AI Tools For Enhancing Employee Experience. *Onomázein.*

Zvarikova, K., Cug, J., & Hamilton, S. (2022). Virtual Human Resource Management in the Metaverse: Immersive Work Environments, Data Visualization Tools and Algorithms, and Behavioral Analytics. *Psychosociological Issues in Human Resource Management, 10*(1), 7–20. doi:10.22381/pihrm10120221

KEY TERMS AND DEFINITIONS

Employee Engagement: Employee engagement is a human resources (HR) concept that describes the level of enthusiasm and dedication a worker feels toward their job.

HR Analytics (HRA): HR analytics is the collection and application of talent data to improve critical talent and business outcomes.

Human Resource Management (HRM): Human resource management is the strategic approach to nurturing and supporting employees and ensuring a positive workplace environment.

Metaverse: The metaverse is a digital reality that combines aspects of social media, online gaming, augmented reality (AR), and virtual reality (VR) to allow users to interact virtually.

Turnover Intention: Turnover intention' refers to an employee's willingness or intention to voluntarily quit their job or leave an organization.

Chapter 7
The Resilient Brand Management Framework as a Responsive Business Strategy in the Industry 4.0 Era

Asik Rahaman Jamader
iD https://orcid.org/0000-0002-6938-5901
Pailan College of Management and Technology, Kolkata, India

Santanu Dasgupta
iD https://orcid.org/0000-0002-3060-4759
Pailan College of Management and Technology, India

Govind Baibhaw
Siliguri Institute of Technology, India

ABSTRACT

The analysis suggests that the application of the sustainability concept underpinning the framework of resilient branding (FRB) has a significant impact on business in contemporary markets, which is supported by the authors' prior narrative, examination, and systematic reflections. The study's practical application is to combine sustainable marketing to improve performance with the psychological capital theory, which emphasizes fostering optimism and personality where the system dynamic model for resilient branding and sigmoid action resilience of brand equity by Heise is used for better results. Future research should consider the suggested theories as worthwhile topics.

DOI: 10.4018/979-8-3693-5868-9.ch007

INTRODUCTION

Modern society is currently undergoing a digital transformation, which is being felt by companies. Modification will impact each sector of sector, irrespective of how much business is being transformed (Jamader, Das & Acharya, 2022). Upwards of simply updating or altering innovation is included in digitalization. Customers, workers, and business partners today all anticipate a technological change. Businesses must embrace advancement because customers favour it over more antiquated, older techniques, as to if they like it or not. What fosters technological change in the corporate setting? The most important factor, in theory, is the customer experience (Majerova et al., 2020). At the nexus of individuals as well as tools, digital revolution happens most quickly. The objective of digital evolution is to create stronger, more intelligent, as well as quicker businesses that can better foresee and customers' requirements. Organizations need new digital leaders and managers, understanding, in addition to administration skills in the direction of arrangement, organise, guide, in addition to direct their socioeconomic movement in the digital age of Industry 4.0. They also must recruit and train staff that can start preparing products to fulfil the requirements of fresh "customers." In order for the organisation to adjust to the shifting customer footpaths in the digital economy, it also needs new marketing knowledge and skills (Jamader et al., 2023). Businesses must be conscious of what clients want in order to logically create a good or service that meets their needs (Brady, 2003). They must then begin producing, pricing, and publicising the service or goods by making an announcement that it is available. In addition, companies must assure service quality both throughout and after the price reduction when delivering their goods or services (Jamader, 2023). A fresh approach to marketing is necessary in this new era. 2023 began with the introduction of a novel marketing strategy known as "FRB 4.0." The fundamental idea behind FRB is that creating "healthier, better, and cheaper" products that meet consumer demands is not the only aspect of sustainable marketing. It is the genuine, vital assets of managing a business, affecting output, igniting creativity, and fostering business collaboration with the economic and social environment. Product positioning provides companies and organisations the assurance as well as power to generate extra by using fewer wherewithal, as captivating interested in consideration the requirements of today's but also tomorrow's millennia of clients as well as a global society.

REVIEW OF LITERATURE

One of the most frequently discussed aspects of sustainable development on a global scale is the sustainability of food production and consumption (Grubor, Milovanov

& O. 2017). As a result, it is necessary to adapt traditional managerial patterns to meet social demands. The revisions that have already been made are mostly general in nature and are based on pertinent production-related details. Moreover, only the method of implementation of conventional managerial postulates changes (Sato et al., 2023). These two facts could be the cause of practical failures in the sustainable management of food products. Brand is one of these conventional managerial ideas (Kamkankaew, 2021). It has been viewed in this context as a CSR (corporate social responsibility) activity facilitator. The environment has changed, though, and there is a strong suspicion that brand loyalty is not a facilitator of sustainable management but rather a hindrance to it. In light of this, it is undeniable that brand loyalty research is crucial for managing food products sustainably. In light of the aforementioned, the main objective of the contribution is to pinpoint relevant brand value sources of loyalty within the context of sustainable brand management of food products. To accomplish this, we have used factor structure to provide statistical evaluation of the data from our own structured questionnaires (Nedergaard & Gyrd-Jones, 2013). We have discovered that when contrasting brands with those that lack devoted customers, the constituents of brand value sources are consistent. A suitable set of recommendations for the theory and application of sustainable brand management of food products has been developed in light of this (Thomas & Capelli, 2023).

Modern scientific literature emphasises the significance of CSR in the sustainable management process, not only generally but also with regard to production sector-specifics. According to this trend, producers of food products should morally pressure their suppliers and encourage consumer participation in the purchasing process (Erdil, 2013). It is important to emphasise the importance of brands and brand management in order to effect these changes in the currently operational stereotypes. However, the fact that alimentary goods are characterised by traditional, habitual purchasing behaviour poses a particular challenge to such an approach because, in this type of purchasing behaviour, consumer loyalty is the primary driving force behind purchases regardless of whether the brand is socially responsible or not (Arbouw et al,. 2019). The main cause of this is that brand managers of food products who represent brands that consumers deem valuable are not sufficiently motivated to act responsibly toward society, and consumers are not sufficiently motivated to participate actively in the process of information search. Even though they are carried out in accordance with the state of knowledge at the time, socially responsible activities in this case are not directly linked with the desired outcome (Jamader et al., 2023) While the main theoretical focus is typically on the issue of sustainable management facilitators, practise indicates the application of the opposite approach that is, a focus on potential barriers to the best possible implementation of managerial patterns is required. Buyers favourably appraise high levels of human contact, especially for vegetables cultivated in vertical cultivation facilities, according to research on the moderating influence of human touch (Son & Hwang, 2023).

This chapter examines brand advantage in great detail as one component of the business case for responsibility. It makes the case that businesses will increasingly be evaluated on factors other than just their financial performance as a result of the socio-political and economic climate that exists today. Their evaluation will be based on how they appear to perform. It is advised that businesses create transparency by engaging in dialogue with stakeholders in order to improve how well they are perceived to be performing. This openness fosters the emergence of trust (Kocyigit & Ringle, 2011).

Brands are effective agents of change today. They have close ties to customers all over the world and are deeply ingrained in their decisions and way of life. Customers express their love for brands by supporting their philosophy and brand image with fervent stances. As a result, businesses that own popular brands with sizable followings of devoted customers have the ability to cause modifications or even a radical change in the way of life, value system, attitudes, and behaviour of consumers. Given that its implementation necessitates changes that will affect the masses rather than individuals, environmentally friendly brands are therefore an essential component of sustainable marketing strategy and sustainability concept. Despite the market's acceptance of socially conscious business practises, there is a significant attitude versus behaviour gap among consumers, which reduces the market for eco-conscious consumers to a niche. Therefore, finding consumers' interest in a sustainable way of life and making it convenient, appealing, and easy to access is the most difficult task for marketing and brand managers (Sarkar, & Singh, 2005). This article aims to emphasise the central position of sustainability in branding theory and practise and to outline strategies for successfully integrating green values into brand management, with a focus on the brand equity construct, by drawing on the findings of research and analysis in the relevant area.

Only a passing mention of the corporate brand's function as a strategic tool for guiding innovation projects has been made in the literature. This article explores the role corporate brands can play in assisting with both the guiding and driving of such innovation processes, as innovation is a key factor in brand growth. In order to create a framework for Sustainable Brand-based Innovation, the article applies the design thinking concept. It is recommended that design thinking, which is linked to intuition and abdicative reasoning, be used in addition to conventional market-oriented strategies (Maio, 2003). A combined theory of what occurs when customers learn regarding brand origin misperceptions (BOM) is developed in this work and experimentally tested. According to the suggested model, consumers' purchase intentions are influenced by discovering a brand's actual origin through cognitive and emotional brand re-evaluations, and these impacts are limited by specific border constraints. The speculated moderated mediation model is supported empirically by a research that involved several product categories and brands and was carried out in the United States. The results show that consumers modify their cognitive and emotional brand assessments in response to knowledge about the real brand origin, but only in the case of affective brand evaluations when the real origin has a poorer country image than the previously supposed (incorrect) origin. Additionally, only customer trust in brand origin moderates the affective implications of learning about BOM, whereas numerous consumer- and brand-related characteristics simply attenuate the psychological effects (Mandler et al., 2023).

The impact of firm sustainability on brand perception a crucial component of brand image in brand management and marketing is assessed in this essay. In order to understand how well-known sustainability activities affect people's perceptions of brands, the paper also reviews relevant literature. The impact of a brand on opportunities for a company's brand image that are driven by sustainability is explained in branding literature (Kale & Öztürk, 2016).

Recent changes in the consumer environment are best exemplified by the intensifying competition between businesses, the rise in brand advertising, and the fragmentation of the media. When brand managers try to express their brand's core associations clearly, these transformations make it more difficult. Customers frequently receive unclear and inconsistent brand messages unintentionally, which causes brand confusion (BC). When consumers are perplexed by a brand, they have a negative opinion of the brand equity, which leads to the dysfunction of the brand. For marketing managers, this occurrence is extremely important because it poses a threat to brand strength (Zhang et al., 2020). Three dimensions have been identified in studies on BC (that is, brand similarity, brand clarity and brand credibility). This study is the first to take five crucial factors into account, giving BC a more comprehensive perspective. The two new fundamental dimensions that we add are brand diversity and brand continuity (Ahmed & Hashim, 2022). This study not only increases the understanding of BC but also demonstrates the strong direct impact of this construct on long-term brand satisfaction (SBS). According to our research, SBS is negatively impacted by BC, which increases consumers' propensity to purchase private label goods and degrades brand equity.

The company conservation as well as commitment progression has a big impact on brand management and has significant implications for it. It generates demands that the self control should adapt to as well as fresh chances for development (Dasgupta, & Jamader, 2022). According to Maio, the concept of "brand" permeates every aspect of a company, and as a result, the brand's values can act as a useful benchmark for all business behaviours, including those in boardrooms, currency sector, worker renegotiations, client relations, as well as discussions with other partners. The organisational components as well as brand management processes that are already present in the majority of corporations can act as efficient conduits for encouraging principles actions as well as trying to measure it (Lee & Park, 2016). By allowing brands to communicate freely with multiple players, digital engagement platforms enable human brands to be more powerful. Athlete brands in particular are on the verge of outperforming traditional brands on digital channels. The investigation analyses performers as well as evaluates the way they perform utilising a case study of a professional athlete brand, drawing on literature from human branding, integrative branding, and performativity concept. To learn more about the co-creation of brand meaning, we use a multi-method approach combining interviews and netnography (Anderski et al., 2023)

Using a quantitative survey-based technique, the current study evaluates the effect of perceived human brand authenticity on brand love across six industries—politics, music, movies, sports, business, and social media. The findings show that, while its ability to forecast varies depending on the kind of individual business, human brand authenticity is a major predictor of brand love. Politics is the area where authenticity has the greatest of an impact, next tunes, films, as well as recreation. Real personality has little bearing on brand love in social media or business. Whereas genuineness is recognised as a potential indicator of positive advertising achievements in existing branding studies, the current study's findings reveal a boundary condition about the environment in which an individual identity functions. Additionally, appreciation for a brand can manifest as a higher propensity to buy self-branded goods from human businesses, providing the human brand with prospects for latent revenue plus market-building (Osorio et al., 2023). Given the prevalence of corporate conspiracies, this study looks at how customer relationships with brands are affected when they are connected to conspiracies. According to our three researches, when consumers think a company is a part of a conspiracy, this perception makes them think the business is machiavellian, which reduces their confidence as well as buy inclinations. Moreover, researchers demonstrate that any time individuals possess a third-party sense of control and think that others are influencing their lives, their conspiracy theories about brands cause them to display decreased purchase intentions for that company. Significantly, the control condition did not show this drop in purchase intentions among those with an external locus of control, proving that consumers only experience the moderating effects of Powerful Others when they believe in a conspiracy. These results contribute to the growing body of marketing research on negative perceptions of brands (Lunardo et al., 2023).

As more people buy for groceries online, it is important to re-evaluate classic marketing strategies to see if they still work and to come up with new ideas that are tailored to online channels. One such cutting-edge strategy would involve suggesting private-label substitutes for goods that customers have already placed to their shopping baskets. According to three studies, when customers are given the option to move from one brand to another, they are more likely to choose the private-label option than the national brand. Private-label products stand to benefit more from these quality signals than national brands from the recommendations, which appear to be quality cues. Customers with low levels of brand loyalty will notice this impact more; whereas, customers with high levels of product commitment will see it less (Volles et al., 2023). Customers' willingness to share their personal information with marketers is undeniably advantageous to them. Data-driven social alliances provide marketers the opportunity to make the most of the data, contribute to the greater good, personalise goods for customers, and increase revenue. In order for marketers to effectively support consumer data donation, it is important to have a deeper knowledge of what motivates consumer data donation to data-driven social partnerships (Loureiro et al., 2023)

It also provides insights into the processes involved in producing this knowledge, including theoretical sources of inspiration and the pivotal role that methodological improvements had in the creation of research streams centred around new kinds. This review concludes by providing a clear roadmap for subsequent studies on how to expand our understanding of existing types, deepen our understanding of their antecedents, moderators, and outcomes, broaden our toolkit of methodological approaches, and define the parameters and structure of consumer-brand connection forms (Alvarez et al., 2023).

THE ASSIMILATION OF RESILIENT IN TO THE STANDARD FRAMEWORK

According to a study of the literature, businessmen as well as the people who might become their customers still have very different ideas about what branding as well as corporation are all about. This paper presents a model of brand management that encourages organisations to adopt principles of sustainability (Jamader, 2022). It is still a problem, though, that customers don't truly comprehend sustainable development. Consequently, the findings of the investigation of the environmental, financial, as well as socioeconomic environment at both the local and global levels allow us to advocate for initiating an educational effort that will result in the introduction of the Sustainable Marketing Model proposed at the intellectual level.

There should be new educational initiatives in the area of sustainable development because resilient is a comparatively novel happening in addition to connected company work plan are static developing. The context of Australian sustainability education might serve as an illustration (Ishaq & Maria, 2020). To determine how they integrate curriculum materials into their curricula, 38 Australian universities were asked to evaluate their graduate programmes. Prospective establishments and society are influenced by universities and the education they provide to their degree holders. Scientists are paying closer interest to the link among what employers of degree holders want and the educational experiences that universities offer. The role of study on ecologic as well as related problems has been studied by Australian universities for more than 40 years. Incorporating such concerns into the creation of sustainable ideas, Australian research is closely connected to the global society. There will be publications which look at the path Australian universities also gone in designing instructional strategies to give educators the capability to contribute against sustainable growth by the explication of learning to enhance (Golob et al., 2022).

An increasing number of studies indicate that genuine leadership has an positive impact on people's life satisfaction as well as job productivity. The characteristics of authentic leaders include being aware of how they act on the way to others, understanding how others see them, understanding their individual principles as well as ethics as well as those of others, having a keen understanding of the communal context within which they work, as well as retaining an elevated level of confidence. An investigation into the connection among genuine management and positive psychological capital led to the discovery that genuine leaders foster employee trust, which in turn boosts achievement. Leadership that is authentic affects behaviour in the workplace, within organisations, as well as resident. The change in the organisational work climate brought about by authentic leadership encourages the development of psychological capital in their supporters. A higher level of effectiveness and efficiency at work is a result of positive psychological states, which are produced by positive psychological capital, according to studies. A connection among personality, wish, enthusiasm, as well as perseverance is how propensity is best defined. It is possible to create and improve the standard of living and productivity of staff at work by pleasing to the eye optimistic psychosomatic assets in an organisation throughout genuine guidance (Podhorska et al., 2021).

System Dynamic Model for Resilient Branding

By illustrating the causal relationships between the components of a system and the evolution of a system over time, system dynamics is a methodology used to study the structures of social or organisational systems. Its goal is to clarify the overall behaviour of a given system using patterns of behaviour among its components and the structures that govern those patterns (Jamader, Chowdhary & Jha 2023). The fundamental tenet of system dynamics is that the accumulation principle governs how dynamically a framework behaves. According to this principle, a platform's transient stability results from the movement of the resources accumulated in stocks, and those movements are governed by the flows of resources entering and leaving

Figure 1. Reserve (Y) inhibited through a flow (X)

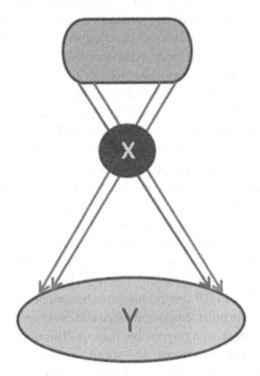

the stocks. The equities figure is a particular causal representation that results from this principle.

In Figure 1, the assessment of the reserve Y is inhibited through flow X. This systematize be able to be uttered next to an equation demonstrating the evolution as of the worth of X starting period M to period M +MZ. This changeover is specified through the Equation 1

$$Y(Z+MZ)=Y(M)+X(M).MZ^{,}X(M)=ZY/ZM \tag{1}$$

RESILIENT BRANDING FRAMEWORK

The Framework of Resilient Branding (FRB) embodies the problems that the marketing sciences face. This same present framework, based on the idea that commitment as well as brand management are mutually exclusive, needs to be changed, and this is a task for both scientists and businesspeople. In order to efficiently put the philosophy of resilient brand management into practise, a representation of business sustainability that links the processes promoting social and economic ties in terms of commitment as well as profitability of the company has been established. In this context, the word "framework" refers to a condensed representation of an enterprise's intricate marketing management process (Schultz & Block, 2015). A complicated current situation is intended to be presented through the renovation suggestion of the framework. The fundamental idea behind FRB is that creating "healthier, better, and cheaper" products that meet consumer demands is not the only aspect of sustainable marketing (Jamader et al., 2023). It is the genuine, vital assets of managing a business, affecting output, igniting creativity, and fostering business collaboration with the economic and social environment. Product positioning provides companies and organisations the assurance as well as power to generate extra by using fewer wherewithal, as captivating interested in consideration the requirements of today's but also tomorrow's millennia of clients as well as a global society. This is done by taking care of the continuing equilibrium among the requirements of individuals, the natural world, as well as the economy's growth (Bartels & Hoogendam, 2011).

On a practical level, the FRB aims to change the behaviour of the top management, employees, and clients in order to improve social and environmental conditions and, as a result, generate profit in a responsible manner. Through creating a company which blends through into economic and social years ahead, it also affects the products and services that the client gets. Eventually, it is crucial to have a say in how products and services are delivered, gratitude to conscientious supervision as well as openness to collaboration in ethical and truthful advertising messages (Rokhim et al., 2021). The concept behind FRB is a great business opportunity that could fulfil customers' desires, improve the effectiveness of the growth of the global societal structure, generate new employment opportunities, and improve both the quality of life now and in the coming decades (Gong et al., 2020).

Utilization of FRB enables organisations to develop a new brand management perspective based on specified fundamentals. According to Figure 2, the recommended FRB is supported by three foundations:

- Conscientious direction,
- A product to facilitate is placed as accountable,
- Popularization of conscientious utilization.

In the area of corporate planning, FRB inspires the field of quality management to be prudently handled in three areas: financial, socio-cultural, as well as environmental, and it specifies that the authority be predicated on the honourable attitude and character of those who are in charge of running the company. Particularly in this day and age, when the concept of business ethics is becoming more and more

Figure 2. The model of resilient brand management

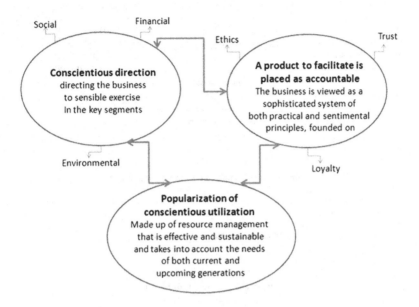

important, prompting every socio-cultural organisation to focus on the general welfare. Leaders of research and practice are becoming more aware of the fact that running an organisation is impossible without ethical principles. It is crucial for the growth of a sustainable business that the leaders assume accountability for the application's achievement in terms of the social, financial, as well as ecologic facets as well. The resilient enterprise should make an effort to manage each link in the product lifecycle, including the advancement of a marketing strategy as well as its allocation, the collision the surroundings, trade growth, as well as the influence on social growth both inside and outside the venture. A business led by a respectable citizen must satisfy the needs of the investor, the consumer, and society at large by utilising the natural resources of the environment in a sustainable manner. The ingrained, well-positioned, in addition to well-managed trademark is another pillar of the FRB. It consists of associations and preferences with the organisation as well as a collection of real-world experiences, referrals, and qualities that define its calibre. A brand is viewed as a sophisticated synthesis of practical and sentimental virtues.

While also being the most important, label is an essential marketing tool. Each business on the industry has a distinctiveness, title, as well as notoriety for their brands. Building a brand is a skill in branding. If a company struggles to build a solid product line, this indicates that its promotional activities are ineffective and not in line with accepted marketing best practises. In an organisation that will use

Figure 3. The sustainable brand management framework that connects to motivation

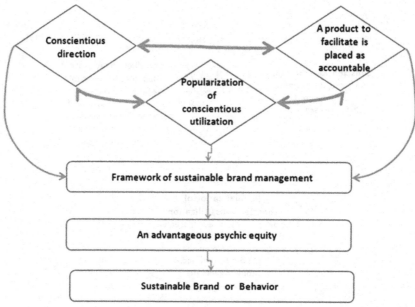

FRB, sustainable marketing will serve as the cornerstone of market action, and brand image will be built on the principles of ethically produced goods, secure and moral trade, ethical business practises, ethical customer relationship management, and cash flow.

Steadily for the past but not least, FRB emphasises the necessity of promoting sustainable consumption by using goods more responsibly and efficiently, advocating a fair resource distribution between the rich and the poor while taking into consideration the needs of both current and future generations of consumers. Through instituting FRB, we should help facilitate usage as a means of satiating needs that are justified by the necessities of a respectable human presence. Utilization is defined as the direct satisfaction of people's desires through the use of resources. The researchers hold the view that manager is the primary tenet of the Sustainable Brand Strategy, based on research-based introspection, more than two decades of branding leadership experience, a review of the literature, and goes back at least own studies. Consequently, we have made an effort to examine administration panel from the standpoint of a positive thinking equity. The FRB tenets as well as the motivational equity methodology are combined in the underlying theory that has been suggested (described in following Figure 3).

Genuine leadership reinforces positive mental wealth within an organisation by fostering a positive impact on meeting people's needs, improving the effectiveness of societal development, and promoting a higher quality of life. According to previous research literature, building up one's psychological capital promotes greater levels of effectiveness and a productive workplace. As a result, the connection between the model of responsible management as well as the growth of positive psychological assets serves as support for sustainable market behaviour (Qureshi et al., 2022). A genuine person inspires peoples choices trust in their capacity to perform by being conscious of and accountable for their actions toward others. As a result, a favourable mental condition of development is produced within an organisation, which increases people's self-efficacy and optimism for achieving both present-day and long-term resilient objectives. Confidence in one's own behaviour as well as in general market hierarchy of authority grows among staff members as well as with customers. All market elements are connected by the ethical principle of leadership, which also enables the Framework of resilient brand management to achieve its objective.

Sigmoid Action for Resilience of Brand Equity

Dignified fundamental diagramming from side to side simplifies statistical result. In Heise's unique formula, contributory system is treated as linear systems. Ψ underlying pointer concentrating as of a capricious Ψ in the direction of a capricious ϵ would articulate a linear task (or linear alteration) of Ψ, i.e.:

$$\Psi \to \Omega \to \epsilon \,{}^{\gg}\, \epsilon = \Omega \cdot \psi \tag{2}$$

Stipulation the correct surface of the correspondence on top of is differentiating $\varphi\epsilon = \Omega.\varphi\,\psi$ is observed. This capital so as to a dissimilarity within Ψ will routinely consequence during a difference into B, scaled through the coefficient Ω. Depending on whether Ω is a coefficient slighter or generously proportioned than the element, the modification into ϵ will be real comparatively finer than that within ψ. The sign of Ω in addition indicates whether the modification caused during ϵ is certainly simultaneous in the direction of the alteration at this time ψ, or depressingly simultaneous. Instantaneous fundamental associations are seen through Heise in a preservative method, i.e.:

$$\Psi \to \Omega \to \epsilon \leftarrow \jmath \leftarrow {}^{\gg}\, \epsilon = \Omega.\psi + \pounds. \sum \tag{3}$$

It is value note so as to Heise's fundamental formulation (Equation 2) takes us in the direction of the next transitive relation (Delbeck, & Heise, 2021).

$$\Psi \to \Omega \to \epsilon \leftarrow \jmath \leftarrow {}^{\gg}\, \pounds = \Omega.\pounds.\psi \tag{4}$$

CONCLUSION

The assessment provided in this research leads one to believe that the application of the resilient theory underpinning FRB has a considerable impact on companies in mature economies. Researchers and industry leaders alike highlight the need for businesses seeking to succeed long-term in the face of global market challenges to be based on ethical behaviour. FRB entails developing official remedies that include an effective conservation framework cantered on the concept of a triple foundation stripe. Top management's example is crucial for the successful implementation of corporate sustainability because most workers adopt their managers' values. Even though staffs are those who will put business ethics into practise in their day-to-day responsibilities, their dedication to implementing the concept is a guarantee of the success of any implemented strategy. In order to successfully build the good bonds that are the foundation of the success of the company, it is also crucial to implement an ongoing, open, and active dialogue with all stakeholders, but particularly with clients.

A good reputation which provides pledge, expresses what individuals may anticipate from a specific company, as well as foretells what might be anticipated among those implicated in offering customers value is at the heart of such a conversation on culpability. By examining events in mature economies, it has been demonstrated that consumers are more likely to embrace the concept of social responsibility when they perceive companies and their employees to wholeheartedly and legitimately trust in whatever the business stands for and to be dedicated to creating value. Communication is a weapon for involving all interested parties in an organization's assets in order to address their needs, enlighten people, as well as learn from them. This enables the business to transform learned information into products and solutions and also organizational operations. Relationship marketing is essential for the growth of eco - efficiency, in which customers actively engage in an array of different activities that build social capital relationships of trust, cooperate, deep connection, as well as interact, offering the business a competitive edge. As a consequence, the built-up trust not only serves as the basis for interpersonal interactions in the relationship between the client and the organisation, but it also affects future generations' chances for social advancement and the creation of a successful global development.

The figure's great framework one of the report's constraints. To get around this limitation, the author's subsequent studies will concentrate on applying the model to control and experimental groups and examining the implications of the FRB and its relationship to healthy personality. This article's focus was strictly on the research methodology necessary to make the figure's idea more understandable. To fully comprehend the favourable psychological development, it is also important to understand cognitive influences on employees' positive behaviour. In order to investigate the impact of the FRB on both employees and consumers, future research should combine both the positive psychology of the stress reduction strategy as well as the behavioural therapy framework. We think that the exacerbating impacts of environmentally sound practices administration, promotional strategies, as well as popularisation of resource conservation act as precursors to favourable mental development (meeting customers' desires, boosting culture's effectiveness, as well as improving life) as well as, as an outcome, strengthen desired attitude. Future research may benefit from a useful framework that is created by introducing mindfulness concepts and examining the developed schema.

Declarations

Funding: The Author declare that they do not have any funding or grant for the manuscript.

    Conflict of Interest: The authors declare that they do not have any conflict of interests that influence the work reported in this paper.

REFERENCES

Ahmed, U., & Hashim, S. (2022). Sustainable Brand Management: The Role of Internal Brand Management and Intrinsic Motivation in Building Employee's Brand Relationship Quality towards Organization's Brand. *Sustainability (Basel)*, *14*(24), 16660. doi:10.3390/su142416660

Alvarez, C., David, M. E., & George, M. (2023). Types of Consumer-Brand Relationships: A systematic review and future research agenda. *Journal of Business Research*, *160*, 113753. doi:10.1016/j.jbusres.2023.113753

Anderski, M., Griebel, L., Stegmann, P., & Ströbel, T. (2023). Empowerment of human brands: Brand meaning co-creation on digital engagement platforms. *Journal of Business Research*, *166*, 113905. doi:10.1016/j.jbusres.2023.113905

Arbouw, P., Ballantine, P. W., & Ozanne, L. K. (2019). Sustainable brand image: An examination of ad–brand incongruence. *Marketing Intelligence & Planning*, *37*(5), 513–526. doi:10.1108/MIP-08-2018-0307

Bartels, J., & Hoogendam, K. (2011). The role of social identity and attitudes toward sustainability brands in buying behaviors for organic products. *Journal of Brand Management*, *18*(9), 697–708. doi:10.1057/bm.2011.3

Brady, A. (2003). How to generate sustainable brand value from responsibility. *Journal of Brand Management*, *10*(4), 279–289. doi:10.1057/palgrave.bm.2540124

Delbeck, S., & Heise, H. M. (2021). Quality assurance of commercial insulin formulations: Novel assay using infrared spectroscopy. *Journal of Diabetes Science and Technology*, *15*(4), 865–873. doi:10.1177/1932296820913874 PMID:32281880

Erdil, T. S. (2013). Strategic brand management based on sustainable-oriented view: An evaluation in Turkish home appliance industry. *Procedia: Social and Behavioral Sciences*, *99*, 122–132. doi:10.1016/j.sbspro.2013.10.478

Golob, U., Burghausen, M., Kernstock, J., & Davies, M. A. (2022). Brand management and sustainability: Exploring potential for the transformative power of brands. *Journal of Brand Management*, *29*(6), 1–7. doi:10.1057/s41262-022-00293-7

Gong, X., Wang, C., Yan, Y., Liu, M., & Ali, R. (2020). What drives sustainable brand awareness: Exploring the cognitive symmetry between brand strategy and consumer brand knowledge. *Symmetry*, *12*(2), 198. doi:10.3390/sym12020198

Grubor, A., & Milovanov, O. (2017). Brand strategies in the era of sustainability. *Interdisciplinary Description of Complex Systems: INDECS*, *15*(1), 78–88. doi:10.7906/indecs.15.1.6

Ishaq, M. I., & Di Maria, E. (2020). Sustainability countenance in brand equity: A critical review and future research directions. *Journal of Brand Management*, *27*(1), 15–34. doi:10.1057/s41262-019-00167-5

Jamader, A. R. (2022). A Brief Report Of The Upcoming & Present Economic Impact To Hospitality Industry In COVID19 Situations. *Journal of Pharmaceutical Negative Results*, 2289–2302.

JamaderA. R. (2023). The Sustainable Ecotourism Strategy: Participation & Combating. *Available at* SSRN 4399894.

Jamader, A. R., Chowdhary, S., Jha, S. S., & Roy, B. (2023). Application of Economic Models to Green Circumstance for Management of Littoral Area: A Sustainable Tourism Arrangement. *SMART Journal of Business Management Studies*, *19*(1), 70–84. doi:10.5958/2321-2012.2023.00008.8

Jamader, A. R., Chowdhary, S., & Shankar Jha, S. (2023). A Road Map for Two Decades of Sustainable Tourism Development Framework. In Resilient and Sustainable Destinations After Disaster: Challenges and Strategies (pp. 9-18). Emerald Publishing Limited. doi:10.1108/978-1-80382-021-720231002

Jamader, A. R., Immanuel, J. S., Ebenezer, V., Rakhi, R. A., Sagayam, K. M., & Das, P. (2023). Virtual Education, Training And Internships In Hospitality And Tourism During Covid-19 Situation. *Journal of Pharmaceutical Negative Results*, 286–290.

Kale, G. Ö., & Öztürk, G. (2016). The importance of sustainability in luxury brand management. *Intermedia. International Journal (Toronto, Ont.)*, *3*(4), 106–126.

Kamkankaew, P. (2021). A Stakeholder-Oriented Sustainability Brand Management: An Introductory Review. วารสาร วิชาการ การ ตลาด และ การ จัดการ มหาวิทยาลัย เทคโนโลยี ราช มงคล ธัญบุรี, *8*(1), 99-129.

Kocyigit, O., & Ringle, C. M. (2011). The impact of brand confusion on sustainable brand satisfaction and private label proneness: A subtle decay of brand equity. *Journal of Brand Management*, *19*(3), 195–212. doi:10.1057/bm.2011.32

Lee, Y. K., & Park, J. W. (2016). Impact of a sustainable brand on improving business performance of airport enterprises: The case of Incheon International Airport. *Journal of Air Transport Management*, *53*, 46–53. doi:10.1016/j.jairtraman.2016.01.002

Loureiro, S. M. C., Friedmann, E., Breazeale, M., & Middendorf, I. (2023). How can brands encourage consumers to donate data to a data-driven social partnership? An examination of hedonic vs. functional categories. *Journal of Business Research*, *164*, 113958. doi:10.1016/j.jbusres.2023.113958

Lunardo, R., Oliver, M. A., & Shepherd, S. (2023). How believing in brand conspiracies shapes relationships with brands. *Journal of Business Research*, *159*, 113729. doi:10.1016/j.jbusres.2023.113729

Maio, E. (2003). Managing brand in the new stakeholder environment. *Journal of Business Ethics*, *44*(2), 235–246. doi:10.1023/A:1023364119516

Majerova, J., Sroka, W., Krizanova, A., Gajanova, L., Lazaroiu, G., & Nadanyiova, M. (2020). Sustainable brand management of alimentary goods. *Sustainability (Basel)*, *12*(2), 556. doi:10.3390/su12020556

Mandler, T., Bartsch, F., & Zeugner-Roth, K. P. (2023). Are brands re-evaluated when consumers learn about brand origin misperceptions? Outcomes, processes, and contingent effects. *Journal of Business Research*, *164*, 113941. doi:10.1016/j.jbusres.2023.113941

Nedergaard, N., & Gyrd-Jones, R. (2013). Sustainable brand-based innovation: The role of corporate brands in driving sustainable innovation. *Journal of Brand Management*, *20*(9), 762–778. doi:10.1057/bm.2013.16

Osorio, M. L., Centeno, E., & Cambra-Fierro, J. (2023). An empirical examination of human brand authenticity as a driver of brand love. *Journal of Business Research, 165*, 114059. doi:10.1016/j.jbusres.2023.114059

Podhorska, I., Sroka, W., & Majerova, J. (2021). *SUSTAINABLE BRAND MANAGEMENT. Sustainable Branding: Ethical.* Social, and Environmental Cases and Perspectives.

Qureshi, F. N., Bashir, S., Mahmood, A., Ahmad, S., Attiq, S., & Zeeshan, M. (2022). Impact of internal brand management on sustainable competitive advantage: An explanatory study based on the mediating roles of brand commitment and brand citizenship behavior. *PLoS One, 17*(3), e0264379. doi:10.1371/journal.pone.0264379 PMID:35275925

Rokhim, R., Mayasari, I., & Wulandari, P. (2021, March). Is brand management critical to SMEs' product sustainability? Qualitative analysis in the context of Indonesia small enterprise environment. [). IOP Publishing.]. *IOP Conference Series. Earth and Environmental Science, 716*(1), 012109. doi:10.1088/1755-1315/716/1/012109

Sarkar, A. N., & Singh, J. (2005). New paradigm in evolving brand management strategy. *Journal of Management Research, 5*(2), 80–90.

Sato, M., Yoshida, M., Doyle, J., & Choi, W. (2023). Consumer-brand identification and happiness in experiential consumption. *Psychology and Marketing, 40*(8), 1579–1592. doi:10.1002/mar.21852

Schultz, D. E., & Block, M. P. (2015). Beyond brand loyalty: Brand sustainability. *Journal of Marketing Communications, 21*(5), 340–355. doi:10.1080/13527266.2013.821227

Son, J., & Hwang, K. (2023). How to make vertical farming more attractive: Effects of vegetable growing conditions on consumer assessment. *Psychology and Marketing, 40*(8), 1466–1483. doi:10.1002/mar.21823

Thomas, F., & Capelli, S. (2023). Increasing purchase intention while limiting binge-eating: The role of repeating the same flavor-giving ingredient image on a front of package. *Psychology and Marketing, 40*(8), 1539–1555. doi:10.1002/mar.21839

Volles, B. K., Van Kerckhove, A., & Geuens, M. (2023). Triggering brand switching in online stores: The effectiveness of recommendations for private labels versus national brands. *Journal of Business Research, 164*, 114020. doi:10.1016/j.jbusres.2023.114020

Zhang, S., Peng, M. Y. P., Peng, Y., Zhang, Y., Ren, G., & Chen, C. C. (2020). Expressive brand relationship, brand love, and brand loyalty for tablet pcs: Building a sustainable brand. *Frontiers in psychology, 11,* 231.

Chapter 8

Sustainable Development of Industry 5.0 and Its Application of Metaverse Practices

Saumendra Das
iD https://orcid.org/0000-0003-4956-4352
GIET University, India

Nayan Deep S. Kanwal
University Putra Malaysia, Malaysia

Udaya Sankar Patro
iD https://orcid.org/0009-0009-9198-3578
Rayagada Autonomous College, India

Tapaswini Panda
iD https://orcid.org/0009-0003-8327-9990
Model Degree College, Rayagada, India

N. Saibabu
iD https://orcid.org/0000-0001-6054-2053
Aditya Institute of Technology and Management, India

Hassan Badawy
Luxor University, Egypt

ABSTRACT

The advent of Industry 5.0 presents new challenges for the design of human communities that have the capacity to be both ecologically and economically sustainable. Industry 5.0 is characterized by its focus on human-centric business, as opposed to Industry 4.0, which prioritizes manufacturing and technology. Machine learning technologies have several applications and play a crucial role in both Industry 4.0 and 5.0. This chapter argues that for Industry 5.0 to really prioritize human needs, it is imperative that humans possess the ability to create, advance, and oversee reliable and morally sound artificial intelligence systems. To tackle this issue, the authors have established an AI ethical framework that aims to offer guidance on the ethical usage of AI in daily activities. The current study is based on the authors' previous research and is being further refined as part of continuing research to validate the proposed framework.

DOI: 10.4018/979-8-3693-5868-9.ch008

INTRODUCTION

Over the course of human history, technical progress has not only changed the ways in which different things are made, but also the entire organization of societies. Throughout the history of technology, there have been four notable phases of industrialization, referred to as "Industrial 1.0 to Industry 4.0" by the scientific community. Despite the ongoing implementation of Industry 4.0 and the increasing adoption of this trend by many firms, discussions regarding Industry 5.0 started several decades ago. Industry 5.0 can be classified in several ways, but it should not be seen as a completely new industrial revolution. Instead, it should be understood as a transitional phase that may precede a potential sixth industrial revolution (Di Nardo & Yu, 2021).

Industry 5.0 represents a shift from the technologically-focused approach of Industry 4.0 to a more human-centred perspective. In this new paradigm, firms are leveraging innovation to achieve objectives that go beyond just commercial efficiency. In this new industrial environment, humans may collaborate with robots and machine learning (ML) technology to enhance their productivity and creativity. While certain studies (Wang L et al., 2021 & Nahavandi, 2021) emphasize the theoretical benefits of Industry 5.0, others (Hekim & Ozdemir, 2021), (Sezen et al., 2021) argue that it entails the establishment of complex and highly interconnected electronic systems, potentially neglecting the administrative challenges arising from human-computer collaboration.

Consequently, it is necessary to tackle certain ethical concerns. In order to address potential ethical issues, it is essential to build appropriate governance and implementation regulations that can tailor the development and deployment of AI technology. Most contemporary scholars (Topcuoglu et al., 2021) (Codini et al., 2020) (Show et al., 2021) have examined the interconnectedness between the features of Industries 5.0 and both the economy and society. These distinctive qualities are not only intended to increase productivity but also to improve the overall quality of life. The participants engaged in a discussion about the possible frameworks and regulations that should be integrated into the realm of technology progress. The aim was to mitigate business risks and promote innovative solutions to address current social issues faced by firms.

Mavrodieva and Shaw (2020) establish a correlation between Industry 5.0 and the notion of a "Super Smart Society," highlighting the distinct requirements and abilities of each individual. The concept involves integrating the tangible world with the internet to efficiently collect more precise and personalized data for improved value creation and problem-solving. This concept is evident in the latest announcement by Microsoft and Facebook on the Metaverse (Krogstise et al., 2022) (Sharma, 2023), which is a system that has the potential to link online assets with real-world economic activities. In other words, the metaverse has the capacity to become a crucial element of Industry 5.0, facilitating the fusion of the real world with computer to provide firms with increased flexibility in their operations.

According to recent research by Umbrello et al (2020), the topic of a value-driven and ethical approach to development in Industry 5.0 is considered significant and sensitive, despite the fact that Industry 5.0 is still portrayed as a conceptual idea. We consider this to be a critical matter because, from an ethical perspective, it highlights the need of both developing new technologies and promoting and maintaining a happy coexistence between humans and machines through collaboration.

Artificially intelligent (AI) systems are a prominent technology element of Industry 5.0. Our study defines artificial intelligence (AI) as a comprehensive concept including several methodologies derived from computer science, psychology science, and analytics. When determining how to facilitate the development and application of these techniques, it is beneficial to perceive them collectively, despite the distinctions among specific terminologies and technologies (e.g., machine learning vs. deep learning or artificial intelligence vs. machine learning) (Jones et al., 2020).

The European Commission has defined many objectives for Industries 5.0, one of which is to adopt a human-centered approach to technical breakthroughs, including intelligent robots. Consequently, they issued a proposition for the regulation of AI (Oatley, 2022). Based on the aforementioned facts, our study posits that with the ongoing progress of artificial intelligence (AI) technologies in tandem with industrial growth, there will be an increased requirement for an ethical framework specifically tailored for AI. The implementation of this system necessitates consideration of several elements, such as economical, ideological, and legal considerations.

This research aims to provide a framework of digital ethical principles while promoting the creativity and collaboration between people and robots as envisioned by Industry 5.0. Our goal is to develop a framework that facilitates the implementation of ethical principles in AI, ensuring their effective and responsible integration into the upcoming generation of technological platforms that will shape Industry 5.0. This study will be broken into two sections: the first piece will examine the moral principles now being studied in AI, while the second section will address the reported implementation concerns identified by previous scientists. The subsequent section will encompass our proposed AI ethical framework.

Currently, Industry 5.0 has not achieved significant recognition or establishment, with discussions mostly centred around Industry 4.0. Industry 5.0 is anticipated to build upon the foundations of Industry 4.0 by prioritizing the integration of state-of-the-art technologies to foster sustainable development. Furthermore, the application of metaverse approaches in Industry 5.0 has the capacity to greatly enhance its capabilities. Presented below is a theoretical overview:

SUSTAINABLE DEVELOPMENT IN INDUSTRY 5.0 AIMS TO ATTAIN OPTIMAL UTILIZATION OF RESOURCES

Industry 5.0 is anticipated to prioritize resource efficiency through the utilization of advanced technologies like the Internet of Things (IoT) and Artificial Intelligence (AI). Adopting eco-friendly behaviors include minimizing waste, reducing energy use, and advocating for circular economic principles.

Sustainable Production: Integrating clean and renewable energy sources into industrial activities. Employing sustainable materials and cutting-edge technologies to minimize environmental impacts.

Cooperative Networks: Industry 5.0 has the potential to facilitate collaborative ecosystems, where companies, government bodies, and the general public work together to achieve sustainable goals. Collaborating to combine resources and knowledge for mutual benefits and sustainable, environmentally-conscious growth Implementing Metaverse methodologies in the context of Industry 5.0.

Virtual Collaboration: It refers to the utilization of metaverse technologies to enable remote interaction among teams that are geographically scattered. Immersive technology has enhanced the convenience of remote work by reducing the requirement for physical effort. Electronic twin refers to the technology that entails the creation of a virtual replica or simulation of a physical object or system. The Metaverse has the potential to facilitate the development and control of digital duplicates of real-world assets, hence improving maintenance efficiency and reducing times of inactivity. Applying analytical and simulation methods in the metaverse can improve efficiency and adaptability.

Education and replication: Utilizing multiverse approaches enables the use of virtual training and simulation, hence enhancing staff skills without the requirement of physical resources in the real world. This might lead to the creation of educational projects that are both more efficient and sustainable.

Improving Supply Chain Transparency: Metaverse technologies enhance transparency throughout the whole supply chain, enabling continuous monitoring and real-time adjustments. This might lead to less waste, improved management, and more environmental accountability. Customer participation is facilitated by platforms like Metaverse, which enable enterprises to build immersive customer experiences and successfully market ethical products and activities. Virtual exhibits and visits have the capacity to reduce the necessity for brick-and-mortar stores and the associated resources.

Independent Production: The utilization of multiverse principles has the capability to augment the concept of decentralized production, where virtual companies may effectively produce goods based on demand, hence reducing the necessity for transportation and storage. The implementation of intelligent urban

Figure 1. History of industrial revolution
Source: Muntaha, 2023

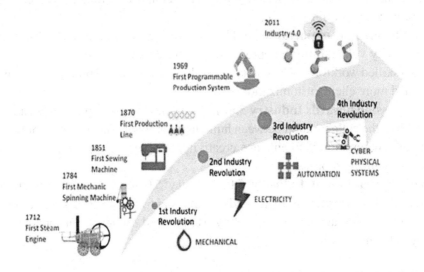

areas and the corresponding physical infrastructure in the form of Metaverse solutions has the potential to accelerate the development of contemporary cities by facilitating efficient energy use, improved transportation systems, and ecologically sustainable infrastructure.

Sustainability Inspection: Metaverse tools can aid in the continuous monitoring and visualization of the environmental consequences of industrial operations, allowing for the proactive deployment of measures to reduce harm. It is crucial to recognize that the advancement of Industrial 5.0 and the integration of metaverse protocols are speculative, and the actual implementation may vary based on technological advancements, societal acceptance, and regulatory frameworks in the future.

EVOLUTION OF INDUSTRY 4.0 TO 5.0 WITH THE METAVERSE APPLICATIONS

Industry 4.0, commonly referred to as the Fourth Industrial Revolution. Industry 4.0 refers to the integration of advanced technologies, exchange of data, and intelligent manufacturing in the industrial sector. The fundamental components include the Internet of Things, cognitive computing, data analytics, artificial intelligence, and automation.

The emergence of Industry 4.0: The emergence of Industry 4.0 marked a shift from traditional production to intelligent and interconnected processes that can adapt and optimize output in real-time.

Challenges and opportunities: The initiation encountered obstacles such as cybersecurity vulnerabilities, apprehensions over data protection, and the need to recruit a skilled workforce. The potential results were enhanced production, reduced costs, and more client customization.

Progressing towards Industry 5.0: Industry 5.0 is a conceptual extension that emphasizes the collaboration between humans and robots. The objective of human-machine collaboration is to enhance creativity, troubleshooting, and flexibility in the manufacturing process.

Salient Features of Industry 5.0: Industry 5.0 focuses on the creation of techniques that prioritize human needs, emphasizing the need of skilled humans working alongside advanced technology. Heightened emphasis on longevity and ecological considerations.

Integration into the Metaverse:

Introduction to the Metaverse: The Metaverse is a convergence of physical and virtual reality, creating a cohesive virtual environment that is shared among users. It includes augmented reality (AR), virtual reality (VR), and other immersive technology breakthroughs.

Utilization of the Metaverse in Manufacturing: The Metaverse, a virtual world, may be employed as a platform to provide instructional simulations, allowing workers to recreate complex scenarios inside a virtual environment.

Collaboration: Geographically distant teams may engage in real-time collaboration inside a virtual environment, hence enhancing interactions and productivity. Industries can utilize the Metaverse for virtual design and prototyping, leading to reduced time and costs associated with physical prototypes.

Progressing towards Industry 5.0 through the Metaverse: Employing Metaverse technology can enhance the level of interaction between humans and machines in Business 5.0. Workers can access the Metaverse to obtain up-to-date information, undergo training, and collaborate as a team to address issues.

Considerations and variables to consider: Addressing privacy issues and security difficulties associated with the vast amounts of data generated and shared inside the Metaverse. Advocating for inclusivity and facilitating accessibility in the digital domain.

Potential benefits: Expanded options enabled by thorough visual representations of data. Intensive instruction and skill improvement in a simulated setting. Improved effectiveness and flexibility in industrial processes. The shift from industrial 4.0

to 5.0, enabled by the integration of Metaverse use, is a seamless and ongoing advancement. The next scenario will be shaped by ongoing progress in technology and industrial processes. Acquiring up-to-date knowledge on the latest advancements in these fields is crucial for gaining a comprehensive understanding. As technology continues to progress, the need of ethics becomes increasingly critical, especially in the context of Industry 5.0. Multiple considerations highlight the need of ethics in Industry.

Industry 5.0: Anthropocentric Approach: Industry 5.0 prioritizes a cooperative partnership between people and robots. Ensuring the integration of technology respects human rights, dignity, and well-being is of utmost importance, and ethical concerns play a vital role in achieving this. It is necessary to create ethical rules to provide direction for the development and application of technologies that improve cooperation between humans and machines.

Data privacy and security: Given the heavy reliance on data-driven technologies in Industry 5.0, it is of utmost importance to prioritize the preservation of people' data privacy and security. Companies must have stringent data protection protocols to deter illegal access and exploitation of personal information.

Openness and responsibility: Ethical issues include the need to openly communicate and disclose the use of sophisticated technology, such as artificial intelligence (AI) and machine learning algorithms. Companies should transparently articulate the use of these technologies and establish responsibility for their activities. Promoting transparency fosters confidence among stakeholders and alleviates concerns related to the use of sophisticated technology.

Equity and inclusiveness: Industry 5.0 need to prioritize equity and inclusiveness in its operations. Ethical issues include the identification and mitigation of biases in algorithms, as well as the equitable distribution of technological advantages across all sectors of society, with the aim of preventing discriminatory consequences. It is imperative to make efforts to reduce the digital gap and guarantee that the advantages of Industry 5.0 are accessible to a wide-ranging and worldwide public.

Ecological Resilience: Environmental effect is included under ethical issues. The development and implementation of Industry 5.0 should prioritize sustainability and aim to minimize adverse environmental impacts. Companies should take into account the whole life cycle of goods and technology, and actively encourage environmentally friendly practices in their production and operational processes.

Employee well-being: In Industry 5.0, the incorporation of technology should give utmost importance to the welfare of the workforce. This includes the resolution of issues pertaining to job displacement, guaranteeing equitable working conditions, and offering prospects for upskilling and reskilling. Ethical practices include the provision of assistance to a workforce that is capable of adjusting to technological advancements without jeopardizing their means of living.

Figure 2. Technology enablers of Industry 5.0
Source: A. (2021, March 29)

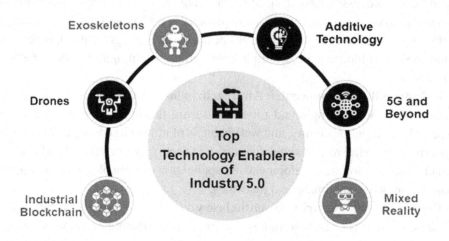

Global norms and guidelines: Industry 5.0 must comply with global ethical norms and legislation. Companies must to proactively participate in conversations and cooperation with regulatory agencies to guarantee the incorporation of ethical issues into industrial operations worldwide.

Ongoing Ethical Assessment: Continuous assessment of ethical implications is crucial due to the ever-changing nature of technology and industry. It is essential for companies to periodically evaluate and revise their ethical principles in light of advancing technology and evolving cultural norms.

Essentially, ethics are of utmost importance in directing the growth and implementation of technologies in Industry 5.0. An approach that prioritizes human interests and is guided by ethical principles is crucial in order to guarantee that technological progress is in line with society values and has a beneficial impact on the well-being of people and the environment.

The concept of Industry 4.0 was first presented at the Dresden Trade Fair in 2011. Its objective is to integrate modern technology into the industrial sector in order to attain optimal levels of productivity and operational efficacy (Sanchez, Exposito, and Aguilar, 2020). Innovation is often highlighted as a tool to improve productivity and efficacy in order to boost profitability in the international marketplace. However, there is also a focus on employing technologies to achieve a particular degree of human-centricity, which is referred to as Operators 4.0. Operator 4.0 refer to operators that get support from technology that alleviate both physical and mental strain, while still maintaining production goals (Romero et al., 2016; Romero, Stahre, and Taisch, 2020; Kaasinen et al., 2020).

Industry 5.0 is a proposed technological shift that involves two main visions:

(i)   human-robot collaboration in the workplace, and
(ii) the utilization of naturally occurring natural assets to remake traditional industries.

This study centres on Enterprise 5.0, which is a factory philosophy and revolutions that emphasizes the significance of technological advancement and research in supporting the sector. It places worker's wellness at the core of the making process (Xu et al., 2021). An effective revolution must address the requirements outlined in the Agricultural Individual Needs Pyramid, encompassing safeguarding at work and fostering a reliable human-machine connection that facilitates optimal confidence and self-actualization, allowing individuals to achieve and achieve their full potential (Lu et al., 2022). The objective is to integrate humans and machinery in a mutually beneficial partnership to enhance efficiency in the industrial sector while also maintaining human employment. Moreover, it aims to cultivate methods that empower individuals to harness their analytical reasoning, ingenuity, and expertise in a particular field. Simultaneously, equipment can be relied upon to independently aid in mundane duties with great productivity, foreseeing the goals and desires of the person who operates them, resulting in less waste and expenses (Nahavandi, 2019; Demir, Döven, and Sezen, 2019; Maddikunta et al., 2022). The ability to communicate and collaborate effectively allows for the establishment of reliable and mutually beneficial partnerships between people and technology. In order to cultivate reliable co-evolutionary connections, platforms must take into account the worker's attributes (such as age, gender, and level of education, among others) as well as the company's goals. An instance of human-machine cooperation is exemplified through the use of cobots for short which coexist in the exact same setting as humans, possess the ability to detect and comprehend human beings, and are capable of separately, concurrently, consecutively, or cooperatively executing tasks (El Zaatari et al., 2019).

To achieve the industry 5.0 vision, it is necessary to reorient the focus from individual innovations to a methodical strategy that reconsiders how to (a) harness the capabilities of machines as well as people, (b) develop digital replicas of entire systems, and (c) extensively utilize AI, via a specific emphasis on generating actionable duties for humans. Although investigation into Industry 5.0 is in its early stages, it has received official endorsement from the European Commission in a paper published in 2021.

AI ETHICS: PROBLEMS IN TRANSLATING CONCEPTS TO PRACTICE

Industry 5.0 is characterized by key ideas such as innovation, cooperation, and human-machine interaction. Considering that AI systems are a crucial technical component of Industry 5.0, it is essential for us to have a deeper understanding of how to progress AI development in a synchronized manner that results in a creative and ethically-driven effective interaction between humans and machines. Recently, there has been a significant interest in the subject of AI ethics from researchers, politicians, AI experts, producers, and the general public. Most studies indicate that the presence of ethics in AI is crucial (Kazim & Koshiyama, 2021), (Floridi, 2021), (Hagendorff, 2020) to mitigate possible hazards associated with AI, such as those pertaining to the labor market, inequalities, biases, and privacy. Additional studies delineated recommendations (Vayena et al., 2019), (Savage et al., 2020) and presented frameworks (Vayena et al., 2021), (Sivarajah et al., 2022) for incorporating ethical principles into artificial intelligence (AI) systems. The consensus among the extensive body of research on ethical principles in artificial intelligence (AI) highlights a fundamental issue about the disparity between theoretical concepts and practical approaches for developing and constructing morally sound AI systems. This study has considered the criteria provided by the European Commission in The Ethics criteria for Trustworthy Artificial Intelligence (Manterlero, 2022). The principles of individual liberty, protection from harm, fairness, and comprehensibility.

Several AI ethical frameworks have been created by both AI corporations (such as Microsoft, Google, etc.) and academic researchers. Almost all of them delineate prerequisites that must be fulfilled in order to classify artificial intelligence as moral. These criteria pertain to core concepts such as confidentiality, fairness, non-discrimination, transparency, security, and accountability. Although the theory is widely accepted, there is still uncertainty and challenges in implementing these frameworks in different businesses. When constructing, implementing, or operating an AI system, several parties may interact with it; as a result, implementing AI ethics necessitates a unified and comprehensive approach. The VDE AI Ethics Group paper categorizes the current challenges of utilizing AI into three main groups: The dependency on context and the nature and usefulness of sociotechnical AI. Furthermore, we encountered an additional challenge related to overall governance that we may potentially apply to this framework, considering its functional perspective, as shown by our previous research (Ciobanu & Meșniță, 2021). Some AI systems has the capability to autonomously adapt or acquire knowledge from previous operations.

Hence, it is imperative that an AI ethical framework, once implemented, maintains its currency by facilitating ongoing feedback loops among developers, consumers, and other stakeholders. Moreover, an AI user or developer should possess the ability to assess the efficiency of a utilized framework for AI ethics and implement enhancements as necessary. This should be a continuous process rather than a one-time effort. Clearly, the issues associated with artificially intelligent systems might vary depending on how, where, and by whom they are used. The EU HLEG initiative identified four main hazard categories that have the potential to impact AI systems throughout their development and deployment stages (Ciobanu & Meşniţă, 2022). Hence, an AI ethical framework must possess the capability to differentiate between different kinds of risks and provide appropriate and differentiated courses of action.

A BLUEPRINT FOR DEVELOPING A FOUNDATION FOR AI ETHICS

The cornerstone of our approach VCIO is founded on the study conducted by the VDE AI Ethics group. This research provided a structure for implementing AI ethical principles by considering factors, needs, metrics, and measures. The VCIO model is a comprehensive approach that tackles the ethical principles of AI across several levels, catering to both AI developers and consumers. Within this essay, we want to progress beyond the current point. Furthermore, considering that an AI ethical system in industry 5.0 needs to be reliable, it is crucial to establish a quantifiable and transparent ethical framework for AI. This framework should also facilitate a real-time feedback loop between the manufacturer and the customer, which directly impacts the model's training process.

The training pattern that forms the foundation of an AI system is a crucial feature. In this phase of the data scientist research lifecycle, operators strive to minimize a loss function throughout its whole forecasting range by adjusting an algorithm with a suitable combination of weight and bias (Ciobanu & Mesnita, 2022). A prototype is created to construct the most precise algebraic representation of the relationship between information aspects and a target designation, such as an AI idea. Our suggested AI moral framework argues that every intended notion should be converted into a Modelling for Instruction in Artificial Intelligence. Thus, the prototype may be validated, scrutinized, and executed.

Figure 1 illustrates a proposed hierarchical structure for our preferred operational AI ethical framework. This is built upon our previous research and will be the main subject of our future inquiry as we aim to confirm its validity. This design framework integrates the four guiding principles defined by the EU HLEG project. It is separated into two layers: AI Desired State Configuration (AI DSC) and AI Embedded Ethics by Design (AI EED), which are coupled by systems API. Based on these two interrelated perspectives, we provide an all-encompassing approach to implementing an AI system that tackles challenges encountered by both AI makers

Figure 3. High-level architecture of a practical AI ethical framework
Source: Ciobanu & Meşniţă (2022)

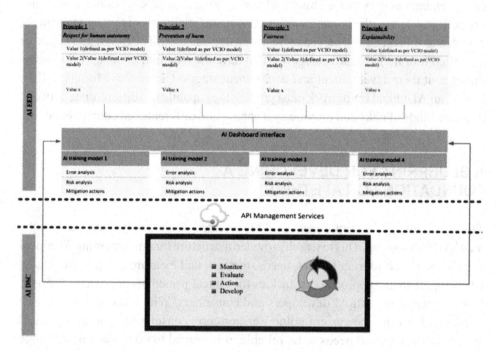

and end-users. They will provide a more comprehensive explanation of this concept and discuss how the framework can effectively manage the two levels (AIDSC and AI EED). We will also discuss the functionality of the API systems and the interoperability between these two levels.

AI EED, OR AI EMBEDDED ETHICS BY DESIGN

Developers and data scientists may utilize the EED component to train their models and datasets in order to meet the required ethical criteria that AI solutions must adhere to. The AI EED layer is designed to be derived from the subsequent procedure:

Programmers and data scientists, whether they work for the AI Manufacturer or the Consumer, have the ability to establish the principles of artificial intelligence based on the VCIO model outlined earlier.

The AI producer will always own an AI Dashboards instrument that may be employed for the training procedure.

The AI platform dashboard enables developers to create training models that instruct the AI system in identifying certain concepts.

Before being implemented, each training model must undergo testing. All mistakes, risk assessments, and potential courses of action to mitigate risks and rectify any errors will be thoroughly considered during the testing process.

The AI EED layer serves as a proactive platform for individuals to utilize before implementing a specific AI system in a production environment. It considers factors such as the industry, social context, potential impacts, and the various stakeholders responsible for maintaining the system post-implementation.

In contrast, the AI DSC serves as a method for ongoing enhancement of the AI system after its implementation, ensuring that the training models on which it relies remain consistently reliable across different situations. In light of the characteristics of Industry 5.0, we strongly believe that every artificial intelligence (AI) system deployed post-migration must be subject to human oversight in order to ensure its traceability, evaluation according to predefined criteria, implementation of relevant measures, and ongoing enhancement. Moreover, this feature will allow non-technical stakeholders (such as police officers, data analysts, etc.) to consistently assess the system and offer suggestions through the AI instrument panel interface. The training model can be repeatedly tested and adjusted based on the provided suggestions.

An API Management System facilitates the technological connection between the two aforementioned levels. Following deployment, the software engineers and data scientists have the option to provide feedback, which can consist of structured or unstructured information sets, to the AI dashboard interface. This input is then used to further enhance the training models. By adopting this approach, we can ensure an all-encompassing strategy in which the AI system continuously adapts to the specific circumstances in which it is implemented. This allows humans to have complete authority over the AI's decisions, enabling them to focus on enhancing their creativity and innovation in their respective areas of expertise.

CONCLUSION

The objective of Industry 5.0 is to shift away from technology-driven productivity approaches and embrace a more human-centric strategy. Ensuring socio-technical compatibility between individuals and AI systems is an essential initial measure. The contemporary occupation, characterized by extensive digitization, is not only a physical one, but rather a digital one. To enhance innovative thinking, it is imperative that individuals prioritize inventiveness. This may be achieved by advancing and implementing technology and artificial intelligence algorithms that are both ethical and reliable. That can only be achieved if humans enforce appropriate controls on the invention, considering sustainability in terms of both the environment and economy, as well as efficiency.

Our research emphasizes the necessity of implementing effective AI regulations in a synchronized manner, considering the different levels of autonomy that AI possesses before, during, and after its adoption, as well as the diverse stakeholders who will interact with these advancements.

Our proposed framework aims to combine the scientific field of defining ethical standards with the technological components that form the foundation of an artificial intelligence (AI) system, using a two-layer approach consisting of AI EED and AI DSC. In addition, we are suggesting a technique (using an API system) where, when the AI engine is put into action, information may be collected and incorporated into the initial training model continuously.

Our post aimed to offer a comprehensive overview of the artificial intelligence architecture. In the subsequent steps, our objective is to develop the AI EED, AI DSC, and the connecting API components of the proposed architecture, while considering the suitability and safety of different AI systems. We are also keen to discover a method of verifying the aforementioned framework in a real-world, pragmatic environment.

ACKNOWLEDGMENT

This research received no specific grant from any funding agency in the public, commercial, or not-for-profit sectors.

REFERENCES

A. (2021, March 29). *Industry 5.0—Bringing Empowered Humans Back to the Shop Floor*. Frost & Sullivan. https://www.frost.com/frost-perspectives/industry-5-0-bringing-empowered-humans-back-to-the-shop-floor/

Allam, Z., Sharifi, A., Bibri, S. E., Jones, D. S., & Krogstie, J. (2022). The metaverse as a virtual form of smart cities: Opportunities and challenges for environmental, economic, and social sustainability in urban futures. *Smart Cities*, 5(3), 771–801. doi:10.3390/smartcities5030040

Aquilani, B., Piccarozzi, M., Abbate, T., & Codini, A. (2020). The role of open innovation and value co-creation in the challenging transition from industry 4.0 to society 5.0: Toward a theoretical framework. *Sustainability (Basel)*, 12(21), 8943. doi:10.3390/su12218943

Ashok, M., Madan, R., Joha, A., & Sivarajah, U. (2022). Ethical framework for Artificial Intelligence and Digital technologies. *International Journal of Information Management, 62*, 102433. doi:10.1016/j.ijinfomgt.2021.102433

Ciobanu, A. C., & Meşniţă, G. (2021). AI ETHICS IN BUSINESS–A Bibliometric APPROACH. *Review of Economic and Business Studies, 14*(28), 169–202. doi:10.47743/rebs-2021-2-0009

Ciobanu, A. C., & Meşniţă, G. (2022, March). AI Ethics for Industry 5.0—From Principles to Practice. In *Proceedings of the Workshop of I-ESA* (Vol. 22). Research Gate.

De Giovanni, P. (2023). Sustainability of the Metaverse: A transition to Industry 5.0. *Sustainability (Basel), 15*(7), 6079. doi:10.3390/su15076079

Demir, K. A., Döven, G., & Sezen, B. (2019). Industry 5.0 and human-robot co-working. *Procedia Computer Science, 158*, 688–695. doi:10.1016/j.procs.2019.09.104

Di Nardo, M., & Yu, H. (2021). Special issue "Industry 5.0: The prelude to the sixth industrial revolution". *Applied System Innovation, 4*(3), 45. doi:10.3390/asi4030045

ElFar, O. A., Chang, C. K., Leong, H. Y., Peter, A. P., Chew, K. W., & Show, P. L. (2021). Prospects of Industry 5.0 in algae: Customization of production and new advance technology for clean bioenergy generation. *Energy Conversion and Management: X*, 10, 100048.

Floridi, L. (2021). Establishing the rules for building trustworthy AI. *Ethics, Governance, and Policies in Artificial Intelligence*, 41-45.

Floridi, L., Cowls, J., Beltrametti, M., Chatila, R., Chazerand, P., Dignum, V., & Vayena, E. (2021). An ethical framework for a good AI society: Opportunities, risks, principles, and recommendations. *Ethics, governance, and policies in artificial intelligence*, 19-39.

Hagendorff, T. (2020). The ethics of AI ethics: An evaluation of guidelines. *Minds and Machines, 30*(1), 99–120. doi:10.1007/s11023-020-09517-8

Jobin, A., Ienca, M., & Vayena, E. (2019). The global landscape of AI ethics guidelines. *Nature Machine Intelligence, 1*(9), 389–399. doi:10.1038/s42256-019-0088-2

Kazim, E., & Koshiyama, A. S. (2021). A high-level overview of AI ethics. *Patterns (New York, N.Y.), 2*(9), 100314. doi:10.1016/j.patter.2021.100314 PMID:34553166

Longo, F., Padovano, A., & Umbrello, S. (2020). Value-oriented and ethical technology engineering in industry 5.0: A human-centric perspective for the design of the factory of the future. *Applied Sciences (Basel, Switzerland)*, *10*(12), 4182. doi:10.3390/app10124182

Mantelero, A. (2022). Regulating AI. In *Beyond Data: Human Rights, Ethical and Social Impact Assessment in AI* (pp. 139–183). TMC Asser Press. doi:10.1007/978-94-6265-531-7_4

Mavrodieva, A. V., & Shaw, R. (2020). Disaster and climate change issues in Japan's Society 5.0—A discussion. *Sustainability (Basel)*, *12*(5), 1893. doi:10.3390/su12051893

Nahavandi, S. (2019). Industry 5.0—A human-centric solution. *Sustainability (Basel)*, *11*(16), 4371. doi:10.3390/su11164371

Oatley, G. C. (2022). Themes in data mining, big data, and crime analytics. *Wiley Interdisciplinary Reviews. Data Mining and Knowledge Discovery*, *12*(2), e1432. doi:10.1002/widm.1432

Özdemir, V., & Hekim, N. (2018). Birth of industry 5.0: Making sense of big data with artificial intelligence, "the internet of things" and next-generation technology policy. *OMICS: A Journal of Integrative Biology*, *22*(1), 65–76. doi:10.1089/omi.2017.0194 PMID:29293405

Procter, R., Glover, B., & Jones, E. (2020). *Research 4.0: Research in the Age of Automation*.

Rességuier, A., & Rodrigues, R. (2020). AI ethics should not remain toothless! A call to bring back the teeth of ethics. *Big Data & Society*, *7*(2), 2053951720942541. doi:10.1177/2053951720942541

Sharma, T. K. (2023). Hybrid Working: The Future of Organizations. In Reshaping the Business World Post-COVID-19 (pp. 41-68). Apple Academic Press.

Xu, X., Lu, Y., Vogel-Heuser, B., & Wang, L. (2021). Industry 4.0 and Industry 5.0—Inception, conception and perception. *Journal of Manufacturing Systems*, *61*, 530–535. doi:10.1016/j.jmsy.2021.10.006

Zengin, Y., Naktiyok, S., Kaygın, E., Kavak, O., & Topçuoğlu, E. (2021). An investigation upon industry 4.0 and society 5.0 within the context of sustainable development goals. *Sustainability (Basel)*, *13*(5), 2682. doi:10.3390/su13052682

Zhou, J., Chen, F., Berry, A., Reed, M., Zhang, S., & Savage, S. (2020, December). A survey on ethical principles of AI and implementations. In *2020 IEEE Symposium Series on Computational Intelligence (SSCI)* (pp. 3010-3017). IEEE. 10.1109/SSCI47803.2020.9308437

Chapter 9
Sustainability Reporting in the Metaverse:
A Multi-Sectoral Analysis

Sunaina Rathore

 https://orcid.org/0000-0002-3289-0963
Central University of Himachal Pradesh, India

Manpreet Arora

 https://orcid.org/0000-0002-4939-1992
Central University of Himachal Pradesh, India

ABSTRACT

Metaverse is a virtual environment where we interact with each other and the world around us. Metaverse integrates the physical environment with the digital environment. In this study, the author explored the extent to which different metaverse technologies have been disclosed in sustainability reports and integrated reports. For this, specific Indian companies have been selected from the Nifty 100 index that have made 'metaverse technologies'-related disclosures in these reports. Further, the sustainability reports of these companies have been extracted to analyse the content to see the extent to which metaverse technologies have been reported by major Indian industries. The study also attempts to highlight important internet of things (IoT), artificial intelligence (AI), and virtual reality (VR) technologies-based platforms, initiatives and projects initiated by Indian industries to improve their productivity and operational efficiency and ensure safety at the workplace.

DOI: 10.4018/979-8-3693-5868-9.ch009

INTRODUCTION

Metaverse is an evolving next-generation internet platform where digital reality integrates physical reality. It is a virtually shared place for people to play, work and socialize (Wang et al., 2022). The word "Metaverse" comes from the "meta-universe" that is an integration of physical and digital space into a virtual universe (Pamucar et al., 2022). There has been a continuous 'platformization' of data infrastructures and digital reality in urban spheres with the advent of the metaverse. Metaverse is such a recent platform project launched by "Meta" as a global platform company (Allam et al. 2022).

Metaverse involves use of Artificial Intelligence (AI), Machine Learning (ML) technologies, Internet of Things (IoT) and Virtual Reality (VR) /Augmented reality (AR). These tools have been consistently applied and implemented by today's organizations in their daily operations. AI tools have been used by companies such as 'Authbase' (Reliance Industries Limited) to mitigate hack and bot attacks in real-time. Reliance has also reported its 'Mygov Corona helpdesk' (by Jio Haptik), which served as a powerful 'ChatBot solution' during COVID-19 pandemic. Similarly, ML technologies have been used by these corporations to forecast the future health of any equipment. The organizations also create Virtual Reality simulators to train the employees to deal with difficult equipment in simulated environments to ensure safety at operations. All these tools are not only making organizations efficient in its operations but also leading them towards sustainability such as Tech Mahindra Limited has been doing water management through "pipeline monitoring". This pipeline monitoring is based on Machine Learning Technologies that automatically detects and predicts any possibility of fault.

Metaverse has a great potential to achieve overall sustainable development. Its 'platformization' should be optimally utilized in achieving United Nations' Sustainable development goals (SDGs). Metaverse is capable of turning imagination into reality with the help of virtual reality, so 'sustainable education' can be achieved as metaverse is free from time and space constraints (Park & Kim, 2022; Lee & Hwang, 2022). It can help in providing a 'game-like experience' for sustainable learning. Innovative educational environments can be created with the help of products of metaverse. So, the United Nations' fourth sustainable development goal (Quality Education) can be achieved with the use of metaverse.

In addition to education, transport also plays a major role in sustainable development. The role of 'transport' in sustainable development was first recognized at the United Nation's Earth Summit in 1992 and was reinforced in the document 'Agenda 21'. But the second Global Sustainable Transport Conference, held in 2021, provided a platform to discuss sustainable transport and propose options for the way forward. It has been recognized that sustainable transport plays a crucial role in achieving SDGs as it provides safe, efficient and resilient mobility infrastructure that will minimize carbon emissions and huge environmental impacts (UN's Interagency Report, 2021). Thus, the metaverse technologies can be used to change transportation systems. It may involve training public transport operation ensuring safety, traffic operation, and 'autonomous driving' using AI to obtain sustainable transportation (Pamucar et al., 2022).

Environmental pollution is also a major unsustainable challenge for the world especially 'megacities' where population burden is heavier. 'Metaverse telework' can help reduce this 'population pressure' in megacities. The telework can positively influence the individual's intention to leave the megacity and relocate to a non-megacity (Choi, 2022). Thus, the metaverse technologies can actually help in achieving overall sustainable development. It can assist in providing sustainable solutions to unstainable challenges. The literature on metaverse is still evolving. Researchers and academicians are consistently providing their insights to it. According to existing literature, the metaverse can transform the way we interact with each other and the world around us. But, the impact of the "metaverse ecosystem" on sustainability reporting is still unclear. This book chapter aims to study the relationship between the metaverse technologies and sustainability reporting with the help of content analysis using MAXQDA software and to provide insights about how the metaverse can be used to promote sustainability reporting practices.

However, this study revolves around the metaverse related disclosures by major corporations listed on NSE. So, this book chapter is aimed at following objectives:

1. To examine the extent to which metaverse technologies have been discussed in sustainability reports/integrated reports across different sectors.
2. To analyse which industry or sector is contributing more to metaverse technologies.

REVIEW OF LITERATURE:

Jauhiainen et al. (2022) in a systematic literature review identified the need to minimize energy consumption, address energy scarcity, and optimize the use of natural and renewable resources within the metaverse. Their literature review highlighted the potential of the metaverse to promote sustained, inclusive, and sustainable economic growth. De Giovanni (2023) also highlighted unsustainable challenges such as environmental impacts of the metaverse technologies. Their study also emphasized on the energy consumption due to use of these digital technologies. However, Vlăduțescu & Stănescu (2023) found that the metaverse reduces environmental pollution as it replaces real-world interactions with 3D virtual and exchanges "physical goods" with digital ones. Jauhiainen et al. (2020) also argued that the metaverse contributes to environmental protection and sustainability but gradually increases e-waste and energy consumption. Moreover, a study suggested that the metaverse can influence "urban planning" also and contribute to reporting "sustainability issues" (Dorostkar & Najarsadeghi, 2023). The study found that the metaverse is an innovative method to reduce the harms of greenhouse gas emissions in the cities of the world.

So, it has become a matter of debate whether metaverse provides solutions to unsustainable challenges or hinders sustainable growth. However, still there are evidences of promotion of sustainable consumption due to metaverse. Pellegrino et al. (2023) provided an understanding of economic and environmental impacts of Metaverse on 'sustainable consumption'. Metaverse has the potential to reduce carbon emissions via replacement of physical goods with digital products (Bibri & Allam, 2022). Moreover, these metaverse products like cloud computing and blockchain technology require significant energy consumption or electricity (Stoll et al., 2022). So, there could be several negative impacts of this meta-universe on the natural environment due to increased energy consumption and carbon emissions. To make this metaverse sustainable, potential malefic impacts of the metaverse technologies must be mitigated by adopting clear regulations and sustainable policies at global level (Vlăduțescu & Stănescu 2023).

It has also led to the creation of data-driven smart cities and enhancing the urban sustainability (Allam et al., 2022). It has been explored that metaverse creates an hypothetical "parallel virtual world" that provide different ways of living and working in such data-driven urban cities. Metaverse has also been improving the quality of life for people around the world by enhancing various industries, including agriculture, manufacturing, construction, energy and service industries (Mozumder et al., 2023). Many companies have been approaching this new reality to see better opportunities for business growth. For instance, robotics technology is being widely used by the businesses to perform repetitive jobs that saves time and bring large economies of scale and efficiency in operations (Bochmann et al., 2017). But still there are key challenges of the metaverse for future smart cities as there are still ethical, environmental, human, social and cultural concerns associated with it (Allam et al., 2022). However, if we see through the lens of big data analytics integrated with sustainability management accounting practices, then there are so many benefits for the organizations to generate value added strategies in terms of managing silos of information, cost reduction, competitive advantage (Abdelhalim, 2023).

In addition to better quality of life and better opportunities for business growth, metaverse has also potential for sustainable growth in many ways. Such metaverse technologies can track the environmental impacts of operations in real-time and also analyse and predict the requirement of adequate resources. Rane et al. (2023) also confirmed the vast potential of metaverse in transforming the world through environmental, economic and social sustainability and transforming the approach to achieve SDGs. Al-Emran (2023) developed a T-EESST (Technology and Environmental, Economic and Social Sustainability theory) and found that technology use significantly impacts the triple bottom line.

Boccia & Covino (2023) opined that adoption of metaverse is capable of providing sustainable opportunities but it may result in some adverse environmental impacts such as energy consumption and CO_2 emissions. These digital technologies may generate huge amount of electronic waste as well that requires proper electronic waste management by the organizations. Besides, organizations must see whether metaverse is a responsible form of technology as Industry 5.0 is (De Giovanni, 2022). Because, industry 5.0 is not just a technology but 'human element' is still there to achieve responsible and fulfilling work experience.

Methods and Data Collection

In this book chapter, the sampling population is all the companies listed on stock exchanges in India. But the target population was taken as companies listed on NSE. The final sample taken for the study is out of Nifty 100 companies. However, the final sample is 34 companies distributed across 15 sectors as appeared on the list of Nifty 100. These 34 companies have been continuously adopting GRI (Global reporting Initiative) a sustainability reporting framework at global level. Only those companies have been selected that have been preparing sustainability and integrated reports according to GRI Standards, 2016, consistently for the past five years. It is deliberate method of sampling. So, specific Indian companies have been selected from the Nifty 100 index that have implemented metaverse technologies in their sustainability reporting.

As far as this study is concerned, it is limited to analysis of only those companies' reports that have been publishing their reports according to GRI reporting framework and have been continuously reporting according to these standards for past few years. Further, the sustainability reports of these companies were extracted to conduct the content analysis to identify the extent to which metaverse technologies-related disclosure has been made in these reports. For this purpose, data as sustainability reports and integrated reports with GRI content index was extracted from the official sources of the nifty companies selected for the study. Then these reports had been imported into MAXQDA software as a metaverse project. Then with the help of "text search and autocode" function, a list of words like 'metaverse', 'Internet of Things', IoT, AI, Artificial Intelligence, Machine learning, internet, Big data, 'Virtual reality' and 'augmented reality' were saved into software to autocode the related segments of the reports on sentence basis. Then the overview of those coded segments was retreived to do further analysis. However, this study is limited to only those

Figure 1. Subcode statistics or subcode system analysis generated through MAXQDA software of the 15 major industries listed on NSE

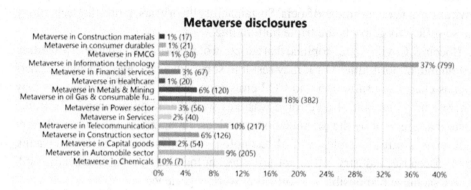

companies' sustainability/integrated reports that have complied with GRI standards for the past five years. Thus, the higher metaverse disclosures in particular sector may be the outcome of higher number of companies in the same sector. Moreover, subjectivity of interpreting especially qualitative content analysis is always there.

1.) **Quantitative Content Analysis & Interpretation:** The quantitative analysis involves the subcode analysis created in the MAXQDA for further analysis. It represents the frequency of the subcodes. The higher the frequency, higher will be the influence of that subcode. Further, the number of documents or sustainability reports in particular sector is also shown here.

Subcode statistics: It is an analysis of the subcodes that are created for conducting the content analysis of the companies reports.

Figure 1 shows a subcode analysis of the subcodes and their coded segments related to metaverse disclosures in each industry, distributed under the top-level code "Metaverse disclosures". Here the coded segments represent those segments of the sustainability reports/integrated reports that highlight metaverse technologies related disclosures. This horizontal bar chart shows that the metaverse technologies related disclosures are higher in Information technology sector, i.e., 37percent of the major industries, followed by Oil& Gas industry (18%) and then by telecommunication sector (10 percent). However, the metaverse technologies disclosures by Chemicals industry of NSE have been found to be negligible.

Table 1 represent the list of codes for which coded segments were generated. The documents represent here the sustainability reports or integrated reports of the companies adopting GRI reporting framework and publishing these consistently too for the last five years. Here, the higher number of documents belong to Information

Table 1. List of "Documents With the Code Names" for which coded segments have been provided

Codes	Frequency	Percentage	Percentage (valid)
Metaverse in Capital goods	6	3.09	4.23
Metaverse in Chemicals	3	1.55	2.11
Metaverse in Construction materials	7	3.61	4.93
Metaverse in consumer durables	6	3.09	4.23
Metaverse in FMCG	8	4.12	5.63
Metaverse in Information technology	31	15.98	21.83
Metaverse in Financial services	11	5.67	7.75
Metaverse in Healthcare	4	2.06	2.82
Metaverse in Metals & Mining	22	11.34	15.49
Metaverse in oil Gas & consumable fuels	23	11.86	16.20
Metaverse in Power sector	5	2.58	3.52
Metaverse in Services	6	3.09	4.23
Metaverse in Telecommunication	4	2.06	2.82
Metaverse in Construction sector	6	3.09	4.23
DOCUMENTS with code(s)	142	73.20	100.00
DOCUMENTS without code(s)	52	26.80	-
ANALYZED DOCUMENTS	194	100.00	-

Technology (IT) sector, that can also be a reason of its greater metaverse related disclosures as compared to other sectors where the documents, i.e., the sustainability reports/integrated reports are less. However, the total analyzed documents were 194.

Table 2 represents the frequency of the coded segments of the extracted reports with the help of MAXQDA software. It shows the higher frequency of coded segments in IT sector (799) related to the metaverse technologies related saved words that became a part of segments query in the reports. However, this frequency can be higher due to the higher number of the documents or higher number of companies in the IT sector. The total amount of coded segments were 1956.

2.) **Qualitative content analysis of the *coded segments* across Indian Industries:**
After completion of the metaverse technologies related words query to look for the related segments, these segments have been analysed to examine the extent to which different Indian industries have been focusing on the metaverse related technologies and what platforms and projects they have reported to

Table 2. Frequency of Segments with code of 15 major Indian industries

Code	Frequency of coded segments	Percentage
Metaverse in Capital goods	54	2.76
Metaverse in Chemicals	7	0.36
Metaverse in Construction materials	17	0.87
Metaverse in consumer durables	21	1.07
Metaverse in FMCG	30	1.53
Metaverse in Information technology	799	40.85
Metaverse in Financial services	67	3.43
Metaverse in Healthcare	20	1.02
Metaverse in Metals & Mining	120	6.13
Metaverse in oil Gas & consumable fuels	382	19.53
Metaverse in Power sector	56	2.86
Metaverse in Services	40	2.04
Metaverse in Telecommunication	217	11.09
Metaverse in Construction sector	126	6.44
TOTAL	1956	100.00

support such technologies. Following is the qualitative content analysis of the extracted or 'retrieved coded segments' for the purpose of this study: *Metaverse in construction sector:*

In 2021 sustainability reports/integrated reports of the companies under construction sector, the information regarding the use of Artificial intelligence (AI), Augmented reality (AR), Virtual Reality (VR), Internet of Things (IoT), and remote inspection in increasing 'construction productivity,' safety and quality has been extensively disclosed. The reports have also mentioned about the automation and IoT technologies in manufacturing and industrial products. There is also an information about "IoT Innovation Hub" by Larsen & Tubro in its Integrated reports. The reports of Larsen & tubro also mentions the training modules or 'safety induction modules' for workmen using Virtual reality (VR). There are more disclosures regarding the use of IoT data to monitor the equipment effectiveness. One more coded segment in the integrated report of Larsen and Tubro are use of Artificial intelligence and Machine learning(ML) based video analytics in training the workmen in utilization of machines with proper safety, in material handling and tracking. The reports also mention about Narrowband Internet of Things (NBIoT) as new communication technology by Larsen and Tubro in construction sector.

Metaverse in Telecommunication Sector

As figure 1 shows the code statistics, where the metaverse related disclosures are higher in telecommunication sector as it has highest number of coded segments (799) related to metaverse as compared to other sectors. In the reports of telecommunication companies, data analytics and artificial intelligence has been mentioned as the tools for empowering digital workforce. The companies of this sector have been extensively focussing on providing best connectivity solutions, cloud services or cloud communications, cybersecurity and IoT. Bharti Airtel in its 2022 integrated report, mentions that it eliminated use of diesel (around 3 million litres) in their tower operations by using AI and ML technologies. It has also launched a 5G platform 'Airtel IoT' for an immediate 5G distribution across all spheres. For this purpose, Airtel's integrated report also discloses about its 'Innovation Lab' that entirely focuses on IoT, digital engineering, AI and ML technologies. Moreover, there are mentions that it has launched a AI based technology 'Vahan' for the job seekers and employers. Also, airtel's another AI based 'Decision tree' tool has also been reported as a tool to help the 'customers service centers' to reply the customers' queries faster.

Metaverse in Services Sector

In the services sector, APSEZ ltd. has been disclosing IoT, AI and automation techniques to enhance operations control and management. With the help of IoT sensors and business analytical tools, it has been capable of real-time monitoring of assets utilisation, locations, health and energy consumption. The APSEZ's integrated report 2022 has disclosed it strategy to use 'big data' to manage the arrivals and departures to reduce congestion in its operations. However, with the use metaverse and IoT, the company has increased its competitiveness. APSEZ ltd has reported its IoT technology based 'smart port' initiative to offer value to its customers. Adani group has also launched a 'Adani skill development centre (ASDC)' that provides training courses like 3D printing, simulation-based crane operators and Augmented reality (AR) based simulator for welding machines.

Metaverse in Power Sector

In power corporations, NTPC ltd. has reported its ART (Augmented/ Virtual reality-based Training) module to manage its turbine operations. NTPC's integrated report 2021 mentions its deployment of various digital, AI/ML tools for its power plant operation to increase efficiency, safety, cost optimization, and reducing any interruptions in the operations. NTPC ltd. has also disclosed its innovative practices like development of VR training modules, online Employee Assistance programs (EAP) to provide 'simulator training'.

Metaverse in Oil Gas and Consumable Fuels Sector

In oil gas sector, Reliance Industries Limited (RIL) disclosed AI/ML-based 'cyberdefense platforms' to monitor the sensor integrity and sensor threat detection. RIL has further reported its industrial IoT technologies for 'Algae to oil' research and development initiative. It has adopted ML technologies for improving 'gasifier reliability' and efficiency. Reliance has been extensively using AI/ML and IoT for seamless communication and ensuring cyber security with help of AI based tools like 'Authbase' to mitigate hack and bot attacks in real-time. Reliance has also reported its 'Mygov Corona helpdesk' (by Jio Haptik) that served as a ChatBot solution during COVID-19 pandemic. It has further disclosed its Integrated IoT and ML solutions in its oil fields and recycled petcoke gasification to utilize the synthesis gas and biomass gasification to generate synthesis gas on a renewable basis. RIL has also reported its 'Mission Kurukshetra' which is an AI-based digital platform where employees collaborate and submit innovative ideas to grow the company. Jio has also been consistently assisting RIL in opting for AI based solutions such as "Digital Oil Field" to generate the big data for RIL's oil and gas operations. In the RIL's integrated report 2021, there are mentions about its bio-innovations in combination with photosynthesis research with the help of AI and ML tools to increase agricultural productivity. The company has also reported that it has been implementing 'Digital Twins' and AI and ML analytical tools to enhance energy efficiency and reduce the carbon footprint.

Also, Indian Oil corporation limited in oil & Gas sector, has just reported that it has been using AI/ML tools, IoT to increase its operational efficiency.

GAIL Limited has reported its IoT application 'Analyser Data' that is directly linked with pollution Control board. Also, the company has implemented an *Industrial-IoT* (IIoT) "online plant emission parameter" and "effluent discharge parameter" that has been linked to Central Pollution Control Board for cloud monitoring. Further the GAIL 's reports also highlights the innovative augmented reality based training module to enhance skills of workforce with the help of simulators. GAIL's reports also disclose the adoption of 'digital transformation' technologies in processing big data sets to streamline the operations.

Drones have been extensively used in surveilling Bharat petroleum corporation limited (BPCL)'s refineries. Robotic cleansing of the confined places, Industrial IoT (IIoT) based wireless Asset monitoring systems have been adopted to enhance safety at workplaces across all business units. In the sustainability report 2022, BPCL Limited discloses use of Virtual reality and augmented reality-based training modules to train workmen regarding functioning of critical equipment, processes and SOPs. BPCL also reports its AI based chatbot 'Urja' to communicate with its customers.

ONGC limited and Coal India Limited have negligible disclosures related to metaverse.

Metaverse in Metals & Mining sector: In metals and mining sector, Tata Steel limited, Steel Authority of India limited, JSW steel limited, Hindalco Industries limited have reported metaverse related disclosures in their sustainability/integrated reports. However, Vedanta Limited and Steel Authority of India Limited (SAIL) have negligible disclosures related to adoption of metaverse. Tata Steel limited has provided several disclosures related to adoption of AI/ML-based technologies and cloud monitoring. It has an 'innovation club' that focusses entirely on the advancement of AI tools, IoT, waste management and alternative fuels. It has also disclosed the AI-based tool 'Digital Twins' for its 'Sinter plants' to reduce CO_2 emissions. The company has also launched an AI-based talent marketplace for employees so that they can perform on cross-functional projects according to their preferences. Furthermore, Tata Steel's sustainability/integrated reports acknowledge the benefits of using data analytics and AI/ML technologies in steel manufacturing. Also, it has identified its stakeholders' stories where Artificial intelligence drives tangible benefits in optimizing operations, logistics management and recruitment. Like other companies as discussed in the above sectors, Tata Steel ltd has also extensively invested in cloud monitoring and cybersecurity capabilities for cyber threat protection and data leak prevention. Tata Steel has also mentioned in its reports about the use of camera feeds as AI-based 'face mask detection systems' to identify people at different places.

JSW ltd has also made several disclosures about its metaverse related projects including deployment of IOT, optimization tools, data modelling and data analytics to solve business issues. In this era of Industry 4.0, the company has deployed various new technologies such as ML, IoT and AI and AR/VR-based simulations in operations to enhance productivity, minimise human intervention and ensuring safety in the operations. JSW has also reported its big data and data analytics-driven real-time models to reduce power consumption and losses (JSW Steel IR 2019, p.19). The company has also used an AI-enabled safety platforms, IoT sensors, big data for efficient business operations. The company has also reported its application of Machine Learning algorithms such as 'tumbler index' for prediction of 'Pellet' and 'Sinter' properties.

Hindalco Industries Limited (HIL) is another major player in Metals and Mining sector. HIL has also adopted Industrial IoT in its manufacturing processes, logistics management. The company has also been adopting AI techniques in predicting the 'asset reliability' of the equipment. HIL has developed a capability development program, 'Digital Shiksha' (DISHA) to make the workforce skilful on IoT, Business

Analytics and AR (HINDALCO INDUSTRIES LTD. > hindalco-integrated-annual-report-2021-22: p. 51). It has also reported its Machine Learning software "Mtell" for monitoring critical condition of any equipment.

Metaverse in Information Technology (IT) Sector

Wipro limited has also made several disclosures about metaverse. The company has IoT enabled platforms to track any equipment on a real-time basis. Wipro ltd. has been making continuous strategic investments through its "Horizon program" on Big data, AI, data engineering, cybersecurity, and Software Defined Everything (SDE) (WIPRO LTD. > sustainability-report-fy-2017-18, p.99).

Tech Mahindra ltd has also made disclosures on its automation platform (GAiA) to provide environment and business solutions, cloud services(mPAC), 'BlueMarble' as a digital telecom platform. The company has also reported the importance of the AI and ML technologies and IoT in ensuring cybersecurity and big data management. It has also reported its solution using Computer Vision technique for cognitive detection' for a medical technology company. The company has also reported its cost optimization with the help of automation and AI technologies during pandemic. Tech Mahindra also acknowledges that "digitisation and AI helps in optimum use of resources and reduce the overall impact of human activities on the environment." (TECH MAHINDRA LTD. > Integrated-report-2021, p.97). the company has been providing continuous water management solutions such as "pipeline monitoring" by using advanced machine learning technologies to detect probability of any fault automatically. Tech Mahindra has reported a comprehensive solution (AI and ML based) "Mhealthy" to enable 'data-driven digital diagnostics' to generate real-time reports (TECH MAHINDRA LTD. > annual-report-2021: 123 - 123). One segment of integrated report Tech Mahindra limited is about integrating technologies like AI, BI, IoT, Block chain with Sustainability towards developing 'Green Solutions' (TECH MAHINDRA LTD. > annual-report-2021, p.166). there are disclosures about its 'TechMNxt' IoT platform solution for solar and wind companies to meet the changing current and future needs of industry. Mindtree has also been reporting extensive metaverse disclosures including IoT solutions, AI/ML technologies, AR and VR, automation systems in its operations. Its IoT solution 'Gladius' is also used for integration of management systems into IT systems.

Tata consultancy services has reported their AI and Automation based 'Machine First delivery Model' that is making technology loads 'self-healing' and IT(information technology) operations & supply chain more robust. The company has been using AI and ML tools to convert the natural language data into structured data. TCS reports its 'TCS Clever Energy', an 'energy and emission management system' that uses IoT based digital twin to help other organizations in managing their energy consumption and reduce carbon emissions. The company has also been adopting various AI-driven cybersecurity and cyber threat prevention and management services. Their disclosures show their commitment to leverage newer advanced technologies to improve efficiency, productivity, security and sustainability across various industries.

Larsen & Tubro infotech ltd has also been disclosing its commitment towards preparedness for adopting this metaverse ecosystem. The company has also invested into "Mosaic Automation platform" covering robotic process automation, ML, Software defined everything (SDE) and design thinking. It has its IIoT lab under AGRIM project where an AI robot 'AVITRA' has been created by the students. The company has also reported its AI-based 'Pharmacovigilance application' developed to automate the narrative of any adverse event.

Metaverse in Healthcare sector: In this sector, Dr Reddy Laboratories Ltd has been disclosing a wide range of digital initiatives and future-oriented digital technologies. Their disclosures include the use of digitalization, analytics, AI/ML, AR and VR and the IIoT across different aspects of their operations. The company has adopted these technologies for optimum utilization of energy, real-time monitoring and tracking, safety measures and for improving the healthcare system. The company has also implemented AI-based tools for faster drug research and development and applying Industry 4.0 technologies to support patients and doctors for better disease management. It has also reported its VR-based events such as 'People development week' which shows its commitment to embrace digital experiences.

Metaverse in Financial Services Sector

In the financial services sector, only two banks have been consistently adopting GRI reporting framework. SBI and Axis Bank have made several disclosures related to use of technologies and innovation. SBI has emphasized on use of business analytics, AI and ML technologies to improve their efficiency and reduce risk and ensure cyber security. The bank has invested in exponential technologies such as cloud monitoring, blockchain technology and AI to enhance its digital banking services. The disclosures also include mentions about SBI's AI-powered ChatBots and Voice assistants to provide better customer service and increase operational efficiency. On the other hand, Axis bank has similarly focused on technology and innovation in AI and ML. it has reported its Robotic Process Automation (RBA) that reduces human intervention and detects and prevents fraud automatically. The reports also mention their awards and accolades received by these banks for their technological advancements.

Metaverse in FMCG sector: In the Fast-moving consumer goods (FMCG) sector, Marico and ITC ltd. have both made significant investments in the metaverse related technologies. Both the companies have been using the metaverse technologies to improve their operational efficiency and customer services. Marico ltd has designed a new AI-based recruitment platform to identify and screen deserving candidates and to also schedule interviews with them to make final selection. The company has reported its ChatBot 'Coach Eddy' as a digital learning tool for employees that provides personalized learning and feedback. ITC ltd is also using the metaverse technologies to improve productivity and its operational efficiency. ITC ltd has also been using VR based training modules to train employees in handling complex machinery.

Metaverse in Consumer Durables Sector

Havells India limited, a home appliance company and Asian paints ltd, a paint manufacturing, both have significantly disclosed its use of metaverse technologies, in the sustainability reports. Havells discloses that it has partnered with 'Treedis' to introduce an innovative solution for their retail tours, and leverage the latest digital twin technology. Such partnership has provided a competitive advantage for Havells India for providing its products beyond physical stores. Furthermore, it has also integrated VR and IoT in its operations for safety training, people management and product development. However, Asian Paints ltd has made negligible metaverse related disclosures. It has just shown insights of VR based safety training.

Metaverse in Construction Materials sector: In this sector, the sustainability reports of Ultratech Cement ltd and Shree Cement ltd mention the use of AI and ML in various aspects of their operations, such as digital transformation initiatives, use of AI in the manufacturing value chain and logistics management and for real-time monitoring. The company has been using robotics technology to detect hazards during operations and improve efficiency. Ultratech's reports also mention their focus on energy efficiency initiatives such as 'improved heat recovery', using alternative fuel and remote monitoring. It has also disclosed its AI technology uses for 'process modelling and optimization' for quality in operations. Both the companies have shown their commitment to contribute to the circular economy with digital transformation.

Metaverse in Chemicals sector: In the chemicals industry, UPL ltd. has made predominant disclosures related to digitalization with metaverse. The company has reported its collaboration with AI-driven 'Seed-X' innovative firm for better seed quality. The company has also collaborated with IoT based sensor 'Telesense' that served as an AI based sensor technology for the company's operations, supply chain and logistics and 'food waste reduction' during storage and transport.

Metaverse in Capital Goods sector: In capital goods industry, Siemens ltd has also made IoT, AI and 'digital twins'-related disclosures. The company finds IoT as capable of providing solutions during crisis as per its sustainability reports. Siemens disclosed its key activities such as cyber-security, digitalization based on its IoT platforms such as 'Mindsphere' and AI, 'decarbonization' and 'climate change action', R&D and automated mobility. According to Siemens sustainability reports, IoT is driving technology behind the digitalization of its industry. With the help of ML and AI technologies, the company has been capable of assisting the plant operators by minimising their stress and increasing their operational efficiency. There are mentions of risk management with the use of analytics in the sustainability reports. The company has also disclosed the potential negative impacts resulting from the increased deployment of artificial intelligence as 'modern slavery', health, safety and labour practices in projects and supply chain, as well as the challenge of responsible decision-making (siemens-sustainability-information-2019, p. 42).

Metaverse in Automobile Sector: The companies in automobile sector, Hero Motocorp ltd., Maruti Sazuki ltd and Bosch ltd., have mentioned their focus on cybersecurity and digitalization. The companies have acknowledged the positive outcomes of use of metaverse technology in form of cyberattack monitoring with the help of AI and sensors. Bosch is heavily investing in metaverse technologies for innovation and consistent growth. It has been developing AI solutions for different applications such as smart home, connected cars and industrial manufacturing. Bosch has developed a code of ethics for AI technology use in responsible manner. The company has reported its improvement in efficiency of manufacturing plants due to AI-assisted automation of tasks. They have also developed automated drivers systems in cars that warn and prevent accidents. Similarly, Hero Motocorp ltd has been focusing on various digital initiatives enhancing cybersecurity, IoT-based projects for connected vehicles, VR-based safety training for unsafe scenarios at workplace through simulation. Maruti Sazuki ltd has also disclosed its use of AI technologies focusing on 'computer vision', AI, vehicle safety, AR and electric vehicles. Maruti Sazuki has adopted AI-based forecasting methods also so that maximum customers have immediate access to Maruti Suzuki Genuine Parts (MGP). The company has also been using simulated VR techniques to incorporate suitable adjustments during the vehicles' model design and development stage. The company has also reported the use of AI in identifying and preventing the entry of suspected people at their premises.

IMPLICATIONS AND CONCLUSION

This study attempts to provide significance to managers, academicians/researchers and practitioners. At managerial level, this study can help managers in aligning their operations with the SDGs. Some of the companies in different industries such as

ONGC limited and Coal India Limited, Asian Paints ltd, Vedanta Limited and Steel Authority of India Limited (SAIL) have made negligible 'metaverse technologies' disclosures. Either they have not been contributed to such technologies or they have not reported them. But these reports are a great matter of discussion for the investors and other stakeholders. So, these companies must contribute and then report about their investments in such technologies of Industry 4.0, however we are approaching Industry 5.0 sooner.

Many companies that became part of this study have made extensive disclosures about their huge investments in IoT, AI and VR based platforms and projects. Their sustainability reports/ integrated reports have immense disclosures on metaverse technologies. They have also reported their VR training modules, AI tools, ML algorithms, ChatBot solutions and Industrial IoT sensors. The content of the reports also highlights how the VR-related training modules and Robotics based automated systems have streamlined their operations.

The companies have given names to their digital projects that are focused on the development of metaverse technologies into their operations. Larsen & tubro (L&T) group of the construction sector have made huge investment in IoT technologies such as L&T's IoT Innovation Hub. It has also made contributions in VR based training modules and video analytics to train workmen for ensuring safety. Almost all the sectors have made several disclosures of their contribution to metaverse technologies through different platforms. For instance, a major company of telecom sector, Bharti Airtel's AI-based 'Vahan' is used for job seekers and employers.

Some companies have developed skill development programs for their workmen and employees to become well proficient in using IoT and analytics such as Hindalco Industries ltd has a capability development program 'Disha' for "digital shiksha". Such programs can be initiated by other companies also for better streamlining of operations and increasing productivity.

IoT based technologies have been widely discussed approximately by all the companies across different industries. However, IoT technologies when merged with the metaverse, various industries can be transformed. IoT also enables "virtual spaces" to effortlessly interact and access the physical world. So, these two technologies complement each other where IoT catalyzes the metaverse industry by providing easy-to-use virtual experiences in different areas such as shopping, gaming, automobiles, real estate etc. Thus, IoT acts as a key pillar of the metaverse infrastructure, and the integration of the two technologies opens up new opportunities for growth and development. APSEZ's 'smart port' initiative is offering greater value to customers. UPL's 'telesense' is a IoT based sensor used for monitoring of food wastage during storage and transport and thus helps in food wastage reduction. GAIL's 'online plant emissions parameter' and 'effluent discharge parameter' is also major IoT based 'Analyser Data' application that directly interacts with pollution control Board. So, it is a real-time display of the emissions by the company. Such technologies can be used by all other companies whose operations can generate higher emissions. It will act as a control to reduce the CO2 emissions. Different industries are investing in the metaverse technologies according to their requirement. Some of the companies in the study are also assisting other companies also in streamlining their operations, such as Tech Mahindra's 'TechMNxt' an IoT-based platform to provide real-time solutions to wind and solar companies to meet their changing current and future needs of the industry. Thus, a responsible decision making should be encouraged by the companies when they invest in such technologies for the sustainable future and steps towards 'sustainable metaverse' should be taken.

Moreover, the negative impacts of these technologies cannot be ignored. The existing literature provides several negative impacts of this meta-universe on the natural environment due to increased energy consumption and carbon emissions. However, in this study, only Seimens ltd., a capital goods company, has disclosed the potential negative impacts resulting from the increased deployment of artificial intelligence technologies such as 'modern slavery', health, safety and labour practices in projects and supply chain. These negative impacts can seriously impact the responsible decision making by companies. There needs to be more discussion on deployment of use of technologies in a responsible manner. Future academicians can research more on the impacts of metaverse on the triple bottom line.

REFERENCES

Allam, Z., Sharifi, A., Bibri, S. E., Jones, D. S., & Krogstie, J. (2022). The metaverse as a virtual form of smart cities: Opportunities and challenges for environmental, economic, and social sustainability in urban futures. *Smart Cities*, 5(3), 771–801. doi:10.3390/smartcities5030040

Allam, Z., Sharifi, A., Bibri, S. E., Jones, D. S., & Krogstie, J. (2022). The metaverse as a virtual form of smart cities: Opportunities and challenges for environmental, economic, and social sustainability in urban futures. *Smart Cities*, 5(3), 771–801. doi:10.3390/smartcities5030040

Bibri, S. E., & Allam, Z. (2022). The Metaverse as a virtual form of data-driven smart cities: The ethics of the hyper-connectivity, datafication, algorithmization, and platformization of urban society. *Computational Urban Science*, 2(1), 22. doi:10.1007/s43762-022-00050-1 PMID:35915731

Boccia, F., & Covino, D. (2023). Knowledge and Food Sustainability: The Metaverse as a New Economic-Environmental Paradigm. *Journal of the Knowledge Economy*, 1–14. doi:10.1007/s13132-023-01626-w

Bochmann, L., Bänziger, T., Kunz, A., & Wegener, K. (2017). Human-robot collaboration in decentralized manufacturing systems: An approach for simulation-based evaluation of future intelligent production. *Procedia CIRP*, *62*, 624–629. doi:10.1016/j.procir.2016.06.021

Choi, H. Y. (2022). Working in the metaverse: Does telework in a metaverse office have the potential to reduce population pressure in megacities? Evidence from young adults in Seoul, South Korea. *Sustainability (Basel)*, *14*(6), 3629. doi:10.3390/su14063629

De Giovanni, P. (2023). Sustainability of the Metaverse: A transition to Industry 5.0. *Sustainability (Basel)*, *15*(7), 6079. doi:10.3390/su15076079

Dorostkar, E., & Najarsadeghi, M. (2023). Sustainability and urban climate: How Metaverse can influence urban planning? *Environment and Planning. B, Urban Analytics and City Science*, *50*(7), 23998083231181596. doi:10.1177/23998083231181596

Jauhiainen, J. S., Krohn, C., & Junnila, J. (2022). Metaverse and Sustainability: Systematic Review of Scientific Publications until 2022 and Beyond. *Sustainability (Basel)*, *15*(1), 346. doi:10.3390/su15010346

Jauhiainen, J. S., Krohn, C., & Junnila, J. (2022). Metaverse and Sustainability: Systematic Review of Scientific Publications until 2022 and Beyond. *Sustainability (Basel)*, *15*(1), 346. doi:10.3390/su15010346

Lee, H., & Hwang, Y. (2022). Technology-enhanced education through VR-making and metaverse-linking to foster teacher readiness and sustainable learning. *Sustainability (Basel)*, *14*(8), 4786. doi:10.3390/su14084786

Mozumder, M. A. I., Armand, T. P. T., Imtiyaj Uddin, S. M., Athar, A., Sumon, R. I., Hussain, A., & Kim, H. C. (2023). Metaverse for Digital Anti-Aging Healthcare: An Overview of Potential Use Cases Based on Artificial Intelligence, Blockchain, IoT Technologies, Its Challenges, and Future Directions. *Applied Sciences (Basel, Switzerland)*, *13*(8), 5127. doi:10.3390/app13085127

Pamucar, D., Deveci, M., Gokasar, I., Tavana, M., & Köppen, M. (2022). A metaverse assessment model for sustainable transportation using ordinal priority approach and Aczel-Alsina norms. *Technological Forecasting and Social Change*, *182*, 121778. doi:10.1016/j.techfore.2022.121778

Park, S., & Kim, S. (2022). Identifying world types to deliver gameful experiences for sustainable learning in the metaverse. *Sustainability (Basel)*, *14*(3), 1361. doi:10.3390/su14031361

Pellegrino, A., Stasi, A., & Wang, R. (2023). Exploring the intersection of sustainable consumption and the Metaverse: A review of current literature and future research directions. *Heliyon*, *9*(9), e19190. doi:10.1016/j.heliyon.2023. e19190 PMID:37681133

Stoll, C., Gallersdörfer, U., & Klaaßen, L. (2022). Climate impacts of the metaverse. *Joule*, *6*(12), 2668–2673. doi:10.1016/j.joule.2022.10.013

United Nations. (2021). *Interagency report for second Global Sustainable Transport Conference*. UN. https://sdgs.un.org/publications/interagency-report-second-global-sustainable-transport-conference

Vlăduțescu, Ș., & Stănescu, G. C. (2023). Environmental Sustainability of Metaverse: Perspectives from Romanian Developers. *Sustainability (Basel)*, *15*(15), 11704. doi:10.3390/su151511704

Wang, Y., Su, Z., Zhang, N., Xing, R., Liu, D., Luan, T. H., & Shen, X. (2022). A survey on metaverse: Fundamentals, security, and privacy. *IEEE Communications Surveys and Tutorials*.

Chapter 10
Metaverse Banking 2.0:
Future Trends and Challenges in Metaverse Banking Strategies

Saurabh Bhattacharya

iD https://orcid.org/0000-0002-2729-1835
Chitkara Business School, Chitkara University, Punjab, India

Babita Singla

iD https://orcid.org/0000-0002-8861-6859
Chitkara Business School, Chitkara University, Punjab, India

ABSTRACT

The metaverse combines with reality and creates an alternate universe. The availability of technological advances enables us to perform new tasks or efficiently complete ordinary duties. The "metaverse," or extended reality, opens up fresh opportunities for fascinating telepathy as well as has the potential to simplify routine tasks. As much as these technologies assist us in this work, education, healthcare, consumption, and pleasure, they also pose several challenges. The chapter tackles the questions of why and when customers will accept an entirely integrated area for a variety of operations, such as buying things and making purchases of Banking services. Examining the potential of Metaverse banking, this study looks into interesting avenues for future development that will influence how financial environments change in virtual spaces. The research anticipates a financial transformation with a focus on Blockchain, virtual assets, smart contracts, decentralized finance (DeFi), and immersive technology.

DOI: 10.4018/979-8-3693-5868-9.ch010

INTRODUCTION

Blockchain, artificial intelligence, and virtual reality are some of the cutting-edge technologies that have been used to construct the intricate virtual environment known as the banking and insurance metaverse. By giving people and companies realistic and engaging experiences, it seeks to streamline relationships and business processes within the banking and finance industries (Bandara et al., 2022). Through VR spectacles, consumers can communicate with simulated possessions and other individuals in worlds of virtual reality through personas. (*(1) Exploring the Potential Impact and Concerns of Metaverse in the Financial Services Industry | LinkedIn*, n.d.)While it's no longer the information technology community's term of choice, the banking sector is starting to take notice of the metaverse (Taylor et al., 2020). Metaverse apps present institutions with distinct chances to cultivate connections with a rising, technologically native clientele that has long supported finance technology, given that the people who use them and their viewership are youthful, proficient in technology, and just starting in adulthood (Cho et al., 2023). To hire people in the future, banks must have access to this potential resource. An all-encompassing, blockchain-powered virtual environment that provides novel social and cultural encounters is known as the dimension of the metaverse. (Hasanova et al., 2019) It opens up a whole new world of communication possibilities by encapsulating decentralized and comprehensive interactions that frequently incorporate virtual reality (VR) and augmented reality (AR). Customers may utilize just one, transferable identification across metaverse applications, and the realm of the metaverse is not defined by a particular business or program. Through the use of illusions and characters, consumers can engage in genuine interactions with both simulated and real-world environments through the realm of metaphysics, which may expand what is real through both virtual and augmented reality. The parallel universe works in tandem with reality to do tasks that would be difficult to complete in the world of reality, like exploring remote areas, offering mental health services, and training members for warfare. Because the metaverse is home to a plethora of complicated and advanced capabilities, such as explicit material, 3D layout, and exciting sensory experiences, visitors could view unwanted and privacy-invading materials as more bothersome and will probably suffer more adverse effects (Kumar et al., 2024). Privacy breaches in the realm of possibility therefore probably carry a greater risk of dire consequences, a phenomenon known as an amplified technical impact. Although the metaverse can drastically change how people interact, socialize, and spend time, it also allows room for the darker sides of human beings, just like any technological advancement that opens up opportunities(Dwivedi et al., 2022). Metaverse Banking 2.0 signifies the next iteration of digital banking, where traditional financial services seamlessly integrate into virtual environments. It goes

Figure 1. Metaverse System

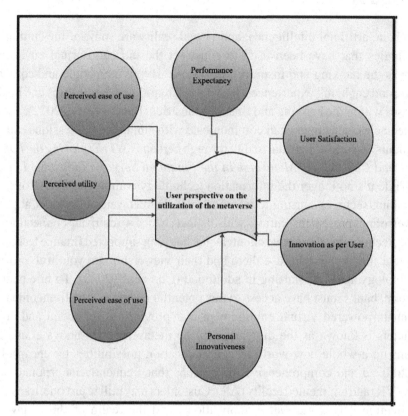

beyond simple online transactions, offering users immersive, 3D experiences where they can interact with financial services and products in real time. This evolution is fueled by advancements in virtual reality (VR), augmented reality (AR), blockchain technology, and artificial intelligence (AI). **Figure 1** below shows the covered Metaverse systems by various authors earlier.

A network of linked, immersive virtual worlds where people may engage with generated by computer settings is called the metaverse (Yaqoob et al., 2023). A metaverse is a fully immersive three-dimensional virtual environment where users can do everyday activities using avatars. This opens up new possibilities for worldwide communication, commerce, and enjoyment. To create a completely immersive, hyper spatiotemporal, and self-sustaining virtual shared place where people may interact, work, and play, metaverse, a newly formed model of the forthcoming Internet, is being built. Thanks to recent developments in cutting-edge fields like blockchain, artificial intelligence, and extended reality, the metaverse is moving from a work of imagination into the near future. Massive privacy violations and safety flaws in the metaverse, nevertheless may prevent its widespread use (Wang et al., 2023).

Background of the Study

The investigation of how virtual reality and blockchain technology may revolutionize the financial sector is known as the "metaverse" research in banking. Users may communicate with digital assets and one other in a virtual world through the decentralized, immersive metaverse. It may make it possible for banking procedures like identity verification and international payments to be more safe, open, and effective. Furthermore, the metaverse may open up new markets for financial services and goods like decentralized finance apps and virtual currencies. Nevertheless, the banking metaverse is still in its infancy, and several obstacles must be removed before it can be widely adopted. Because blockchain technology and virtual reality have the potential to completely change the financial sector, understanding the metaverse is essential. The decentralized, immersive environment provided by the metaverse can improve transaction security, identity verification, and overall efficiency in banking operations. New financial services and products, such as virtual currencies and decentralized finance apps, are also made possible by this. But as this idea is still in its infancy, several important issues need to be resolved before the metaverse is widely used in the banking industry (Mishra, n.d.) (*Banking in the Metaverse: Evolving Opportunity - Spiceworks*, n.d.) (*3D Avatars and Blockchain Integration: The Future of Virtual Identity in Metaverse - Digital Transformation News | The Financial Express*, n.d.)

Modern Issues of Metaverse 2.0

A wide range of topics are covered by current Metaverse 2.0 issues, including the effect of the web3 metaverse on the digital economy, moral design guidelines for AR/VR and Metaverse centers, the potential of mixed reality to empower frontline employees, and the difficulties banks face in meeting customer expectations because of technological constraints.

The impact of the metaverse on customer-facing operations, the difficulty of meeting customer expectations due to technological constraints, and the shift in focus away from the metaverse and towards other technologies are some of the challenges banks are facing as they attempt to adapt to the metaverse (*De-Risking Banking in the Metaverse*, n.d.) ("Metaverse in Banking - Thematic Intelligence," n.d.) (Srivastava, 2023) (Glenk, 2023)

Key Metaverse Statistics

Market Size for Metaverse: The market is anticipated to develop at a 33.6% compound annual growth rate (CAGR) to reach $82.27 billion in 2023 (*In the next 25 Years Ground-Breaking Tech Will Change India's Banking Industry; Here's How*, 2023). Following are some of the key statistics according to (Mileva, 2022)

1) Key players like Meta, Nvidia, Roblox, and others control the majority of the worldwide metaverse market, and growth in the gaming sector is anticipated in the upcoming years.
2) According to estimates, the metaverse has enormous business potential, with growth in AR, VR, and MR technologies expected to reach billions of dollars.
3) The number of AR and VR headset shipments predicted for 2023, 2024, and 2025 is 23.22 million, 32.76 million, and an anticipated 43.87 million. It is anticipated that the market will bring in $31.12 billion in 2023 and $52.05 billion by 2027.
4) By 2030, it's expected that the AR and VR gear market for the metaverse will have grown to $3.19 billion, with a compound annual growth rate of 17.71%.
5) By 2023, the worldwide market value of the metaverse is expected to be $82 billion, and by 2030, it will have grown exponentially to $936.6 billion.
6) By 2024, there will be 1.7 billion mobile augmented reality users globally, up from 200 million in 2015.
7) Sixty-seven percent of customers in the 16–44 age range are familiar with AR.

RESEARCH METHODOLOGY

The chapter is the outcome of a rigorous study of carefully selected 30 high-quality journals. A systematic literature review was carried out on the selected articles(Jahan et al., n.d.). The chapter will cover the current trends, challenges, and future of Metaverse, especially in the banking sector. The following Database was used to shortlist the articles for the study.

RQ1: What is the status of banking-related metaverse studies today?

RQ2: What are the current trends and challenges of Metaverse in the Banking industry?

Following are the inclusion and exclusion criteria that were followed for this article.

Table 1. Database Used for the Search

Source	Website
Scopus	https://www.scopus.com
IEEE Xplore	https://ieeexplore.ieee.org
Google Scholar	https://scholar.google.com
Springer	https://www.springer.com
ScienceDirect	https://www.sciencedirect.com

LITERATURE REVIEW

Trends Shaping Metaverse Banking

Even while there is a plethora of options, it may occasionally be challenging to envision the ways it can affect the banking sector. Let's explore different ways that the banking sector may be affected by the metaverse. Banking and finance businesses may gain insight into the requirements and tastes of their consumers and deliver a better user experience by utilizing analytics and data analysis (*Metaverse in Banking*, n.d.). Chatbots, virtual assistants, and artificial intelligence can be implemented in the metaverse to help users with their budgetary requirements (Singla et al., 2023).

Figure 2. Selection process of the final study

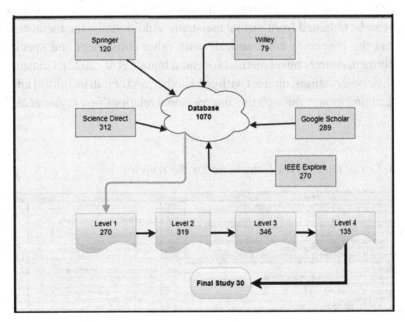

Table 2. Inclusion and exclusion criteria

No	Code	Description	To exclude if	To include if
1	It is Duplicate	There was a duplicate post discovered.	Google Scholar, IEEE Explore, Springer, Science Direct, Willey, and Scopus may use different distinguishing narratives.	
2	It is non-English	Non-English article	Abstract if non-English	
3	It yields no outcomes.	If there are no outcomes in the article	If the article fails to provide worthwhile outcomes and just offers opinions	
4	The study is not on VR, AR, Banking	The text with no recommendations for VR, AR, Metaverse, or Blockchain research.	The manuscript without VR or AR Metaverse or Banking or Finance or Blockchain or Behaviour research was omitted.	
5	Determinants and outcomes have not been found.	Metaverse and Finance or banking are mentioned in this publication.	Restricted articles with no behavioral or perspective, desire, influence, or adaptation to VR or AR.	Incorporated is a study article that includes several things like: -Banking, Blockchain -VR, AR, Preferences, -Intention, Banking, -Spending, Defi -Influence
6	The intended audience	The paper focuses on a particular demographic.	Articles are excluded if any of the listed conditions are met: Users under the legal age of 18 and individuals who are unaware of the use of Metaverse. Exclude Grey Studies	Incorporate these categories of writing: -Students -Elderly - Any geographical location

Customized guidance on investing techniques, budgeting, and other goods and services can be obtained from virtual assistants. Additionally, the metaverse might offer users the chance to communicate with other consumers and specialists in finance through entirely novel methods (Renduchintala et al., 2022). Consumers can discuss their observations, interact with one another, and obtain insightful knowledge about managing money through this interpersonal relationship (Taylor et al., 2020).

Figure 3. List of top articles considered for the review

Title	Year	Journal	Citations	ABDC Status	SJR Status
Marketing in the Metaverse: Conceptual understanding, framework, and research agenda	2023	Journal of Business Research	217	A	Q1
Metaverse Banking Service: Are We Ready to Adopt? A Deep Learning-Based Dual-Stage SEM-ANN Analysis	2023	Human Behavior and Emerging Technologies	12		Q1
Shaping the metaverse into reality: a holistic multidisciplinary understanding of opportunities, challenges, and avenues for future investigation	2023	Journal of Computer Information Systems	127	A	Q1
A Review of Blockchain Architecture and Consensus Protocols: Use Cases, Challenges, and Solutions	2019	Symmetry	249		Q2
Towards an understanding of metaverse banking: a conceptual paper	2023	Journal of Financial Reporting and Accounting	16	C	Q2
Blockchain Revolution: How the Technology/Behind Bitcoin is Changing Money, Business, andthe World	2018	Quality Management Journal	117	B	Q2
Metaverse beyond the hype: Multidisciplinary perspectives on emerging challenges, opportunities, and agenda for research, practice and policy	2022	International Journal of Information Management	935	A*	Q1
Blockchain, adoption, and financial inclusion in India: Research opportunities	2020	International Journal of Information Management	348	A*	Q1
A Comprehensive Study on Metaverse and Its Impacts on Humans	2022	Advances in Human-Computer Interaction	39		Q3
A systematic literature review of blockchain cyber security	2020	Digital Communications and Networks	580		Q1
Banking with blockchain-ed big data	2018	Journal of Management Analytics	279	C	Q1
Metaverse Shape of Your Life for Future: Abibliometric snapshot	2021	Journal of Metaverse	277		

This study sheds light on the intricate future fabric of metaverse banking as it reshapes the financial industry. Financial institutions must embrace developing trends, overcome obstacles, and navigate new routes to prosper in the fast-paced world of virtual finance. This section will include the Literature Review. Researchers can obtain a logical and ordered view regarding what has been written in a certain body of literature throughout the measured period by using the systematic literature review (SLR) approach. This method is widely used by researchers in all fields to fill in the gaps in the literature and produce a representation of a certain issue. Considering a variety of investigated themes or sections will surface throughout an SLR study, researchers can identify the niche that needs to be addressed. Additionally, researchers can advance information and provide light on scholarly disagreements (Milian et al., 2019). A decision to not embrace the use of metaverse is strongly correlated with efficiency, safety, and psychological dangers. The relationship between performance risk, social risk, psychological risk, and non-adoption intention towards the corporate metaverse is mediated by mistrust, and this impact is stronger in people with high technostress than in those with low technostress. (Kumar et al., 2023).Consumers will adopt AR and VR as alternate methods for transactions by 2030, according to 47% of financiers (Abbott, 2022).

Employing the keywords "metaverse" "banking" or "blockchain" in the article's title fields, this analysis uses statistics from the Scopus collection. Since the database maintained by Scopus serves as one of the well-known and reliable resources for researchers, it is utilized. Additionally, it features extensive information from a variety of subjects, fields, and publishing slots in addition to a dependable updating schedule (regular). The development of digital financial services, such as neobanks, has been facilitated by technological advancements in recent times (Shi et al., 2023). For these branchless banks to succeed, their customers must accept them. One study sought to comprehend how prospective and existing neobank customers in Hungary would make decisions in 2022. Through a poll of 475 respondents, researchers discovered that attitudes toward utilizing neobank products had a direct impact on people's intentions to utilize them. Trust, perceived utility, and perceived simplicity of use all have a beneficial impact on this mindset. Therefore, to foster favorable opinions about their services, neobanks ought to place a high priority on establishing credibility, dependability, usability, and simplicity of usage (Nagy et al., 2024).

Virtual Branches and Spaces

Metaverse Banking introduces the concept of virtual branches, where users can engage with banking services in a spatial environment. Virtual spaces mimic physical branches, fostering a sense of community and interaction among users. Virtual branches and spaces represent a pivotal trend within the realm of Metaverse

Figure 4. The graphics in this visual depiction are licensed and free to use
This cover has been designed using assets from https://www.freepik.com/(Freepik Company, n.d.)

Banking, signifying a departure from traditional brick-and-mortar banking structures towards immersive and interactive digital environments. This innovative approach seeks to redefine the user experience, offering a spatial context to financial services that transcend the limitations of physical locations. Virtual branches, in the context of Metaverse Banking, are digital replicas of traditional bank branches manifested within immersive virtual environments. These environments often leverage virtual reality (VR) or augmented reality (AR) technologies to create realistic and engaging spaces where users can interact with banking services, products, and representatives. (Koohang et al., 2023)

Acknowledgment

The writers express their gratitude to the group of freepik.com. Pictures with license are taken

Key Features of Virtual Branches

Spatial Design: Virtual branches are meticulously designed to replicate the layout and aesthetics of physical bank branches. Users navigate these spaces using avatars, experiencing a three-dimensional representation that mimics the real-world banking environment (Koohang et al., 2023) (Wang et al., 2023).

Interactive Interfaces: The virtual branches feature interactive interfaces where users can access a range of financial services. From conducting transactions to consulting with virtual bankers, these interfaces provide a seamless and intuitive way for users to engage with banking activities.

Community Engagement: To enhance the sense of community, virtual branches often include spaces for social interactions. Users can engage with each other, attend financial seminars, or participate in virtual events, fostering a community atmosphere within the metaverse.

Customer Support: Virtual branches incorporate AI-driven customer support features. Virtual assistants guide users through transactions, answer queries, and assist, creating a dynamic and responsive customer support experience.

Advantages of Virtual Branches

Global Accessibility: Virtual branches break down geographical barriers, allowing users from around the world to access banking services without the need for physical proximity to a branch.

Immersive User Experience: The spatial design and interactive interfaces offer users a unique and immersive banking experience. This goes beyond the transactional nature of traditional online banking, creating a more engaging and memorable interaction (Fussell & Truong, 2022).

Cost-Efficiency: Virtual branches can be more cost-effective than maintaining physical locations. There are reduced overhead costs associated with building and maintaining brick-and-mortar structures.

Challenges and Considerations

User Adoption: The success of virtual branches hinges on user adoption. Financial institutions must ensure that users are comfortable and willing to engage with banking services in a virtual space(Dwivedi et al., 2022).

Technology Requirements: Virtual branches require users to have access to compatible hardware such as VR headsets or AR-enabled devices. Ensuring widespread access may pose a challenge (Ismail & Materwala, 2019).

Security Concerns: As with any digital space, security is paramount. Safeguarding user data and transactions within virtual branches is a critical consideration that financial institutions must address.

Digital Asset Integration

This section examines how technical innovations like as blockchain, smart contracts, and immersive experiences are propelling innovation in Metaverse Banking, emphasizing the role of cutting-edge technology. It looks at how they could change transactional procedures, security standards, and user experiences. (Pilkington: 11 Blockchain Technology: Principles... - Google Scholar, n.d.). Anyone involved in

Metaverse Banking needs to anticipate trends. We explore the new trends, such as the impact of decentralized finance (DeFi), the integration of artificial intelligence, and non-fungible tokens (NFTs). Comprehending these patterns is crucial for banks seeking to maintain a competitive edge in the swiftly changing financial landscape. The Metaverse is a cutting-edge technology that integrates various advanced tools such as virtual reality, augmented reality, blockchain, AI, and the Internet of Things. It offers users an immersive and personalized experience, leading businesses to explore its potential for transforming customer interactions. However, according to surveys and health experts, prolonged use of the Metaverse may have adverse impacts on mental and physical health. (Bale et al., 2022). Notably, the most commonly employed techniques by corporations are networking, optimism, and assurance which underscore the distinct advantages of the metaverse, including embodiment, interaction, and navigability (Kang & Ki, 2024). Companies successfully build and maintain connections with their audiences by utilizing the engrossing qualities of the metaverse. In addition to offering the payment tracks that underpin digital transactions and reinventing them for a 3D world, banks operating in the metaverse will also profit from a plethora of innovative possibilities, such as interacting with staff in novel ways, luring in youthful ability, and discovering fresh, practical methods of connecting and interacting with clients via the internet. It's critical to comprehend user attitudes and actions. The interaction between people and financial services in the metaverse is examined in this part, with a focus on user preferences, concerns, and the factors driving the uptake of virtual banking solutions. The main obstacles are those related to technology, experience gaps, health, security, privacy of data, and legal concerns. (Jung et al., 2024).

Digital Asset Integration stands as a transformative trend within the Metaverse, reshaping into the immersive realms of virtual environments. This evolution not only empowers users with unprecedented control over their financial portfolios but also aligns with the broader movement towards decentralized finance (DeFi), fostering a new era of financial inclusivity. (Ismail & Materwala, 2019). To handle digital money like cryptocurrencies, NFTs, and other digital tokens, securities businesses can leverage the metaverse. To make it simpler for traders to buy and sell these securities, an extensive system is provided for their storage and trading. (Shi et al., 2023) Financial service providers may use the metaverse to teach their clients as well. Attending conferences and online classes on economic subjects, including pension and planning for investments, may help consumers understand how to manage their own money (Cao, 2022) (Karaarslan & Yazici Yilmaz, 2023). Additionally, it might present novel purchasing alternatives to investors, including virtual assets or buildings. The ability to purchase and sell these assets throughout the metaverse opens up an entirely novel industry for investors (Caldarelli & Ellul, 2021).

International transactions can also be made simpler by using the metaverse. It offers an environment for businesses related to foreign exchange and transfers of funds. To handle digital money like cryptocurrencies, NFTs, and various other digital tokens, securities businesses can leverage the metaverse. To make it simpler for traders to buy and sell these securities, an extensive system is provided for their storage and trading(Guo & Liang, 2016). Financial services may use the metaverse to teach their clients as well. Attending conferences and online classes on economic subjects, including pension and investing strategies, may help consumers understand how to manage their own money(Radziwill, 2018b).

Additionally, it might present novel purchasing alternatives to investors, including virtual assets or buildings. The ability to purchase and sell these assets throughout the metaverse opens up an entirely novel industry for investors. International transactions can also be made simpler by using the metaverse. It offers an environment for businesses related to foreign exchange

The Technological Backbone: Blockchain Facilitation

At the heart of Digital Asset Integration lies the utilization of blockchain technology, the decentralized ledger system that underpins most cryptocurrencies. Blockchain's transparent, secure, and decentralized nature serves as the facilitator for the seamless incorporation of digital assets into the metaverse. This technology ensures the integrity and traceability of transactions within the virtual financial ecosystem (Guo & Liang, 2016). The basic idea in the metaverse is being in your possession. Blockchain technology powers the decentralized digital universe, allowing users to access data and manage their virtual assets in a transparent environment. Simulated replicas of real-world things can be created by corporations, and individuals can develop personas along with additional digital material. Because of non-fungible tokens (NFTs), possession in the metaverse is secure (Schuetz & Venkatesh, 2020). These tokens are distinct and contain info that identifies the person who owns them. Throughout the blockchain, NFTs serve as possession documents (Lu, 2018) (Niranjanamurthy et al., 2019) (Lu, 2018)

Seamless Incorporation of Cryptocurrencies

One of the primary facets of Digital Asset Integration is the incorporation of cryptocurrencies into the metaverse. Users can now navigate virtual environments and engage in financial transactions using digital currencies such as Bitcoin, Ethereum, and an array of altcoins. This shift enables users to participate in a myriad of financial activities within the metaverse using their preferred cryptocurrencies (Antipin et al., 2022) (Guo & Liang, 2016).

Unprecedented User Control: Digital Asset Integration places users at the helm of their financial destinies within the metaverse. The integration empowers users with unprecedented control over their digital assets, enabling them to manage, trade, and invest within virtual spaces (Manser Payne et al., 2021). This user-centric approach aligns with the ethos of decentralized finance, where individuals have direct control over their financial decisions without reliance on traditional intermediaries. In the metaverse right now, some of the most well-liked coins are:(The Impact Of The Metaverse In Banking And Finance | Definme, n.d.)

Ether: The Ethereum blockchain is the foundation for the majority of metaverse systems. Ether, the primary coin of Ethereum, is used by users to run decentralized apps and construct NFTs. On the marketplaces, immediate payments may also be made with Ether.

MANA: This is the native token of Decentraland, an Ethereum-powered 3D virtual world where users may play games, purchase property, create personas, and display their NFTs. In the area, MANA is used by users to make payments. Furthermore, MANA gives token owners the ability to participate in platform leadership and cast votes on initiatives.

SAND: Sandbox is the cryptocurrency associated with a well-known metaverse application. Sandbox is an Ethereum-based platform that provides users with immersive 3D experiences, much to Decentraland. The SAND token, which is utilized for administration and purchases, drives ecological activity.

Decentralized Finance Opportunities

The trend towards Digital Asset Integration seamlessly intertwines with the broader movement of decentralized finance. In the metaverse, users can access decentralized financial services, including lending, borrowing, and yield farming, all powered by smart contracts. This decentralized approach democratizes financial opportunities, allowing users to participate in financial activities traditionally reserved for institutions(Taylor et al., 2020) (Damar, 2021).

Advantages of Digital Asset Integration

Global Accessibility: Users across the globe can access and utilize digital assets within the metaverse, transcending geographical barriers and fostering financial inclusivity(Giang Barrera & Shah, 2023).

Security and Transparency: Blockchain's inherent security features ensure the integrity and transparency of transactions. Users can trust the immutability of their financial activities within the metaverse.

Financial Empowerment: Digital Asset Integration empowers users by granting them control over their financial portfolios. This shift aligns with the principles of self-sovereignty and financial autonomy.

Challenges and Considerations

Regulatory Landscape: The integration of digital assets brings forth regulatory challenges. Governments and regulatory bodies are grappling with the need to define and enforce regulations within the metaverse(Koohang et al., 2023).

User Education: As digital assets gain prominence within the metaverse, there is a need for extensive user education to ensure individuals understand the intricacies of managing and securing their digital assets.

Interoperability: Ensuring interoperability between different digital assets and virtual platforms is a technical challenge that needs to be addressed for a seamless user experience. Digital Asset Integration in the metaverse represents a groundbreaking shift towards a more inclusive, user-centric, and decentralized financial future. As blockchain technology continues to underpin these integrations, users find themselves at the forefront of financial innovation within immersive virtual environments, signaling a new era where financial empowerment knows no bounds.

AI-Powered Financial Advisors in the Metaverse

AI-Powered Financial Advisors represent a pivotal advancement within Metaverse Banking, revolutionizing the way users engage with financial services in immersive virtual environments. These virtual assistants, infused with artificial intelligence (AI) capabilities, offer personalized and real-time guidance, shaping a user experience that goes beyond conventional banking.

The Core Mechanism

Machine Learning Algorithms: At the heart of AI-Powered Financial Advisors lies the intricate interplay of machine learning algorithms. These algorithms serve as the brainpower, enabling virtual assistants to analyze vast datasets, discern patterns, and comprehend user behavior within the metaverse. The continuous learning and adaptation afforded by machine learning are fundamental to the personalized guidance these advisors provide.

Understanding User Preferences

AI-driven virtual financial advisors excel in understanding user preferences within the dynamic metaverse banking landscape. Through continuous interaction and analysis, these advisors build a nuanced understanding of individual user behaviors, financial goals, risk tolerance, and preferences. This contextual awareness allows them to tailor their guidance to each user's unique financial profile.

Real-Time Guidance and Decision Support

The hallmark of AI-Powered Financial Advisors is their ability to offer real-time guidance. Whether users are navigating investment decisions, exploring financial products, or seeking advice on budgeting, these virtual assistants provide instantaneous support. The integration of real-time data and machine learning ensures that the advice is not only personalized but also contextually relevant to the current financial landscape.

Personalized Financial Advice

The crux of AI-Powered Financial Advisors' capabilities lies in their capacity to offer personalized financial advice. By synthesizing user data, market trends, and individual preferences, these virtual assistants generate recommendations that align with users' financial objectives. Whether it's optimizing investment portfolios, suggesting budget adjustments, or providing insights into financial planning, the advice is tailored to suit each user's unique circumstances.

Benefits of AI-Powered Financial Advisors

Personalization: Users experience a level of personalization that transcends traditional banking services, as AI adapts to individual preferences and financial behaviors.

Efficiency: AI-driven virtual financial advisors operate in real-time, providing swift and efficient guidance, and reducing the time required for decision-making.

Continuous Learning: Machine learning algorithms ensure that virtual assistants continuously learn and adapt, refining their advice over time based on user interactions and evolving financial landscapes.

Challenges and Considerations

Data Privacy: The use of extensive user data raises concerns about data privacy. Financial institutions must implement robust security measures to protect user information within the metaverse.

Explainability: The opacity of AI decision-making processes poses a challenge in gaining user trust. There is a need for transparent communication on how AI arrives at specific financial recommendations.

User Adoption: User comfort with AI-powered financial advice is pivotal. Financial institutions must address any hesitancy or skepticism through education and transparent communication about the benefits and limitations of virtual financial advisors. AI-Powered Financial Advisors stand as a testament to the transformative potential of AI in redefining the metaverse banking experience (Zainurin et al., 2023). As these virtual assistants continue to evolve, learning from user interactions and offering increasingly sophisticated guidance, they play a pivotal role in shaping a future where financial advice is not only accessible but also deeply personalized within the dynamic landscape of the metaverse(Bale et al., 2022).

Decentralized Finance (DeFi) in the Metaverse

The fusion of Decentralized Finance (DeFi) with the metaverse represents a revolutionary progression in the banking landscape, introducing a paradigm shift in how financial transactions and services are conducted within immersive virtual environments. This convergence brings forth not only the principles of decentralization but also ushers in a new era of automation, efficiency, and transparency in financial interactions.

The Pillars of DeFi in the Metaverse

Decentralization: At the core of DeFi in the metaverse lies the principle of decentralization. Traditional financial systems are replaced by decentralized protocols and smart contracts that operate on blockchain technology. This shift eliminates the need for intermediaries, placing greater control and autonomy in the hands of users.

Automation: Smart contracts, self-executing agreements with the terms of the contract directly written into code, play a central role in DeFi within the metaverse. These contracts automate various financial processes, from lending and borrowing to trading and yield farming. Automation ensures swift and accurate execution of transactions without the need for manual intervention.

Automated Lending and Borrowing

DeFi in the metaverse introduces automated lending and borrowing mechanisms. Users can leverage their digital assets as collateral to access loans without traditional intermediaries. Smart contracts execute lending agreements, determining interest rates, loan terms, and collateral management autonomously. This democratized approach to lending enhances financial inclusivity within the metaverse.

Automated Trading

The convergence of DeFi with the metaverse facilitates automated trading through decentralized exchanges (DEXs). Smart contracts execute trades based on predefined conditions, providing users with a seamless and efficient trading experience. This automated trading mechanism operates 24/7, removing the constraints of traditional market hours.

Yield Farming and Liquidity Provision

DeFi introduces novel concepts like yield farming and liquidity provision within the metaverse. Users can contribute their digital assets to liquidity pools, earning yields in return. Smart contracts automate the distribution of rewards, creating a decentralized and automated ecosystem where users actively participate in the growth and liquidity of decentralized platforms(Radziwill, 2018a).

Efficiency and Transparency

Efficiency: DeFi in the metaverse streamlines financial processes by eliminating intermediaries and automating transactions. This efficiency translates into faster transaction processing, reduced costs, and increased accessibility for users engaging in various financial activities.

Transparency: Blockchain's transparent and immutable nature ensures that all financial transactions within the metaverse are verifiable and traceable. Users can audit and verify transaction histories, promoting a level of transparency that is often elusive in traditional banking systems(Ismail & Materwala, 2019).

Challenges and Considerations

Smart Contract Risks: The reliance on smart contracts introduces risks such as vulnerabilities and coding errors. Thorough auditing and testing of smart contracts are crucial to mitigate these risks and ensure the security of financial transactions.

Regulatory Uncertainty: The decentralized nature of DeFi in the metaverse poses challenges in terms of regulatory clarity. Governments and regulatory bodies are navigating the complexities of applying existing regulations to these novel financial ecosystems.

The impact of Decentralized Finance in the metaverse on banking is profound, redefining the very essence of financial transactions. As automation, decentralization, and transparency become the pillars of financial interactions within immersive virtual environments, the metaverse emerges as a frontier where traditional banking structures are replaced by a more inclusive, efficient, and user-centric financial paradigm(Dwivedi et al., 2022) (Nguyen et al., 2023).

Cross-Platform Financial Integration in Metaverse Banking

Cross-Platform Financial Integration in Metaverse Banking signifies a transformative shift, acknowledging the interconnected fabric of the digital age. This trend transcends the limitations of singular metaverse platforms, empowering users to partake in a unified banking experience seamlessly across diverse virtual environments. At its core, this evolution reflects a commitment to providing users with unparalleled flexibility and choice in their interactions with financial services within the metaverse(Schuetz & Venkatesh, 2020).

Unified Banking Experience Across Platforms

Breaking Platform Barriers: Cross-platform financial integration dismantles the traditional boundaries that confined users to a single metaverse platform. Users now have the freedom to traverse multiple virtual environments while maintaining a consistent and cohesive banking experience. This liberation from platform constraints is foundational to the trend's significance.

Comprehensive Banking Services: Regardless of the metaverse platform chosen, users gain access to a comprehensive suite of banking services. These include account management, transactional activities, investment options, and customer support. The integration ensures that users don't encounter fragmented or disparate financial experiences as they navigate diverse virtual landscapes.

Flexibility and User Choice

Platform-Agnostic Banking: Users are no longer tethered to the features of a specific metaverse platform for their banking needs. The trend promotes platform-agnostic banking services, allowing users to choose their preferred metaverse while enjoying a consistent and cohesive banking experience. This platform-agnostic approach exemplifies a user-centric philosophy.

Multi-Metaverse Engagement: Cross-platform financial integration facilitates multi-metaverse engagement. Users can seamlessly transition between different virtual environments, each catering to specific aspects of their preferences. For instance, one metaverse might be chosen for social interactions, while another, with distinct features, could be selected for financial transactions.

Technological Facilitators of Integration

APIs and Middleware: The integration is made possible through the utilization of Application Programming Interfaces (APIs) and middleware. These technological components act as bridges, facilitating communication and data exchange between diverse metaverse platforms and the banking systems. APIs enable the seamless flow of information, ensuring a cohesive user experience.

Blockchain Interoperability: The application of blockchain technology enhances the interoperability of financial transactions and data. Blockchain's decentralized and transparent nature ensures that user data remains consistent and verifiable across various metaverse environments. This interoperability contributes to the seamless integration of banking services(Hassani et al., 2018).

Advantages of Cross-Platform Financial Integration

User Empowerment: The trend empowers users by offering them the freedom to choose their preferred metaverse platforms without compromising their banking experience. This user-centric approach enhances overall satisfaction and engagement (Damar, 2021).

Global Accessibility: Cross-platform integration ensures global accessibility. Users from diverse geographical locations can access banking services without being restricted by the choice of a specific metaverse platform, fostering inclusivity.

Challenges and Considerations

Security Measures: Ensuring the security of user data and transactions across multiple metaverse platforms requires robust security measures. Implementation of encryption, authentication protocols, and secure APIs is paramount to safeguarding user information.

Standardization Efforts: Achieving a standardized approach to cross-platform integration poses challenges due to the diverse technological infrastructures of different metaverse platforms. Collaborative standardization efforts are essential to streamline integration processes. Cross-Platform Financial Integration in Metaverse Banking is not merely a technological advancement; it represents a paradigm shift in user engagement. Financial institutions embracing this trend are positioned to deliver a level of service that adapts to the diverse preferences of users, emphasizing choice, flexibility, and a unified banking experience across the expansive metaverse landscape. As this trend evolves, it is set to redefine the way users interact with financial services in the ever-expanding digital universe(Taylor et al., 2020).

POSSIBILITIES FOR METAVERSE BANKING IN THE YEARS TO COME TOMORROW

Combining Cryptocurrencies and Virtual Assets

The future of cryptocurrency and virtual assets integration is closely related to that of metaverse banking (Truong et al., 2023). The emergence of non-fungible tokens (NFTs) has led to the metaverse developing into a central location for exclusive digital assets, such as in-game goods and virtual real estate. This section examines how banks might use blockchain technology to enable safe virtual asset management, trading, and storage, opening up new financial services and income opportunities inside the metaverse (Mohamed & Faisal, 2024).

Banking Process Automation and Smart Agreements

It is predicted that smart contracts, which are self-executing contracts with their terms encoded directly into code, would be essential to the development of metaverse banking. By automating financial operations like as transaction execution and agreement enforcement, these contracts can decrease the need for middlemen and increase efficiency. This section explores the possible automation of intricate financial procedures by looking at how smart contracts might simplify banking operations in the metaverse (Gadekallu et al., 2022).

Optimized User Experiences With Immersion Technologies

Transactions alone won't define Metaverse Banking in the future; immersive user experiences will be included (Liu et al., 2023). Technologies like virtual reality (VR) and augmented reality (AR) are anticipated to be crucial in developing customized and interesting banking environments in the metaverse. The potential for these immersive technologies to change how people engage with their finances is covered in this section. Examples include individualized financial consultations in virtual settings and virtual branch experiences.(Balcerzak et al., 2022)

Drawbacks Associated With the Metaverse

Many researchers have focused attention on the numerous drawbacks of society's acceptance of the metaverse and its effects on particular demographic groups, even though most of the literature on the metaverse has formed a story centered on its advantages and difficulties. Numerous incidents of racism, brutal conduct, harassment, explicit sexual content appearance, threats of assault, training of youngsters on the VR Chatting system, and virtual-world obsession have been reported (Quach et al., 2022). In addition to providing new avenues for social engagement through avatar use, the metaverse's heightened holistic and tactile sensation may also provide victims of sexual misconduct a sense of realism in virtual reality. To fully comprehend many of the behavioral ramifications of the metaverse's broad acceptance, its impact begs for further transdisciplinary study. (Bale et al., 2022) (Dwivedi et al., 2023)

CONCLUSION

The Metaverse's innovations in several disciplines, particularly commerce and education, will keep altering the globe. In particular, the Metaverse in conjunction with other forms of technology will play a critical role in educational endeavours. Educational methodologies will be greatly impacted by the growing inventiveness and use of VR and AR in educational environments. The study found that people's propensity to use the Metaverse is significantly influenced by their Innovativeness (PI). The PI is influenced by both perceived benefits and simplicity of usage. By illustrating how acquisition attributes like perceived reliability, perceived visibility, and what is considered tribality affect Metaverse acceptance, some study contributes to our understanding of technological acquisition. An important factor in determining whether or not a user plans to use the metaverse is their level of happiness. Whenever it pertains to behavior change studies in consumer-related disciplines, the outcomes of similar studies carried out in real-world settings usually resemble those in virtual reality contexts. Virtual reality (VR) can be utilized to evaluate treatments in a more controlled and efficient setting (Singla et al., 2023). Numerous consumer-related businesses, such as clothing, food, financial services, and vacationing, have shown that virtual reality (VR) can facilitate changes in behavior. The future particular audience is in the metaverse. The metaverse fosters teamwork and imaginative thought, much like the real-world Zoom environment. The subsequent development in financing and accounting may be seen in the effects of the metaverse on the banking and finance sectors. The result of this is that advisers are becoming more knowledgeable on a variety of digital tokens other than both of the most prominent ones, ether, and bitcoin. Virtual property instruction and courses are being developed by professionals in response to the growing demand from consultants who feel compelled to train them to offer accessibility to this emerging sector of assets.

The trends shaping Metaverse Banking underscore the industry's commitment to innovation and user-centricity. These trends are not isolated features but interconnected elements of a broader narrative that envisions a future where banking transcends physical limitations. As financial institutions embrace these trends, they embark on a journey that promises not just evolution but a revolution in the way we perceive and engage with banking services.

To prepare for technological changes and seize possibilities, business executives in the banking industry must implement four essential transformations as a result of the management implications of Metaverse 2.0. However, the sources that are now accessible do not provide a clear explanation of the precise constraints or future directions associated with Metaverse 2.0 in banking. To gain a thorough comprehension of these facets, one should refer to certain studies or papers that concentrate on Metaverse 2.0 within the banking sector.

REFERENCES

Abbott, M. (2022, April 20). *Prepare for the metaverse with our ultimate guide.* Accenture Banking Blog. https://bankingblog.accenture.com/ultimate-guide-to-banking-in-the-metaverse

Antipin, D., Morozevich, O., Deitch, V., & Gomboeva, A. (2022). Blockchain Technology as a Factor Affecting the Digitalization of the Financial Sector. In A. Gibadullin (Ed.), *Digital and Information Technologies in Economics and Management* (pp. 202–212). Springer International Publishing., doi:10.1007/978-3-030-97730-6_18

Sriram, P. H. (2023). 3D avatars and blockchain integration: The future of virtual identity in metaverse—Digital Transformation News. *The Financial Express.* https://www.financialexpress.com/business/digital-transformation-3d-avatars-and-blockchain-integration-the-future-of-virtual-identity-in-metaverse-3265057/

Balcerzak, A. P., Nica, E., Rogalska, E., Poliak, M., Klieštik, T., & Sabie, O.-M. (2022). Blockchain Technology and Smart Contracts in Decentralized Governance Systems. *Administrative Sciences*, *12*(3), 3. doi:10.3390/admsci12030096

Bale, A. S., Ghorpade, N., Hashim, M. F., Vaishnav, J., & Almaspoor, Z. (2022). A Comprehensive Study on Metaverse and Its Impacts on Humans. *Advances in Human-Computer Interaction*, *2022*, 1–11. doi:10.1155/2022/3247060

Bandara, E., Shetty, S., Mukkamala, R., Liang, X., Foytik, P., Ranasinghe, N., & De Zoysa, K. (2022). Casper: A blockchain-based system for efficient and secure customer credential verification. *Journal of Banking and Financial Technology*, *6*(1), 43–62. doi:10.1007/s42786-021-00036-3

Banking in the Metaverse: Evolving Opportunity—Spiceworks. (n.d.). Spice Works. https://www.spiceworks.com/finance/fintech/guest-article/banking-in-the-metaverse/

Caldarelli, G., & Ellul, J. (2021). The Blockchain Oracle Problem in Decentralized Finance—A Multivocal Approach. *Applied Sciences (Basel, Switzerland)*, *11*(16), 16. doi:10.3390/app11167572

Cao, L. (2022). Decentralized AI: Edge Intelligence and Smart Blockchain, Metaverse, Web3, and DeSci. *IEEE Intelligent Systems*, *37*(3), 6–19. doi:10.1109/MIS.2022.3181504

Cho, J., tom Dieck, M. C., & Jung, T. (2023). What is the Metaverse? Challenges, Opportunities, Definition, and Future Research Directions. In T. Jung, M. C. tom Dieck, & S. M. Correia Loureiro (Eds.), *Extended Reality and Metaverse* (pp. 3–26). Springer International Publishing. doi:10.1007/978-3-031-25390-4_1

Damar, M. (2021). Metaverse Shape of Your Life for Future: A bibliometric snapshot. *Journal of Metaverse*, *1*(1), 1.

Dwivedi, Y. K., Hughes, L., Baabdullah, A. M., Ribeiro-Navarrete, S., Giannakis, M., Al-Debei, M. M., Dennehy, D., Metri, B., Buhalis, D., Cheung, C. M. K., Conboy, K., Doyle, R., Dubey, R., Dutot, V., Felix, R., Goyal, D. P., Gustafsson, A., Hinsch, C., Jebabli, I., & Wamba, S. F. (2022). Metaverse beyond the hype: Multidisciplinary perspectives on emerging challenges, opportunities, and agenda for research, practice and policy. *International Journal of Information Management*, *66*, 102542. doi:10.1016/j.ijinfomgt.2022.102542

Dwivedi, Y. K., Kshetri, N., Hughes, L., Rana, N. P., Baabdullah, A. M., Kar, A. K., Koohang, A., Ribeiro-Navarrete, S., Belei, N., Balakrishnan, J., Basu, S., Behl, A., Davies, G. H., Dutot, V., Dwivedi, R., Evans, L., Felix, R., Foster-Fletcher, R., Giannakis, M., & Yan, M. (2023). Exploring the Darkverse: A Multi-Perspective Analysis of the Negative Societal Impacts of the Metaverse. *Information Systems Frontiers*, *25*(5), 2071–2114. doi:10.1007/s10796-023-10400-x PMID:37361890

Fussell, S. G., & Truong, D. (2022). Using virtual reality for dynamic learning: An extended technology acceptance model. *Virtual Reality (Waltham Cross)*, *26*(1), 249–267. doi:10.1007/s10055-021-00554-x PMID:34276237

Gadekallu, T. R., Huynh-The, T., Wang, W., Yenduri, G., Ranaweera, P., Pham, Q.-V., da Costa, D. B., & Liyanage, M. (2022). *Blockchain for the Metaverse: A Review* (arXiv:2203.09738). arXiv. https://doi.org//arXiv.2203.09738 doi:10.48550

Giang Barrera, K., & Shah, D. (2023). Marketing in the Metaverse: Conceptual understanding, framework, and research agenda. *Journal of Business Research*, *155*, 113420. doi:10.1016/j.jbusres.2022.113420

Glenk, S. (2023, July 7). *The Metaverse: Dreamland or Dystopia?* SAP News Center. https://news.sap.com/2023/07/metaverse-art-exhibition/

Guo, Y., & Liang, C. (2016). Blockchain application and outlook in the banking industry. *Financial Innovation*, *2*(1), 24. doi:10.1186/s40854-016-0034-9

Hasanova, H., Baek, U., Shin, M., Cho, K., & Kim, M.-S. (2019). A survey on blockchain cybersecurity vulnerabilities and possible countermeasures. *International Journal of Network Management*, *29*(2), e2060. doi:10.1002/nem.2060

Hassani, H., Huang, X., & Silva, E. (2018). Banking with blockchain-ed big data. *Journal of Management Analytics*, *5*(4), 256–275. doi:10.1080/23270012.2018.1528900

Ismail, L., & Materwala, H. (2019). A Review of Blockchain Architecture and Consensus Protocols: Use Cases, Challenges, and Solutions. *Symmetry*, *11*(10), 10. doi:10.3390/sym11101198

Jahan, N., Naveed, S., Zeshan, M., & Tahir, M. A. (2016, November 4). (n.d.). How to Conduct a Systematic Review: A Narrative Literature Review. *Cureus*, *8*(11), e864. doi:10.7759/cureus.864 PMID:27924252

Jung, T., Cho, J., Han, D.-I. D., Ahn, S. J., Gupta, M., Das, G., Heo, C. Y., Loureiro, S. M. C., Sigala, M., Trunfio, M., Taylor, A., & tom Dieck, M. C. (2024). Metaverse for service industries: Future applications, opportunities, challenges and research directions. *Computers in Human Behavior*, *151*, 108039. doi:10.1016/j.chb.2023.108039

Kang, D., & Ki, E.-J. (2024). Relationship cultivation strategies in the metaverse. *Public Relations Review*, *50*(1), 102397. doi:10.1016/j.pubrev.2023.102397

Karaarslan, E., & Yazici Yilmaz, S. (2023). Metaverse and Decentralization. In F. S. Esen, H. Tinmaz, & M. Singh (Eds.), *Metaverse: Technologies, Opportunities and Threats* (pp. 31–44). Springer Nature., doi:10.1007/978-981-99-4641-9_3

Koohang, A., Nord, J. H., Ooi, K.-B., Tan, G. W.-H., Al-Emran, M., Aw, E. C.-X., Baabdullah, A. M., Buhalis, D., Cham, T.-H., Dennis, C., Dutot, V., Dwivedi, Y. K., Hughes, L., Mogaji, E., Pandey, N., Phau, I., Raman, R., Sharma, A., Sigala, M., & Wong, L.-W. (2023). Shaping the Metaverse into Reality: A Holistic Multidisciplinary Understanding of Opportunities, Challenges, and Avenues for Future Investigation. *Journal of Computer Information Systems*, *63*(3), 735–765. doi:10.1080/0887441 7.2023.2165197

Kumar, A., Shankar, A., & Nayal, P. (2024). Metaverse is not my cup of tea! An investigation into how personality traits shape metaverse usage intentions. *Journal of Retailing and Consumer Services*, *77*, 103639. doi:10.1016/j.jretconser.2023.103639

Kumar, A., Shankar, A., Shaik, A. S., Jain, G., & Malibari, A. (2023). Risking it all in the metaverse ecosystem: Forecasting resistance towards the enterprise metaverse. *Information Technology & People*. doi:10.1108/ITP-04-2023-0374

Liu, S., Xie, J., & Wang, X. (2023). QoE enhancement of the industrial metaverse based on Mixed Reality application optimization. *Displays*, *79*, 102463. doi:10.1016/j. displa.2023.102463

Lu, W. (2018). Blockchain Technology and Its Applications in FinTech. In I. Traore, I. Woungang, S. S. Ahmed, & Y. Malik (Eds.), *Intelligent, Secure, and Dependable Systems in Distributed and Cloud Environments* (pp. 118–124). Springer International Publishing. doi:10.1007/978-3-030-03712-3_10

Manser Payne, E. H., Dahl, A. J., & Peltier, J. (2021). Digital servitization value co-creation framework for AI services: A research agenda for digital transformation in financial service ecosystems. *Journal of Research in Interactive Marketing*, *15*(2), 200–222. doi:10.1108/JRIM-12-2020-0252

Metaverse in Banking: An Initiative for Banking Transformation from Emerging Country Prospective - ProQuest. (n.d.). Proquest. https://www.proquest.com/openview/ ad29e7b2bfafe34b5a85d2f61ab652d3/1?pq-origsite=gscholar&cbl=38744

Mileva, G. (2022). *48 Metaverse Statistics*. Influencer Marketing Hub. https:// influencermarketinghub.com/metaverse-stats/

Milian, E. Z., Spinola, M. D. M., & Carvalho, M. M. D. (2019). Fintechs: A literature review and research agenda. *Electronic Commerce Research and Applications*, *34*, 100833. doi:10.1016/j.elerap.2019.100833

Mishra, A. (n.d.). How is the Technology of Metaverse Transforming the Future of Banks. *The Times of India*. https://timesofindia.indiatimes.com/blogs/voices/how-is-the-technology-of-metaverse-transforming-the-future-of-banks/

Mohamed, A., & Faisal, R. (2024). Exploring metaverse-enabled innovation in banking: Leveraging NFTS, blockchain, and smart contracts for transformative business opportunities. *International Journal of Data and Network Science*, *8*(1), 35–44. doi:10.5267/j.ijdns.2023.10.020

Nagy, S., Molnár, L., & Papp, A. (2024). Customer Adoption of Neobank Services from a Technology Acceptance Perspective – Evidence from Hungary. *Decision Making: Applications in Management and Engineering*, *7*(1), 1. doi:10.31181/dmame712024883

Nguyen, L.-T., Duc, D. T. V., Dang, T.-Q., & Nguyen, D. P. (2023). Metaverse Banking Service: Are We Ready to Adopt? A Deep Learning-Based Dual-Stage SEM-ANN Analysis. *Human Behavior and Emerging Technologies*, *2023*, e6617371. doi:10.1155/2023/6617371

Niranjanamurthy, M., Nithya, B. N., & Jagannatha, S. (2019). Analysis of Blockchain technology: Pros, cons and SWOT. *Cluster Computing*, *22*(6), 14743–14757. doi:10.1007/s10586-018-2387-5

Quach, S., Thaichon, P., Martin, K. D., Weaven, S., & Palmatier, R. W. (2022). Digital technologies: Tensions in privacy and data. *Journal of the Academy of Marketing Science*, *50*(6), 1299–1323. doi:10.1007/s11747-022-00845-y PMID:35281634

Radziwill, N. (2018a). Blockchain Revolution: How the Technology Behind Bitcoin is Changing Money, Business, and the World. *The Quality Management Journal*, *25*(1), 64–65. doi:10.1080/10686967.2018.1404373

Radziwill, N. (2018b). Mapping Innovation: A Playbook for Navigating a Disruptive Age. *The Quality Management Journal*, *25*(1), 64–64. doi:10.1080/10686967.2018.1404372

Renduchintala, T., Alfauri, H., Yang, Z., Pietro, R. D., & Jain, R. (2022). A Survey of Blockchain Applications in the FinTech Sector. *Journal of Open Innovation*, *8*(4), 185. doi:10.3390/joitmc8040185

Schuetz, S., & Venkatesh, V. (2020). Blockchain, adoption, and financial inclusion in India: Research opportunities. *International Journal of Information Management*, *52*, 101936. doi:10.1016/j.ijinfomgt.2019.04.009

Shi, F., Ning, H., Zhang, X., Li, R., Tian, Q., Zhang, S., Zheng, Y., Guo, Y., & Daneshmand, M. (2023). A new technology perspective of the Metaverse: Its essence, framework and challenges. *Digital Communications and Networks*. doi:10.1016/j. dcan.2023.02.017

Singla, B., Bhattacharya, S., & Naik, N. (2023). Introduction to Metaverse and Consumer Behaviour Change: Adoption of Metaverse Among Consumers. In P. Keikhosrokiani (Ed.), (pp. 113–129). Advances in Marketing, Customer Relationship Management, and E-Services. IGI Global., doi:10.4018/978-1-6684-7029-9.ch006

Srivastava, S. (2023, February 9). Web3 and the Metaverse: Building a Stronger Digital Economy. *Appinventiv*. https://appinventiv.com/blog/web3-metaverse-for-digital-economy/

Taylor, P. J., Dargahi, T., Dehghantanha, A., Parizi, R. M., & Choo, K.-K. R. (2020). A systematic literature review of blockchain cyber security. *Digital Communications and Networks*, 6(2), 147–156. doi:10.1016/j.dcan.2019.01.005

Truong, V. T., Le, L., & Niyato, D. (2023). Blockchain Meets Metaverse and Digital Asset Management: A Comprehensive Survey. *IEEE Access : Practical Innovations, Open Solutions*, 11, 26258–26288. doi:10.1109/ACCESS.2023.3257029

Wang, Y., Su, Z., Zhang, N., Xing, R., Liu, D., Luan, T. H., & Shen, X. (2023). A Survey on Metaverse: Fundamentals, Security, and Privacy. *IEEE Communications Surveys and Tutorials*, 25(1), 319–352. doi:10.1109/COMST.2022.3202047

Yaqoob, I., Salah, K., Jayaraman, R., & Omar, M. (2023). Metaverse applications in smart cities: Enabling technologies, opportunities, challenges, and future directions. *Internet of Things : Engineering Cyber Physical Human Systems*, 23, 100884. doi:10.1016/j.iot.2023.100884

Zainurin, M. Z. L., Haji Masri, M., Besar, M. H. A., & Anshari, M. (2023). Towards an understanding of metaverse banking: A conceptual paper. *Journal of Financial Reporting and Accounting*, 21(1), 178–190. doi:10.1108/JFRA-12-2021-0487

Chapter 11
Unlocking the Metaverse and Navigating Legal Implications in the NFT Landscape

Nitika Sharma
Chitkara University, Punjab, India

Sridhar Manohar
iD https://orcid.org/0000-0003-0173-3479
Chitkara University, Punjab, India

ABSTRACT

The problem of intellectual property and legality in NFTs has gotten little attention thus far and requires additional research because of the increasingly digital nature of financial investments and the rapid growth of technology. Because NFTs are dynamic and ever-evolving and have an array of outcomes and impacts on digital ownership, technology, law, and various other aspects of society—both positive and negative—this chapter aims to examine NFTs in the context of the metaverse. The implications for digital intellectual property rights law will play a major role in this chapter. Research is required since previous studies have not sufficiently covered the rights of ownership of NFTs through digital intellectual property.

INTRODUCTION

Metaverse in recent years has gained significant attention due to its involvement in various technologies that provide a virtual world similar to the real world (Lee et al., 2021). Through the virtual world of metaverse people can engage in activities

DOI: 10.4018/979-8-3693-5868-9.ch011

such as socializing, entertainment, learning, artistic work and can even experience real time shopping (Chen et al., 2023). Jasmini et al. (2023) defined metaverse as the "futuristic virtual world beyond the universe" while also predicting that most of the population in coming years will significantly ease tasks through use of metaverse and the organizations will also develop products and services centric to metaverse technology. The metaverse holds ample opportunities with a blend of the virtual social world and a significant space for businesses and investors (Singh & Sisodia, 2023). The rise of metaverse and its significance has built an opportunity for investors and businesses to enter into virtual space and expand their arenas.

The metaverse integrates with decentralized finance (DeFi) to offer various services in the virtual space such as financial services ease through cryptocurrency and blockchain technology, artistic opportunities and opportunities to build businesses (Kumar et al., 2023). It enables investing and trading through cryptocurrencies, virtual banking, virtual currency exchange and in fact virtual insurance services as well (Kaur et al., 2023). The blockchain technology used in the metaverse has a major contribution in empowering the digital management of assets offering a safe and secure distribution mechanism (Gadekallu et al., 2022). One aspect of these digital assets is that of Non- Fungible Tokens (NFTs) which have a unique feature of non-transferability (Razi et al., 2023), irreplaceability in the virtual world (Aksoy & Uner, 2021) unlike the other cryptocurrencies. NFTs also help in community development and cooperation by establishing virtual landscape, real estate, and creative ownership (Chalmers et al., 2022). The popularity of NFTs has been evergrowing since its prevalence, particularly in the artwork sector. Furthermore, because NFTs in the metaverse rely on decentralized technology to function, they assist artists in directly monetizing their unique creations without the need for middlemen (Kharitonova, 2024). Through the use of smart contracts included into NFTs, creators will receive a percentage of the proceeds from selling of their developed digital assets. According to Timucin and Birogul (2023), smart contracts provide a secure and efficient means of carrying out agreements and transactions in a decentralized environment. An environment that is more equal and transparent with respect to creators' assistance is made possible by this automated system. All good things though, come with a drawback. Looking at the emerging use of NFTs and the Metaverse, it is important to take digital intellectual property rights into account. The rights of creators need to be given more attention as the era of the internet progresses with advancements and digitization to gain the trust of people. Going backwards to the early days of the internet, fewer technological developments also helped to minimize dishonest behavior and scams. As we dig deeper into the digital transformation, we see that the virtual world evolved as an important aspect. The change from Web 2.0 to Web 3.0 is now the one that needs to be given attention. The platform offered by Web 3.0 is more user-centric. It is mostly dependent on blockchain technology, which necessitates a radical shift from conventional to contemporary investing methods. Web 3.0 represents a big change in data privacy, data management, and technology. This promotes a move toward a more helpful and advanced manner for consumers to interact with the internet.

WEB 3.0 AND ITS ROLE IN SHAPING THE METAVERSE

Looking back at the transformation of various stages of the internet, it has evolved immensely through the years heading a way to new technologies and revolution (Zhang et. al., 2008). The internet initially emerged as HTML and later the introduction of two way communication began the second generation of internet with the prevalence of Web 2.0 in 2004 (Ibrahim, 2021). Web 2.0 applications take advantage of the network as platform, spanning all connected devices, by delivering software as a constantly-updated service that gets better the more people use it, consuming and remixing data from multiple sources, including individual users, and providing their own data and services in a form that allows remixing by others (O'Reilly, 2005). Prominent instances of Web 2.0 include Facebook, Outlook, Instagram, and many others. The usage of Web 2.0 has increased connection and accessibility of the virtual world (Ibrahim, 2021). Additionally, finance and technology has seen advancement due to the increased availability and utilization of tech. The emergence of the traditional web in the field of finance and banking has eradicated the need for physical presence in banks or depositories for financial transactions. Instead, all activities can be conducted through the use of these technologies (Giglio, 2021). Nevertheless, the option that offers numerous advantages also entails certain disadvantages. The ability of Web 2.0 to effectively facilitate the swift distribution of information has experienced notable growth in recent years. According to Rani et al. (2022), individuals have a transforming process that changes system and belief, resulting in an impact on them. Moreover, Despite the implementation of strong cyber security by banks, hackers get loopholes through which they can gain illegal access to this data (Ali et al., 2021). Additionally, Web 3.0 offers a platform that prioritizes user-centricity. The system heavily depends on the utilization of blockchain technology. Metaverse has transformed into actual reality from fiction, paving a new way for the digital era in terms of art, finance, banking, gaming, businesses and much more. Through these endless and unveiling opportunities, it has the potential of replicating the actual world with the virtual world, headed by great advancements in technology.

The famous cryptocurrencies Bitcoin and Ethereum play a crucial role in the making of the Metaverse also called the Di fi world. NFTs are an important aspect in this context (Kabanda et al., 2022). NFTs can be seen as a way of ownership of various digital assets. The rise in variety of NFTs has merged with the emergence of good business opportunities (Ali et al., 2023). Unlike Bitcoin or any other cryptocurrency, NFTs are non- fungible digital assets which are not same rather every NFT has a unique identity (Thomas & David, 2022). NFTs have become increasingly popular in recent years due to their unique characteristics. The development of blockchain technology and the idea of digital ownership have contributed to the evolution of NFTs. Initially, NFTs were mainly associated with the art world, providing artists with a new way to generate income from their digital creations and offering collectors verifiable evidence of ownership. However, as de fi has emerged and the metaverse has grown, NFTs have expanded beyond art. Today, NFTs are used in various industries, from gaming to virtual real estate, allowing people to buy, sell, and trade unique digital assets in a safe and transparent manner. The evolution of these tokens has led to a shift in the way we view and engage with digital assets, providing a shot into the future of digital ownership in the virtual world.

The combination of NFTs into the metaverse has a good way to the virtual world. But what exactly is the Metaverse? Dionisio et al. (2013) have defined it as, *"The word Metaverse is a portmanteau of the prefix "meta" (meaning "beyond") and the suffix "verse" (shorthand for "universe")."* It means a non-physical universe. This "universe beyond" is a computer-generated world. The metaverse is a virtual world that is parallel to the actual world. The embodiment of NFTs into the metaverse helps the establishment of a decentralized and user-focused economic system. According to Kabanda et al. (2022), the use ofNFTs enables users to establish ownership of their virtual assets within the metaverse. Additionally, metaverse helps in trading of these tokens making it easy for users to do peer-to-peer lending providing a flexible and user centric platform for the financial investors, opening up new investment ways.

NFTS AND DIGITAL OWNERSHIP

From using blockchain technology securing ownership rights, to providing a unique representation for digital assets, NFTs prevent the ease of copying and stealing of these digital assets in the metaverse secondary market (Raman & Raj, 2021) having a huge potential to change the concept of digital ownership in numerous ways. They can create a digital ecosystem driven by gaming, art & collectables, real estate etc along with an essential advantage of authentication enabling ease in collection of royalties by the original owner (Tomić et al., 2023).

Uses of NFTs

A) **Blockchain Gaming:** With the evolution of virtual realm blockchain technology emerges as a force for digital gaming which enables data safety and establishes trust among its users. (Stamatakis et al., 2024). Additionally, NFTs in blockchain-based games possess a diverse array of applications. Applications for non-fungible tokens include in-game currency, which lets users buy skills, upgrades, and other exclusive items. Additionally, they let players to possess exclusive goods like armor or weapons, or tradeable goods like virtual land.

B) **Art Galleries:** NFTs help artists with creative ways of showing their creations in the virtual world. They let investors purchase, sell digital art that is available in online galleries. They provide new avenues for digital art experiences within the metaverse for both collectors and artists.

C) **Virtual Real Estate:** Within the metaverse, non-fungible tokens offer a safe means of acquiring, exchanging, and storing virtual land and structures. These real estate NFTs are ideal for representing virtual real estate because they are safe and not copyable and counterfeit-proof. These tokens can be purchased for various uses in the metaverse, including getting into groups, or creating spaces with other holders.

With this revolution of decentralized finance and digital assets, the concept of businesses, possessions and ownership is also developing rapidly (Belk et al., 2022). Several research focuses on the ever evolving metaverse digital realm (Schumacher, 2022; Tukur et al., 2024; Li et al., 2021) and the ownership of NFTs (Rehman et al., 2021; Razi et al., 2023; Valeonti et al., 2021). But what is it that people actually own when they hold an NFT? It is not the physical assets of artwork or real estate that an individual owns when buying NFTs. It is the right that one buys to hold a rare and unique digital creation that has monetary value (Belk et al., 2022) similar to buying shares of a company, which do not have physical presence but hold monetary value. Along with the ownership of these assets comes the digital intellectual property rights which serve as a regulating ownership in the virtual space. These laws have been created to systematically regulate the ownership and creation of digital assets in order to prevent misconduct in the ever evolving digital era (Bonnet & Teuteberg, 2023). However, possessing the asset right does not usually mean the transfer of royalties of those assets. Royalty benefits of digital creations usually remain with the creator itself and merely the property rights transfer when transferring the possession (Savale & Savale, 2016). The existence of IP rights in NFTs enables a transparent environment for the creators heading a reliable and safe way of protecting their unique creations (Bamakan et al., 2022). However, the challenges faced in the digital space regarding the copyright of these assets is the one that has to be looked upon. Counterfeiting is also a matter of concern pertinent to this area which has to be looked upon.

LEGAL FRAMEWORK FOR NFTS

The lack of regulators in the blockchain has made it slightly difficult for creators and investors to rely on its benefits and the vast opportunities it provides. There still remains a lack of comprehensive overview of the legal framework for NFTs. Transactions in NFTs create legal questions related to copyrights, ownership rights which vary from country to country (Aksoy & Uner, 2021). The legality of NFTs is an evolving area and currently is tied to the intellectual property laws across jurisdictions. It is imperative to create a clear and effective framework for the legal framework that governs digital assets. As the NFTs market is growing, creators and investors need to know the importance of monetizing their digital creations. However, as monetization increases, so does the concern about digital ownership and copyright. The consideration of digital intellectual property rights is crucial in light of the expanding utilization of non-fungible tokens (NFTs) and the Metaverse ecosystem. As digital creation is being tokenized at a greater pace, a need for awareness and understanding of legal and ethical considerations also increases (Guadamuz, 2021). Issues pertaining to copyright infringement rights in the digital world need to be carefully seen and addressed.

With the growing emergence of metaverse in the digital realm, the social scope of people has also extended which makes NFTs one of the most prominent ways of achieving this which provides a means of verifying ownership of digital assets (Behl et al., 2024). The emerging NFT identity dilemma presents a unique challenge that requires careful examination and thoughtful solutions to ensure a seamless and sustainable experience for the users in this evolving digital landscape. The question that arises is, if the existing privacy security protection is enough to cope up with the counterfeiting activities of the scammers?

NFTs were initially developed to establish a technologically sophisticated domain for artists. However, unscrupulous scammers have tainted this domain by illicitly appropriating the artwork of fellow creators (Collier, 2022). The intellectual property rights concerning these digital assets is a matter of concern for the creators as blockchain helps in providing protection against the information security against these assets but to look at the copyright part, there is no prevailing law which will help the creators get the right of copyright holders against their unique artwork (Kulakova, 2022). With the help of copyrights and trademarks, transparency for the creators can be promoted (Bamakan et al., 2022). Therefore, the scope or potential NFTs have in intellectual property is one that should be looked upon which most importantly provides a right to original ownership to the creators or NFTs holders. Furthermore, the fear of artwork counterfeiting can be eliminated among creators, making NFTs a good financial investment avenue. The diminishing concern about counterfeiting among creators paves the way for new investment opportunities in the Web 3.0 domain.

Copyright Protection of NFTs

There is a lack of set security based standard in case of NFTs when it comes to copyright protection (Aksoy & Uner, 2021). The decentralized nature of blockchain, which makes it difficult to track information makes the copyright claims a difficult task (Makridakis & Christodoulou, 2019). As discussed in the previous section, the possession of NFTs brings along intellectual property rights as well; however, it is at times crucial to get to the creator of these unique assets in the first place. There is a possibility of counterfeiting which further results in frauds such as selling NFTs which are not owned by the seller (Bhujel & Rahulamathavan, 2022). Moreover, issues of ownership remain a matter of concern in the digital world which raises questions of copyright claims among investors and participants of metaverse.

However, the current copyright law is not fully applicable and compatible to regulate the Web 3.0 environment. A need to study the legal issues concerning NFTs is a vital factor in research. Certain steps to supervise the copyright protection which might not be major to the existing web 3.0 environment but can result in a number of changes such as optimized platforms which automatically detect the counterfeited or infringed work can result into a major revolution for the creators and legitimacy of metaverse environment, especially NFTs. In addition to this, creators can be provided with unique numbers which they would have to clarify before moving forward with copyrights etc. Addressing the challenges and issues relating to copyright laws provides practical implications solving a major problem among the academicians as well as practitioners.

Blockchain Technology and Smart Contracts

Blockchain is the foundation of the entire functionality of non-fungible tokens, recording transactions across the system (Hammi et al., 2023). This reason makes the NFTs to be unique from each other forming the digital scarcity which mitigates the risk of manipulation (Bhujel & Rahulamathavan, 2022). In order to do so, NFTs utilize the smart contracts which govern the ownership and transferability of these assets, generally eradicating the need for a middleman, thus making it decentralized.

But what are smart contracts? As it is known, blockchain technology heavily relies on coding and decentralization through which it ensures a cryptographic mechanism in order to create self executing agreements that are known as smart contracts (Singh et al., 2020). Due to its automation it nullifies the transaction costs or need for intermediaries, as required in traditional financial transactions. Additionally, smart contracts also facilitate automation in the royalty payments to original creators of NFTs.

Legal Issues and Challenges

The major challenge faced by digital assets is that of counterfeiters. These are people who copy or steal work of creators and sell it as their own making it very difficult for anyone to identify between real or fake (Mochram, 2022). What happens if counterfeited NFTs are bought? The intellectual property right that pertains with the possession of NFTs is missing if fake NFTs are bought which makes it valueless and impossible to legally trade it further (Rawat et al., 2022). Despite the efforts of technology and smart contracts on metaverse to prevent counterfeiting, it still happens which becomes a major loophole in web 3.0. This gap exists due to various reasons, major reason being the global usage of blockchain and metaverse (Truong et al., 2023). Even though different platforms have their authentication processes to make it difficult for any legal issues to pertain, however the demand, lack of awareness, evolving technology and many other reasons makes it difficult to track or stop counterfeiting activities (Razi et al., 2023).

Unless the issue of counterfeiting pertains to a great extent, the trust or reliability of creators and investors shall remain questionable. Looking at the bigger picture, regulations on metaverse still remain a difficult task to do, however there are numerous measures that can prevent such malpractices. The major need of the clock is consumer awareness which stands behind drastically in this context. Despite the evolving technology and interest in NFTs, there is a lack of awareness or knowledge associated with digital assets which lets the misleading information or duplicate websites take advantage of it. Apart from this, a common decentralized regulatory system in the context of digital space is required which may diminish the problems related to metaverse space.

BUSINESS SCOPE AND CASE STUDIES

The ever-growing scope of NFTs has expanded various business and investment opportunities. According to (Razi et al, 2023), NFTs market size is estimated to grow from $21.39 billion to $212 billion by 2030 with a thriving compounded annual

Figure 1. Cryptopreneurs NFT original NFTs collection[1]

growth rate (CAGR) of 33.7% which depicts the market opportunities and growth in the realm of NFTs. Additionally, exploring business opportunities or expanding existing business through Web 3.0 tools, such as, cryptocurrency and NFTs adds up an advantage of working from anywhere, anytime virtually. Opportunists need not look for physical spaces or excessive fundings in order to build up a business or generate an income through Web 3.0. Apart from business opportunities, Web 3.0 has also opened up doors for diversifying investments, cryptocurrencies and NFTs being the vital participants. As the future scope of NFTs evolution can be clearly seen in the upcoming years, an early awareness, access and investment into it can turn out to be fruitful in the upcoming years. Similarly, understanding the business scope and seizing the opportunities it presents will be vital for success in this flourishing digital landscape.

Below are a few case studies of flourishing NFT business models that are trending in the emerging hype of NFTs:

Cryptopreneurs NFT:

The business model of Cryptopreneurs NFT incorporates an escrow system to facilitate transactions in cryptocurrencies, ensuring seamless transactions and protecting creators from fraudulent activities. The company primarily caters to Web 3.0 creators and entrepreneurs who are interested in purchasing and vending NFTs or Web 3.0-based services.

It is a digital collectible platform that unites NFT creators into a community. Additionally, the platform offers instructional materials on finance and investments for Web 2.0 and Web 3.0 platforms to support community upgradation and the development of stronger businesses. In order to support a business model that is fully virtual and unrestricted by its digitalization, they also offer digital marketing services and skill enhancement in this area. Furthermore, as illustrated in Figure 1 above, they have their original collectible NFTs, whose purpose is to encourage creators to produce their original work and list it on the website to safeguard it against fraudulent activities.

Figure 2. Metropoly ecosystem²

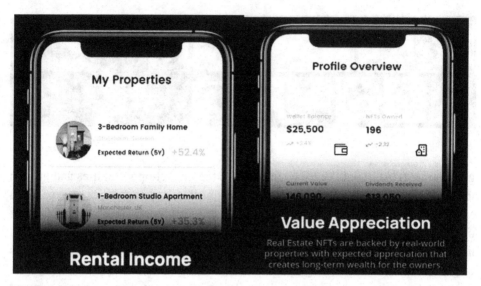

Metropoly:

Blockchain based business model called Metropoly NFT deals with popular real estate properties as NFTs. Every property is uploaded to the blockchain network and tokenized, making it accessible from any location at any time. With the help of the Metropoly business model, investors and users can diversify their portfolios by purchasing real estate and generating passive income. Furthermore, investors can meet their immediate needs with high liquidity from this investment.

For those looking to make real estate investments, Metropoly is a great business model. The benefits offered include non-fungible tokens (NFTs) supported by physician properties, a platform for trading real estate NFTs, and the opportunity to access new properties before they become available on the secondary market. The above Figure 2 reflects the various features of Metropoly.

Pudgy Penguins:

Using the Ethereum blockchain to store ownership of 8,888 NFT collections, Pudgy Penguins is an NFT brand on the Web 3.0 platform of original digital art that accelerates innovation through the use of intellectual property and community empowerment. The images in Figure 3 below were taken from Pudgy Penguins' website. The figure makes it apparent that in addition to the brand's clothing collection, the website offers the option to purchase media GIFs.

There is an endless list of NFT projects and business models that have emerged in the last few years. This demonstrates the enormous potential that NFTs have in the metaverse. As previously mentioned, the virtual world of the metaverse is a copy of

Figure 3. Pudgy Penguins collection[3]

the real world, providing countless chances for possible businesses to succeed. Even though these platforms state to offer copyright and intellectual property protection, a strong law with authority backing would be of additional benefit to users and would make them trustworthy sources for investments and businesses.

FUTURE SCOPE

The growing popularity of the metaverse indicates that NFTs will be crucial in determining how business is conducted in this virtual realm in the future. The existing literature has not explored the potential of NFTs in the context of legality. NFTs creators can directly commercialize their work with the help of a platform and most importantly, without need of a middleman which is very difficult in case of traditional businesses and traditional finance. This direct connection between the creators and investors can revolutionize the scenario of how digital content is bought and sold, heading a new path for creativity and businesses. In addition to this, NFTs pave a new way for creators and entrepreneurs the opportunity to offer their customers unique experiences as they work to establish goodwill of their businesses and creations in the metaverse.

Legal Concerns of NFTs

NFTs embibe a number of complex issues related to intellectual rights, taxation, awareness and much more. NFTs enable creators to work and build business realms virtually which raises a question regarding the copyright and ownership rights (Dong & Wang, 2023). Determining the actual owner or creator is difficult to determine which drastically affects the business profits of such creators as investors or consumers restrict themselves from investing. Although there is an option of smart contracts available on the blockchain, that also gets restricted due to legal constraints of different countries. There remains a major lack in the existing literature regarding the legal concerns which makes it crucial for further studies to consider legal aspects of NFTs. The research questions that can be framed for further research are:

FRQ1: How can legal framework affect the interest of creators and investors in NFTs?

FRQ2: How do evolving laws related to copyright and intellectual property adapt to the challenges posed by NFTs in terms of ownership?

Awareness: a Challenge

While NFTs offer numerous opportunities for investors and creators, the lack of knowledge freedom and awareness stands as a big challenge (David & Won, 2022). The research questions that can be formulated are:

FRQ3: What can be the measures and impact to promote awareness related to NFTs and how can it affect the decision making process?

FRQ4: Does lack of awareness lead to behavioral biases among creators and investors? How significantly does it affect decision making?

Traditional vs. Digital

While there are a number of studies on comparison among traditional finance vs the digital finance or traditional businesses vs metaverse businesses (Gomber et al., 2017; Klein et al., 2019; Nair & Menon, 2017), however the impact it creates in the long term on the economy or wealth of investors is an area that can be worked upon. The following research questions can be addressed:

FRQ5: What are the long-term implications of NFTs in comparison to the traditional businesses or traditional investments?

FRQ6: Does early adoption of NFTs have a significant impact on the wealth creation of investors?

CONCLUSION

The past literature has addressed a number of studies on NFTs and the metaverse, however there remains a major gap in addressing the legality issue related to copyright protection of intellectual property rights. This study addresses some of these issues and provides a scope for further research in this domain. The past literatures have also taken into consideration the matter of counterfeiters, however measures to stop counterfeiting activities still remain missing. In addition to this, awareness among the creators and investors can significantly impact the entire scenario of web 3.0 environment and irregularities can significantly be improved. This study provides a basis for future research to dig deeper into NFTs and its practical implications.

REFERENCES

Bamakan, S. M. H., Nezhadsistani, N., Bodaghi, O., & Qu, Q. (2022). Patents and intellectual property assets as non-fungible tokens; key technologies and challenges. *Scientific Reports*, *12*(1), 2178. doi:10.1038/s41598-022-05920-6 PMID:35140251

Behl, A., Pereira, V., Nigam, A., Wamba, S., & Sindhwani, R. (2024). Knowledge development in non-fungible tokens (NFT): a scoping review. *Journal of Knowledge Management,* *28*(1), 232-267. doi/ doi:10.1108/JKM-12-2022-0937

Belk, R., Humayun, M., & Brouard, M. (2022). Money, possessions, and ownership in the Metaverse: NFTs, cryptocurrencies, Web3 and Wild Markets. *Journal of Business Research, 153*, 198–205. doi:10.1016/j.jbusres.2022.08.031

Bhujel, S., & Rahulamathavan, Y. (2022). A survey: Security, transparency, and scalability issues of nft's and its marketplaces. *Sensors (Basel), 22*(22), 8833. doi:10.3390/s22228833 PMID:36433429

Bonnet, S., & Teuteberg, F. (2023). Impact of blockchain and distributed ledger technology for the management, protection, enforcement and monetization of intellectual property: A systematic literature review. *Information Systems and e-Business Management, 21*(2), 229–275. doi:10.1007/s10257-022-00579-y

Çağlayan Aksoy, P., & Özkan Üner, Z. (2021). Nfts And Copyright: Challenges And Opportunities. *Journal Of Intellectual Property Law And Practice, 16*(10), 1115–1126. doi:10.1093/jiplp/jpab104

Chalmers, D., Fisch, C., Matthews, R., Quinn, W., & Recker, J. (2022). Beyond the bubble: Will NFTs and digital proof of ownership empower creative industry entrepreneurs? *Journal of Business Venturing Insights, 17*, e00309. doi:10.1016/j.jbvi.2022.e00309

Chen, H., Duan, H., Abdallah, M., Zhu, Y., Wen, Y., Saddik, A. E., & Cai, W. (2023). Web3 Metaverse: State-Of-The-Art And Vision. *ACM Transactions on Multimedia Computing Communications and Applications*, 20(4), 1–42. doi:10.1145/3630258

David, L. E. E., & Won, L. S. (2022). Nft of nft: Is our imagination the only limitation of the metaverse?. *The Journal of The British Blockchain Association*. https://doi.org/ doi:10.31585/jbba-5-2-(2)2022

Dionisio, J. D. N., Iii, W. G. B., & Gilbert, R. (2013). 3d Virtual Worlds And The Metaverse: Current Status And Future Possibilities. *ACM Computing Surveys*, 45(3), 1–38. doi:10.1145/2480741.2480751

Dong, Y., & Wang, C. (2023). Copyright protection on NFT digital works in the Metaverse. *Security and Safety*, 2, 2023013. doi:10.1051/sands/2023013

Gadekallu, T. R., Huynh-The, T., Wang, W., Yenduri, G., Ranaweera, P., Pham, Q. V., & Liyanage, M. (2022). Blockchain for the metaverse: A review. *arXiv preprint arXiv:2203.09738*. Doi: https://doi.org//arXiv.2203.09738 doi:10.48550

Giglio, F. (2021). Fintech: A Literature Review. *European Research Studies Journal*, 24(2b), 600–627. doi:10.5539/ibr.v15n1p80

Gomber, P., Koch, J. A., & Siering, M. (2017). Digital Finance and FinTech: Current research and future research directions. *Journal of Business Economics*, 87, 537–580. doi:10.1007/s11573-017-0852-x

Guadamuz, A. (December, 2021). Non-Fungible Tokens (Nfts) And Copyright, *Wipo Magazine*. https://www.wipo.int/wipo_magazine/en/2021/04/article_0007.html

Hammi, B., Zeadally, S., & Perez, A. J. (2023). Non-fungible tokens: A review. *IEEE Internet of Things Magazine*, 6(1), 46–50. doi:10.1109/IOTM.001.2200244

Ibrahim, A. K. (2021). Evolution Of The Web: From Web 1.0 To 4.0. *Qubahan Academic Journal*, 1(3), doi: . doi:20-28

Jaimini, U., Zhang, T., Brikis, G. O., & Sheth, A. (2022). iMetaverseKG: Industrial Metaverse Knowledge Graph to Promote Interoperability in Design and Engineering Applications. *IEEE Internet Computing*, 26(6), 59–67. doi:10.1109/ MIC.2022.3212085

Jaimini, U., Zhang, T., Brikis, G. O., & Sheth, A. (2022). iMetaverseKG: Industrial Metaverse Knowledge Graph to Promote Interoperability in Design and Engineering Applications. *IEEE Internet Computing*, 26(6), 59–67. doi:10.1109/ MIC.2022.3212085

Kaur, N., Saha, S., Agarwal, V., & Gulati, S. (2023, February). Metaverse and Fintech: Pathway for Innovation and Development. In *2023 3rd International Conference on Innovative Practices in Technology and Management (ICIPTM)* (pp. 1-6). IEEE. doi: 10.1109/ICIPTM57143.2023.10117956

Kharitonova, Y. (2024). Tokenization of the Creative Industries: The Intersection Between Emerging Technologies and Sustainability. *Digital Technologies and Distributed Registries for Sustainable Development: Legal Challenges*, 59-75. doi:10.1007/978-3-031-51067-0_4

Klein, M., Neitzert, F., Hartmann-Wendels, T., & Kraus, S. (2019). Start-up financing in the digital age: A systematic review and comparison of new forms of financing. *The Journal of Entrepreneurial Finance (JEF), 21*(2), 46-98. http://hdl.handle.net/10419/264405

Kulakova, O. S. (2022). Digital Art In The Light Of Nft: Market Role And Legal Uncertainty. *Digital Lj, 3*, 36. doi:10.38044/2686-9136-2022-3-2-36-50

Kumar, S., Sureka, R., Lucey, B. M., Dowling, M., Vigne, S., & Lim, W. M. (2023). MetaMoney: Exploring the intersection of financial systems and virtual worlds. *Research in International Business and Finance, 102195*. doi:10.1016/j.ribaf.2023.102195

Lee, L. H., Braud, T., Zhou, P., Wang, L., Xu, D., Lin, Z., & Hui, P. (2021). All One Needs To Know About Metaverse: A Complete Survey On Technological Singularity, Virtual Ecosystem, And Research Agenda. *Arxiv Preprint Arxiv:2110.05352*. Doi: https://doi.org//arXiv.2110.0535 doi:10.48550

Makridakis, S., & Christodoulou, K. (2019). Blockchain: Current challenges and future prospects/applications. *Future Internet, 11*(12), 258. doi:10.3390/fi11120258

Mochram, R. A. A., Makawowor, C. T., Tanujaya, K. M., Moniaga, J. V., & Jabar, B. A. (2022, September). Systematic literature review: Blockchain security in nft ownership. In *2022 International Conference on Electrical and Information Technology (IEIT)* (pp. 302-306). IEEE. doi: 10.1109/IEIT56384.2022.9967897

Nair, V. M., & Menon, D. G. (2017). Fin Tech firms-A new challenge to Traditional Banks: A Review. *International Journal of Applied Business and Economic Research, 15*(Special Issue), 173–184.

Razi, Q., Devrani, A., Abhyankar, H., Chalapathi, G. S. S., Hassija, V., & Guizani, M. (2023). Non-fungible tokens (NFTs)-survey of current applications, evolution and future directions. *IEEE Open Journal of the Communications Society.*

Razi, Q., Devrani, A., Abhyankar, H., Chalapathi, G. S. S., Hassija, V., & Guizani, M. (2023). Non-Fungible Tokens (Nfts)-Survey Of Current Applications, Evolution And Future Directions. *IEEE Open Journal of the Communications Society*. doi:10.1109/OJCOMS.2023.3343926

Rehman, W., Zainab, H., Imran, J., & Bawany, N. Z. (2021, December). NFTs: Applications and challenges. In *2021 22nd International Arab Conference on Information Technology (ACIT)* (pp. 1-7). IEEE. doi: 10.1109/ACIT53391.2021.9677260

Savale, S. K., & Savale, V. K. (2016). Intellectual property rights (IPR). *World Journal of Pharmacy and Pharmaceutical Sciences, 5,* 2559–2592. doi:10.20959/wjpps20166-7102

Schumacher, P. (2022). The metaverse as opportunity for architecture and society: Design drivers, core competencies. *Architectural Intelligence, 1*(1), 11. PMID:35993030

Singh, A., Parizi, R. M., Zhang, Q., Choo, K. K. R., & Dehghantanha, A. (2020). Blockchain smart contracts formalization: Approaches and challenges to address vulnerabilities. *Computers & Security, 88,* 101654. doi:10.1016/j.cose.2019.101654

Singh, S., & Sisodia, H. (2023). Building Blocks for the Metaverse: Virtual Worlds, Marketplaces, and Tools. In Concepts, Technologies, Challenges, and the Future of Web 3 (pp. 198-221). IGI Global. doi:10.4018/978-1-6684-9919-1.ch011

Stamatakis, D., Kogias, D. G., Papadopoulos, P., Karkazis, P. A., & Leligou, H. C. (2024). Blockchain-Powered Gaming: Bridging Entertainment With Serious Game Objectives. *Computers, 13*(1), 14. doi:10.3390/computers13010014

Timuçin, T., & Bıroğul, S. (2023). The Evolution Of Smart Contract Platforms: A Look At Current Trends And Future Directions. *Mugla Journal Of Science And Technology, 9*(2), 46–55. doi:10.22531/muglajsci.1280985

Tomić, N., Todorović, V., & Jakšić, M. (2023). Future Tendencies of Non-fungible Tokens. *Naše gospodarstvo/Our economy, 69*(2), 60-67. oi:10.2478/ngoe-2023-0012

Truong, V. T., Le, L. B., & Niyato, D. (2023). *Blockchain meets metaverse and digital asset management: A comprehensive survey.* IEEE. doi:10.1109/ACCESS.2023.3257029

Tukur, M., Schneider, J., Househ, M., Dokoro, A. H., Ismail, U. I., Dawaki, M., & Agus, M. (2024). The metaverse digital environments: A scoping review of the techniques, technologies, and applications. *Journal of King Saud University. Computer and Information Sciences*, *101967*. doi:10.1016/j.jksuci.2024.101967

Valeonti, F., Bikakis, A., Terras, M., Speed, C., Hudson-Smith, A., & Chalkias, K. (2021). Crypto collectibles, museum funding and OpenGLAM: Challenges, opportunities and the potential of Non-Fungible Tokens (NFTs). *Applied Sciences (Basel, Switzerland)*, *11*(21), 9931. doi:10.3390/app11219931

Vidal-Tomás, D. (2022). The New Crypto Niche: Nfts, Play-To-Earn, And Metaverse Tokens. *Finance Research Letters*, *47*, 102742. doi:10.1016/j.frl.2022.102742

Zhang, G. Q., Zhang, G. Q., Yang, Q. F., Cheng, S. Q., & Zhou, T. (2008). Evolution Of The Internet And Its Cores. *New Journal of Physics*, *10*(12), 123027. doi:10.1088/1367-2630/10/12/123027

ENDNOTES

[1] Source: Cryptopreneurs NFT https://cryptopreneursnft.com/
[2] Source: Metropoly https://www.metropoly.io/
[3] Source: Pudgy Penguins https://pudgypenguins.com/

Chapter 12
The Role and Future of Metaverse in Travel Agencies

Emre Yaşar
Isparta University of Applied Sciences, Turkey

Erge Tür
Istanbul Esenyurt University, Turkey

Eda Yayla
Bitlis Eren University, Turkey

Nesrin Aydın Alakuş
ⓘ https://orcid.org/0000-0001-7263-4457
Suleyman Demirel University, Turkey

ABSTRACT

The primary objective of this study is to discern the role of the metaverse, specifically within travel agencies, and to unveil potential future trends in this context. Through an empirical approach, the research aims to contribute valuable insights into the practical implications and applications of the metaverse within travel agencies, shedding light on its evolving significance in the tourism sector. In general, it is seen that the opinions of travel agency employees about Metaverse are positive. As a result of the analysis, it was determined that Metaverse can make positive contributions to travel agency activities. It is also seen that the use of Metaverse may vary according to the profiles of the customers, but it is possible to provide a positive experience to the customers in general.

DOI: 10.4018/979-8-3693-5868-9.ch012

INTRODUCTION

Rapid and striking developments in information and communication technologies have affected many sectors and have led the tourism sector to change drastically. The digital paradigm of these developments reflected in the tourism sector is the concept of metaverse tourism after concepts such as e-tourism and smart tourism (Gretzel, 2021; Gretzel & Koo, 2021; Koo et al., 2023). The metaverse is a term coined by Neal Stephenson in his science fiction novel Snow Crash in 1992. In the perspective of that novel, the metaverse is an all-encompassing virtual world parallel to the physical world (Koo et al., 2023). On the other hand, Dwivedi et al. (2022) define the metaverse as a technology that has the potential to enhance the physical world using augmented and virtual reality technologies, allowing users to interact seamlessly in actual and simulated environments using avatars and holograms. Virtual environments and immersive games are precursors of the metaverse (Koo et al., 2023). The different transfer of reality to virtual environments explains the Metaverse.

The tourism sector is seen as a sector where metaverse applications will be used frequently, as it is a highly experiential field that requires people to search for information intensively (Dwivedi et al., 2022). Metaverse refers to exploration and participation in large, virtually shared environments that simulate immersive travel experiences through virtual avatars (Shin & Kang, 2024). Tourism products and experiences are difficult to evaluate because they are intangible. Touristic consumers seek information from different sources to experience and compare possible options (Buhalis et al., 2023). Metaverse offers travelers the opportunity to experience destinations and operations before they arrive (Buhalis et al., 2022). Metaverse tours are built on existing virtual tours that use these technologies with 360-degree or 3D modality. By facilitating simultaneous interaction with other agents and objects in a virtual destination, psychological and physiological experience is allowed through the embodiment of the avatar. Thus, travelers, i.e. touristic consumers, have the chance to get to know tourism services. Accordingly, their expectations and intentions to participate are shaped.

In the tourism sector, the metaverse empowers access to virtual resources to enhance consumer experience and destination satisfaction while physically in destinations. For example, visitors can use augmented (XR) devices to experience an ancient ceremony in an archaeological temple or a volcano eruption (Rauschnabel, 2022). On the other hand, virtual concerts, digital shopping, exhibitions are actively organized in the metaverse world (Wang et al., 2022). Metaverse tourism can also be a sustainable form of tourism that reduces environmental and ecological damages caused by excessive tourism (Go & Kang, 2023). In addition, socially vulnerable groups, such as people with disabilities or physical challenges, may consider metaverse travel as an alternative form of travel. Metaverse is important in terms of expanding the scope of tourism activities.

With the use of the Metaverse in the travel sector, consumers can benefit from the ability to try and evaluate travel alternatives comprehensively, and it can play a role in facilitating experiential consumption in tourist activities such as skydiving. Navigating the digital twin, which can replicate a destination, accommodation business, or cultural heritage site, allows users to choose the one that best suits their needs and preferences (Buhalis et al., 2023). Gürsoy et al. (2022) point out that the metaverse affects the stages of tourism experiences and consumer behavior, leading to marketing and operational strategy improvements. Moreover, people who experience destinations and tourism activities tend to be physically motivated to visit. Overall, the metaverse is likely to become an indispensable part of the tourism industry with innovative tourism experiences in the future (Gursoy et al., 2022). In particular, intensive technological developments may accelerate the level of use of the Metaverse.

Exploring the metaverse within the tourism sector is currently in its early stages (Buhalis et al., 2023). Existing research primarily centers around conceptual discussions concerning the metaverse (Go & Kang, 2023; Gursoy et al., 2022; Ko et al., 2022; Buhalis et al., 2023). Empirical studies in this domain are notably limited (Shin & Kang, 2024). Against this backdrop, the primary objective of this study is to discern the role of the metaverse, specifically within travel agencies, and to unveil potential future trends in this context. Through an empirical approach, the research aims to contribute valuable insights into the practical implications and applications of the metaverse within travel agencies, shedding light on its evolving significance in the tourism sector.

BACKGROUND

Tourism and Metaverse

The recent rebranding of Facebook to Meta has thrust the concept of the Metaverse into the spotlight, underscoring its growing significance (Bolar, 2022). The term "meta," meaning beyond, combined with "verse" in the sense of the universe, conveys the notion of going beyond the universe (Çolakoğlu et al., 2022). The Metaverse represents a technological realm that offers unique and captivating experiences within both virtual and physical environments (Buhalis et al., 2023). The Metaverse extends physical boundaries by leveraging augmented and virtual reality technologies, enabling individuals to engage in interactive experiences grounded in both virtual and real-world contexts (Dwivedi et al., 2022). With its transformative features, the

Metaverse is poised to introduce innovations and opportunities across various social domains and industries, although it also presents several challenges, particularly concerning effective business utilization (Dwivedi et al., 2023). Among the sectors expected to derive substantial benefits from the Metaverse is the tourism sector, where it contributes to resource diversification and fosters sustainable tourism practices (Goo & Kang, 2023).

Metaverse is one of the influential factors in changing the behavior patterns of individuals in the tourism sector (Gürsoy et al., 2022). Tourists can experience the hotel or destination with the Metaverse before their holiday. Thus, the experience of tourists increases and diversifies even before the holiday begins (Buhalis et al., 2022). This experience can contribute positively to tourists' purchasing behavior but also negatively impact them. If tourists are disappointed with their experiences or their expectations are not satisfied, they may not engage in purchasing behavior (Buhalis et al., 2023). The Metaverse generally helps tourists, especially before and during their holiday.

Metaverse provides tourists with the opportunity to experience destinations and places to stay before their holiday. Thus, it is possible for tourists to evaluate their holiday options comprehensively (Monaco & Sacchi, 2023). Tourists who experience holiday options with the Metaverse make purchasing decisions (Flavian et al., 2021). Because the Metaverse offers tourists the opportunity to travel virtually beyond the real world, allowing them to explore destinations more closely and experience new cultures. Similarly, Metaverse also helps tourists during their holidays. While visiting a cultural site in a destination, tourists can access information visually and audibly using Metaverse and see the cultural site in past periods (Buhalis & Karatay, 2022). Metaverse can present before and after versions of cultural sites. Tourists can experience the development of the cultural and historical site over time with Metaverse. After the holiday, tourists can help other potential tourists by sharing their experiences and knowledge.

The Metaverse is pivotal in destination promotion and marketing, becoming an essential tool for travel agencies and destinations (Volchek & Brysch, 2023). Utilizing the Metaverse, these entities can engage potential tourists by creating original and captivating digital content. Virtual reality videos, augmented reality experiences, and interactive digital tours go beyond merely offering a glimpse of an authentic holiday experience; they heighten interest in destinations (Ioannidis & Kontis, 2023). By leveraging the Metaverse, tourism destinations enhance their marketing practices, establishing a foundation for conveying a sense of trust to potential tourists. These advantages prompt significant shifts in destinations and businesses' business and management models (Koo et al., 2023). Notably, user satisfaction levels within the Metaverse, particularly in smart tourism destinations, are reported to be high (Suanpang et al., 2022). Additionally, the potential for reducing overtourism in destinations is highlighted as a tangible outcome of incorporating the Metaverse (Kouroupi & Metaxas, 2023).

Hotels can promote their services and prepare advertisements in the Metaverse. A virtual tour of the hotel can be designed for potential customers, and personalizations can be arranged according to customer profiles. Thus, the hotel is promoted, and brand awareness is strengthened (Adel, 2023). Abass and Zohry (2022) state that hotels use Metaverse technology, but customers are unaware of it. Uçgun and Şahin (2023) state that the traditional structure of the tourism sector will be affected using Metaverse. In the same study, it is explained that Metaverse has both positive and negative contributions. The positive aspects of Metaverse are that it improves sales and marketing activities, creates opportunities for disadvantaged individuals to participate in tourism activities, and creates new employment opportunities in the tourism sector. In the negative aspects of Metaverse, legal and personal concerns are emphasized (Uçgun & Şahin, 2023). Metaverse can also be used in museums. Virtual exhibitions can be created using Metaverse in museums, and visitors can experience art products differently and impressively (Wei, 2023).

Digital Transformation of Travel Agencies

The rapid pace of digitalization is ushering in significant transformations in people's lifestyles, economies, and societies. Research indicates that the momentum in the development and evolution of automation and artificial intelligence technologies is set to intensify, with projections extending until 2030 (Samaan, 2021). Concurrently, a Google Travel study highlights that 74% of travelers utilize digital media for trip planning. Consequently, these shifts are anticipated to impact consumer choices and the business models and marketing strategies embraced by various industries (Nevmerzhitskaya, 2013).

This paradigm shift is encapsulated by the concept of digital transformation, defined as the reorganization of business models and processes, coupled with increased investments in technological initiatives to generate novel value for both customers and employees (Solis, 2020). These developments underscore the inevitability of changes in business models, prompting businesses to revitalize their processes in alignment with the imperatives of digital transformation.

The World Economic Forum (2020) and Accenture (2018) highlight that the tourism sector stands out as the most rapidly and actively adapting industry to global digital transformation. This sentiment is reinforced by Buhalis and Law (2008), who, in their research investigating technology integration in tourism businesses, assert that the pace of technological adoption in the tourism sector surpasses that of other industries. Consequently, in the tourism sector, characterized by a swift and dynamic experience of digital transformation, it has become imperative for tourism businesses to incorporate digital strategies. This ensures a competitive edge and serves as a means to enhance customer satisfaction and drive revenue growth by effectively integrating digital transformation initiatives.

Travel agencies serve as a fundamental pillar in the tourism sector, comprising a complex service network deeply influenced by the ongoing wave of digital transformation. Insights derived from a digitalization survey conducted within the travel agency domain reveal that 70% of these agencies anticipate highly positive contributions to the tourism sector and business outcomes through digitalization and technological investments. Moreover, a substantial 73% of respondents stressed the indispensability of digitalization in establishing a distinctive presence in a competitive marketplace. Notably, online travel agencies allocate a significant portion, specifically 73%, of their marketing budgets to digital marketing strategies (TÜRSAB, 2019). These statistics underscore the central role played by digital transformation in shaping the trajectory of travel agencies.

The infusion of artificial intelligence and chatbots stands out as a pivotal development in enhancing personalized holiday planning and customer support throughout the travel journey. A noteworthy example is "Hello Hipmunk," a virtual travel agency leveraging calendar and email data to provide tailored recommendations. Another instance is Thomas Cook-Jem, a service previously employed by Thomas Cook, offering features such as travel planning through a Chatbot, continuous customer support during vacations, and destination-specific recommendations. Furthermore, Thomas Cook integrates customer information analysis seamlessly into its sales strategy (TÜRSAB, 2019). These illustrations illuminate the evolving landscape of travel agencies, illustrating the integration of innovative technologies to elevate both customer experiences and operational efficiency.

On the other hand, artificial intelligence chatbots such as Chat-GPT, which are used today, have become able to create travel programs according to the user's wishes. As can be seen from the examples, the artificial intelligence technology that travel agencies integrate into their business processes in digitalization enables applications such as 24/7 automatic service, personalization of services, and pricing optimization through chatbots. Pricing optimization contributes to travel agencies minimizing the uncertainty related to seasonality. In addition, travel agencies that integrate AI technology into their business processes have the benefits of increasing customer satisfaction and loyalty, achieving cost efficiency through personalized recommendations, and increasing profit rates (Demir & Demir, 2023).

The pervasive impact of digitalization across various sectors has led to a surge in research studies evaluating digital transformation within specific industries. A notable contribution in this regard comes from Perelygina et al. (2022), who delved into digital business models within the travel industry. Their study systematically and comprehensively categorized various digital business configurations within the travel sector, shedding light on a broad spectrum of value drivers. Examples of digital business models, including online travel agencies, lead generation, and online travel marketplaces, were systematically classified, and sample companies were examined. Another noteworthy study focuses on evaluating the innovation adoption process from the perspective of travel agencies. This research explores the adoption and utilization of versatile platforms by travel agencies. The study's findings reveal that travel agencies tend to adopt versatile platforms that are easy, fast, and cost-effective, allowing them to digitalize their business models seamlessly without disrupting existing routines and operations (Aamir et al., 2023). These studies contribute valuable insights into the evolving digital transformation landscape within the travel industry.

Aboushouk and Elsawy (2020) investigated how user-generated content promotes the digital transformation of Egyptian travel agencies. The results showed that user-generated digital content has a weak positive impact on the digital transformation of Egyptian travel agencies. Liyushiana et al. (2022) examined digital transformation in tourism from the perspective of travel agencies. The study's results revealed that digital transformation in travel agencies is closely related to organizational culture, technology use, and processes. Based on this result, emphasis was placed on the application of the technology-organization-environment framework in the digital transformation process. A similar study was conducted by Chang et al. (2021). The researchers studied Taiwan travel agencies to identify critical success factors in digital transformation. As a result, they used the technology-organization-environment-culture dimensions to develop the impact dimensions and factors of digital transformation and created a preliminary framework for the impact factors of digital transformation in the tourism industry.

MAIN FOCUS OF THE CHAPTER

Research Method

As can be seen in the information provided in the literature section, the Metaverse has several effects on the stakeholders of the tourism sector. It is seen that businesses in the tourism sector, such as hotels and travel agencies, can use the Metaverse as a digital resource to provide quality service, persuade customers, and promote themselves. However, there is limited research on the potential effects of Metaverse on travel agencies and their customers. This research aims to fill this research gap. This research comprehensively examines the impressions of the Metaverse from the perspective of travel agency employees and the effects of the Metaverse on travel agencies and customers.

A qualitative research methodology was employed in this research, as it was imperative to gather in-depth insights into the perspectives of travel agency employees regarding the Metaverse. The qualitative research approach comprehensively explores individuals' thoughts on a particular subject (Creswell, 2013). The chosen method for this research involved the application of a semi-structured interview technique within the qualitative framework to elicit the viewpoints of travel agency employees regarding the Metaverse. The semi-structured interview format commences with predefined questions by the researcher and unfolds organically based on the participant's responses (Brinkmann, 2014). To facilitate this process, an interview form was meticulously devised.

The interview form includes five demographic questions and eight questions to learn the participants' thoughts about the Metaverse. These questions were inspired by the studies of Buhalis et al. (2022, 2023) to understand the opinions of travel agency employees about the Metaverse. The first question was created to determine the general impressions and thoughts of the employees about the Metaverse. Three questions between 2-4 were prepared to determine the possible effects of the Metaverse on the functioning of travel agencies. Two questions between 5-6 were designed to understand the possible effects of the Metaverse on travel agency customers. Two questions between 7-8 are designed to determine the future of Metaverse in travel agencies. The questions in the interview form are as follows;

1.   How do you evaluate Metaverse in the travel industry? What are your thoughts?
2.   What are your thoughts on integrating Metaverse into business processes?
3.   How can Metaverse affect the business activities of travel agencies?
4.   How can Metaverse affect competition among travel agencies?
5.   To what extent can Metaverse offer customers an enriched travel experience?
6.   To what extent do you think customers will prefer to use Metaverse?
7.   How do you assess the future role of Metaverse in travel agencies?
8.   What would you recommend for travel agencies to use Metaverse effectively?

Sample and Data Collection

Purposive sampling was used in the research. In purposive sampling, it is essential to select participants within the scope of specific criteria for the research (Bernard, 2017). In this research, there are some criteria for choosing the participants. First of all, the participants included in the research are the employees of a travel agency that continues its activities in Antalya and has activities in many fields in Turkey. Another criterion for including these employees in the research is that they know Metaverse. The research did not include employees who have not heard of Metaverse and do not know what it is. Within these criteria, interviews were conducted with seven travel agency employees.

In the qualitative research method, there is no need to increase the number of participants when the interviews continue within an inevitable repetition, and the researcher realizes that they have reached sufficient data saturation (Miles & Huberman, 1994). Marshall (1996) states that the interviews should be completed when the participants' responses become repetitive. Creswell (2013) explains that 5-25 participants are sufficient for interviews. Based on this information, the interviews were completed with 7 participants.

The interviews were conducted between 27.12.2023-21.01.2024 at the convenience of the participants and the researcher. The interviews were completed in an average of 23 minutes. Before the interviews started, the participants were informed about the research topic. The participants who participated in the interviews participated in the research on a voluntary basis. After the interviews were completed, the recordings were transcribed.

The obtained records underwent a thematic analysis, a method in which researchers identify and code themes based on relevant literature. For this research, Braun and Clarke's (2006) approach was employed to define themes and codes. The analysis involved several steps: recognizing the data, creating initial codes to extract content, identifying recurrent themes, conducting theme checks, defining and naming the themes, finalizing the analysis, and preparing the report (Braun & Clarke, 2006). The collaborative effort of four authors was employed for data control and analysis. Two academicians, well-versed in the research subject, conducted the final verification.

Demographic characteristics of the participants are shown in Table 1. Four of the participants were male, and three were female. The age range of the participants varies between 21-28 years. Participants have undergraduate or postgraduate education. The working years of the participants vary between 3-6 years. The duration of the interview varied between 15-30 minutes.

Results

As a result of analyzing the responses obtained from the participants, four main themes were identified in the research. These main themes are general thoughts about the Metaverse, the potential impacts of the Metaverse on travel agencies, the potential impacts of the Metaverse on customers, and the future of the Metaverse in travel agencies. The main theme of general thoughts about the Metaverse includes participants' general perceptions of the Metaverse and their thoughts about its advantages or disadvantages. Table 2 shows the sub-themes and codes related to the main theme of general thoughts about Metaverse.

Table 1. Demographic characteristics of the participants

Participant	Gender	Age	Education	Working Time	Interview Time
P1	Male	26	Undergraduate	3 years	20 minutes
P2	Male	27	Postgraduate	4 years	25 minutes
P3	Female	27	Undergraduate	5 years	30 minutes
P4	Male	21	Undergraduate	3 years	23 minutes
P5	Male	27	Undergraduate	6 years	15 minutes
P6	Female	26	Postgraduate	5 years	25 minutes
P7	Female	28	Doctorate	3 years	26 minutes

Participants have a positive view of Metaverse in the travel industry. P7 emphasizes that Metaverse will be used primarily in travel agencies in the future. P7 states, *"I think that over time, Metaverse and other applications will be used in travel agencies and will make a difference."* P2 thinks that Metaverse can provide broader access to tourist destinations. P2 states, *"For example, I cannot go to the Colosseum in Italy, but thanks to Metaverse, I will be able to visit it."* P1 argues that the density in cultural areas can be reduced with Metaverse. P1 says, *"For example, we can attend a live event on the other side of the world or visit historical cultural sites from where we sit. In this case, the density in cultural areas will decrease."* It is also stated that the metaverse will make it easier to overcome travel barriers and provide prior knowledge. P4 says, *"In the future, due to the creation of cultural areas with artificial intelligence in the Metaverse, it will be possible to go and see those places. It will be much better in terms of prior knowledge."*

Table 2. General thoughts about the metaverse

Main Theme	Sub Themes	Sub Codes	
		Positive Views	Negative Views
General Thoughts About the Metaverse	Potential Advantages and Disadvantages of the Metaverse	Providing easy access to destinations	Harm local economies by reducing physical visitation
		Reducing density in cultural areas	Limited impact due to its fictional nature
		Providing the opportunity to visit cultural sites virtually	
		Providing preliminary information about destinations and cultural sites	

Table 3. The potential impacts of the metaverse on travel agencies

Main Theme	Sub Themes	Sub Codes	
		Positive Views	**Negative Views**
The Potential Impacts of the Metaverse on Travel Agencies	Metaverse Integrated Fields	Tour programs	It is difficult to integrate because of the lack of infrastructure
		Destination promotions	
		Sales and marketing processes	
	Impact of Metaverse on Business Operations	It can increase sales	It can reduce sales
		Customer convincing time may be shorter	
	Impact of the Metaverse on Competition	Agencies using Metaverse can gain a competitive advantage	-

On the other hand, negative participants expressed concern that the Metaverse could harm the local economy by reducing physical travel. P1 states, *"Reducing the density in cultural areas can be a negative situation as well as a positive one. In the negative sense, the need for personnel may be eliminated and the sense of curiosity in those regions may be lost due to the virtual visit of the locations."* In addition, those who think that the Metaverse is more of a fictional process stated that its impact will be limited and that it can only be effective at the sales stage. P5 says, *"I think it is more of a fictional process. It can be used in the future to persuade people about the places they will visit and see during the sales phase."* The participants defending this view argued that Metaverse is not open to development in the domestic market and stated that the integration of technologies such as Metaverse can be considered in the future. P6 states, *"The travel industry is a market that continues to evolve, but from what I have observed, it is not a market that is open to development, at least in the domestic market."*

The main theme of the potential impacts of the Metaverse on travel agencies describes the determination of what kind of impacts the Metaverse will have on travel agencies. The sub-themes and codes related to the main theme are shown in Table 3.

Most participants express the view that Metaverse can be seamlessly incorporated into the operations of travel agencies. P2 envisions the possibility of enhancing bookings by showcasing trailers of tour programs and introducing destinations to customers through Metaverse. P2 emphasizes, *"It should be ensured that they can preview the places they will visit through Metaverse like a trailer. If it can be integrated, their persuasiveness will increase, and an uptick in bookings will be observed."* P3, P5, and P7 propose that Metaverse can find utility in sales and marketing. P3 asserts, *"I believe it can be integrated into the sales phase. During online tours or reservations, people can be provided with an experiential preview of the places they will visit."* Conversely, P1 contends that integrating Metaverse is currently unfeasible due to the absence of the necessary infrastructure, P1, *"It can be integrated but in the future. Because I don't think our country has such an infrastructure right now."*

Participants, except P4, think that Metaverse will contribute positively to business activities in travel agencies. These positive contributions are increased sales and easier customer persuasion processes. For example, P5 argues that Metaverse will increase visualization, and this will increase sales. P5 states, *"It affects positively. Sales will increase since the places to visit, hotels, and destinations will be visually conveyed."* Similarly, P6 also thinks that sales will increase. P6 states, *"It can give the feeling of being there and the sales phase can take a shorter time. Guest persuasion rate will increase. At the same time, an increase in agency bookings will be observed."* Some participants argue that with Metaverse, customer persuasion processes will occur quickly. P2 states, *"Persuasion processes will be shorter for employees who make reservations/tour sales in the agency."*

P4 thinks that the Metaverse may negatively affect business activities. He argues that the Metaverse may badly affect one-to-one relationships and claims that an artificial environment will not affect human emotions. He even emphasizes that sales will decrease with the use of Metaverse. P4 states, *"It will affect one-to-one relationships badly because human beings are full of emotions. Interviews and trips with an artificial environment will not be effective, and this may cause a decrease in sales."*

According to the participants' standard view, travel agencies that use Metaverse will gain a competitive advantage. Using Metaverse, travel agencies can give customers a first impression, create a sense of trust, and show destinations in detail. In this way, agencies can increase customer satisfaction. P2 states, *"There will be a big difference between travel agencies that use Metaverse and those that do not. It is important to offer a first impression because we want to see and feel safe as human beings. Seeing what I am going to do attracts me there."* Especially for those who can take a limited number of vacations per year, visiting and seeing destinations through the virtual universe can help them make their vacation plans more conscious. This may attract the attention of agencies because it may contribute to more customer efficiency. P1 states, *"It creates a competitive advantage. For example, I am in Antalya and want to visit China. I can visit and see the place through the virtual universe; thus, when I go there, I can have my vacation/tour without difficulties. I can know what or what kind of image is waiting for me."* Agencies using the Metaverse can share more visual information and create appeal through effective advertising strategies. This can increase bookings and make agencies stand out from others regarding revenue and advertising. P5 states, *"Those who use it will be in a more advantageous situation*

Table 4. The potential impacts of the metaverse on customers

Main Themes	Sub Themes	Sub Codes	
		Positive Views	Negative Views
The Potential Impacts of the Metaverse on Customers	Customers' Travel Experience	Travel experience will increase	The travel experience may not change according to customers' profiles
	Customers' Use of Metaverse	Customers with knowledge about Metaverse will use	Customers in middle age and above may not use

than those who do not. Concretely, since there will be more information sharing in a visual sense, if it can be well advertised, attractiveness will be created.''

The main theme of the potential impacts of the Metaverse on customers refers to how the Metaverse can create changes in customers' expectations and preferences. The sub-themes and codes related to the main theme are shown in Table 4.

Participants suggest that the Metaverse has the potential to provide customers with a travel experience enriched with content, but they emphasize the importance of considering customer profiles. Offering up-to-date and technological expertise may lead to satisfaction, especially for newer generations. However, for individuals with extensive travel experience and specific preferences, the impact of the Metaverse may be limited. Mainly, customers with well-established preferences may not view the Metaverse positively. P6 expresses, *''I think this situation is relative. For example, I would like to visit and feel the region even if I like digital media. But some people think otherwise. But as far as I see in the agency I work for, most middle-aged people in the segment we address favor going and seeing the place on the spot.''* Similarly, P5 states, *''I can say that it can offer a partial travel experience. This issue is relative. It may vary according to customers and their preferences.''*

P2 states that Metaverse will provide customers with a good travel experience. It is emphasized that thanks to Metaverse, it is possible to experience the place to be traveled in advance and solve any problems in advance, enriching the travel experience. P2 states, *"For example, when I want to go somewhere now, only the name of the destination is known, but by seeing it through Metaverse with a 360-degree view, I will set off in a planned and programmed way, as if I had been there before I went. In other words, I will have a trip with much content. Metaverse will provide a lot of comfort to agencies and customers.''*

Participants state that those who know Metaverse or those who are curious about Metaverse are more likely to use Metaverse during their vacation. P7 says, *"I think that customers who have prior knowledge about Metaverse will use it, but it will take time for others to use it.''* Participants such as P4-P6 state that customers will use

Metaverse, but those who use it will remain a minority. P4 states, *"A certain segment will use it, and I think this segment will be in the minority. People take vacations to see, travel, and feel the places they are going to, but this will not happen in the virtual environment. For the simplest example, there is a big difference between feeling the breeze of the wind in a hotel and feeling it in artificial intelligence."*

P2 emphasizes that customers will frequently use Metaverse. P2 says, *"Let's take the orange blossom festival in Adana. I have never been there but can see the festival through Metaverse. During this screening, I will be able to visit the restaurants and markets in the areas I visited through Metaverse when I go to the location. I can do this while there, which will also affect the surrounding destinations and companies. We will not waste time because we will know the businesses in the neighborhood before we go. We will be less likely to make a mistake because we will have experienced it beforehand. Sometimes, we go to a restaurant and regret it, so we will be less likely to have problems. For this reason, I think it will be highly preferred."*

Customers' generations are also seen as influential in the use of Metaverse. P3 points out that customers who are above middle age and have certain habits will tend not to use Metaverse. P3 says, *"I think very, very few middle-aged and older customers will prefer Metaverse. It is difficult to differentiate travel preferences and the selection process for middle-aged and older customers. For example, although it is now possible to make a reservation through websites or Call Centers without going to a branch, the middle and elderly people still go on vacation by meeting with a person at the branch and choosing a hotel based on the pictures (computer) they show them."*

The main theme of the future of Metaverse in travel agencies addresses the status of Metaverse in travel agencies in the future. The sub-themes and codes related to the main theme are shown in Table 5.

Participants such as P2, P3, P5, and P7 state that Metaverse will be frequently used in travel agencies in the future. It is even claimed that with the use of Metaverse, the business models of travel agencies will change, and new departments will be created. P2 states, *"It will even change the way travel agencies do business."* P3 says, *"I can say that it is our inevitable end. Maybe we will not even be needed in the future. This may, of course, lead to unemployment. Of course, different business lines will be opened, but this will be for those who understand technology better. If it can be used in a effective way, a breakthrough can be made in the sector, and it can be popularized as one of the types of tourism."*

Metaverse's use in travel agencies will be limited in the future according to P4 and P6. P6 states, *"It can be used in sales and marketing stages. It's not my belief that it can be utilized during the operation and planning stages.* P1 believes that it's too early to make any definitive statements on the future use of Metaverse in travel agencies. P1 says, *"It would be very wrong to answer this question right now. This*

Table 5. The future of the metaverse in travel agencies

Main Themes	Sub Themes	Sub Codes	
		Positive Views	Negative Views
The Future of the Metaverse in Travel Agencies	Future Role and Use of the Metaverse	It can change business models	Metaverse usage will remain limited
		New departments can be created	
		Preferred by agencies	
	Advice to Travel Agencies about Metaverse	Metaverse team should be formed	
		Staff should be trained	-
		Planning should be done	
		Content should be kept up to date	

issue is new because Metaverse is still in the development stage and has not been integrated with tourism.''

Regarding what travel agencies need to do to use Metaverse effectively and successfully, participants emphasize the creation of a new team, training personnel, planning, and keeping Metaverse content up-to-date. P1 underscores the need for a particular team to use Metaverse. P1 says, *"A team should be formed, and there should be someone who only deals with it, updating the software and checking new locations.''* P3 believes that the staff should be trained and knowledgeable about Metaverse. P3 states, *"First, the personnel using it should be trained. P3 states. P7 suggests that agencies should first plan for the use of Metaverse and then complete staff training.''* P7 states, *"Travel agencies should first plan to use Metaverse and other artificial intelligence applications. Then staff training is important.''* P5 emphasizes that a team should deal with Metaverse, and the content should be updated. P5 says, *"The timeliness of such applications should be well controlled. Any inaccuracy means wrong information given to the customer, and this means an unsatisfied and lost customer.''*

SOLUTIONS AND RECOMMENDATIONS

While articulating their overall perspectives on Metaverse, travel agency employees delved into the advantages and disadvantages of this emerging technology. Participants highlighted that the advantages of the Metaverse include facilitating access to destinations, alleviating congestion in cultural areas, providing the opportunity for virtual visits to cultural sites, and offering preliminary information about the intended locations. On the downside, two main concerns were emphasized the Metaverse's diminishing physical visitation, leading to economic losses for local communities, and its limited impact due to its fictional nature. Despite the numerous advantages mentioned by travel agency employees, such as enhanced accessibility to destinations, virtual exploration, capacity management, and acquiring prior information about places to be visited, Tayfun et al. (2022) underscored in their study that the adoption of Metaverse technology poses potential threats. These threats encompass employment issues in the tourism industry, declining revenues, businesses struggling to adapt to technological advancements, and security vulnerabilities.

On the other hand, Demir (2022) examined Metaverse technology in terms of the hotel industry and found that this technology enables revenue growth, brand loyalty, and individual guest experience. As can be understood from these studies, Metaverse can cause an increase in revenue, but it can also cause economic loss in this field. Within the scope of this study, since travel agency employees stated that there would be a decrease in the expected revenue from tourism in the touristic region due to the reduction of travel to the touristic destination due to the Metaverse technology, it is seen that the study findings are supporting and opposing this disadvantage in the literature.

In their views on the potential effects of Metaverse technology on travel agencies, travel agency employees they were stated that Metaverse can provide a competitive advantage to travel agencies. Accordingly, it is possible that travel agencies using Metaverse technology can gain a competitive advantage over rival businesses. A similar result to this judgment was found in the study by Gursoy et al. (2023). The authors found that Metaverse technology effectively creates a sustainable competitive advantage for businesses operating in the tourism industry. Within the scope of this study, travel agency employees concluded that Metaverse can shorten the process of convincing customers and thus increase the travel agency's sales. Similarly, Ercan (2022) found that with Metaverse technology, tourism businesses generate additional revenue from virtual tours, events, and tourist product sales.

Thapa (2023) contends that Metaverse technology presents a significant opportunity for enhancing the marketing efforts of travel and hospitality businesses. Additionally, Uçgun and Şahin (2023) underscore the potential of Metaverse in elevating sales and marketing activities, indicating a substantial role for this technology in these domains. In the context of the present study, it has been observed that Metaverse provides an advantage in travel agencies' sales and marketing activities. Consequently, it can be asserted that Metaverse positively impacts travel agencies in terms of sales and profitability. Nevertheless, there are concerns about the potential adverse effects of Metaverse technology on travel agencies, particularly in the form of decreased sales.

This might be attributed to the challenges some travel agencies face in adapting to Metaverse technology in the tourism industry.

Travel agency employees stated that Metaverse will provide a travel experience in their answers regarding the potential effects of Metaverse technology on customers. A similar finding to this result obtained within the scope of the research can be found in the study conducted by Kaya et al. (2022). In their study, the authors state that Metaverse technology enriches the travel experiences of touristic consumers by offering virtual travel and virtual hotel tours. Thus, it is possible for touristic consumers using the Metaverse to travel with a virtual tour without the need for a physical visit. In addition, tourists can first experience the destination with Metaverse and then travel for a physical visit. In both cases, it can be stated that Metaverse enriches the travel experience.

Another finding in the current study is that Metaverse technology provides a travel experience, but this experience is determined by customer profiles. It is stated that especially middle-aged and older customer profiles may have difficulty using Metaverse technology. Similar to this judgment, Ağaoğlu et al. (2022) stated that the elderly population who do not have much knowledge about technology adaptation may have difficulty in using Metaverse. Travel agency employees also stated that only people who have knowledge in this field can use Metaverse technology and that middle-aged and older people will have difficulty in using this technology. For this reason, the findings of Ağaoğlu et al. (2022) and the findings of the current study are similar in this respect.

Travel agency employees mentioned Metaverse's future role and suggested that travel agencies use this technology. They stated that business models may change with the Metaverse technology, new departments may be formed, and many travel agencies may prefer this technology. Volchek and Brysch (2023) concluded that Metaverse technology and the tourism industry are conceptually compatible. From this point of view, Metaverse and tourism can become integrated. New business models and departments may emerge with the compatibility of these two concepts, as stated by travel agency employees. In addition, Buhalis et al. (2023) state that the Metaverse is a technology that will revolutionize travel and tourism management in terms of marketing in the future. Therefore, the fact that travel agency employees stated that many travel agencies would prefer Metaverse in the future within the scope of this study coincides with the judgment expressed by Buhalis et al. (2023).

Within the scope of this study, travel agency employees offered suggestions to travel agencies, stating that a Metaverse team should be formed in the businesses, staff training and planning should be given importance and virtual content should be kept up to date. Koo et al. (2023) state that tourists who experience Metaverse technology may have more realistic expectations and that the Metaverse offers new business models in a creative economy. At this point, it is essential to employ a professional Metaverse team in travel agencies, train staff, plan for further development of Metaverse, and keep Metaverse content up-to-date. Tourists may more likely be satisfied with the Metaverse experience when these efforts are fulfilled. In addition, it can be stated that as a result of all these efforts, new business departments may be created in travel agencies, which may also contribute economically to the business and employees.

Theoretical Implications

As can be understood from the information in the literature section of this study, the Metaverse has a number of effects on stakeholders operating in the tourism sector. It is noteworthy that tourism businesses such as hotels and travel agencies operating in the tourism sector can apply Metaverse technology to prioritize quality in service, to persuade touristic consumers and to use it as a digital resource in promotional activities. However, it is seen that research on the potential effects of the Metaverse on travel agencies and their customers is limited. This study aims to fill this gap in the related literature. This study provides a comprehensive overview of the impressions of Metaverse technology from the perspective of travel agency employees and the impacts of Metaverse on travel agencies and customers. The study clearly reveals the impacts of Metaverse on both travel agents and customers.

This study encompasses findings categorized under four main themes derived from the relevant literature. First and foremost, travel agency employees express their opinions on the potential advantages and disadvantages of the Metaverse. They highlight the advantages, including facilitating access to destinations, alleviating congestion in cultural areas, enabling virtual tours of cultural sites, and offering preliminary information about destinations. Conversely, they note the disadvantage of the Metaverse reducing physical visits to destinations, potentially harming local economies, and its limited impact due to its fictional nature. Secondly, travel agency employees assess the potential effects of the Metaverse on travel agencies. Within this context, they express positive views on the Metaverse's capability to showcase tour programs, promote destinations, enhance sales and marketing processes, boost sales, expedite customer persuasion, and provide a competitive advantage to agencies leveraging this technology.

The negative views expressed by travel agency employees in this section are that Metaverse is cumbersome to integrate due to a lack of infrastructure and has the potential to reduce sales. Thirdly, travel agency employees revealed the potential impacts of Metaverse on customers. In this section, travel agency employees expressed positive opinions that tourists' travel experiences would increase and that customers who know Metaverse would use this technology. The negative views of travel agency employees in the related section are that there is a possibility that travel experiences may not change according to the profiles of tourists and that middle-aged or older adults may not be successful in using Metaverse technology. Finally, the travel agency employees assessed the future of Metaverse technology in travel agencies. This section referred to the future role and use of Metaverse technology. They expressed positive views about Metaverse, stating that this technology can change business models, create new departments, and be preferred by agencies. However, they also said a negative view that the use of Metaverse may remain limited. In the related section, it is also seen that suggestions were made for the formation of a Metaverse team in travel agencies, training personnel, planning for the use of Metaverse, and keeping Metaverse content up to date.

Practical Implications

This study offers several practical contributions to the related literature. Firstly, it is seen that the sales and marketing processes are accelerated by promoting the destination to customers by showing trailers of Metaverse's tour programs. This may shorten the customer persuasion process and increase sales. Therefore, using Metaverse can be considered an essential factor for travel agencies to increase their profitability in generating revenue and earnings. Secondly, Metaverse provides a competitive advantage among travel agencies. As a result of this situation, travel agencies can get ahead of rival businesses in terms of brand and prestige through the use of Metaverse. As a result, travel agencies using Metaverse technology can be recognized in the tourism sector. Thirdly, Metaverse technology contributes to customers' travel experiences. Therefore, travel agencies operating Metaverse should enrich the content of this technology.

Successful integration of the Metaverse could position travel agencies as pioneers in the travel industry, creating awareness and establishing a distinct identity for those adepts at utilizing Metaverse technology effectively. The suggestions provided by travel agency employees highlight the importance of forming a dedicated Metaverse team, conducting training programs for employees, strategizing the proper use of Metaverse, and ensuring the continuous updating of Metaverse content. Fulfilling these conditions can significantly contribute to the success of travel agencies. These contributions encompass executing tasks correctly by employing skilled personnel in the Metaverse field, proactively identifying and addressing potential issues through robust planning, maintaining organizational excellence through trained staff, and continuously improving Metaverse technology to achieve success in the travel agency sector. The study's findings offer valuable insights for travel agencies and industry professionals, emphasizing the need for operational development and the pivotal role of Metaverse technology in this ongoing process.

FUTURE RESEARCH DIRECTIONS

The research conducted in this study employed a qualitative research method, and thus, the insights provided are based on the statements of the interviewees. Future research endeavors may explore the topic using quantitative research methods to complement and expand upon the qualitative findings. Additionally, the current study focused on travel agency employees situated in the Antalya destination. Subsequent research could enhance the breadth of findings by including employees from diverse destinations. Furthermore, this study specifically targeted travel agency employees. Future research initiatives may broaden the scope by incorporating employees from various sectors within the tourism industry. This inclusive approach could provide a more comprehensive understanding of the broader implications of Metaverse technology across different facets of the tourism sector.

CONCLUSION

Travel agencies should contemplate the incorporation of Metaverse as a determinant impacting their financial success. Utilizing Metaverse can furnish travel agencies with a competitive edge, propelling them forward within the industry. Capitalizing on the positive impacts of Metaverse technology on business operations enables swift customer persuasion and an upsurge in sales. Moreover, integrating Metaverse into sales and marketing initiatives, destination promotions, and tour programs can be a strategic approach. Implementing these strategies may empower travel agencies utilizing Metaverse to attain substantial profits in the sector and position themselves as financially successful entities.

Travel agency employees have stated that using Metaverse significantly positively affects customers. While the Metaverse can contribute to travel agencies in terms of profitability, prestige, brand, and financial success, it can also contribute to customers. These contributions are in terms of customers' travel experience and their in-depth knowledge of the Metaverse. In addition, it was found that travel agencies with Metaverse technology can change their business models and have new business departments in the future. This may enable travel agencies to use a technology that is in line with the era's requirements, and as a result, they can effectively apply Metaverse in their business activities. In addition, factors such as professionalism, training, planning, and timeliness are also seen to be important in the development of the Metaverse. These factors can be considered as the headings of suggestions for businesses by travel agency employees about Metaverse.

To provide a comprehensive evaluation, participants generally expressed positive views about the Metaverse. However, there were also negative opinions, such as concerns that Metaverse technology could negatively impact local economies by reducing physical visitation, its limited impact due to its fictional nature, challenges in integration due to infrastructure gaps, potential sales reduction, and difficulties faced by middle-aged and older individuals in adapting to this technology. There is an opportunity for travel agencies to enhance the use of Metaverse in the future and work towards ensuring accessibility for people of all age groups. For instance, recognizing the challenges middle-aged and older individuals face in using Metaverse, informative discussions or training sessions about Metaverse could be organized for this age group. Hence, in our digital age, efforts should be made to ensure that individuals from all age segments can effectively use Metaverse without encountering difficulties.

REFERENCES

Aamir, S., Atsan, N., & Khan, M. S. (2023). Going digital with multisided-platforms: Assessing the innovation adoption process from the perspectives of travel agents. *Tourism and Hospitality Research, 14673584231186535*, 14673584231186535. doi:10.1177/14673584231186535

Abass, M. N., & Zohry, M. A. F. (2022). Mixed reality drama towards metaverse technology in smart hotels: An exploratory study on Egyptian hotels evidence from guests' perspectives. *Journal of Association of Arab Universities for Tourism and Hospitality, 23*(2), 130–154. doi:10.21608/jaauth.2022.177500.1411

Aboushouk, M. A., & Elsawy, T. M. (2020). The impact of user-generated content on digital transformation of tourism and travel services: Evidence from the Egyptian travel agencies. *International Journal of Heritage. Tourism and Hospitality, 14*(3 (Special Issue)), 12–30. doi:10.21608/ijhth.2020.106168

Adel, M. (2023). The Role of Metaverse to Create an Interactive Experience for Tourists. *Journal of Association of Arab Universities for Tourism and Hospitality, 24*(1), 242–269. doi:10.21608/jaauth.2023.216690.1473

Ağaoğlu, F. O., Ekinci, L. O., & Tosun, N. (2022). Metaverse ve sağlık hizmetleri üzerine bir değerlendirme. *Erzincan Binali Yıldırım Üniversitesi İktisadi ve İdari Bilimler Fakültesi Dergisi, 4*(1), 95–102. doi:10.46482/ebyuiibfdergi.1133902

Buhalis, D., & Karatay, N. (2022). Mixed reality (MR) for generation Z in cultural heritage tourism towards metaverse. In *Information and Communication Technologies in Tourism 2022: Proceedings of the ENTER 2022 eTourism Conference,* (pp. 16-27). Springer International Publishing. 10.1007/978-3-030-94751-4_2

Buhalis, D., & Law, R. (2008). Progress in information technology and tourism management: 20 years on and 10 years after the Internet—The state of eTourism research. *Tourism Management, 29*(4), 609–623. doi:10.1016/j.tourman.2008.01.005

Buhalis, D., Leung, D., & Lin, M. (2023). Metaverse as a disruptive technology revolutionising tourism management and marketing. *Tourism Management, 97,* 104724. doi:10.1016/j.tourman.2023.104724

Buhalis, D., Lin, M. S., & Leung, D. (2022). Metaverse as a driver for customer experience and value co-creation: Implications for hospitality and tourism management and marketing. *International Journal of Contemporary Hospitality Management, 35*(2), 701–716. doi:10.1108/IJCHM-05-2022-0631

Chang, M., Gu, S., Huang, L., & Hsiao, T. Y. (2021). Constructing the Critical Success Factors in Digital Transformation for Taiwan's Travel Agencies. *Frontiers, 2*(11).

Çolakoğlu, Ü., Anış, E., Esen, Ö., & Tuncay, C. S. (2023). The evaluation of tourists' virtual reality experiences in the transition process to Metaverse. *Journal of Hospitality and Tourism Insights*. doi:10.1108/JHTI-09-2022-0426

Demir, Ç. (2022). Metaverse teknolojisinin otel sektörünün geleceğine etkileri üzerine bir inceleme. *Journal of Tourism and Gastronomy Studies, 10*(1), 542–555.

Demir, M., & Demir, Ş. Ş. (2023). Is ChatGPT the right technology for service individualization and value co-creation? evidence from the travel industry. *Journal of Travel & Tourism Marketing, 40*(5), 383–398. doi:10.1080/10548408.2023.2255884

Ercan, F. (2022). Metaverse teknolojisinin gelecekte turizm sektörüne olası etkilerini belirlemeye yönelik bir araştırma. *Anadolu Üniversitesi Sosyal Bilimler Dergisi, 22*(4), 1063–1092. doi:10.18037/ausbd.1225882

Flavián, C., Ibáñez-Sánchez, S., & Orús, C. (2021). Impacts of technological embodiment through virtual reality on potential guests' emotions and engagement. *Journal of Hospitality Marketing & Management, 30*(1), 1–20. doi:10.1080/1936 8623.2020.1770146

Go, H., & Kang, M. (2023). Metaverse tourism for sustainable tourism development: Tourism agenda 2030. *Tourism Review, 78*(2), 381–394. doi:10.1108/TR-02-2022-0102

Gretzel, U. (2021). Conceptualizing the smart tourism mindset: Fostering utopian thinking in smart tourism development. *Journal of Smart Tourism, 1*(1), 3–8. doi:10.52255/smarttourism.2021.1.1.2

Gretzel, U., & Koo, C. (2021). Smart tourism cities: A duality of place where technology supports the convergence of touristic and residential experiences. *Asia Pacific Journal of Tourism Research, 26*(4), 352–364. doi:10.1080/10941665.2021.1897636

Gursoy, D., Malodia, S., & Dhir, A. (2022). The metaverse in the hospitality and tourism industry: An overview of current trends and future research directions. *Journal of Hospitality Marketing & Management, 31*(5), 527–534. doi:10.1080/19368623.2022.2072504

Ioannidis, S., & Kontis, A. P. (2023). Metaverse for tourists and tourism destinations. *Information Technology & Tourism, 25*(4), 483–506. doi:10.1007/s40558-023-00271-y

Kaya, B., Bayar, S. B., & Meydan Uygur, S. (2022). *Is Metaverse a comfortable parallel universe for the tourism industry or a nightmare full of fear?* University of South Florida (USF) M3 Publishing.

Koo, C., Kwon, J., Chung, N., & Kim, J. (2023). Metaverse tourism: Conceptual framework and research propositions. *Current Issues in Tourism, 26*(20), 3268–3274. doi:10.1080/13683500.2022.2122781

Kouroupi, N., & Metaxas, T. (2023). Can the Metaverse and Its Associated Digital Tools and Technologies Provide an Opportunity for Destinations to Address the Vulnerability of Overtourism? *Tourism and Hospitality, 4*(2), 355–373. doi:10.3390/tourhosp4020022

Liyushiana, L., Rustanto, A. E., Ulfah, M., Akbar, R. A., & Imran, I. (2023). Digital Transformation in Tourism: Capturing the Perspective of a Travel Agency. *International Journal of Artificial Intelligence Research, 6*(1.1).

Monaco, S., & Sacchi, G. (2023). Travelling the metaverse: Potential benefits and main challenges for tourism sectors and research applications. *Sustainability (Basel), 15*(4), 3348. doi:10.3390/su15043348

Nevmerzhitskaya, J. (2013). *Scenarios of the future work of business travel agencies.* [Master's thesis, Haaga-Helia University of Applied Sciences, Helsinki, Finland].

Özdemir Uçgun, G., & Şahin, S. Z. (2023). How does Metaverse affect the tourism industry? Current practices and future forecasts. *Current Issues in Tourism,* 1–15. doi:10.1080/13683500.2023.2238111

Perelygina, M., Kucukusta, D., & Law, R. (2022). Digital business model configurations in the travel industry. *Tourism Management, 88,* 104408. doi:10.1016/j. tourman.2021.104408

Rauschnabel, P. (2022). XR in tourism marketing. In D. Buhalis D (Ed.), Encyclopedia of tourism management and marketing. Edward Elgar Publishing. doi:10.4337/9781800377486.xr.in.tourism

Samaan, D. K. (2021). Job Scenarios 2030: How the World of Work Has Changed Around the Globe. *Managing Work in the Digital Economy: Challenges, Strategies and Practices for the Next Decade,* 47-71. Springer. doi:10.1007/978-3-030-65173-2_4

Shin, H., & Kang, J. (2024). How does the metaverse travel experience influence virtual and actual travel behaviors? Focusing on the role of telepresence and avatar identification. *Journal of Hospitality and Tourism Management, 58,* 174–183. doi:10.1016/j.jhtm.2023.12.009

Suanpang, P., Niamsorn, C., Pothipassa, P., Chunhapataragul, T., Netwong, T., & Jermsittiparsert, K. (2022). Extensible metaverse implication for a smart tourism city. *Sustainability (Basel), 14*(21), 14027. doi:10.3390/su142114027

Tayfun, A., Silik, C. E., Şimşek, E., & Dülger, A. S. (2022). Metaverse: Turizm için bir fırsat mı? Yoksa bir tehdit mi? (Metaverse: An opportunity for tourism? Or is it a threat?). *Journal of Tourism and Gastronomy Studies, 10*(2), 818–836. doi:10.21325/jotags.2022.1017

Thapa, P. (2023). Metaverse and tourism industry: A conceptual proposition. *In How the Metaverse Will Reshape Business and Sustainability* (pp. 131-137). Singapore: Springer. *Nature in Singapore.* doi:10.1007/978-981-99-5126-0_12

TURSAB. (2019). *Turizm Sektörü Dijitalleşme Yol Haritası Giriş.* TURSAB. https:// www.tursab.org.tr/apps//Files/Content/ad5f3ddb-5a11-410f-9e3c-fe8b2dc4df8b.pdf

Volchek, K., & Brysch, A. (2023, January). Metaverse and tourism: From a new niche to a transformation. In *ENTER22 e-Tourism Conference* (pp. 300–311). Springer Nature Switzerland. doi:10.1007/978-3-031-25752-0_32

Wang, Y., Su, Z., Zhang, N., Xing, R., Liu, D., Luan, T. H., & Shen, X. (2022). A survey on metaverse: Fundamentals, security, and privacy. *IEEE Communications Surveys and Tutorials, 25*(1), 319–352. doi:10.1109/COMST.2022.3202047

WEF. (2020, July). *Digital Transformation: Powering the Great Reset Switzerland.* Davos Forum. http://www3.weforum.org/docs/ _Great_Reset_2020.pdf.

Wei, W. (2023). A buzzword, a phase or the next chapter for the Internet? The status and possibilities of the metaverse for tourism. *Journal of Hospitality and Tourism Insights*. doi:10.1108/JHTI-11-2022-0568

ADDITIONAL READING

Buhalis, D., Leung, D., & Lin, M. (2023). Metaverse as a disruptive technology revolutionising tourism management and marketing. *Tourism Management*, *97*, 104724. doi:10.1016/j.tourman.2023.104724

Buhalis, D., Lin, M. S., & Leung, D. (2022). Metaverse as a driver for customer experience and value co-creation: Implications for hospitality and tourism management and marketing. *International Journal of Contemporary Hospitality Management*, *35*(2), 701–716. doi:10.1108/IJCHM-05-2022-0631

KEY TERMS AND DEFINITIONS

Metaverse: The digital world beyond reality.

Travel Agency: A business that prepares and offers a comprehensive tourism product.

Chapter 13
Embarking on Virtual Journeys:
The Evolutionary Dynamics of Travel Vlogs and the Integration of Virtual Reality

Md. Tariqul Islam
ⓘ https://orcid.org/0000-0002-7367-2989
Taylor's University, Malaysia

Jeetesh Kumar
ⓘ https://orcid.org/0000-0001-9878-1228
Taylor's University, Malaysia

Siti Rahayu Hussin
Universiti Putra Malaysia, Malaysia

Foong Yee Wong
Universiti Putra Malaysia, Malaysia

ABSTRACT

A travel vlog is short for a travel video blog, which includes footage of the vlogger exploring different places, trying local foods, engaging in different activities, and interacting with the local culture. It plays a significant role in tourism by influencing and inspiring potential travellers. It is a powerful tool for promoting destinations, influencing travel decisions, and fostering a global community of adventure-seekers. Travel vlogs are commonly shared on video-sharing platforms such as YouTube and social media. This chapter delves into the evolutionary journey of travel vlogs, examining their roots in traditional word-of-mouth communication and their progression through electronic word-of-mouth (e-WoM), online consumer reviews (OCRs), and travel blogs. The chapter envisions the potential of virtual reality (VR) to redefine how travel stories are told and foster a deeper connection between creators and viewers. Finally, this study highlights the significance of travel vlogs in the tourism industry.

DOI: 10.4018/979-8-3693-5868-9.ch013

INTRODUCTION

Travel vlogs have emerged as an effective and influential medium, significantly influencing how individuals engage with and adopt travel-related content. Travel vlogs provide a dynamic platform for vloggers (creators of travel videos) to share their experiences and perceptions of various destinations as individuals get more accustomed to visual and immersive experiences (Dewantara et al., 2023). Through the integration of audio, videos, and personal narratives, travel vlogs provide viewers with an immersive experience that is distinct from typical travel blogs or reviews (He et al., 2022). These engaging videos demonstrate picturesque landscapes and tourist attractions and capture the essence of a destination's cultural encounters, local cuisines, and overall ambience. According to Dewantara et al. (2023), vloggers connect with viewers looking for authentic and genuine travel experiences by providing a personal touch to their content.

Travel vlogs have a more profound significance than an ordinary form of entertainment; they provide prospective travellers with helpful information and inspiration (He et al., 2022). Viewers may virtually travel destinations, comprehend the ins and outs of travel, and obtain an understanding of other traveller's authentic experiences. This type of user-generated content (UGC) is becoming a significant factor in determining where to go, how to get there, and how to enhance the travel experience. The increasing significance of travel vlogs in the tourism industry is important for many stakeholders. The tourism industry, content creators, marketers, and researchers benefit from a comprehensive study of travel vlogs (Xu et al., 2021). This study explores the distinctive features of travel vlogs and their impact on the hospitality and tourism industry. Travel vlogs are important for destination marketing organisations, accommodation providers, and tourism professionals as they become a popular source of travel-related information.

Moreover, virtual reality (VR) has added a new dimension to travel vlog videos. Therefore, it is important to study the evolution of travel vlogs, their importance in the tourism industry, and how VR has transformed travel vlogs. This chapter aims to provide a brief insight into the evolution of travel vlogs and the emergence of virtual reality (VR) in travel vlogs. The chapter has been developed by reviewing the literature on each heading and subheading. This chapter starts with the introduction, followed by the literature review section, where the evolution of travel vlogs will be briefly discussed. Later on, the importance of vlogs in tourism and the integration of VR with travel vlogs will be discussed. Finally, the chapter will be concluded with the discussion and conclusion sections.

LITERATURE REVIEW

Evolution of Travel Vlog

Innovative modern technologies are utilised in the hospitality and tourist industry to attract prospective consumers. Travel vlogs have emerged as a type of visual travel blog which includes information regarding tourist destinations, accommodation, cuisine, touristic activities, mode of accessibility, etc. (Peralta, 2019). Travel vlogs are perceived as more attractive than travel blogs as vlogs contain more information, including audio, video, photo, and, most importantly, real-life stories in visual mode (Cheng et al., 2020). Travel vlogs are considered a video form of online consumer review, usually generated by tourists and shared most on social media platforms. Moreover, vlogs are the updated version of word of mouth (WoM), where the consumer provides a review or share their experience regarding the products or services they have consumed (Cheng et al., 2020). In the current section, the evolution of travel vlogs will be described briefly, and how tourism word of mouth (WoM) has been transformed into travel vlogs after passing a long route.

Word of Mouth (WoM)

The term "word of mouth" can be described as the process in which information is transmitted and received face to face (Arndt, 1967). Word of Mouth is an informal communication method to convey information about goods and services among people. WoM is a type of interactive communication through face-to-face interaction; moreover, it happens free of financial motivations (Candrasari, 2020). WoM is considered a credible, accurate, and trusted communication method as those communications happen in person. In addition, consumer-generated WoM is considered more trustworthy. When making a purchase decision, customers like to perceive word of mouth as a more effective than usual way of marketing and promotion. Generally, WoM communication occurs within a close, trusting relationship between friends and family members, significantly reducing perceived risks and uncertainty (Talwar et al., 2021). This is because consumers discuss their self-experiences and are not motivated to provide false information. Katz et al. (2017) explored interpersonal influence and explained how information and impact are transferred between people within social systems. The previous scholars demonstrated that word of mouth is one of human history's most potent information-sharing modes.

In the current study, Word-of-mouth has been investigated from the point of view of a tourist. Moore (2020) examined the importance of the sender-receiver relationship by examining the effect of WoM on the receiver's purchasing choices. WoM significantly influences recipients when actively seeking information. Furthermore, past research has found that individual information sources, such as word of mouth (WoM), are perceived as the lowest controversial sources of marketing information. WoM is considered more persuading and trustworthy than information from commercial sources. With the new advancements in technology and the wide accessibility of the internet, word of mouth (WoM) has transformed into electronic word of mouth (e-WOM), which is transmitted over the Online platform with the help of the internet. Researchers have argued that consumer-generated e-WOM is more significant and influential in the tourism industry than traditional WoM (Tran & Strutton, 2020). E-WoM expands the range of options available to customers while seeking information about products or services. Moreover, e-WOM is more effective as it is more associated and connected with consumer purchase behaviour.

WoM to e-WoM

Hennig-Thurau et al. (2004) describe electronic word of mouth (e-WoM) as "any good or negative comment made by prospective, existing, or past consumers regarding any specific product or service or organisation that is accessible to a large number of people and organisations through the internet". E-WoM is the informal communication between consumers through Internet-based technologies, which indicates the qualities of specific products and services. Individuals can utilise the internet to explore different online platforms and obtain information shared by others. The fastest growth of Internet technology during the 1990s resulted in the emergence of a unique form of WoM known as e-WoM. Communication is a message-transferring activity between two or more persons to elicit a response. The concept of e-WoM was initially studied in relationship marketing to discuss the challenges and possibilities for business development with the growth of online customers. The internet enables new communication methods among consumers who have not previously connected. E-WoM consists of positive or negative reviews and feedback from potential, existing, or past customers. It is an excellent method of acquiring such information, thereby minimising the decision-making process (Kim & Hwang, 2022). E-WoM is gaining popularity and being used more extensively by consumers. It has been developed as one of the significant information sources on products and services as consumers recognise its abundance of information. It is one of the reasons why the majority of offline decisions are based on the information obtained from online.

Moreover, e-WoM is disseminated on online review sites, providing individuals with an open forum to discuss their thoughts and experiences. Additionally, electronic word-of-mouth (e-WoM) can take place on several platforms, enabling customers to assess, evaluate, and share their opinions on any product on review sites, discussion forums, bulletin board systems, and social networking platforms (Nilashi et al., 2021). E-WoM is rapidly becoming a more popular information resource for customers and marketers. Customers place greater importance on information obtained from online sources than they do from marketers' websites. Because they believe that E-WoM sources provide more accurate information than traditional sources, consumers prefer to get information about products and services from these sources. Nevertheless, Ngarmwongnoi et al. (2020) further asserted that the outcomes apply to individuals inquiring about products and services or interested in acquiring further knowledge regarding stated products and services.

E-WoM provides several benefits over traditional WoM for both customers and marketers. A broader range of information sources, such as reviews, ratings, and user recommendations, are available to customers through e-WoM. They may receive more in-depth and unbiased information about products and services. e-WoM makes it convenient for marketers to monitor and analyse customer feedback and enables them to respond and resolve any problems or complaints promptly. Moreover, as e-WoM has the potential to become viral and generate significant involvement on social media platforms, it can reach a larger audience and make an even more significant impact. According to Vergura et al. (2021), e-WoM is a crucial information source for academics and industry professionals. E-WoM may reach a larger audience than traditional WoM through social media, blogs, and online forums. This facilitates the dissemination of favourable reviews and fosters the development of a good reputation for scholarly work, products, or services. Moreover, e-WoM gives entrepreneurs insightful information for customer insights and market research, allowing them to customise their products according to customer requirements. E-WoM promotes and expands businesses more efficiently and effectively than traditional methods, making it an indispensable instrument for success in the current digital age.

E-WoM to Online Consumer Reviews (OCRs)

Online consumer reviews (OCRs) are a kind of e-WOM. Based on the review providers' point of view, OCRs can be either positive or negative. Huseynov (2020) defined OCRs as "the peer-generated product assessments posted on organisations' or third-party websites or platforms." In addition, OCRs can be described as exchanging personal views, suggestions, and customer complaints about products, services, and brands. OCRs assist the consumer in making buying choices by providing past consumers' opinions and experiences. Broad reviews and recommendations posted by the consumer provide the review readers with more valuable information.

Houser and Wooders (2006) stated that consumers carefully seek information and online feedback shared by others while determining purchase choices. Indeed, when customers cannot physically evaluate a product or service, they often depend on online consumer reviews (OCRs). The prior study has found that OCRs are a subcategory of e-WoM, and it is more highly accessible than e-WoM as they are often uploaded on commercial or retailer sites without restriction. In contrast, social networking platforms like Facebook control who access the information, and only Facebook friends can access the information shared. OCRs provide two functions in social influence: they serve as informants and recommenders to consumers (Elwalda & Lu, 2016).

Customers put a higher value on reviews from previous customers who have experienced that product or service rather than the random reviewers, as they consider the anonymous customers' feedback to be unbiased, and those are not part of the company's marketing strategy. In addition, OCRs do not necessitate a substantial marketing budget. OCRs are a significant marketing mix component that provides free marketing assistance. OCRs have already been established as an important source of information for consumer purchase and consumption (Siddiqui et al., 2021). The number of customers who depend on online reviews to evaluate products and services before purchasing has been increasing rapidly in recent years because of the noticeable growth in the popularity of review platforms (Lin et al., 2018). Online reviews are uncertain, and customers must deal with this uncertainty because services are intangible. Therefore, customers rely on third-party reviews to ascertain their degree of confidence. OCRs have motivated academics to study in this field as it is a significant type of E-WoM. Numerous previous studies have explored the influence of OCRs on consumer decision-making (Fox et al., 2018; Hernandez-Ortega, 2019).

Elwalda et al. (2016) investigated the perceived information qualities of OCRs and found that they had a beneficial effect on developing trust and purchasing intentions. Consumers conduct information searches on the search engine to get the information that they are looking for. At the start of the internet era, online discussion forums facilitated customer interaction. Blogs have been established over time. Consumers can make a blog regarding their experiences and make them accessible for others to read. Social media has become a trendy platform for sharing consumer reviews. Challa et al. (2021) described social media as a web-based app developed based on the concept and technical underpinnings of Web 2.0 and enables its users to interact with each other and share User-Generated Content. Previously, researchers examined consumer behaviour using a variety of social media platforms, including discussion forums (Dwityas & Briandana, 2017), blogs (Yilmaz, 2020), and consumer review websites (Erkan & Evans, 2018). Online consumer reviews have replaced electronic word-of-mouth (e-WoM), significantly impacting customers and marketers. Nowadays, customers can access many product and service reviews from other customers, offering insightful information to help with decision-making.

Online reviews also allow marketers to interact directly with consumers, resolve problems, and foster brand loyalty by generating positive feedback. The e-WoM transformations have improved market transparency to the advantage of both advertisers and customers.

Online Reviews in the Tourism Industry

Consumers can now exchange information with each other due to the advancement in Information technology. Travelers frequently utilise Web 2.0 applications to gather information before or during their trips. Social media has been considered an effective information exchange platform that enables consumers to attach and communicate. OCRs are attractive sites that fascinate tourists and impact their travel planning procedures. Consumer review platforms named TripAdvisor are the most popular social media platforms for getting information about travel and tourism (Casado-Díaz et al., 2020).

Internet websites assist in advertising tourist items and contacting prospective consumers without geographical constraints. The primary objective of OCRs, particularly online travel websites, is to promote and provide information regarding alternate options to customers. Alhemimah (2019) described OCRs in the context of the travel industry as the travel information regarding a destination that is provided either directly or indirectly based on previous experience. Information is presented to justify the perception based on prior travel experiences. Tour information and personal travel experience can shape potential tourists' perceptions.

Tourists' recommendations have long been recognised as highly significant in the travel industry. On the other hand, consumers prefer to read and discuss with their peers regarding trip experiences rather than receive feedback from travel service providers. Numerous studies mentioned that OCRs on travel websites assist customers in making decisions by offering additional information (Chan et al., 2017; Lee et al., 2021). As a result, OCRs have developed into a valuable source of information for tourists and significantly impact their tour plans. The previous literature in the hospitality industry has focused on the influence of OCRs on consumers' attitudes toward accommodation and tourist destinations (Chakraborty & Biswal, 2020) and consumer decision-making (Bigne et al., 2020). Additionally, several researchers have examined the influence of OCRs on travel decision-making (Filieri et al., 2021; Mariani et al., 2019). For example, Zhu et al. (2020) stated that hotels with high ratings are more trustworthy. Several studies have examined OCRs in the tourism sector to identify, search, tour planning, and purchasing choices. Mauri and Minazzi (2013) examined the impact of OCRs on consumer purchasing intentions in tourism. They found that more than 75% of respondents considered the previous ratings and reviews before reserving a hotel room. According to Gretzel et al. (2007), OCRs are essential when customers browse travel websites to gather information and evaluate various options throughout the planning stage. 92.3 per cent of respondents used travel review websites like Lonely Planet and TripAdvisor when planning vacations.

Consumers and marketers acknowledge online reviews' growing importance in the hospitality and tourism industry. Online reviews provide travellers with insightful information and helpful advice from other travellers, assisting them in making decisions about where to stay, where to dine, and what activities to engage in. In addition, these reviews allow travellers to discuss their experiences and advise future travellers. Online reviews provide helpful feedback and insights marketers can utilise to enhance their goods and services. They also present chances for consumer interaction and brand loyalty building. Positive reviews can boost a business's exposure and trustworthiness, increasing financial status and bookings. Furthermore, as OCRs are economical and strategic marketing tools, travel agencies must keep an eye on, respond to, and comprehend OCRs' impact when they want to grow.

Travel Blog in Tourism

Travel blogs are a platform where individuals share and discuss their upcoming, present, or previous travel in written form, sometimes including photos (Xu & Zhang, 2021). Travel blogs can be considered as the internet version of personal diaries, consisting of one or more posts related to a similar theme (for example, a travel itinerary or the purchasing of a round-the-world ticket). The most popular travel blog platforms include travelblog.org, travelpod.com, blog.realtravel.com, yourtraveljournal.com, and travelpost.com (Martins & Costa, 2022). Numerous travel blogs were also seen to be affiliated with the digital and virtual travel community, e.g., realtravel.com, igougo.com, travelpod.com, and virtualtourist.com. Tripadvisor. com, holidaycheck.com, and cosmotourist.de are also renowned as specialised travel review platforms (Li et al., 2019). Renowned travel guides such as lonelyplanet. com, community.roughguides.com, and frommers.com allow tourists to share their travel stories (Wu & Pearce, 2016). Travel-related blogs can also be shared on a diary-style platform like livejournal.com or bloggerspot.com.

The most prominent type of blog in tourism is written by travellers who share their experiences and online feedback in the form of trip diaries or product reviews (Oliveira et al., 2020). The main stories in travel blogs are based on the weather, food, accessibility, and attractions of any region or country. Travel blogs often focus on particular topics such as accommodation, dining, and quality of service (Zadeh et al., 2021). Tourists consider travel blogs as archives of their trip experiences. Blogs are detailed descriptions that include information about numerous tourists' experiences and share important information with the blog reader. Naipeng et al. (2021) indicated the importance of posted pictures in assisting visitors' post-travel remembering and recall of prior experiences. Blogs may also be regarded as something for tourists to remember after returning.

Previous studies emphasised the importance of using blogs for management and marketing (Xu & Zhang, 2021). Most of the research offered empirical support for using travel blogs as sources of information for destination marketing organisations to understand better visitors' attitudes, behaviours, and engagements within a particular destination. In addition, travel blogs have gained importance among tourists in making decisions about where to go and developing perceptions about the locations they intend to go. Ali and Anwar (2021) stated that blogs have transformed the way of communication among consumers with each other. A blog story can influence many prospective tourists and develop an image of any particular destination in their imaginations.

Travel blogs are essential to the tourism sector since they provide several benefits. It gives travellers the information they need to thoroughly learn about destinations, accommodation options, dining options, and activities before making reservations. Travel blogs help them make well-informed decisions and enjoy their trip better. Furthermore, travel blogs provide genuine and distinctive viewpoints, frequently from locals or experienced travellers, which might motivate and enthral prospective visitors. Moreover, travel blogs give organisations in the tourism industry a platform to advertise their goods and draw in prospective consumers through sponsored content and partnerships. Travel blogs are an efficient way of online advertisements and are considered more effective in interpreting advertising messages, significantly influencing the tourists' purchase intention of travel products (Choi & Lee, 2021). Several authors identified the value of travel blogs for brand and promotion management and research (Chang et al., 2021; Maggiore et al., 2022). Moreover, the benefits of blogging are consumer profiling, customer acquisition, customer engagement, brand awareness, brand reinforcement, reputation management, and customer service.

Travel Vlog in Tourism

The term "vlog" is a very recent term that is formed with the words "video" and "blog" (Wang & Chang, 2020). Travel vlogs integrate components of travel videos and blogs, emphasising video creators' attributes and the engagement of the viewers and audience. Existing literature indicated that travel videos have a significant role in consumers' decision-making procedures and more than sixty per cent of individuals like to watch travel videos before planning a tour, and more than a third of passengers narrow down their options after watching relevant travel videos online (Cheng et al., 2020). The "vloggers," "influencers," or "microcelebrities" can generate revenue by making travel vlogs, as travel vlog videos are perceived as the most popular form of travel video that people watch on YouTube or any social media (Mohanty et al., 2022). Prior research has investigated the influence of microcelebrity endorsement on customers' hotel booking intentions (Zhang et al., 2019). Due to the tremendous promotional opportunities, travel vlogs have acquired great interest from hospitality and tourism stakeholders.

Recently, researchers began to explore the impact of travel vlogs on individuals' decision-making while planning tours. For example, Le and Hancer (2021) performed qualitative research to evaluate how travel vlogs influenced viewers and found that travel vlogs deliver beneficial information, significantly promoting viewers' travel intention. Online travel videos inspire viewers' imagination and help in viewers' trip planning by sharing videos and information exchange. As travel vlogs are a kind of travel video, the empirical results of travel videos can yield insights into travel vlogs. As a result, the conclusion that informative and appealing travel vlogs can assist viewers in their decision-making procedure can be drawn. Travel vlogs are very different from other types of videos or programs, such as TV shows, because they have interesting and quality content and are easy to share (Cheng et al., 2020).

Visitors are transformed from inexperienced to experienced regarding the destinations in terms of destination selection by watching promotional videos. Moreover, the languages used in the videos can also create a significant difference. Multilingual travel vlogs assist in advertising the destination and native culture and making the foreigners understand. Zhumadilova (2016) also demonstrates that travel vlogs regarding any destination influence viewers' attitudes, perceptions, cognitive images, and buying behaviours toward that destination. People are inclined to watch and believe the travel vlogs and want to visit those places and experience the services recommended in the travel vlog. Trinh and Nguyen (2019) found that the travel vlog's information usefulness, credibility, and source originality significantly positively impact the prospective tourist. In contrast, official promotional videos significantly improve destination image. Moreover, travel vlogs can effectively enhance the perceived destination image. A video blog is a type of user-generated content (UGC) that combines storytelling with audio. The travel vlog-sharing platforms can be corporate or personal websites, but those are generally virtual content communities, especially YouTube.

Regarding content, vlogs are like text blogs but with videos. Vloggers present their surroundings, describe the scenario, review products, and convey their perceptions in travel vlogs. Travel vlogs have been considered influential in promoting tourism and destinations. Firstly, People who watch vlogs can gain knowledge more efficiently and simply than people who read conventional text blogs because of their multisensory characteristics and simple information presentation method (Trinh & Nguyen, 2019). While body language, facial expression, and language are provided in the vlog for viewing, the viewer can utilise these for a better understanding. Secondly, vlogging is very effective for generating travel ideas and planning (Liang & Gössling, 2020). Travel vlogs are the most popular videos to connect with on YouTube. Each month, YouTube receives 100 million searches for seeking travel information, receiving four times more social engagement than other forms of tourist video (Mowat, 2017). Thirdly, vlogs transmit emotions and experiences better than different reviews (Huertas, 2018). Vlogs can evoke emotions, stimulate attitudes, and increase viewers' desire to visit the presented. Finally, travel vlogs are user-generated content (UGCs) that show actual tourist experiences while maintaining a high standard of quality and originality. Moreover, travel vlog videos are more credible than videos generated by marketers. In addition, independent videos are more successful than commercial videos in grabbing viewers' attention (Zhumadilova, 2016). Travel vlog videos have grown in popularity recently, greatly influencing travellers' decisions on where to go. Offering genuine, motivating, and instructive insights into the tourist locations travellers visit significantly influences their choice of destinations. They are essential for destinations to market themselves to prospective tourists since they foster trust and impact viewers' decisions.

Elevating Travel Vlogs through Virtual Reality

Combining advanced virtual reality (VR) technology with conventional travel vlogs provides new narrative and audience engagement opportunities in the constantly evolving content creation arena (Bilgihan & Ricci, 2023). Content creators can transform viewers from observers to active participants in their travel experiences by utilising VR's immersive qualities. Using 360-degree videos is one of the most effective methods to incorporate virtual reality into a travel vlog. 360-degree videos give viewers complete control over their perspective by capturing their surroundings (Vettehen et al., 2019). With the audience at the centre of the journey, this immersive experience allows them to explore landscapes, historical places, and colourful cultures as if they were there. To do this, creators can use specialised 360-degree cameras, simultaneously capturing footage in all directions (Vettehen et al., 2019). Viewers can swivel and pan to experience the entire world from all angles, whether traversing historic monuments, strolling through crowded marketplaces, or hiking lovely trails.

Moreover, adding specialised VR experiences to conventional travel vlogs enhances immersion. Virtual reality (VR) experiences can encompass anything from guided tours to moment recreations, giving users an intense sensation of presence. VR headsets are helpful for content creators who want to immerse their audience in a virtual environment. This makes travel material engaging and unforgettable (Rahimizhian et al., 2020). This sensation becomes an experience through virtual reality, going beyond mere visuals. Virtual reality (VR) provides a potent narrative tool to travel vloggers, enabling them to portray a destination's appearance and sensation

(Bilgihan & Ricci, 2023). VR video platforms like YouTube VR or specialised virtual reality applications are excellent ways to share these immersive experiences. Using virtual reality headsets, viewers may immerse themselves in these virtual worlds, strengthening their bond with the individuals who created them and their content.

A coherent viewer experience requires a smooth transition between traditional and virtual reality content. Start the trip with a typical travel vlog that provides information about the location, shares personal thoughts, and develops a story. Viewers can immerse themselves in the virtual world as the story effortlessly flows into VR portions. This dynamic strategy considers different audiences' preferences while maintaining the storytelling's interest. Virtual reality storytelling improves travel vlogs to a level that has never been achieved before. Creators can transcend geographical borders by using immersive 360-degree videos and customised VR experiences, which bring viewers closer to the destinations and develop a stronger relationship with the content (Ranieri et al., 2022). The integration of virtual reality and travel vlogging has the potential to transform how we experience and share our journeys completely.

The Importance of Travel Vlogs in Tourism

Travel vlogs are an essential part of the tourism industry since they are an effective way to enlighten, motivate, and interact with prospective tourists (Xu et al., 2021). Travel vlogs offer a visual and engaging experience beyond typical textual information. Viewers can see destinations, landmarks, and activities firsthand, making imagining themselves in those places more straightforward. Travel vlogs are also helpful for discovering new places, and viewers can gain information about regional traditions, customs, and experiences, which inspires people to go beyond the usual tourist destinations (He et al., 2022). Vloggers provide a more genuine and appealing view by frequently sharing personal experiences. By adding a personal touch, the vlogger builds a stronger emotional bond with his or her audience, increasing the viewers' trust and confidence when making travel plans.

Vlogs also provide helpful information that can assist with planning, such as recommendations on accommodation, transportation, and proposed itineraries (Dewantara et al., 2023). Because of this, travel vlogs are an excellent tool for those who want guidance on organising their trips. Travel vlogs may adapt to new platforms and formats, such as virtual and augmented reality, due to the advancement of technology advances. Due to their adaptability, travel vlogs maintain their significance and ability to captivate audiences in the dynamic digital media environment. Travel trends can be significantly influenced by the recommendations of successful travel vloggers, who frequently have a substantial following (He et al., 2022). Popular vlogs may generate greater interest in and visitation towards the accommodations, destinations, and activities they feature.

In addition, travel agencies, lodging facilities, and other travel-related organisations recognise the promotional benefits of collaborating with travel vloggers (Gholamhosseinzadeh, 2023). Expanding an organisation's prospective consumers and audience can enhance brand exposure through strategic collaborations. Additionally, vloggers have the chance to advance ethical and sustainable tourism practices. They can stimulate the adoption and recognition of sustainable tourism practises by emphasising environmentally friendly accommodations, conservation initiatives, and ethical travel behaviour. According to Gholamhosseinzadeh (2023), viewers frequently interact with travel vlogs by commenting, asking queries, and sharing their experiences. This content created by users fosters a feeling of community and gives the vlogger and prospective tourists more information. By highlighting the variety of people, customs, and ways of life throughout the world, travel vlogs promote cultural exchange. This exposure improves one's appreciation and comprehension of various cultures, encouraging a more friendly and receptive perspective on travel. Travel vlogs are a powerful and dynamic resource for the tourism industry. They provide a captivating fusion of information, inspiration, and interpersonal relationships that motivate and guide tourists in exploring the world.

DISCUSSION

With the dynamic character of information dissemination in the tourism sector, travel-related content has evolved from traditional word-of-mouth (WoM) to online consumer reviews (OCRs), travel blogs, and travel vlogs. Due to the extensive use of the internet and technological advances, there has been a significant evolution from conventional word-of-mouth (WoM) to electronic word-of-mouth (E-WoM). E-WoM enables users access to a wider variety of information sources and accelerates the sharing of ratings and reviews. OCRs are becoming essential to decision-making in the hospitality and travel industries. They provide insightful opinions from other travellers, enabling individuals to make well-informed decisions on accommodation, transportation, and travel locations. OCRs also give individuals a platform to discuss their experiences, promoting more market transparency. Travel plans are influenced by OCRs, which also influence travellers' attitudes. The information shared on these platforms significantly impacts individuals' confidence and decision-making, frequently based on personal experiences.

Travel blogs give detailed information on destinations, lodging options, and activities with written descriptions of the writer's travel experiences. They are useful for individuals seeking reliable and comprehensive information regarding numerous travel-related topics. The most recent advancement in the sharing of travel experiences is travel vlogs. With the popularity of video content growing, vlogs provide a multisensory experience that allows viewers to interact more deeply with the destination. Since travel vlogs are so popular, influencers have more significant opportunities to generate revenue from their content. Studies revealed that travel vlogs have a significant influence on viewers' decision-making. Vlogs are effective and appealing methods for disseminating information, generating travel ideas, and stimulating individuals' behaviour. Vlogs effectively influence perceptions and desire to visit a particular destination due to their authenticity and user-generated content. The study provides several implications. Destination managers and content creators can utilize VR technology in travel vlogs, which will improve the connection between viewers and vloggers. Moreover, the government can take the initiative to educate travel-related content creators on emerging technology, such as VR, to enhance the quality of their videos. The authorities should pay more concentration to privacy, standards, and guidelines to utilize VR technology in an ethical way.

CONCLUSION

The evolution of travel vlogs from traditional word-of-mouth to their present form has been characterised by persistent innovation and adaptability to technological improvements. Consumers today can access various information sources, each providing a distinct perspective on travel experiences. Online platforms influencing consumer behaviour and decision-making, such as travel blogs, travel vlogs, and OCRs, have become essential components of the tourism industry. Mainly, travel vlogs' multimodal form provides an immersive experience that goes beyond what can be achieved with standard text-based content. Travel service providers can benefit from monitoring and engaging with online reviews, collaborating with travel bloggers, and exploring partnerships with influential travel vloggers. The evolution of travel-related content reflects the growing importance of user-generated and multimedia-rich information in the tourism industry. Navigating this dynamic landscape requires a nuanced understanding of consumer preferences, technological trends, and the evolving role of influencers in shaping travel experiences. Future studies can be conducted to identify the level of satisfaction and engagement or challenges with VR from the perspective of both viewers and content creators. Moreover, future studies can focus on the issues of trust and authenticity of VR-integrated travel vlog videos.

REFERENCES

Alhemimah, A. (2019). *The Influence of Online Reviews on Saudi Consumers' Tourism Destination Choices* [Thesis, University of Plymouth]. https://pearl. plymouth.ac.uk/handle/10026.1/15206

Ali, B. J., & Anwar, G. (2021). Marketing Strategy: Pricing strategies and its influence on consumer purchasing decision. *International Journal of Rural Development. Environment and Health Research, 5*(2), 26–39. doi:10.22161/ijreh.5.2.4

Arndt, J. (1967). *Word of mouth advertising: A review of the literature.* Advertising Research Foundation.

Bigne, E., Chatzipanagiotou, K., & Ruiz, C. (2020). Pictorial content, sequence of conflicting online reviews and consumer decision-making: The stimulus-organism-response model revisited. *Journal of Business Research, 115*, 403–416. doi:10.1016/j. jbusres.2019.11.031

Bilgihan, A., & Ricci, P. (2023). The new era of hotel marketing: Integrating cutting-edge technologies with core marketing principles. *Journal of Hospitality and Tourism Technology.* doi:10.1108/JHTT-04-2023-0095

Candrasari, Y. (2020). Mediated Interpersonal Communication: A New Way of Social Interaction in the Digital Age. *Proceedings of the 2nd International Media Conference 2019 (IMC 2019).* IEEE. 10.2991/assehr.k.200325.041

Casado-Díaz, A. B., Andreu, L., Beckmann, S. C., & Miller, C. (2020). Negative online reviews and webcare strategies in social media: Effects on hotel attitude and booking intentions. *Current Issues in Tourism, 23*(4), 418–422. doi:10.1080/1368 3500.2018.1546675

Chakraborty, U., & Biswal, S. K. (2020). Impact of Online Reviews on Consumer's Hotel Booking Intentions: Does Brand Image Mediate? *Journal of Promotion Management, 26*(7), 943–963. doi:10.1080/10496491.2020.1746465

Challa, V. N. S. K., Padmalatha, P., & Burra, V. K. (2021). Influence of Relationship Marketing Variables on Social Media Marketing. *Empirical Economics Letters, 20*(4), 241249. https://www.researchgate.net/publication/357516260

Chan, I. C. C., Lam, L. W., Chow, C. W. C., Fong, L. H. N., & Law, R. (2017). The effect of online reviews on hotel booking intention: The role of reader-reviewer similarity. *International Journal of Hospitality Management, 66*, 54–65. doi:10.1016/j. ijhm.2017.06.007

Chang, W., Chao, R.-F., & Chien, G. (2021). Impacts of Online Social Support and Perceived Value in Influential Travel Blogs. *International Journal of Research in Business and Social Science (2147- 4478)*, *10*(4), 339–348. doi:10.20525/ijrbs.v10i4.1190

Cheng, W., Tian, R., & Chiu, D. K. (2023). Travel vlogs influencing tourist decisions: Information preferences and gender differences. *Aslib Journal of Information Management*. doi:10.1108/AJIM-05-2022-0261

Cheng, Y., Wei, W., & Zhang, L. (2020). Seeing destinations through vlogs: Implications for leveraging customer engagement behavior to increase travel intention. *International Journal of Contemporary Hospitality Management*, *32*(10), 3227–3248. doi:10.1108/IJCHM-04-2020-0319

Choi, H.-Y., & Lee, Y. K. (2021). View of The Influence of Travel Blog Quality on User Satisfaction and Intention to Revisit. *NVEO - Natural Volatiles & Essential Oils*, *8*(4), 848–861. https://www.nveo.org/index.php/journal/article/view/225/202

Dewantara, M. H., Gardiner, S., & Jin, X. (2023). Travel vlog ecosystem in tourism digital marketing evolution: A narrative literature review. *Current Issues in Tourism*, *26*(19), 3125–3139. doi:10.1080/13683500.2022.2136568

Dwityas, N. A., & Briandana, R. (2017). Social Media in Travel Decision Making Process. *International Journal of Humanities and Social Science*, *7*(7). https://www.researchgate.net/publication/322749479

Elwalda, A., & Lu, K. (2016). The impact of online customer reviews (OCRs) on customers' purchase decisions: An exploration of the main dimensions of OCRs. *Journal of Customer Behaviour*, *15*(2), 123–152. doi:10.1362/147539216X14594362873695

Elwalda, A., Lü, K., & Ali, M. (2016). Perceived derived attributes of online customer reviews. *Computers in Human Behavior*, *56*, 306–319. doi:10.1016/j.chb.2015.11.051

Erkan, I., & Evans, C. (2018). Social media or shopping websites? The influence of eWOM on consumers' online purchase intentions. *Journal of Marketing Communications*, *24*(6), 617–632. doi:10.1080/13527266.2016.1184706

Filieri, R., Lin, Z., Pino, G., Alguezaui, S., & Inversini, A. (2021). The role of visual cues in eWOM on consumers' behavioral intention and decisions. *Journal of Business Research*, *135*, 663–675. doi:10.1016/j.jbusres.2021.06.055

Fox, A. K., Deitz, G. D., Royne, M. B., & Fox, J. D. (2018). The face of contagion: Consumer response to service failure depiction in online reviews. *European Journal of Marketing, 52*(1–2), 39–65. doi:10.1108/EJM-12-2016-0887

Gholamhosseinzadeh, M. S. (2023). Theorising vloggers' approaches and practices in travel vlog production through grounded theory. *Journal of Hospitality Marketing & Management, 32*(2), 196–223. doi:10.1080/19368623.2023.2164392

Gretzel, U., Yoo, K. H., & Purifoy, M. (2007). *Online travel review study: Role and impact of online travel reviews.*

He, J., Xu, D., & Chen, T. (2022). Travel vlogging practice and its impacts on tourist experiences. *Current Issues in Tourism, 25*(15), 2518–2533. doi:10.1080/136835 00.2021.1971166

Hennig-Thurau, T., Gwinner, K. P., Walsh, G., & Gremler, D. D. (2004). Electronic word-of-mouth via consumer-opinion platforms: What motivates consumers to articulate themselves on the internet? *Journal of Interactive Marketing, 18*(1), 38–52. doi:10.1002/dir.10073

Hernandez-Ortega, B. (2019). Not so positive, please!: Effects of online consumer reviews on evaluations during the decision-making process. *Internet Research, 29*(4), 606–637. doi:10.1108/INTR-07-2017-0257

Houser, D., & Wooders, J. (2006). Reputation in auctions: Theory, and evidence from eBay. *Journal of Economics & Management Strategy, 15*(2), 353–369. doi:10.1111/j.1530-9134.2006.00103.x

Huertas, A. (2018). How live videos and stories in social media influence tourist opinions and behaviour. *Information Technology & Tourism, 19*(1), 1–28. doi:10.1007/s40558-018-0112-0

Huseynov, F., & Dhahak, K. (2020). The Impact of Online Consumer Reviews (OCR) on Online Consumers Purchase Intention. *Journal of Business Research - Turk, 12*(2), 990–1005. doi:10.20491/isarder.2020.889

Katz, E., Lazarsfeld, P. F., & Roper, E. (2017). Personal influence: The part played by people in the flow of mass communications. In *Personal Influence: The Part Played by People in the Flow of Mass Communications.* Routledge. doi:10.4324/9781315126234

Kim, J., & Hwang, J. (2022). Who is an evangelist? Food tourists' positive and negative eWOM behavior. *International Journal of Contemporary Hospitality Management, 34*(2), 555–577. doi:10.1108/IJCHM-06-2021-0707

Le, L. H., & Hancer, M. (2021). Using social learning theory in examining YouTube viewers' desire to imitate travel vloggers. *Journal of Hospitality and Tourism Technology*, *12*(3), 512–532. doi:10.1108/JHTT-08-2020-0200

Lee, M., Kwon, W., & Back, K. J. (2021). Artificial intelligence for hospitality big data analytics: Developing a prediction model of restaurant review helpfulness for customer decision-making. *International Journal of Contemporary Hospitality Management*, *33*(6), 2117–2136. doi:10.1108/IJCHM-06-2020-0587

Li, L., Lee, K. Y., & Yang, S. B. (2019). Exploring the effect of heuristic factors on the popularity of user-curated 'Best places to visit' recommendations in an online travel community. *Information Processing & Management*, *56*(4), 1391–1408. doi:10.1016/j.ipm.2018.03.009

Liang, A., & Gössling, S. (2020). *Exploring the Formation and Representation of Destination Images in Travel Vlogs on Social Media*. Lund University. https://lup.lub.lu.se/student-papers/record/9012220

Lin, X., Featherman, M., Brooks, S. L., & Hajli, N. (2018). Exploring Gender Differences in Online Consumer Purchase Decision Making: An Online Product Presentation Perspective. *Information Systems Frontiers*, *21*(5), 1187–1201. doi:10.1007/s10796-018-9831-1

Maggiore, G., lo Presti, L., Orlowski, M., & Morvillo, A. (2022). In the travel bloggers' wonderland: Mechanisms of the blogger – follower relationship in tourism and hospitality management – a systematic literature review. *International Journal of Contemporary Hospitality Management*, *34*(7), 2747–2772. doi:10.1108/IJCHM-11-2021-1377

Mariani, M., Ek Styven, M., & Ayeh, J. K. (2019). Using Facebook for travel decision-making: An international study of antecedents. *International Journal of Contemporary Hospitality Management*, *31*(2), 1021–1044. doi:10.1108/IJCHM-02-2018-0158

Martins, M. R., & da Costa, R. A. (2022). Backpackers' Sociodemographic Characteristics, Travel Organisation and the Impact of New Technologies. *The Backpacker Tourist: A Contemporary Perspective*. Emerald. doi:10.1108/978-1-80262-255-320221006

Mauri, A. G., & Minazzi, R. (2013). Web reviews influence on expectations and purchasing intentions of hotel potential customers. *International Journal of Hospitality Management*, *34*(1), 99–107. doi:10.1016/j.ijhm.2013.02.012

Mohanty, S., Pradhan, B. B., & Sahoo, D. (2022). A Study to Investigate Consumer's Resonance Experience Effect and Engagement Behaviour on Travel Vlogs. *NMIMS Management Review*, *30*(02), 35–57. doi:10.53908/NMMR.300203

Moore, S. G., & Lafreniere, K. C. (2020). How online word-of-mouth impacts receivers. *Consumer Psychology Review*, *3*(1), 34–59. doi:10.1002/arcp.1055

Mowat, J. (2017, May 21). *Why travel brands win with a video first marketing strategy*. Hurricane. https://www.hurricanemedia.co.uk/blog/news/travel-brands-lead-video-first-marketing-strategy/

Ngarmwongnoi, C., Oliveira, J. S., AbedRabbo, M., & Mousavi, S. (2020). The implications of eWOM adoption on the customer journey. *Journal of Consumer Marketing*, *37*(7), 749–759. doi:10.1108/JCM-10-2019-3450

Nilashi, M., & Asadi, S. (2021). Recommendation agents and information sharing through social media for coronavirus outbreak. *Telematics and Informatics*, *61*, 101597. doi:10.1016/j.tele.2021.101597 PMID:34887615

Oliveira, T., Araujo, B., & Tam, C. (2020). Why do people share their travel experiences on social media? *Tourism Management*, *78*, 104041. doi:10.1016/j.tourman.2019.104041 PMID:32322615

Peralta, R. L. (2019). How vlogging promotes a destination image: A narrative analysis of popular travel vlogs about the Philippines. *Place Branding and Public Diplomacy*, *15*(4), 244–256. doi:10.1057/s41254-019-00134-6

Rahimizhian, S., Ozturen, A., & Ilkan, M. (2020). Emerging realm of 360-degree technology to promote tourism destination. *Technology in Society*, *63*, 101411. doi:10.1016/j.techsoc.2020.101411

Ranieri, M., Luzzi, D., Cuomo, S., & Bruni, I. (2022). If and how do 360 videos fit into education settings? Results from a scoping review of empirical research. *Journal of Computer Assisted Learning*, *38*(5), 1199–1219. doi:10.1111/jcal.12683

Siddiqui, M. S., Siddiqui, U. A., Khan, M. A., Alkandi, I. G., Saxena, A. K., & Siddiqui, J. H. (2021). Creating electronic word of mouth credibility through social networking sites and determining its impact on brand image and online purchase intentions in India. *Journal of Theoretical and Applied Electronic Commerce Research*, *16*(4), 1008–1024. doi:10.3390/jtaer16040057

Talwar, M., Talwar, S., Kaur, P., Islam, A. K. M. N., & Dhir, A. (2021). Positive and negative word of mouth (WOM) are not necessarily opposites: A reappraisal using the dual factor theory. *Journal of Retailing and Consumer Services*, *63*, 102396. doi:10.1016/j.jretconser.2020.102396

Tran, G. A., & Strutton, D. (2020). Comparing email and SNS users: Investigating e-servicescape, customer reviews, trust, loyalty and E-WOM. *Journal of Retailing and Consumer Services*, *53*, 101782. doi:10.1016/j.jretconser.2019.03.009

Trinh, V. D., & Nguyen, D. Y. L. (2019). How to Change Perceived Destination Image Through Vlogging on Youtube. SSRN *Electronic Journal*. doi:10.2139/ssrn.3426968

Vergura, D. T., Luceri, B., & Zerbini, C. (2021). The Effect of Social EWOM on Consumers' Behaviour Patterns in the Fashion Sector. In *The Art of Digital Marketing for Fashion and Luxury Brands* (pp. 221–242). Springer International Publishing. doi:10.1007/978-3-030-70324-0_10

Vettehen, P. H., Wiltink, D., Huiskamp, M., Schaap, G., & Ketelaar, P. (2019). Taking the full view: How viewers respond to 360-degree video news. *Computers in Human Behavior*, *91*, 24–32. doi:10.1016/j.chb.2018.09.018

Wang, X., & Chang, B. (2020). The Impact of the Audience's Continuance Intention Towards the Vlog: Focusing on Intimacy, Media Synchronicity and Authenticity. *International Journal of Contents*, *16*(2), 65–77. doi:10.5392/IJOC.2020.16.2.065

Wu, M.-Y., & Pearce, P. L. (2016). Tourism Blogging Motivations. *Journal of Travel Research*, *55*(4), 537–549. doi:10.1177/0047287514553057

Xu, D., Chen, T., Pearce, J., Mohammadi, Z., & Pearce, P. L. (2021). Reaching audiences through travel vlogs: The perspective of involvement. *Tourism Management*, *86*, 104326. doi:10.1016/j.tourman.2021.104326

Xu, W., & Zhang, X. (2021). Online expression as Well-be(com)ing: A study of travel blogs on Nepal by Chinese female tourists. *Tourism Management*, *83*, 104224. doi:10.1016/j.tourman.2020.104224

Yilmaz, E. S. (2020). The Effects on Consumer Behavior of Hotel Related Comments on the TripAdvisor Website: An Istanbul Case. [AHTR]. *Advances in Hospitality and Tourism Research*, *8*(1), 1–29. doi:10.30519/ahtr.536303

Zadeh, G., Sadegh, M., Chapuis, J.-M., & Lehu, J.-M. (2021). Tourism netnography: How travel bloggers influence destination image. *Tourism Recreation Research*, 1–17. doi:10.1080/02508281.2021.1911274

Zhang, L., Kuo, P.-J., & McCall, M. (2019). Microcelebrity: The Impact of Information Source, Hotel Type, and Misleading Photos on Consumers' Responses. *Cornell Hospitality Quarterly*, *60*(4), 285–297. doi:10.1177/1938965519851461

Zhu, L., Lin, Y., & Cheng, M. (2020). Sentiment and guest satisfaction with peer-to-peer accommodation: When are online ratings more trustworthy? *International Journal of Hospitality Management*, *86*, 102369. doi:10.1016/j.ijhm.2019.102369

Zhumadilova, A. (2016). The impact of TV shows and video blogs on tourists' destination choice. *Tourism Today (Nicosia)*, *166*, 148–168.

Chapter 14
Enhancing Instructional Effectiveness Using the Metaverse:
An Empirical Analysis of the Role of Attitude and Experience of Participants

Sridevi Nair

https://orcid.org/0000-0002-1529-4297
School of Business and Management, CHRIST University, India

Tanvi Tare
Incture Technologies, India

ABSTRACT

The Metaverse has been gaining importance, with businesses looking to adopt the same for processes ranging from onboarding to customer experience. The current study has been conducted to evaluate the impact of learner characteristics on motivation to participate in metaverse-based training programs across various organizations. Based on literature and theory, two main characteristics were identified: attitude towards the metaverse and experience with the technology. Data for the study was collected using a structured questionnaire and 103 responses were collected from employees belonging to various organizations in India. The analysis and interpretation of the data was done using statistical techniques through the tool of SPSS. The study found out that both the learner characteristics have a strong positive relationship with each other, and attitude towards metaverse has a stronger relationship with learner motivation than the experience of use. The findings suggest organizations focus more on the manner in which they should introduce metaverse at the workplaces and need to keep the employee attitude towards any kind of change; more of a technological change in mind when they are strategizing to implement metaverse-based training programs.

DOI: 10.4018/979-8-3693-5868-9.ch014

INTRODUCTION

The exponential growth of cyberspace, symbolic of the internet's extensive reach, has made the online world a significant part of modern existence. Humans are becoming increasingly reliant on digital interfaces, making interaction with the digital world practically unavoidable. Recent times have witnessed a surge in the advancement of digital technologies, propelling their integration across diverse sectors and institutions. From artificial intelligence and machine learning to blockchain, IoT, and cloud computing, these technologies have become integral components in the operations of numerous organizations. Their adoption promises increased efficiency, streamlined processes, and innovative solutions. As society marches forward, the symbiotic relationship between humanity and the digital realm continues to evolve, shaping our daily personal and professional lives. As humans, our communication keeps evolving, and therefore, virtual communication also takes a new shape in the form of a metaverse (Ning et al., 2023).

The popularity of Metaverse has recently increased due to Facebook's rebranding to Meta and its focus on developing the Metaverse (Krauss et al., 2022). This strategic move by one of the tech industry's biggest names has significantly elevated the interest in the concept. Despite being in its initial stages, rapid advancements in virtual reality (VR) technologies are promoting interest in and acceptance of the metaverse. These innovations are increasingly blurring the lines between the physical and digital worlds, offering immersive and interactive experiences. The refinement of VR headsets, haptic feedback systems, spatial computing and augmented reality (AR) integrations are key contributors to the evolution of the Metaverse. These advancements are laying the groundwork for a multifaceted digital space where individuals can interact, socialize, work, play and create.

The COVID-19 pandemic has also contributed to the realization of opportunities for the use of Metaverse in the workplace, shifting its focus from entertainment to professional use (Dwivedi et al., 2022). The main idea behind the Metaverse is to create a digital space that mimics the social interaction of physical contexts. Regular video conferencing fails to replicate the in-person meeting experience, which affects collaboration among employees. Metaverse has the potential to enhance remote working by replicating physical work contexts and encouraging camaraderie, leading to increased creativity and productivity (Karlsson & Shamoun, 2022).

The evolution of the metaverse within the framework of a workspace reflects the dynamic shift in how we perceive and engage with work environments. With the transition of workspaces into online domains, companies have undergone a significant transformation in monitoring and managing employee activities. As workspaces continue to evolve within the metaverse, there is a pressing need for a more balanced approach that prioritizes employee wellbeing alongside organizational goals, fostering an environment where individuals can thrive while contributing meaningfully to their work (Pinnington & Ayoko, 2021). This understanding has encouraged a shift of focus from the technology to the audience of the technology. Something that Davis's (1989) TAM model has been advocating for a long time.

Indeed, the characteristics of learners play an important role in their ability to adapt to new learning environments, including those presented by metaverse technology. Metaverse technology has the potential to create immersive, flexible, and interactive learning environments that can enhance motivation, engagement, and active involvement in the learning process (Collins, 2008). Learners who are open to new experiences, willing to experiment and collaborate, and who are comfortable with technology are likely to thrive in such environments. However, it is also important to note that the use of metaverse technology for learning should be designed with accessibility and inclusivity in mind, ensuring that all learners have equal access and opportunity to participate and learn in these environments (Kye et al., 2021).

Research shows how the metaverse has been taking over the workplace and also how employees are sceptical towards being a part of such advanced technologies (Karlsson & Shamoun, 2022). If employees do not have an acceptance towards a metaverse-based training model, the whole agenda of implementing the same would be quite futile. Therefore, this study looks at two personal factors that could impact the motivation of the employees to undergo a metaverse-based program.

What is Metaverse: Why and How It Came Into the Picture

Metaverse, a combination of two words- 'Meta' meaning 'combination', and 'verse' meaning 'universe' is an application/software which merges the real and the digital world and creates a mirror image of the world we live in (Chua & Yu, 2023). It is a method through which the virtual world is combined with the real world and is integrated with the social, economic and identity system to live in it, produce content and make the utmost use of this technology (Ning et al., 2021). Users of the Metaverse can not only inhabit this digital space but also actively engage within it, generate content, and leverage its multifaceted capabilities. This convergence of realities offers unprecedented opportunities for creativity, collaboration, and exploration across various domains, transcending the traditional confines of physical existence. As this technology evolves, the potential of the Metaverse to reshape social dynamics, economic landscapes, and individual experiences is increasingly apparent, heralding a new era of interconnectedness between the real and the digital.

It all came into direct focus when the CEO of Facebook, Mark Zuckerberg announced the change in the name of Facebook to 'Meta' in October 2021. This announcement made quite an impact in the business world as it denoted a significant change in the business model of a company as huge as Facebook.

Zuckerberg described it as a three-dimensional space which provides an overlap of virtual and augmented reality (Kraus et al., 2021). The renaming of the company encapsulated a strategic pivot towards investing heavily in building and nurturing the Metaverse—a comprehensive digital environment facilitating immersive interactions, social connections, and multifaceted experiences. This move signalled Facebook's commitment to spearheading the development and integration of technologies such as virtual reality (VR) and augmented reality (AR) into a cohesive, interconnected platform. Zuckerberg's portrayal of the Metaverse as a spatial, interactive realm underscored the company's aspirations to evolve beyond traditional social networking paradigms, marking a profound step toward reshaping digital interactions and the way individuals engage with technology on a global scale.

The term 'metaverse', was first used in a novel by Neal Stephenson in the year 1992, where humans in the novel enter into a parallel universe. The metaverse would allow the users to access spaces and environments virtually, which might not be possible physically, and allow them to be digital citizens of a place. It has been constantly evolving and has been given various names such as 'second life', '3D virtual worlds', and 'life-logging' (Wang et al., 2022). To summarize the metaverse is a spatiotemporal space, with full immersion and is a blend of the physical, the digital and the human worlds under one space. It serves as a convergence point, enabling individuals to traverse boundaries and engage in activities that might be unattainable in the physical world. This multifaceted environment fosters a sense of presence and connectivity, allowing users to interact, create, socialize, and conduct various activities, mirroring and often enhancing real-life experiences. The metaverse concept defines a vision of a boundless digital frontier where the physical, digital, and human worlds coexists harmoniously, redefining how we perceive, interact, and navigate through immersive digital landscapes (Qadir & Fatah, 2023).

Integration of Metaverse Into Workspace

Since the late 1970s, companies and industries have become more interested in remote working due to the advent of digital ways of working (Vilhelmson & Thulin, 2016). A type of working that occurs outside of the office, away from coworkers, and depends on modern technology for communication is called remote working, sometimes known as teleworking, telecommuting, or flexible work (Martino & Wirth, 1990). With the advancement of information and communications technology throughout the years, remote working has been feasible by facilitating communication across physical borders (Wang et al., 2021). The idea of virtual realities has been studied since the 1960s and 1970s (Dionisio et al., 2013). However, with the advancements in information and communications technology, virtual realities have gained increasing attention for their diverse range of potential applications.

The concept of Metaverse has gained significant attention in recent years. Metaverse is a virtual reality idea where users create avatars that exist in a three-dimensional virtual world (Diónisio et al., 2013). The concept is believed to be an ongoing evolution, and with the growing trend of remote working, companies like Facebook and Microsoft see the potential of its application to enhance the remote working experience for employees (Kim, 2021).

The rise in popularity and creation of the Metaverse can be attributed to a fundamental shift in people's needs and desires in the face of the ubiquitous impact of the digital era. The rapid advancement of technology has brought about a shift in people's expectations and interactions with digital platforms. In response to these changing demands, the Metaverse offers a multidimensional digital environment that goes beyond conventional bounds. In an age where everything is connected, where communication happens instantly, and where the real and virtual worlds coexist, people want experiences that are more full, interactive, and immersive. By offering a dynamic environment where users can engage, create, collaborate, and interact in ways that reflect the complexity of modern life, the Metaverse meets these expectations. It caters to the desire for enhanced connectivity, personalized experiences, and the ability to navigate diverse digital landscapes seamlessly. This rise of the Metaverse signifies a paradigm shift in how people perceive and engage with technology, driven by the necessity to fulfil the ever-changing needs and desires of individuals navigating the digital landscape. Due to the COVID-19 pandemic, people have developed a greater need for flexibility, freedom, and the ability to connect and collaborate easily while maintaining the social aspects of remote work (Fernandez, 2022). Companies that fail to recognize this changing trend risk falling behind and losing credibility. Therefore, it is essential to keep up with the development of Metaverse to ensure that businesses are prepared for its implementation in the workplace in the future (Karlsson & Shamoun, 2021). For companies, Metaverse offers possibilities of new revenue streams, land ownership, office customization, and scalability to cater to their specific needs. Furthermore, virtual currencies and NFTs introduce a new way of transacting and monetizing the virtual world, opening up new opportunities for businesses (Alvim, 2022).

An educational metaverse has the potential to revolutionize the way we approach education and professional training. By providing a virtual space where learners can engage in hands-on experiences and simulations, it can offer opportunities that may not be available in the real world due to limitations in resources, costs, or risks. This can lead to more effective and cost-efficient training and development programs, as well as provide access to education for individuals who may face barriers in accessing traditional educational settings. Additionally, an educational metaverse can foster collaboration and community-building among learners and educators from all over the world, further enhancing the learning experience (Mitra, 2023).

Metaverse can effectively utilize its strong simulation capabilities for teaching and training learners or employees of organizations. However, it is crucial to consider users' attitudes toward these technological advancements as they can either amplify the benefits of working from home or highlight its negative aspects (Yarberry & Sims, 2021). Research has shown a strong correlation between employee happiness and engagement, which ultimately leads to organizational success. Therefore, taking employees' attitudes towards organizational change into account is critical in predicting the success of such changes (Jeon, 2021).

This study aims to establish if there is a relationship between learner characteristics and the motivation to participate in a metaverse-based training program. The model designed for this study has taken up two independent and one dependent variable. Experience with technological interfaces and attitude towards the metaverse are the independent variables, and Learner Motivation is the dependent variable that needs to be analysed. This model has been designed keeping in mind the employees in an organization and their inclination to participate in a metaverse-based training program based on the two independent variables taken.

Experience with technological interfaces and attitude towards technology have been borrowed from the TETEM model. The TAM framework (Davis, 1989) is adapted to include learning and development through the technology-enhanced training effectiveness model, or TETEM. TETEM, initially designed for evaluating training effectiveness in virtual environments, draws inspiration from Baldwin and Ford's (1988) training effectiveness model. They proposed that the primary predictors of training outcomes include trainee characteristics, work climate, and training design, with these factors subsequently influencing training transfer. As the workplace undergoes significant transformations with technological advancements, the necessity to evaluate the impact of these factors on the acceptance levels of the audience becomes crucial.

In this evolving landscape, Landers and Callan (2012) identified three crucial factors for enhancing the learning experience through technological tools. First, at the organizational level, the culture plays a pivotal role in determining the effectiveness of technologically enhanced learning modules. An organization with a sceptical or unresponsive attitude towards technology could prevent the acceptance of such training. This can be assessed through the organizational climate and the level of supervisory support. Secondly, and more importantly, at the individual level, the learner's attitude towards technology and their prior technological experience are key influencers of training effectiveness. These individual factors act as moderators, shaping the relationship between training design and the learner's motivation to engage in technologically enhanced learning experiences.

Applying this model to the realm of gamification, Landers and Armstrong (2015) introduced a parallel framework. According to their adaptation, two sets of characteristics predict a learner's motivation to participate in a gamified learning experience. The first set encompasses organizational factors such as organizational climate and supervisory support. The second set focuses on individual characteristics, specifically the learner's experience with video games and their attitude towards game-based learning. These individual attributes are expected to moderate the relationship between training design and pre-training valence, consequently influencing reactions to the training and subsequent learning outcomes. Empirical evidence supporting the application of TETEM to gamified learning contexts was obtained through a study conducted on students.

At its core, the TETEM model recognizes that the effectiveness of training programs, whether in virtual environments or gamified settings, is intricately tied to both organizational and individual factors. On an individual level, learners' attitudes towards technology and their prior experiences with technological tools shape their motivation to engage in the learning experiences. In the context of gamification, the inclusion of factors like experience with video games and attitude towards game-based learning adds a layer of complexity to the relationship between training design and learner motivation.

TETEM serves as a versatile framework that transcends traditional training environments, adapting to the changing dynamics of the modern workplace. It highlights the significance of individual factors in shaping the effectiveness of training interventions, whether in virtual environments or gamified scenarios. As organizations continue to navigate the evolving landscape of technology-enhanced learning, the TETEM model offers valuable insights into optimizing training programs for maximum impact and success.

Through the TETEM, Landers and Callan (2012) emphasized a crucial component of technology adoption that if consumers are uncomfortable or inexperienced with the technology, using new technologies may not produce the desired results. This claim emphasizes how important user competence and familiarity are in assessing how well technology is used. The degree of comfort and prior experience people have with a new technical tool or platform greatly affects how well they are able to use and navigate it. In the current study the two variables are proposed to be predictors of the level of learner motivation levels. The conceptual framework for the study is given in Figure 1.

METHODOLOGY

The objective of the current research is to study the impact of the experience of use of technology and attitude towards metaverse on learner motivation. For the same, the researchers adopted a quantitative, survey-based approach. The methodology was

Figure 1. Conceptual framework

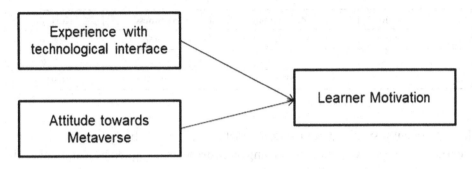

adapted from the study by Landers and Callan (2017). In their study, the researchers evaluated the technology-enhanced training effectiveness model (TETEM) in the context of gamification. The approach was found to be suitable for the given study as well.

Participants

The respondents for the current study were chosen from among employees in Indian organizations. The majority (53%) of the respondents were males. More than 70% of the respondents belonged to the age group of 18-25 years. In terms of educational qualifications, the majority of the respondents 23% claimed to be post-graduates. Post-cleaning of the data, 103 complete responses were found and used for the final analysis.

Data Collection

Data for the current study was collected using a structured questionnaire. The questionnaire was designed keeping in mind the conceptual framework of the study. The questionnaire also included a video attached which was shown to the respondents, post which they were asked to respond to the questions that followed. The video inserted within the questionnaire showed how metaverse has been taking over workplaces and how training programs and working life are being given an immersive experience owing to the use of metaverse. The first section of the questionnaire collected the demographic details of the respondent and the remaining three sections consisted of 15 questions based on the three variables taken for the study and respondents were expected to mark their responses on a five-point Likert scale.

The statements for experience with technology and attitude towards the metaverse were adapted from Bourgonjon et al., (2009). Sample statements included statements

Table 1. Descriptive statistics

	Mean	Std. Deviation	Skewness	Kurtosis
A	3.140	1.125	-0.166	-0.911
E	2.980	1.029	0.039	-0.528
M	3.377	0.988	-0.284	-0.939

like "I am enthusiastic about using the metaverse" and "I like using technology". Learner motivation was measured using an instrument designed by Zaniboni et al., (2011). The T-VIES-it scale included statements like "Attending training activities, I want to improve technical/practical knowledge in my job", "If I am involved in training activities, I am confident I can improve my ability of initiative" and "Acquiring new skills thanks to training activities, positively influences my performances".

RESULTS

Prior to testing the hypotheses, the researcher examined the spread of the data to understand if the use of parametric tests was appropriate. The descriptive statistics of the variables have been provided in Table 1.

The skewness and kurtosis values of the variables, attitude towards the metaverse (A), experience with the metaverse (E) and motivation (M) were found to be within the acceptable limits of +3 and -3. This suggests that the data can be treated as normally distributed and parametric tests can be applied (Kline, 2005).

The next step in the analysis involved the analysis of the correlation between the variables. The results of the same, have been presented in Table 2.

The correlation between all the variables was found to be significant with $p < 0.05$. Motivation to participate in a training program was found to be very strongly correlated to the attitude of the participant towards the metaverse (0.826) and the participant's experience with technology (0.712). Having established a correlation,

Table 2. Correlation Analysis

	M	A	E
M	1		
A	.826**	1	
E	.712**	.703**	1

**. Correlation is significant at the 0.01 level (2-tailed).

Table 3. Regression analysis

Predictor	R	R Square	Adjusted R Square	F	Sig.
E	0.712[a]	0.507	0.502	103.833	.000[b]
A	0.826[a]	0.682	0.679	217.095	.000[b]
Coefficients					
		B	Std. Error	T	Sig.
1	(Constant)	1.338	0.148	11.038	0.000
	E	0.684	0.069	0.491	0.000
2	(Constant)	1.091	0.165	6.623	0.000
	A	0.726	0.049	14.734	0.000

the researchers proceeded to evaluate the impact through a regression analysis. The results of the analysis have been presented in Table 3.

The regression analysis suggests that the characteristics of experience with technology and attitude towards the metaverse have a significant impact on the learner's motivation to participate in the metaverse-based training program. Experience with technology was found to predict a 50% variance in the level of learner motivation ($p<0.05$). the attitude towards the metaverse was found to predict close to 68% variance in the level of motivation ($p<0.05$). Both variables showed significant and strong impacts on the level of learner motivation.

DISCUSSION

The current study analysed data collected from working professionals. The first step in the analysis involved evaluating the distribution of the data. The skewness and kurtosis values of the dataset. The values were found to be between +3 and -3, allowing the use of parametric tests. The researchers then proceeded to check the correlation. As the data could be considered as normally distributed, Pearson's correlation was analysed and it was found to be significant and strong. The correlation between motivation and experience with technology was found to be 0.712 and the between motivation and attitude towards technology was found to be 0.826. Similarly, both experience with technology and attitude towards technology were found to significant predicting the level of motivation; as seen from the regression analysis. Attitude was found to predict approximately 68 percent of variance in the level motivation and experience was found to predict approximately 50 percent variance in motivation levels. These results are further discussed in this section.

The dramatic rise of the metaverse underscores its significance in the evolving technological landscape. However, as with any transformative technological shift, the certainty of its success remains ambiguous. Since Fred Davis introduced the Technology Acceptance Model (TAM) in 1985, there has been a continuous effort to comprehend and anticipate the adoption of new technologies. TAM proposed that users' intention to use technology, as well as their actual usage, is primarily determined by two key factors: perceived usefulness and perceived ease of use. According to this model, individuals are more inclined to embrace a technology if they perceive it as beneficial and if its utilization is easy and familiar. This model has been instrumental in understanding user behaviour and adoption patterns across various technological innovations. In the context of the metaverse, the applicability of TAM suggests that its widespread acceptance and integration into daily life depends on the user's perceptions of its utility and the ease with which they can navigate and engage with the technology. The successful adoption of the metaverse may, thus, depend on how effectively it addresses these critical aspects—usefulness and user-friendliness (Davis, 1985).

Technology-enhanced training effectiveness model or TETEM extends the TAM framework to learning and development. TETEM focuses on the acceptance of technology for learning purposes only. Landers and Callan (2012) highlighted an essential aspect of technology adoption wherein the utilization of new technologies might not result in the expected outcomes if users lack comfort or experience with the technology. This assertion highlights the significance of user familiarity and proficiency in determining the effectiveness of technology use. When individuals encounter a new technological tool or platform, their level of comfort and prior experience significantly influences their ability to navigate and leverage these tools effectively. A lack of familiarity or discomfort with the technology may lead to reduced proficiency, hindering the user's capability to harness its full potential. This can result in reduced efficiency, errors in operation, or an inability to explore and utilize all features and functionalities. Consequently, these factors may prevent users from obtaining the maximum benefits or achieving the best outcomes from the technology. Therefore, facilitating user comfort, providing adequate training, and ensuring a user-friendly interface are crucial in ensuring the successful integration and utilization of new technologies, allowing individuals to leverage them to their fullest potential and yield more favourable outcomes.

Landers and Armstrong (2015), applied the TETEM to a gamified learning experience and found that the attitude towards game-based learning and experience with video games would moderate the impact of gamification on the pre-training valence of the participant. The current study borrowed the learner characteristic variables from their study and evaluated the impact of attitude towards the metaverse and experience with technology on the motivation to participate in a metaverse-based training program. The findings suggest that the variables significantly predicted the level of motivation.

One explanation for this relationship can be found in the cognitive load theory by Sweller (1988). When learners encounter a learning module designed with unfamiliar technology, their cognitive load increases as they grapple with navigating and comprehending the new tools or platform. This heightened cognitive demand, stemming from the need to understand and operate the unfamiliar technology, can potentially dampen the learner's motivation to actively engage in the program. The cognitive resources that would otherwise be dedicated to absorbing the learning content are diverted towards grappling with the mechanics of the new technology, thereby diminishing the learner's enthusiasm and willingness to participate fully. Conversely, when learners possess prior experience with the medium or technology used in the module, their cognitive load is significantly reduced. Familiarity enables learners to channel their cognitive resources more effectively toward the learning objectives rather than expending effort on navigating the technology itself. As a result, having experience with the medium leads to a smoother learning experience, allowing learners to focus more on the educational content, participate more enthusiastically, and consequently achieve better learning outcomes. Therefore, integrating familiar technology or providing adequate training and support for unfamiliar technology within learning modules becomes crucial in fostering a conducive environment for optimal engagement and improved learning results.

The second relationship proposed by the current study is that the attitude towards the metaverse would have a significant impact on the level of learner motivation. This is supported by the constructivist theory of learning which states that learning can only happen if the learner believes that the training is meaningful (Kraiger, 2002). In other words, the attitude of the learner would impact the level of motivation to participate in the training and thereby influence the learning outcomes of the program.

While both experience and attitude were found to have a significant impact, the attitude was found to have a stronger impact. A study by Karlsson and Shamoun (2022) found that employees who had prior experience with virtual environments exhibited more positive attitudes toward the metaverse. This familiarity was linked to higher levels of acceptance and enthusiasm for metaverse technologies in the workplace.

However, the attitude towards the metaverse is not all positive. Research by Woldemichael (2019) highlighted that employees are worried about data privacy, online harassment, and potential breaches of sensitive information. Another survey also found that the use of metaverse technology raises concerns about employee privacy and data collection, with a significant number of workers expressing concern that their employers may monitor their location and screen activity. Interestingly, the survey found that workers were more likely to trust Microsoft and Google than Meta (formerly Facebook) to lead the way in virtual workplace technology (Barr, 2022).

In one of the other surveys, around 53% of people did not know what a metaverse is, and are unaware of it, and thus comes a question of the success of the implementation of metaverse in workplaces (Bale et al., 2022). The attitude and perceptions of the employees were also reflected in the said survey. The survey results suggest that there is a significant concern among people regarding the potential negative impact of metaverse on physical human interactions. Many individuals believe that the immersive nature of the metaverse could lead to the development of a dual personality and affect how people behave in real-life conversations. This effect is similar to what is observed in existing social media platforms, where people tend to be more comfortable having virtual conversations but struggle to communicate effectively in person. Nearly 38.2% of individuals felt that metaverse could harm human interactions, while only a small percentage of people believed that it would have no effect. These findings highlight the importance of considering the potential social and psychological implications of emerging technologies like metaverse (Bale et al., 2022). The survey results indicate that a majority of people (65.3%) believe that a metaverse would reduce physical activity in humans, which could have negative consequences for their health in the long run.

Considering how people currently view the metaverse and the study's findings, it is clear that companies must first work to change the attitudes of their workforce before launching any metaverse-based learning programmes. One way to counter the same is **by** outlining a subtle strategy in which the switch to a metaverse-based platform is a methodical, progressive deployment rather than a sudden change. Instead of moving a whole training programme to the metaverse, companies can progressively integrate it with conventional training techniques. This guarantees that employees have the option of an alternative form of training and do not feel compelled to take up only the metaverse based training.

The phased transition will also allow employees the opportunity to familiarize themselves with the metaverse at a pace that aligns with their comfort levels and learning preferences. By providing multiple training options, organizations acknowledge the diverse needs of their workforce, creating an inclusive environment that caters to different learning styles. Employees can be encouraged to explore the nuances of using the metaverse as a learning tool, fostering a sense of agency and empowerment in their digital skill development journey. This approach is pivotal in dispelling apprehensions and building a positive attitude towards incorporating metaverse technologies in the workplace.

Based on the understanding that adaptation to technologies requires time and support, organizations can leverage this gradual integration to ensure that the user experience with metaverse interfaces remains consistently high. This involves investing in user-friendly designs, intuitive interfaces, and comprehensive training programs that equip employees with the necessary skills to navigate the metaverse seamlessly. The objective is not just to introduce a new technological dimension but to elevate the overall experience of employees, fostering a sense of confidence and competence in utilizing the metaverse as a tool for learning.

As employees become more adept at using the metaverse for training and collaboration, it can be positioned as an extended dimension of the workplace. This goes beyond viewing the metaverse as a mere technological platform and transforms it into an integral component of the organizational ecosystem. By integrating the metaverse into the broader context of the workplace, organizations can capitalize on its potential as a space for enhanced collaboration, communication, and creativity. The metaverse becomes a virtual extension of the physical workspace, providing opportunities for seamless interaction and productivity irrespective of geographical boundaries.

In this manner when the metaverse is introduced gradually and thoughtfully, it has the potential to revolutionize the workplace by serving as an extended dimension. Organizations must recognize that changing employee attitudes towards the metaverse is a fundamental prerequisite for successful implementation. The phased transition strategy, offering multiple training options, and ensuring a positive user experience. It also paves the way for a seamless integration of the metaverse into the professional landscape. By embracing the metaverse as an extended workplace dimension, organizations can usher in a new era of collaboration, innovation, and adaptive learning, positioning themselves at the forefront of the evolving work paradigm.

Limitations

One of the biggest limitations of the current study is that it relies on survey data. Surveys rely on self-report data, which can be subject to various biases such as social desirability bias, recall bias, and response bias. Respondents may provide answers they believe are expected rather than reflecting their true feelings or experiences. To encourage genuine responses, the respondents were not asked for any personal data like name or email. However, the findings of the current study would gain validity if supported by an experimental study that observed the levels of learning.

Additionally, survey information records motivations, experiences, and attitudes at a particular moment in time. The study's ability to take temporal dynamics into account may be limited by changes in organisational contexts, technology use, or individual circumstances throughout time that are not well reflected.

Lastly, even though survey results offer quantitative insights, it's possible that they miss some of the complexity and depth of participant experiences. Integrating qualitative techniques with survey data can provide a more comprehensive picture of the topic being studied. Open-ended survey questions, focus groups, and interviews are examples of qualitative methods that enable participants to express their experiences in their own words and provide nuanced viewpoints that quantitative measurements could miss. The validity and depth of the findings can be improved and a more comprehensive understanding of the relationships between learner motivation levels in organisational settings, attitudes towards technology, and experience with technology can be achieved by triangulating both qualitative and quantitative data. A more in-depth analysis of the phenomenon being studied and a more sophisticated interpretation of the survey data are made possible by this mixed-methods approach.

Scope for Future Research

The current manuscript is only a preliminary study that attempts to identify some personal factors that could predict the success of an initiative to include the metaverse in the functioning of the organization. This may be applied to any function or section of the organization. Future research could evaluate the personal characteristics of attitude towards technology and experience with technology across the different demographic segments; age and gender. This would provide a deeper understanding to how these variables function and how the relationship differs across categories.

Another dimension that could be explored is to expand the model to take into consideration other variables that are specific to difference contexts. For example, while studying the use of metaverse in the field of learning, the context of the training, perceived organizational support, attitude of leadership etc., could also be evaluated.

Another aspect that could be explored is to adapt the model to understand if it can be used to predict effectiveness in other contexts like health and wellbeing. One such application was explored i=by Garcia et al., (2022). In their study, they explored the possibility of creating a virtual dietician for gym and fitness enthusiasts.

CONCLUSION

The ever-changing nature of the modern workplace is undoubtedly driving the trend towards metaverse-based training programmes and work environments. Organisations are realising more and more that they need creative ways to adjust to the evolving nature of work, and the metaverse is emerging as a game-changing answer. However, how employees feel about using metaverse-based interfaces will have a big impact on how well this shift goes.

Implementing metaverse-based programmes successfully depends on comprehending and meeting the expectations and concerns of employees. According to research, companies should handle this shift gradually so that staff members may become used to the new paradigm. Offering a variety of training opportunities within the metaverse allows staff members to acquaint themselves with the subtleties of this state-of-the-art technology. This method not only lessens opposition but also gives people the confidence to use the metaverse as a tool for cooperation and learning. Moreover, the phased transition approach enables organizations to identify and address potential challenges as they arise. This iterative process allows for continuous improvement based on feedback from employees, ensuring that any issues are promptly resolved. Proactive management of concerns, coupled with open communication channels, can contribute to a culture of collaboration and transparency during the metaverse adoption journey.

The key to a successful metaverse integration also lies in ensuring that employees have a positive and user-friendly experience with the technological interfaces. Employees used to traditional work environments should find it easy to transfer to the metaverse with the help of user-friendly interfaces. This means making investments in elements that improve the user experience overall, such as responsive design and easy navigation. Organisations can greatly boost workforce adoption of metaverse-based programmes by emphasising the user experience.

Creating a positive experience for employees within the metaverse goes beyond technical proficiency; it involves fostering a supportive and inclusive environment. Prioritising training and development initiatives can help organisations improve the digital literacy of their workforce and provide them the confidence and empowerment to successfully navigate the metaverse. In addition to making, it easier for users to adopt metaverse-based platforms, this investment in skill development gives staff members useful digital skills that are becoming more and more important in the fast-changing workplace of today.

Organisations can use the revolutionary potential of metaverse interfaces as employees gain greater comfort with them. Opportunities to rethink training programmes, teamwork, and work processes are presented by the metaverse. Employing a metaverse-based strategy can help companies promote a change to more adaptable and dynamic work practices. This puts companies at the forefront of innovation and appeals to top personnel looking for progressive and forward-thinking environments. It also fits in with the current trends in remote and hybrid work.

In conclusion, the transition to metaverse-based training programs and workplaces is a strategic move for organizations seeking to adapt to the changing face of the workplace. The phased approach, coupled with a focus on user experience and employee development, ensures a smoother integration and fosters a positive attitude towards the metaverse. By taking these considerations into account, organizations can successfully navigate the transformative journey towards a metaverse-enabled future, unlocking new possibilities for collaboration, learning, and work.

REFERENCES

Alvim, L. (2022). How the metaverse could impact the world and the future of technology.

Baldwin, T. T., & Ford, J. K. (1988). Transfer of training: A review and directions for future research. *Personnel Psychology, 41*(1), 63–105. doi:10.1111/j.1744-6570.1988. tb00632.x

Bale, A. S., Ghorpade, N., Hashim, M. F., Vaishnav, J., & Almaspoor, Z. (2022). A comprehensive study on Metaverse and its impacts on humans. *Advances in Human-Computer Interaction, 2022*, 2022. doi:10.1155/2022/3247060

Barr, M., & Copeland-Stewart, A. (2022). Playing video games during the COVID-19 pandemic and effects on players' well-being. *Games and Culture, 17*(1), 122–139. doi:10.1177/15554120211017036

Bourgonjon, J., Valcke, M., Soetaert, R., & Schellens, T. (2009, November). Exploring the acceptance of video games in the classroom by secondary school students. In *17th International Conference on Computers in Education* (pp. 651-658). Hong Kong: Asia-Pacific Society for Computers in Education.

Collins, C. (2008). Looking to the future: Higher education in the Metaverse. *EDUCAUSE Review, 43*(5), 50–52.

Davis, F. D. (1985). *A technology acceptance model for empirically testing new end-user information systems: Theory and results* [Doctoral dissertation, Massachusetts Institute of Technology].

Di Martino, V., & Wirth, L. (1990). Telework: A new way of working and living. *Int'l Lab. Rev., 129*, 529.

Dionisio, J. D. N., Iii, W. G. B., & Gilbert, R. (2013). 3D virtual worlds and the metaverse: Current status and future possibilities. *ACM Computing Surveys, 45*(3), 1–38. doi:10.1145/2480741.2480751

Dwivedi, Y. K., Hughes, L., Baabdullah, A. M., Ribeiro-Navarrete, S., Giannakis, M., Al-Debei, M. M., Dennehy, D., Metri, B., Buhalis, D., Cheung, C. M. K., Conboy, K., Doyle, R., Dubey, R., Dutot, V., Felix, R., Goyal, D. P., Gustafsson, A., Hinsch, C., Jebabli, I., & Wamba, S. F. (2022). Metaverse beyond the hype: Multidisciplinary perspectives on emerging challenges, opportunities, and agenda for research, practice and policy. *International Journal of Information Management, 66*, 102542. doi:10.1016/j.ijinfomgt.2022.102542

Fernandez, P. (2022). Facebook, Meta, the metaverse and libraries. *Library Hi Tech News*, *39*(4), 1–5. doi:10.1108/LHTN-03-2022-0037

Garcia, M. B., Revano, T. F., Loresco, P. J. M., Maaliw, R. R., Oducado, R. M. F., & Uludag, K. (2022, December). Virtual Dietitian as a Precision Nutrition Application for Gym and Fitness Enthusiasts: A Quality Improvement Initiative. In *2022 IEEE 14th International Conference on Humanoid, Nanotechnology, Information Technology, Communication and Control, Environment, and Management (HNICEM)* (pp. 1-5). IEEE. 10.1109/HNICEM57413.2022.10109490

Jeon, J. E. (2021). The effects of user experience-based design innovativeness on user-metaverse platform channel relationships in South Korea. *Journal of Distribution Science*, *19*(11), 81–90.

Karlsson, L., & Shamoun, M. (2022). *Virtual Realities for Remote Working: Exploring employee's attitudes toward the use of Metaverse for remote working.*

Kim, J. (2021). Advertising in the metaverse: Research agenda. *Journal of Interactive Advertising*, *21*(3), 141–144. doi:10.1080/15252019.2021.2001273

Kraiger, Kurt. (2002). Decision-based evaluation. *Improving Training Effectiveness in Work Organizations*, 291-322.

Kraus, S., Kanbach, D. K., Krysta, P. M., Steinhoff, M. M., & Tomini, N. (2022). Facebook and the creation of the metaverse: Radical business model innovation or incremental transformation? *International Journal of Entrepreneurial Behaviour & Research*, *28*(9), 52–77. doi:10.1108/IJEBR-12-2021-0984

Kye, B., Han, N., Kim, E., Park, Y., & Jo, S. (2021). Educational applications of metaverse: Possibilities and limitations. *Journal of Educational Evaluation for Health Professions*, *18*, 18. doi:10.3352/jeehp.2021.18.32 PMID:34897242

Landers, R. N., & Armstrong, M. B. (2017). Enhancing instructional outcomes with gamification: An empirical test of the Technology-Enhanced Training Effectiveness Model. *Computers in Human Behavior*, *71*, 499–507. doi:10.1016/j.chb.2015.07.031

Landers, R. N., & Callan, R. C. (2012). Training evaluation in virtual worlds: Development of a model. *Journal of Virtual Worlds Research*, *5*(3). doi:10.4101/jvwr.v5i3.6335

Landers, R. N., & Callan, R. C. (2017). An Experiment on Anonymity and Multi-User Virtual Environments: Manipulating Identity to Increase Learning. In *Transforming Gaming and Computer Simulation Technologies across Industries* (pp. 80–93). IGI Global. doi:10.4018/978-1-5225-1817-4.ch004

Mitra, S. (2023). Metaverse: A Potential Virtual-Physical Ecosystem for Innovative Blended Education and Training. *Journal of Metaverse, 3*(1), 66–72. doi:10.57019/jmv.1168056

Ning, H., Wang, H., Lin, Y., Wang, W., Dhelim, S., Farha, F., & Daneshmand, M. (2023). A Survey on the Metaverse: The State-of-the-Art, Technologies, Applications, and Challenges. *IEEE Internet of Things Journal.*

Pinnington, A. H., & Ayoko, O. B. (2021). Managing physical and virtual work environments during the COVID-19 pandemic: Improving employee well-being and achieving mutual gains. *Journal of Management & Organization, 27*(6), 993–1002. doi:10.1017/jmo.2022.2

Qadir, A. M. A., & Fatah, A. O. (2023). Platformization and the metaverse: Opportunities and challenges for urban sustainability and economic development. *EAI Endorsed Transactions on Energy Web, 10*(1).

Sweller, J. (1988). Cognitive load during problem solving: Effects on learning. *Cognitive Science, 12*(2), 257–285. doi:10.1207/s15516709cog1202_4

Vilhelmson, B., & Thulin, E. (2016). Who and where are the flexible workers? Exploring the current diffusion of telework in Sweden. *New Technology, Work and Employment, 31*(1), 77–96. doi:10.1111/ntwe.12060

Wang, Y., Su, Z., Zhang, N., Xing, R., Liu, D., Luan, T. H., & Shen, X. (2022). A survey on metaverse: Fundamentals, security, and privacy. *IEEE Communications Surveys and Tutorials.*

Woldemichael, H. T. (2019). Emerging Cyber Security Threats in Organization. *International Journal of Scientific Research in Network Security and Communication, 7*(6), 7–10.

Zaniboni, S., Fraccaroli, F., Truxillo, D. M., Bertolino, M., & Bauer, T. N. (2011). Training valence, instrumentality, and expectancy scale (T-VIES-it) Factor structure and nomological network in an Italian sample. *Journal of Workplace Learning, 23*(2), 133–151. doi:10.1108/13665621111108792

Chapter 15
Use of Virtual Academic Environments During the Coronavirus Pandemic

Kadir Uludag

ⓘ https://orcid.org/0000-0003-3713-4670

Shanghai Jiao Tong University Mental Health Center, China

ABSTRACT

The coronavirus pandemic has had a significant impact on academic settings, disrupting normal routines and limiting social interactions among students. In response to this challenge, educational systems have implemented temporary measures to improve the quality of education and communication in online learning environments. While online learning communities have gained popularity, they often lack the immersive aspects provided by virtual reality (VR) and augmented reality (AR), resulting in decreased motivation and engagement compared to traditional classroom settings facilitated by web applications. This chapter aimed to explore how virtual academic environments, incorporating augmented reality elements, could improve educational outcomes by fostering social learning gains. By leveraging augmented reality features, virtual academic environments, including the Metaverse, have the potential to enhance academic productivity during situations like the coronavirus pandemic or future outbreaks by facilitating improved social interaction.

INTRODUCTION

The progress in state-of-the-art virtual reality (VR) and artificial intelligence (AI) technologies has given rise to a range of novel applications that aim to enhance our perception of reality and offer unique learning experiences. Augmented reality (AR),

DOI: 10.4018/979-8-3693-5868-9.ch015

virtual reality, and metaverse platforms hold the capability to completely transform the settings where educational activities take place. (Lee, 2012). The accessibility of VR technology has unlocked a multitude of fresh and captivating prospects for delivering education with exceptional effectiveness (Carruth, 2017). However, students using AR may experience cognitive overwhelm due to the extensive volume of information they come across (Wu, Lee, Chang, & Liang, 2013). Overall, the book chapter highlights the transformative impact of VR and AI technologies on education and the promising prospects they offer in the context of pandemic situations such as Coronavirus epidemic. We will also discuss some of the disadvantages or limitations that come with the adoption of new technologies in education.

The utilization of Metaverses for human interaction, similar to the interactions in platforms like Second Life, is becoming a popular trend due to its ability to facilitate meaningful interactions among people. This technology is valuable as it enables individuals to engage and connect with each other in virtual environments (Vernaza, Armuelles, & Ruiz, 2012) following the announcement by the Facebook company to rebrand itself as Metaverse, driven by a renewed passion and vision, they aim to reshape Facebook into a virtual environment. This decision highlights their commitment to embracing the concept of the Metaverse and signifies their ambition to transform the way people experience and interact within online spaces.

As the popularity of VR continues to rise, it becomes crucial to evaluate the obstacles associated with transitioning traditional classrooms into virtual learning environments. It is essential to recognize the distinctions between the benefits and drawbacks of online learning and in-person instruction (Jefferson & Arnold, 2009). According to a study, a virtual community in the healthcare field refers to a collective of individuals utilizing telecommunication methods to deliver educational services (Demiris, 2006). Engaging in collaborative learning or working enables individuals to interact with others, leading to increased motivation levels (Phon, Ali, & Abd Halim, 2014).

Moreover, considering behavioral psychology perspectives, augmented reality can facilitate learning through the utilization of multi-sensory systems. However, there remains controversy regarding the extent to which this innovative medium can effectively fulfill educational objectives (Kabát, 2016). Additional research is required to gain a comprehensive understanding of the implementation of VR tools in educational settings, as psychological and cultural variations can introduce specific challenges. A study has indicated that community trust plays a paramount role in fostering collaboration among researchers. (Pang & Capek, 2020). Numerous applications have been developed to enhance interactivity through augmented reality (AR) applications. A research paper explores how museums and cultural institutions are transitioning to platforms like Second Life to expand their presence and engagement with audiences (Hazan, 2010). Furthermore, a virtual physics laboratory has been developed, providing students with the capability to manipulate and control various aspects of the laboratory environment. This immersive platform offers a hands-on learning experience for students in the field of physics (Loftin, Engleberg, & Benedetti, 1993). Also, VR applications can be used in the field of mathematics (Kaufmann, Schmalstieg, & Wagner, 2000) languages (Golonka, Bowles, Frank, Richardson, & Freynik, 2014; Khoshnevisan & Le, 2018; Sadler & Thrasher, 2021), engineering education (Cibulka & Giannoumis, 2017; Sulbaran & Baker, 2000) and geometry (Gargrish, Mantri, & Kaur, 2020; Kaufmann & Schmalstieg, 2002).

In order to assess how students retain science knowledge when presented with auditory and visual information, a study utilized a between-subjects design, comparing AR and VR conditions. The results suggest that VR provides a highly immersive experience, while AR demonstrates greater effectiveness in conveying auditory information (Huang et al., 2019).

The literature also acknowledges various limitations associated with the use of such applications. One notable drawback is that it presents new challenges for educators in terms of technological, pedagogical, and psychological aspects when implementing AR in educational settings. A specific concern is the potential information overload experienced by students in AR environments (Wu et al., 2013). Additionally, a study revealed that the most commonly reported challenge is the difficulty students face when using AR technology (Akçayır & Akçayır, 2017). Furthermore, ethical dilemmas encompass critical aspects such as identity, privacy, and confidentiality. These concepts raise significant concerns and challenges in various contexts (Demiris, 2006). These ethical considerations are crucial in determining how individuals are treated, how their personal information is handled, and how their identities are respected in different contexts.

Main Focus of Book Chapter

The main focus of the book chapter is the integration of VR and AR as potential solutions to address the limitations of online learning communities. The chapter explores how VR and AR can enhance the sense of reality, motivation, and active participation in academic discussions. It also highlights the advancements in technology that allow for the creation of 3D environments and Metaverse experiences for educational purposes. However, the chapter also emphasizes the importance of recognizing and addressing potential risks, such as addiction and excessive dependence on virtual experiences, associated with virtual academic environments.

METHODS

The SANRA (a scale for the quality assessment of narrative review articles) narrative review methodology was employed in the study (Baethge, Goldbeck-Wood, & Mertens, 2019). The study employed the SANRA as the methodological framework for conducting the review. We did not utilize a systematic review approach.

MAIN RESULTS AND MAIN FINDINGS

The findings revealed that a significant number of studies primarily engaged in speculating about the potential applications of VR. Furthermore, assessing the advantages of VR poses a challenge in terms of quantification and evaluation during pandemic scenarios.

However, when it came to investigating its impact on specific areas or aspects using a research design, only a limited number of research articles were identified. Additionally, it should be noted that a systematic investigation of previous studies using a specific methodology was not conducted in this research.

DISCUSSION

The use of virtual academic environments has emerged as a potential solution to address the limitations of online learning during the coronavirus epidemic. The pandemic has disrupted traditional academic settings, leading to decreased social interactions and challenges in maintaining student engagement. While online learning communities have been widely adopted, they often lack the immersive experiences that virtual reality (VR) and augmented reality (AR) can provide. By incorporating VR and AR technologies into virtual academic environments, educational systems can offer students a more engaging and interactive learning experience. These technologies have the potential to enhance motivation, increase student engagement, and bridge the gap between online and traditional classroom settings. However, it is essential to explore and evaluate the effectiveness of these virtual environments to ensure they effectively meet the educational needs of students during the pandemic and beyond. By assessing and refining VR applications we can optimize their educational value and ensure their relevance.

Virtual Reality Applications and Psychology

The intersection of metaverse applications and psychology has gained significant attention as researchers explore the psychological implications and psychological benefits and drawbacks of immersive virtual environments especially during pandemic situations. Amidst the COVID-19 pandemic, approximately 40% of the worldwide population experienced a decline in their depressive mood, according to reports (Borisova et al., 2022). It is essential to consider potential solutions to address this issue.

For many years, researchers and practitioners have employed VR as a tool to gain insights into attitudes and behaviors related to climate change (Markowitz & Bailenson, 2021). VR holds the capacity to revolutionize the evaluation, comprehension, and management of mental health issues (Freeman et al., 2017). VR creates a secure and regulated setting for certain therapeutic interventions, thereby expanding the potential to provide individualized mental healthcare. However, the literature on VR reality and personalized psychology is limited. A previous study mentioned virtual reality exposure therapy for veterans with posttraumatic stress disorder (Rothbaum, Hodges, Ready, Graap, & Alarcon, 2001). Also, in other studies related to anxiety (Grillon, Riquier, Herbelin, & Thalmann, 2006; Maples-Keller, Bunnell, Kim, & Rothbaum, 2017; Powers & Emmelkamp, 2008), pain reduction (Malloy & Milling, 2010), phobias (Parsons & Rizzo, 2008), social cognition training (Kandalaft, Didehbani, Krawczyk, Allen, & Chapman, 2013), and psychotherapy (Riva, 2005) the impact of VR was mentioned.

In general, the utilization of virtual training for non-technical skills in healthcare education is a relatively recent development that has witnessed a notable rise since 2010 (Bracq, Michinov, & Jannin, 2019). The significance of VR in education extends to its importance in psychological research as well. Virtual reality applications offer valuable training opportunities for psychologists, enabling them to enhance their skills and expertise in a realistic and immersive environment. Additionally, VR can be employed in psychiatric settings to assist and support psychiatric patients within the context of their treatment. VR applications hold particular relevance during pandemics, as they can serve as effective tools in providing remote and accessible mental health support and interventions. VR can be utilized to train staff members in emergency situations effectively.

In conclusion, in psychiatric settings, VR can be utilized to support and assist mental health patients as part of their treatment. Particularly during pandemics, virtual reality applications are essential, providing remote and accessible mental health support and interventions. It is imperative to conduct additional research prior to the emergence of any future pandemics.

Virtual Reality Applications and Education

The relationship between virtual technologies and trends in education is becoming increasingly intertwined and related technologies were designed to improve educational output. Virtual reality has the ability to captivate individuals' attention (Martín-Gutiérrez, Mora, Añorbe-Díaz, & González-Marrero, 2017). A previous mentioned several main aspects: the organization of learning content within the current domain structure, the design elements of VR, and the underlying learning theories that form the basis for effective VR-based learning (Radianti, Majchrzak, Fromm, & Wohlgenannt, 2020). In conclusion, the integration between VR and education shows a promising trend aimed at enhancing educational results.

Drawbacks of Virtual Reality in Education

Despite the potential for advancements, the widespread integration of virtual reality (VR) in psychiatry has yet to take place due to technical challenges like motion sickness and ocular dryness (Park, Kim, Lee, Na, & Jeon, 2019). A previous review also mentioned concerns regarding the challenges associated with using VR, such as potential side effects and the transferability of skills acquired in the virtual environment to real-world settings (Weiss & Jessel, 1998). Nevertheless, the available literature on this subject is scarce, highlighting the need for future studies to thoroughly investigate and assess the potential drawbacks of this technology.

Conclusion

Virtual academic environments, including the Metaverse, have the potential to significantly enhance academic productivity, particularly in times of potential epidemic situations. In such circumstances, the utilization of augmented reality can play a crucial role in improving social communication and educational outcomes. However, it is important to approach this technology with a balanced perspective, considering both its positive and negative aspects.

While VR applications can provide valuable learning experiences, it is essential to acknowledge that it cannot fully replace real-life experiences. It is crucial for students to be well-informed about the potential drawbacks and limitations associated with virtual education applications. By being aware of these potential negative impacts, students can make informed decisions and actively navigate the virtual academic environment.

Furthermore, educators and institutions have a responsibility to address these concerns and provide guidance to students regarding the appropriate use of augmented reality technologies. This includes promoting a healthy balance between virtual and real-world experiences, emphasizing the importance of face-to-face interactions, and encouraging critical thinking skills to navigate the virtual learning environment effectively.

By considering both the benefits and limitations of augmented reality in education, and by providing proper guidance and support, virtual academic environments can be leveraged to enhance academic productivity during potential epidemic situations while ensuring a well-rounded educational experience for students.

Suggestions for Future Studies

As indicated in the preceding study, adopting a conceptual perspective of AR would yield greater educational benefits. Emphasizing the conceptual understanding of AR rather than focusing solely on the technological aspects can enhance the overall educational outcomes (Wu et al., 2013). The global outbreak of the coronavirus pandemic has had wide-ranging impacts on health, political, and social systems worldwide (Uludag, 2022) and AR solutions should prioritize addressing the systems that are susceptible to the impacts of an epidemic.

For instance, virtual applications like a virtual dietitian (Garcia et al., 2022) can be developed to assist individuals in maintaining a healthy lifestyle during an epidemic. Similar health applications can also support sleep quality of individuals. These applications could provide personalized guidance, nutrition advice, and exercise advices tailored to the specific needs and circumstances of individuals during pandemic.

Furthermore, it is crucial to calculate and anticipate future potential pandemic scenarios, taking into account the lessons learned from the current situation. Precautions should be proactively established to mitigate the impact of future outbreaks on academic settings. This includes developing robust contingency plans, investing in technology infrastructure to support virtual academic environments, and providing adequate training to educators and students in utilizing online learning tools effectively.

Limitations

Our manuscript requires the inclusion of both quantitative and qualitative approaches to confirm the manuscript. The chapter does not qualify as a systematic review. Furthermore, pandemic conditions can vary significantly, and it is important to acknowledge the existence of numerous potential pandemic scenarios.

The manuscript might not have adequately mentioned the diverse needs of individuals across different disciplines, age groups, or cultural backgrounds, potentially limiting the applicability of the pandemic situation findings. This limitation could restrict the generalizability and application of our findings, as the impact of pandemic situations can vary greatly depending on these factors. To enhance the relevance and inclusivity of our study, future research should consider a broader range of perspectives and demographics.

REFERENCES

Akçayır, M., & Akçayır, G. (2017). Advantages and challenges associated with augmented reality for education: A systematic review of the literature. *Educational Research Review*, *20*, 1–11. doi:10.1016/j.edurev.2016.11.002

Baethge, C., Goldbeck-Wood, S., & Mertens, S. (2019). SANRA—A scale for the quality assessment of narrative review articles. *Research Integrity and Peer Review*, *4*(1), 5. doi:10.1186/s41073-019-0064-8 PMID:30962953

Borisova, N., Moore, N., Sira Mahalingappa, S., Cumming, P., Dave, S., Abraham, S., & Syunyakov, T. (2022). Virtual Reality-Based Interventions for Treating Depression in the Context of COVID-19 Pandemic: Inducing the Proficit in Positive Emotions as a Key Concept of Recovery and a Path Back to Normality. *Psychiatria Danubina*, *34*(Suppl 8), 276–284. PMID:36170742

Bracq, M. S., Michinov, E., & Jannin, P. (2019). Virtual Reality Simulation in Nontechnical Skills Training for Healthcare Professionals: A Systematic Review. *Simulation in Healthcare*, *14*(3), 188–194. doi:10.1097/SIH.0000000000000347 PMID:30601464

Carruth, D. W. (2017). Virtual reality for education and workforce training. *Paper presented at the 2017 15th International Conference on Emerging eLearning Technologies and Applications (ICETA)*. IEEE. 10.1109/ICETA.2017.8102472

Cibulka, J., & Giannoumis, G. A. (2017). *Augmented and virtual reality for engineering education*. Research Gate.

Demiris, G. (2006). The diffusion of virtual communities in health care: Concepts and challenges. *Patient Education and Counseling*, *62*(2), 178–188. doi:10.1016/j.pec.2005.10.003 PMID:16406472

Freeman, D., Reeve, S., Robinson, A., Ehlers, A., Clark, D., Spanlang, B., & Slater, M. (2017). Virtual reality in the assessment, understanding, and treatment of mental health disorders. *Psychological Medicine*, *47*(14), 2393–2400. doi:10.1017/S003329171700040X PMID:28325167

Garcia, M. B., Revano, T. F., Loresco, P. J. M., Maaliw, R. R., Oducado, R. M. F., & Uludag, K. (2022). Virtual Dietitian as a Precision Nutrition Application for Gym and Fitness Enthusiasts: A Quality Improvement Initiative. *Paper presented at the 2022 IEEE 14th International Conference on Humanoid, Nanotechnology, Information Technology, Communication and Control, Environment, and Management (HNICEM)*. IEEE. 10.1109/HNICEM57413.2022.10109490

Gargrish, S., Mantri, A., & Kaur, D. P. (2020). Augmented reality-based learning environment to enhance teaching-learning experience in geometry education. *Procedia Computer Science, 172*, 1039–1046. doi:10.1016/j.procs.2020.05.152

Golonka, E. M., Bowles, A. R., Frank, V. M., Richardson, D. L., & Freynik, S. (2014). Technologies for foreign language learning: A review of technology types and their effectiveness. *Computer Assisted Language Learning, 27*(1), 70–105. doi:10.1080/09588221.2012.700315

Grillon, H., Riquier, F., Herbelin, B., & Thalmann, D. (2006). Virtual reality as a therapeutic tool in the confines of social anxiety disorder treatment. *International Journal on Disability and Human Development: IJDHD, 5*(3), 243–250. doi:10.1515/IJDHD.2006.5.3.243

Hazan, S. (2010). *Musing the metaverse. Heritage in the Digital Era, Multi-Science Publishing, Brentwood*. Esse.

Huang, K.-T., Ball, C., Francis, J., Ratan, R., Boumis, J., & Fordham, J. (2019). Augmented versus virtual reality in education: An exploratory study examining science knowledge retention when using augmented reality/virtual reality mobile applications. *Cyberpsychology, Behavior, and Social Networking, 22*(2), 105–110. doi:10.1089/cyber.2018.0150 PMID:30657334

Jefferson, R. N., & Arnold, L. W. (2009). Effects of virtual education on academic culture: Perceived advantages and disadvantages. *Online Submission, 6*(3), 61–66.

Kabát, M. (2016). Teaching Metaverse. What and how to (not) teach using the medium of virtual reality. *Edutainment, 1*(1).

Kandalaft, M. R., Didehbani, N., Krawczyk, D. C., Allen, T. T., & Chapman, S. B. (2013). Virtual reality social cognition training for young adults with high-functioning autism. *Journal of Autism and Developmental Disorders, 43*(1), 34–44. doi:10.1007/s10803-012-1544-6 PMID:22570145

Kaufmann, H., & Schmalstieg, D. (2002). Mathematics and geometry education with collaborative augmented reality. Paper *presented at the ACM SIGGRAPH 2002 conference abstracts and applications*. ACM. 10.1145/1242073.1242086

Kaufmann, H., Schmalstieg, D., & Wagner, M. (2000). Construct3D: A virtual reality application for mathematics and geometry education. *Education and Information Technologies, 5*(4), 263–276. doi:10.1023/A:1012049406877

Khoshnevisan, B., & Le, N. (2018). Augmented reality in language education: A systematic literature review. *Adv. Glob. Educ. Res, 2*, 57–71.

Lee, K. (2012). Augmented Reality in Education and Training. *TechTrends*, *56*(2), 13–21. doi:10.1007/s11528-012-0559-3

Loftin, R. B., Engleberg, M., & Benedetti, R. (1993). Applying virtual reality in education: A prototypical virtual physics laboratory. *Paper presented at the Proceedings of 1993 IEEE Research Properties in Virtual Reality Symposium.* IEEE. 10.1109/VRAIS.1993.378261

Malloy, K. M., & Milling, L. S. (2010). The effectiveness of virtual reality distraction for pain reduction: A systematic review. *Clinical Psychology Review*, *30*(8), 1011–1018. doi:10.1016/j.cpr.2010.07.001 PMID:20691523

Maples-Keller, J. L., Bunnell, B. E., Kim, S.-J., & Rothbaum, B. O. (2017). The use of virtual reality technology in the treatment of anxiety and other psychiatric disorders. *Harvard Review of Psychiatry*, *25*(3), 103–113. doi:10.1097/HRP.0000000000000138 PMID:28475502

Markowitz, D. M., & Bailenson, J. N. (2021). Virtual reality and the psychology of climate change. *Current Opinion in Psychology*, *42*, 60–65. doi:10.1016/j.copsyc.2021.03.009 PMID:33930832

Martín-Gutiérrez, J., Mora, C. E., Añorbe-Díaz, B., & González-Marrero, A. (2017). Virtual technologies trends in education. *Eurasia Journal of Mathematics, Science and Technology Education*, *13*(2), 469–486.

Pang, J., & Capek, J. (2020). Factors Influencing Researcher Cooperation in Virtual Academic Communities Based on Principal Component Analysis. *Acta Informatica Pragensia*, *9*(1), 4–17. doi:10.18267/j.aip.128

Park, M. J., Kim, D. J., Lee, U., Na, E. J., & Jeon, H. J. (2019). A Literature Overview of Virtual Reality (VR) in Treatment of Psychiatric Disorders: Recent Advances and Limitations. *Frontiers in Psychiatry*, *10*, 505. doi:10.3389/fpsyt.2019.00505 PMID:31379623

Parsons, T. D., & Rizzo, A. A. (2008). Affective outcomes of virtual reality exposure therapy for anxiety and specific phobias: A meta-analysis. *Journal of Behavior Therapy and Experimental Psychiatry*, *39*(3), 250–261. doi:10.1016/j.jbtep.2007.07.007 PMID:17720136

Phon, D. N. E., Ali, M. B., & Abd Halim, N. D. (2014). Collaborative augmented reality in education: A review. *Paper presented at the 2014 International Conference on Teaching and Learning in Computing and Engineering.* IEEE. 10.1109/LaTiCE.2014.23

Powers, M. B., & Emmelkamp, P. M. (2008). Virtual reality exposure therapy for anxiety disorders: A meta-analysis. *Journal of Anxiety Disorders, 22*(3), 561–569. doi:10.1016/j.janxdis.2007.04.006 PMID:17544252

Radianti, J., Majchrzak, T. A., Fromm, J., & Wohlgenannt, I. (2020). A systematic review of immersive virtual reality applications for higher education: Design elements, lessons learned, and research agenda. *Computers & Education, 147*, 103778. doi:10.1016/j.compedu.2019.103778

Riva, G. (2005). Virtual reality in psychotherapy. *Cyberpsychology & Behavior, 8*(3), 220–230. doi:10.1089/cpb.2005.8.220 PMID:15971972

Rothbaum, B. O., Hodges, L. F., Ready, D., Graap, K., & Alarcon, R. D. (2001). Virtual reality exposure therapy for Vietnam veterans with posttraumatic stress disorder. *The Journal of Clinical Psychiatry, 62*(8), 617–622. doi:10.4088/JCP. v62n0808 PMID:11561934

Sadler, R., & Thrasher, T. (2021). *Teaching languages with virtual reality: Things you may need to know.* CALICO Infobytes.

Sulbaran, T., & Baker, N. C. (2000). Enhancing engineering education through distributed virtual reality. Paper presented at the *30th Annual Frontiers in Education Conference.* IEEE. 10.1109/FIE.2000.896621

Uludag, K. (2022). 'Coronary Blindness: Desensitization after excessive exposure to coronavirus-related information '. *Health Policy and Technology.*

Vernaza, A., Armuelles, V. I., & Ruiz, I. (2012). Towards to an open and interoperable virtual learning enviroment using Metaverse at University of Panama. Paper presented at the *2012 Technologies Applied to Electronics Teaching (TAEE).* IEEE. 10.1109/ TAEE.2012.6235458

Weiss, P. L., & Jessel, A. S. (1998). Virtual reality applications to work. *Work (Reading, Mass.), 11*(3), 277–293. doi:10.3233/WOR-1998-11305 PMID:24441599

Wu, H.-K., Lee, S. W.-Y., Chang, H.-Y., & Liang, J.-C. (2013). Current status, opportunities and challenges of augmented reality in education. *Computers & Education, 62*, 41–49. doi:10.1016/j.compedu.2012.10.024

Compilation of References

A. (2021, March 29). *Industry 5.0—Bringing Empowered Humans Back to the Shop Floor*. Frost & Sullivan. https://www.frost.com/frost-perspectives/industry-5-0-bringing-empowered-humans-back-to-the-shop-floor/

Aamir, S., Atsan, N., & Khan, M. S. (2023). Going digital with multisided-platforms: Assessing the innovation adoption process from the perspectives of travel agents. *Tourism and Hospitality Research, 14673584231186535*, 14673584231186535. doi:10.1177/14673584231186535

Abass, M. N., & Zohry, M. A. F. (2022). Mixed reality drama towards metaverse technology in smart hotels: An exploratory study on Egyptian hotels evidence from guests' perspectives. *Journal of Association of Arab Universities for Tourism and Hospitality, 23*(2), 130–154. doi:10.21608/jaauth.2022.177500.1411

Abbott, M. (2022, April 20). *Prepare for the metaverse with our ultimate guide*. Accenture Banking Blog. https://bankingblog.accenture.com/ultimate-guide-to-banking-in-the-metaverse

Aboushouk, M. A., & Elsawy, T. M. (2020). The impact of user-generated content on digital transformation of tourism and travel services: Evidence from the Egyptian travel agencies. *International Journal of Heritage. Tourism and Hospitality, 14*(3 (Special Issue)), 12–30. doi:10.21608/ijhth.2020.106168

Adel, M. (2023). The Role of Metaverse to Create an Interactive Experience for Tourists. *Journal of Association of Arab Universities for Tourism and Hospitality, 24*(1), 242–269. doi:10.21608/jaauth.2023.216690.1473

Ağaoğlu, F. O., Ekinci, L. O., & Tosun, N. (2022). Metaverse ve sağlık hizmetleri üzerine bir değerlendirme. *Erzincan Binali Yıldırım Üniversitesi İktisadi ve İdari Bilimler Fakültesi Dergisi, 4*(1), 95–102. doi:10.46482/ebyuiibfdergi.1133902

Ahmed, U., & Hashim, S. (2022). Sustainable Brand Management: The Role of Internal Brand Management and Intrinsic Motivation in Building Employee's Brand Relationship Quality towards Organization's Brand. *Sustainability (Basel), 14*(24), 16660. doi:10.3390/su142416660

Akçayır, M., & Akçayır, G. (2017). Advantages and challenges associated with augmented reality for education: A systematic review of the literature. *Educational Research Review, 20*, 1–11. doi:10.1016/j.edurev.2016.11.002

Compilation of References

Alhemimah, A. (2019). *The Influence of Online Reviews on Saudi Consumers' Tourism Destination Choices* [Thesis, University of Plymouth]. https://pearl.plymouth.ac.uk/handle/10026.1/15206

Ali, B. J., & Anwar, G. (2021). Marketing Strategy: Pricing strategies and its influence on consumer purchasing decision. *International Journal of Rural Development. Environment and Health Research, 5*(2), 26–39. doi:10.22161/ijreh.5.2.4

Allam, Z., Sharifi, A., Bibri, S. E., Jones, D. S., & Krogstie, J. (2022). The metaverse as a virtual form of smart cities: Opportunities and challenges for environmental, economic, and social sustainability in urban futures. *Smart Cities, 5*(3), 771–801. doi:10.3390/smartcities5030040

Alvarez, C., David, M. E., & George, M. (2023). Types of Consumer-Brand Relationships: A systematic review and future research agenda. *Journal of Business Research, 160*, 113753. doi:10.1016/j.jbusres.2023.113753

Alvim, L. (2022). How the metaverse could impact the world and the future of technology.

Andersen, M. K. (2017). Human capital analytics: The winding road. *Journal of organisational Effectiveness. People and Performance, 4*(2), 133–136.

Anderski, M., Griebel, L., Stegmann, P., & Ströbel, T. (2023). Empowerment of human brands: Brand meaning co-creation on digital engagement platforms. *Journal of Business Research, 166*, 113905. doi:10.1016/j.jbusres.2023.113905

Andronie, M., Iatagan, M., Uță, C., Hurloiu, I., Dijmărescu, A., & Dijmărescu, I. (2023). Big data management algorithms in artificial Internet of Things-based fintech. *Oeconomia Copernicana, 14*(3), 769–793. doi:10.24136/oc.2023.023

Antipin, D., Morozevich, O., Deitch, V., & Gomboeva, A. (2022). Blockchain Technology as a Factor Affecting the Digitalization of the Financial Sector. In A. Gibadullin (Ed.), *Digital and Information Technologies in Economics and Management* (pp. 202–212). Springer International Publishing., doi:10.1007/978-3-030-97730-6_18

Aquilani, B., Piccarozzi, M., Abbate, T., & Codini, A. (2020). The role of open innovation and value co-creation in the challenging transition from industry 4.0 to society 5.0: Toward a theoretical framework. *Sustainability (Basel), 12*(21), 8943. doi:10.3390/su12218943

Arbouw, P., Ballantine, P. W., & Ozanne, L. K. (2019). Sustainable brand image: An examination of ad–brand incongruence. *Marketing Intelligence & Planning, 37*(5), 513–526. doi:10.1108/MIP-08-2018-0307

Arndt, J. (1967). *Word of mouth advertising: A review of the literature.* Advertising Research Foundation.

Arora, M., & Sharma, R. L. (2021). Repurposing the Role of Entrepreneurs in the Havoc of COVID-19. In Entrepreneurship and Big Data (pp. 229-250). CRC Press. doi:10.1201/9781003097945-16

Arora, M., Kumar, J., & Valeri, M. (2023). Crises and Resilience in the Age of Digitalization: Perspectivations of Past, Present and Future for Tourism Industry. In Tourism Innovation in the Digital Era (pp. 57-74). Emerald Publishing Limited.

Arora, M. (2016). Creative dimensions of entrepreneurship: A key to business innovation. *Pacific Business Review International*, *1*(1), 255–259.

Arora, M., Dhiman, V., & Sharma, R. L. (2023). Exploring the dimensions of spirituality, wellness and value creation amidst Himalayan regions promoting entrepreneurship and sustainability. *Journal of Tourismology*, *9*(2), 86–96.

Arora, M., & Sharma, R. L. (2022). Integrating Gig Economy and Social Media Platforms as a Business Strategy in the Era of Digitalization. In *Integrated Business Models in the Digital Age: Principles and Practices of Technology Empowered Strategies* (pp. 67–86). Springer International Publishing. doi:10.1007/978-3-030-97877-8_3

Arora, M., & Sharma, R. L. (2023). Artificial intelligence and big data: Ontological and communicative perspectives in multi-sectoral scenarios of modern businesses. *Foresight*, *25*(1), 126–143. doi:10.1108/FS-10-2021-0216

Ashok, M., Madan, R., Joha, A., & Sivarajah, U. (2022). Ethical framework for Artificial Intelligence and Digital technologies. *International Journal of Information Management*, *62*, 102433. doi:10.1016/j.ijinfomgt.2021.102433

Baethge, C., Goldbeck-Wood, S., & Mertens, S. (2019). SANRA—A scale for the quality assessment of narrative review articles. *Research Integrity and Peer Review*, *4*(1), 5. doi:10.1186/s41073-019-0064-8 PMID:30962953

Balcerzak, A. P., Nica, E., Rogalska, E., Poliak, M., Klieštik, T., & Sabie, O.-M. (2022). Blockchain Technology and Smart Contracts in Decentralized Governance Systems. *Administrative Sciences*, *12*(3), 3. doi:10.3390/admsci12030096

Baldwin, T. T., & Ford, J. K. (1988). Transfer of training: A review and directions for future research. *Personnel Psychology*, *41*(1), 63–105. doi:10.1111/j.1744-6570.1988.tb00632.x

Bale, A. S., Ghorpade, N., Hashim, M. F., Vaishnav, J., & Almaspoor, Z. (2022). A Comprehensive Study on Metaverse and Its Impacts on Humans. *Advances in Human-Computer Interaction*, *2022*, 1–11. doi:10.1155/2022/3247060

Bamakan, S. M. H., Nezhadsistani, N., Bodaghi, O., & Qu, Q. (2022). Patents and intellectual property assets as non-fungible tokens; key technologies and challenges. *Scientific Reports*, *12*(1), 2178. doi:10.1038/s41598-022-05920-6 PMID:35140251

Bandara, E., Shetty, S., Mukkamala, R., Liang, X., Foytik, P., Ranasinghe, N., & De Zoysa, K. (2022). Casper: A blockchain-based system for efficient and secure customer credential verification. *Journal of Banking and Financial Technology*, *6*(1), 43–62. doi:10.1007/s42786-021-00036-3

Banking in the Metaverse: Evolving Opportunity—Spiceworks. (n.d.). Spice Works. https://www.spiceworks.com/finance/fintech/guest-article/banking-in-the-metaverse/

Barr, M., & Copeland-Stewart, A. (2022). Playing video games during the COVID-19 pandemic and effects on players' well-being. *Games and Culture, 17*(1), 122–139. doi:10.1177/15554120211017036

Bartels, J., & Hoogendam, K. (2011). The role of social identity and attitudes toward sustainability brands in buying behaviors for organic products. *Journal of Brand Management, 18*(9), 697–708. doi:10.1057/bm.2011.3

Bassi, L. (2011). Raging debates in HR analytics. *People Strategy, 34*(2), 14–18.

Baumruk, R. (2004). The missing link: The role of employee engagement in business success. *Workspan, 47*, 48–52.

Behl, A., Pereira, V., Nigam, A., Wamba, S., & Sindhwani, R. (2024). Knowledge development in non-fungible tokens (NFT): a scoping review. *Journal of Knowledge Management, 28*(1), 232-267. doi/ doi:10.1108/JKM-12-2022-0937

Belk, R., Humayun, M., & Brouard, M. (2022). Money, possessions, and ownership in the Metaverse: NFTs, cryptocurrencies, Web3 and Wild Markets. *Journal of Business Research, 153*, 198–205. doi:10.1016/j.jbusres.2022.08.031

Ben-Gal, C. H. (2019). An ROI-based review of HR analytics: Practical implementation tools. *Personnel Review*.

Bhatnagar, J. (2009). Exploring psychological contract and employee engagement In India. In Budhwar, P.S. and Bhatnagar, J (Eds.) The changing face of people management in India. London: Routledge: Taylor and Francis doi:10.4324/9780203884867.pt4

Bhatnagar, J. (2007). Talent management strategy of employee engagement of Indian ITES employees: Key to retention. *Employee Relations, 29*(6), 640–663. doi:10.1108/01425450710826122

Bhattacharyya, D. K. (2017). *HR Analytics: Understanding Theories and Applications*. SAGE Publications.

Bhujel, S., & Rahulamathavan, Y. (2022). A survey: Security, transparency, and scalability issues of nft's and its marketplaces. *Sensors (Basel), 22*(22), 8833. doi:10.3390/s22228833 PMID:36433429

Bibri, S. E., & Allam, Z. (2022). The Metaverse as a virtual form of data-driven smart cities: The ethics of the hyper-connectivity, datafication, algorithmization, and platformization of urban society. *Computational Urban Science, 2*(1), 22. doi:10.1007/s43762-022-00050-1 PMID:35915731

Bigne, E., Chatzipanagiotou, K., & Ruiz, C. (2020). Pictorial content, sequence of conflicting online reviews and consumer decision-making: The stimulus-organism-response model revisited. *Journal of Business Research, 115*, 403–416. doi:10.1016/j.jbusres.2019.11.031

Bilgihan, A., & Ricci, P. (2023). The new era of hotel marketing: Integrating cutting-edge technologies with core marketing principles. *Journal of Hospitality and Tourism Technology*. doi:10.1108/JHTT-04-2023-0095

Bloomberg. (2023). Metaverse Market Size Worth $678.8 Billion by 2030: Grand View Research, Inc. Bloomberg. https://www.bloomberg.com/press-releases/2022-03-09/metaverse-market-size-worth-678-8-billion-by-2030-grand-view-research-inc

Boakye, A., & Lamptey, A. Y. (2020). The Rise of HR Analytics: Exploring Its Implications from a Developing Country Perspective. *Journal of Human Resource Management, 8*(3), 181–189. doi:10.11648/j.jhrm.20200803.19

Boccia, F., & Covino, D. (2023). Knowledge and Food Sustainability: The Metaverse as a New Economic-Environmental Paradigm. *Journal of the Knowledge Economy*, 1–14. doi:10.1007/s13132-023-01626-w

Bochmann, L., Bänziger, T., Kunz, A., & Wegener, K. (2017). Human-robot collaboration in decentralized manufacturing systems: An approach for simulation-based evaluation of future intelligent production. *Procedia CIRP, 62*, 624–629. doi:10.1016/j.procir.2016.06.021

Bonnet, S., & Teuteberg, F. (2023). Impact of blockchain and distributed ledger technology for the management, protection, enforcement and monetization of intellectual property: A systematic literature review. *Information Systems and e-Business Management, 21*(2), 229–275. doi:10.1007/s10257-022-00579-y

Borisova, N., Moore, N., Sira Mahalingappa, S., Cumming, P., Dave, S., Abraham, S., & Syunyakov, T. (2022). Virtual Reality-Based Interventions for Treating Depression in the Context of COVID-19 Pandemic: Inducing the Proficit in Positive Emotions as a Key Concept of Recovery and a Path Back to Normality. *Psychiatria Danubina, 34*(Suppl 8), 276–284. PMID:36170742

Boudreau, J., & Cascio, W. (2017). Human capital analytics: Why are we not there? *J Organ Eff, 4*(2), 119–126. doi:10.1108/JOEPP-03-2017-0021

Bourgonjon, J., Valcke, M., Soetaert, R., & Schellens, T. (2009, November). Exploring the acceptance of video games in the classroom by secondary school students. In *17th International Conference on Computers in Education* (pp. 651-658). Hong Kong: Asia-Pacific Society for Computers in Education.

Bracq, M. S., Michinov, E., & Jannin, P. (2019). Virtual Reality Simulation in Nontechnical Skills Training for Healthcare Professionals: A Systematic Review. *Simulation in Healthcare, 14*(3), 188–194. doi:10.1097/SIH.0000000000000347 PMID:30601464

Brady, A. (2003). How to generate sustainable brand value from responsibility. *Journal of Brand Management, 10*(4), 279–289. doi:10.1057/palgrave.bm.2540124

Buhalis, D., & Karatay, N. (2022). Mixed reality (MR) for generation Z in cultural heritage tourism towards metaverse. In *Information and Communication Technologies in Tourism 2022: Proceedings of the ENTER 2022 eTourism Conference,* (pp. 16-27). Springer International Publishing. 10.1007/978-3-030-94751-4_2

Buhalis, D., Lin, M. S., & Leung, D. (2023b). Metaverse as a driver for customer experience and value co-creation: Implications for hospitality and tourism management and marketing. *International Journal of Contemporary Hospitality Management.* doi:10.1108/IJCHM-05-2022-0631

Buhalis, D., & Law, R. (2008). Progress in information technology and tourism management: 20 years on and 10 years after the Internet—The state of eTourism research. *Tourism Management, 29*(4), 609–623. doi:10.1016/j.tourman.2008.01.005

Buhalis, D., Leung, D., & Lin, M. (2023a). Metaverse as a disruptive technology revolutionising tourism management and marketing. *Tourism Management, 97*(1), 1–11. doi:10.1016/j.tourman.2023.104724

Çağlayan Aksoy, P., & Özkan Üner, Z. (2021). Nfts And Copyright: Challenges And Opportunities. *Journal Of Intellectual Property Law And Practice, 16*(10), 1115–1126. doi:10.1093/jiplp/jpab104

Calandra, D., Oppioli, M., Sadraei, R., Jafari-Sadeghi, V., & Biancone, P. P. (2023). Metaverse meets digital entrepreneurship: A practitioner-based qualitative synthesis. *International Journal of Entrepreneurial Behaviour & Research.*

Caldarelli, G., & Ellul, J. (2021). The Blockchain Oracle Problem in Decentralized Finance—A Multivocal Approach. *Applied Sciences (Basel, Switzerland), 11*(16), 16. doi:10.3390/app11167572

Candrasari, Y. (2020). Mediated Interpersonal Communication: A New Way of Social Interaction in the Digital Age. *Proceedings of the 2nd International Media Conference 2019 (IMC 2019).* IEEE. 10.2991/assehr.k.200325.041

Cao, L. (2022). Decentralized AI: Edge Intelligence and Smart Blockchain, Metaverse, Web3, and DeSci. *IEEE Intelligent Systems, 37*(3), 6–19. doi:10.1109/MIS.2022.3181504

Carruth, D. W. (2017). Virtual reality for education and workforce training. *Paper presented at the 2017 15th International Conference on Emerging eLearning Technologies and Applications (ICETA).* IEEE. 10.1109/ICETA.2017.8102472

Casado-Díaz, A. B., Andreu, L., Beckmann, S. C., & Miller, C. (2020). Negative online reviews and webcare strategies in social media: Effects on hotel attitude and booking intentions. *Current Issues in Tourism, 23*(4), 418–422. doi:10.1080/13683500.2018.1546675

Chakraborty, U., & Biswal, S. K. (2020). Impact of Online Reviews on Consumer's Hotel Booking Intentions: Does Brand Image Mediate? *Journal of Promotion Management, 26*(7), 943–963. doi:10.1080/10496491.2020.1746465

Challa, V. N. S. K., Padmalatha, P., & Burra, V. K. (2021). Influence of Relationship Marketing Variables on Social Media Marketing. *Empirical Economics Letters, 20*(4), 241249. https://www.researchgate.net/publication/357516260

Chalmers, D., Fisch, C., Matthews, R., Quinn, W., & Recker, J. (2022). Beyond the bubble: Will NFTs and digital proof of ownership empower creative industry entrepreneurs? *Journal of Business Venturing Insights, 17*, e00309. doi:10.1016/j.jbvi.2022.e00309

Chang, W., Chao, R.-F., & Chien, G. (2021). Impacts of Online Social Support and Perceived Value in Influential Travel Blogs. *International Journal of Research in Business and Social Science (2147- 4478)*, *10*(4), 339–348. doi:10.20525/ijrbs.v10i4.1190

Chang, M., Gu, S., Huang, L., & Hsiao, T. Y. (2021). Constructing the Critical Success Factors in Digital Transformation for Taiwan's Travel Agencies. *Frontiers*, *2*(11).

Chan, I. C. C., Lam, L. W., Chow, C. W. C., Fong, L. H. N., & Law, R. (2017). The effect of online reviews on hotel booking intention: The role of reader-reviewer similarity. *International Journal of Hospitality Management*, *66*, 54–65. doi:10.1016/j.ijhm.2017.06.007

Chaturvedi, O. (2022). *Miller lite super bowl commercial running in the metaverse*. Techstory. https://techstory.in/miller-lite-super-bowl-commercial-running-in-the-metaverse/

Cheng, W., Tian, R., & Chiu, D. K. (2023). Travel vlogs influencing tourist decisions: Information preferences and gender differences. *Aslib Journal of Information Management*. doi:10.1108/AJIM-05-2022-0261

Cheng, Y., Wei, W., & Zhang, L. (2020). Seeing destinations through vlogs: Implications for leveraging customer engagement behavior to increase travel intention. *International Journal of Contemporary Hospitality Management*, *32*(10), 3227–3248. doi:10.1108/IJCHM-04-2020-0319

Chen, H., Duan, H., Abdallah, M., Zhu, Y., Wen, Y., Saddik, A. E., & Cai, W. (2023). Web3 Metaverse: State-Of-The-Art And Vision. *ACM Transactions on Multimedia Computing Communications and Applications*, *20*(4), 1–42. doi:10.1145/3630258

Choi, H.-Y., & Lee, Y. K. (2021). View of The Influence of Travel Blog Quality on User Satisfaction and Intention to Revisit. *NVEO - Natural Volatiles & Essential Oils*, *8*(4), 848–861. https://www.nveo.org/index.php/journal/article/view/225/202

Choi, H. Y. (2022). Working in the metaverse: Does telework in a metaverse office have the potential to reduce population pressure in megacities? Evidence from young adults in Seoul, South Korea. *Sustainability (Basel)*, *14*(6), 3629. doi:10.3390/su14063629

Cho, J., tom Dieck, M. C., & Jung, T. (2023). What is the Metaverse? Challenges, Opportunities, Definition, and Future Research Directions. In T. Jung, M. C. tom Dieck, & S. M. Correia Loureiro (Eds.), *Extended Reality and Metaverse* (pp. 3–26). Springer International Publishing. doi:10.1007/978-3-031-25390-4_1

Choudhury, H. A., & Barman, A. (2016). Human Resource Analytics-Discovering Research Issues Posited in its Milleu in India organisation. *Discovering Research Issues in Applications of HRA in India*, (5-2016), 1-19.

Cibulka, J., & Giannoumis, G. A. (2017). *Augmented and virtual reality for engineering education*. Research Gate.

Cifci, I., Rather, R., Taspinar, O., & Altunel, G. (2023). Demystifying destination attachment, self-congruity and revisiting intention in dark tourism destinations through the gender-based lens. *Tourism Recreation Research*, 1–17. doi:10.1080/02508281.2023.2190280

Ciobanu, A. C., & Meşniţă, G. (2022, March). AI Ethics for Industry 5.0—From Principles to Practice. In *Proceedings of the Workshop of I-ESA* (Vol. 22). Research Gate.

Ciobanu, A. C., & Meşniţă, G. (2021). AI ETHICS IN BUSINESS–A Bibliometric APPROACH. *Review of Economic and Business Studies*, *14*(28), 169–202. doi:10.47743/rebs-2021-2-0009

Çolakoğlu, Ü., Anış, E., Esen, Ö. and Tuncay, C.S. (2023). The evaluation of tourists' virtual reality experiences in the transition process to Metaverse. *Journal of Hospitality and Tourism Insights*. doi:10.1108/JHTI-09-2022-0426

Collins, C. (2008). Looking to the future: Higher education in the Metaverse. *EDUCAUSE Review*, *43*(5), 50–52.

Damar, M. (2021). Metaverse Shape of Your Life for Future: A bibliometric snapshot. *Journal of Metaverse*, *1*(1), 1.

Daneshfar, F., & Jamshidi, M. B. (2023). An octonion-based nonlinear echo state network for speech emotion recognition in Metaverse. *Neural Networks*, *163*, 108–121. doi:10.1016/j.neunet.2023.03.026 PMID:37030275

Davenport, T. H., Harris, J. G., & Morison, R. (2010). *Analytics at Work: Smarter Decisions, Better Results*. Harvard Business School Press.

David, L. E. E., & Won, L. S. (2022). Nft of nft: Is our imagination the only limitation of the metaverse?. *The Journal of The British Blockchain Association*. https://doi.org/ doi:10.31585/jbba-5-2-(2)2022

Davis, F. D. (1985). *A technology acceptance model for empirically testing new end-user information systems: Theory and results* [Doctoral dissertation, Massachusetts Institute of Technology].

De Giovanni, P. (2023). Sustainability of the Metaverse: A transition to Industry 5.0. *Sustainability (Basel)*, *15*(7), 6079. doi:10.3390/su15076079

De Jaegher, H., Di Paolo, E., & Gallagher, S. (2010). Can social interaction constitute social cognition? *Trends in Cognitive Sciences*, *14*(10), 441–447. https://doi.org/. 06.009 doi:10.1016/j.tics.2010

de Oliveira, L. B., Cavazotte, F., & Alan Dunzer, R. (2019). The interactive effects of organisational and leadership career management support on job satisfaction and turnover intention. *International Journal of Human Resource Management*, *30*(10), 1583–1603. doi:10.1080/09585192.2017.1298650

Delbeck, S., & Heise, H. M. (2021). Quality assurance of commercial insulin formulations: Novel assay using infrared spectroscopy. *Journal of Diabetes Science and Technology*, *15*(4), 865–873. doi:10.1177/1932296820913874 PMID:32281880

Demir, Ç. (2022). A Review on the Effects of Metaverse Technology on the Future of the Hotel Sector. *Journal of Tourism and Gastronomy Studies*, *10*(1), 542–555.

Demir, Ç. (2022). Metaverse teknolojisinin otel sektörünün geleceğine etkileri üzerine bir inceleme. *Journal of Tourism and Gastronomy Studies, 10*(1), 542–555.

Demiris, G. (2006). The diffusion of virtual communities in health care: Concepts and challenges. *Patient Education and Counseling, 62*(2), 178–188. doi:10.1016/j.pec.2005.10.003 PMID:16406472

Demir, K. A., Döven, G., & Sezen, B. (2019). Industry 5.0 and human-robot co-working. *Procedia Computer Science, 158*, 688–695. doi:10.1016/j.procs.2019.09.104

Demir, M., & Demir, Ş. Ş. (2023). Is ChatGPT the right technology for service individualization and value co-creation? evidence from the travel industry. *Journal of Travel & Tourism Marketing, 40*(5), 383–398. doi:10.1080/10548408.2023.2255884

Dewantara, M. H., Gardiner, S., & Jin, X. (2023). Travel vlog ecosystem in tourism digital marketing evolution: A narrative literature review. *Current Issues in Tourism, 26*(19), 3125–3139. doi:10.1080/13683500.2022.2136568

Dhiman, V., & Arora, M. (2023). *How foresight has evolved since 1999? Understanding its themes, scope and focus. Foresight.* EarlyCite. doi:10.1108/FS-01-2023-0001

Dhiman, V., & Arora, M. (2024). *Exploring the linkage between business incubation and entrepreneurship: understanding trends, themes and future research agenda. LBS Journal of Management & Research.* EarlyCite. doi:10.1108/LBSJMR-06-2023-0021

Di Martino, V., & Wirth, L. (1990). Telework: A new way of working and living. *Int'l Lab. Rev., 129*, 529.

Di Nardo, M., & Yu, H. (2021). Special issue "Industry 5.0: The prelude to the sixth industrial revolution". *Applied System Innovation, 4*(3), 45. doi:10.3390/asi4030045

Dionisio, J. D. N., Iii, W. G. B., & Gilbert, R. (2013). 3D virtual worlds and the metaverse: Current status and future possibilities. *ACM Computing Surveys, 45*(3), 1–38. doi:10.1145/2480741.2480751

Dong, Y., & Wang, C. (2023). Copyright protection on NFT digital works in the Metaverse. *Security and Safety, 2*, 2023013. doi:10.1051/sands/2023013

Dorostkar, E., & Najarsadeghi, M. (2023). Sustainability and urban climate: How Metaverse can influence urban planning? *Environment and Planning. B, Urban Analytics and City Science, 50*(7), 23998083231181596. doi:10.1177/23998083231181596

Dwityas, N. A., & Briandana, R. (2017). Social Media in Travel Decision Making Process. *International Journal of Humanities and Social Science, 7*(7). https://www.researchgate.net/publication/322749479

Dwivedi, Y. K., Hughes, L., Baabdullah, A. M., Ribeiro-Navarrete, S., Giannakis, M., Al-Debei, M. M., Dennehy, D., Metri, B., Buhalis, D., Cheung, C. M. K., Conboy, K., Doyle, R., Dubey, R., Dutot, V., Felix, R., Goyal, D. P., Gustafsson, A., Hinsch, C., Jebabli, I., & Wamba, S. F. (2022). Metaverse beyond the hype: Multidisciplinary perspectives on emerging challenges, opportunities, and agenda for research, practice and policy. *International Journal of Information Management, 66*, 102542. doi:10.1016/j.ijinfomgt.2022.102542

Dwivedi, Y. K., Kshetri, N., Hughes, L., Rana, N. P., Baabdullah, A. M., Kar, A. K., Koohang, A., Ribeiro-Navarrete, S., Belei, N., Balakrishnan, J., Basu, S., Behl, A., Davies, G. H., Dutot, V., Dwivedi, R., Evans, L., Felix, R., Foster-Fletcher, R., Giannakis, M., & Yan, M. (2023). Exploring the Darkverse: A Multi-Perspective Analysis of the Negative Societal Impacts of the Metaverse. *Information Systems Frontiers, 25*(5), 2071–2114. doi:10.1007/s10796-023-10400-x PMID:37361890

Dwivedi, Y., Hughes, L., Wang, Y., Alalwan, A. A., Ahn, S., Balakrishnan, J., Barta, S., Belk, R., Buhalis, D., Dutot, V., Felix, R., Filieri, R., Flavi'an, C., Gustafsson, A., Hinsch, C., Hollensen, S., Jain, V., Kim, J., Krishen, A., & Wirtz, J. (2023). How metaverse will change the future of marketing: Implications for Research and Practice. *Psychology and Marketing*. doi:10.1002/mar.21767

ElFar, O. A., Chang, C. K., Leong, H. Y., Peter, A. P., Chew, K. W., & Show, P. L. (2021). Prospects of Industry 5.0 in algae: Customization of production and new advance technology for clean bioenergy generation. *Energy Conversion and Management: X, 10*, 100048.

Elwalda, A., & Lu, K. (2016). The impact of online customer reviews (OCRs) on customers' purchase decisions: An exploration of the main dimensions of OCRs. *Journal of Customer Behaviour, 15*(2), 123–152. doi:10.1362/147539216X14594362873695

Elwalda, A., Lü, K., & Ali, M. (2016). Perceived derived attributes of online customer reviews. *Computers in Human Behavior, 56*, 306–319. doi:10.1016/j.chb.2015.11.051

Enache, M. C. (2022). Metaverse Opportunities for Businesses. *Annals of the University Dunarea de Jos of Galati: Fascicle: I, Economics & Applied Informatics, 28*(1).

Ercan, F. (2022). Metaverse teknolojisinin gelecekte turizm sektörüne olası etkilerini belirlemeye yönelik bir araştırma. *Anadolu Üniversitesi Sosyal Bilimler Dergisi, 22*(4), 1063–1092. doi:10.18037/ausbd.1225882

Erdil, T. S. (2013). Strategic brand management based on sustainable-oriented view: An evaluation in Turkish home appliance industry. *Procedia: Social and Behavioral Sciences, 99*, 122–132. doi:10.1016/j.sbspro.2013.10.478

Erkan, I., & Evans, C. (2018). Social media or shopping websites? The influence of eWOM on consumers' online purchase intentions. *Journal of Marketing Communications, 24*(6), 617–632. doi:10.1080/13527266.2016.1184706

Falletta, S. V. (2014). In search of HR intelligence: Evidence-based HR Analytics practices in high performing companies. *People Strategy, 36*(4), 28–37.

Falletta, S. V., & Combs, W. L. (2021). The HR analytics cycle: A seven-step process for building evidence-based and ethical HR analytics capabilities. *Journal of Work-Applied Management*, *13*(1), 51–68. doi:10.1108/JWAM-03-2020-0020

Fernandez, P. (2022). Facebook, Meta, the metaverse and libraries. *Library Hi Tech News*, *39*(4), 1–5. doi:10.1108/LHTN-03-2022-0037

Fernandez, V., & Gallardo-Gallardo, E. (2021). Tackling the HR digitalization challenge: Key factors and barriers to HR analytics adoption. *Competitiveness Review*, *31*(1), 162–187. doi:10.1108/CR-12-2019-0163

Filieri, R., Lin, Z., Pino, G., Alguezaui, S., & Inversini, A. (2021). The role of visual cues in eWOM on consumers' behavioral intention and decisions. *Journal of Business Research*, *135*, 663–675. doi:10.1016/j.jbusres.2021.06.055

Flavián, C., Ibáñez-Sánchez, S., & Orús, C. (2021). Impacts of technological embodiment through virtual reality on potential guests' emotions and engagement. *Journal of Hospitality Marketing & Management*, *30*(1), 1–20. doi:10.1080/19368623.2020.1770146

Floridi, L. (2021). Establishing the rules for building trustworthy AI. *Ethics, Governance, and Policies in Artificial Intelligence*, 41-45.

Floridi, L., Cowls, J., Beltrametti, M., Chatila, R., Chazerand, P., Dignum, V., & Vayena, E. (2021). An ethical framework for a good AI society: Opportunities, risks, principles, and recommendations. *Ethics, governance, and policies in artificial intelligence*, 19-39.

Forbes. (2022). Will The Metaverse Revolutionize The Hospitality Industry? *Forbes*. https://www.forbes.com/sites/forbestechcouncil/2022/01/10/will-the-metaverse-revolutionize-the-hospitality-industry/?sh=307cca4a25e7 (accessed 4 December 2023).

Fox, A. K., Deitz, G. D., Royne, M. B., & Fox, J. D. (2018). The face of contagion: Consumer response to service failure depiction in online reviews. *European Journal of Marketing*, *52*(1–2), 39–65. doi:10.1108/EJM-12-2016-0887

Frank, F. D., Finnegan, R. P., & Taylor, C. R. (2004). The race for talent: Retaining and engaging workers in the 21st century. *Human Resource Planning*, *27*(3), 12–25.

Fred, M.O. & Kinange U.M. (2015). *Overview of HR Analytics to maximize Human capital investment*. Research Gate.

Freeman, D., Reeve, S., Robinson, A., Ehlers, A., Clark, D., Spanlang, B., & Slater, M. (2017). Virtual reality in the assessment, understanding, and treatment of mental health disorders. *Psychological Medicine*, *47*(14), 2393–2400. doi:10.1017/S003329171700040X PMID:28325167

Fussell, S. G., & Truong, D. (2022). Using virtual reality for dynamic learning: An extended technology acceptance model. *Virtual Reality (Waltham Cross)*, *26*(1), 249–267. doi:10.1007/s10055-021-00554-x PMID:34276237

Gadekallu, T. R., Huynh-The, T., Wang, W., Yenduri, G., Ranaweera, P., Pham, Q.-V., da Costa, D. B., & Liyanage, M. (2022). *Blockchain for the Metaverse: A Review* (arXiv:2203.09738). arXiv. https://doi.org//arXiv.2203.09738 doi:10.48550

Garcia, M. B., Revano, T. F., Loresco, P. J. M., Maaliw, R. R., Oducado, R. M. F., & Uludag, K. (2022, December). Virtual Dietitian as a Precision Nutrition Application for Gym and Fitness Enthusiasts: A Quality Improvement Initiative. In *2022 IEEE 14th International Conference on Humanoid, Nanotechnology, Information Technology, Communication and Control, Environment, and Management (HNICEM)* (pp. 1-5). IEEE. 10.1109/HNICEM57413.2022.10109490

Gargrish, S., Mantri, A., & Kaur, D. P. (2020). Augmented reality-based learning environment to enhance teaching-learning experience in geometry education. *Procedia Computer Science*, *172*, 1039–1046. doi:10.1016/j.procs.2020.05.152

Gates, S. (2002). *Value at work: The risks and opportunities of human capital measurement and reporting*. Conference Board.

Gawke, J. C., Gorgievski, M. J., & Bakker, A. B. (2017). Employee intrapreneurship and work engagement: A latent change score approach. *Journal of Vocational Behavior*, *100*, 88–100. doi:10.1016/j.jvb.2017.03.002

George-Reyes, C. E., Ramírez-Montoya, M. S., & López-Caudana, E. O. (2023). Imbrication of the Metaverse in the complexity of education 4.0: Approach from an analysis of the literature. Pixel-Bit. *Revista de Medios y Educación*, *66*, 199–237. doi:10.12795/pixelbit.97337

Geraghty, L., Lee, T., Glickman, J., & Rainwater, B. (2022). *Cities and the metaverse*. National League of Cities, Centre for City Solutions. https://www.nlc.org/wp-content/uploads/2022/04/CS-Cities-and-the-Metaverse_v4-Final-1.pdf

Gholamhosseinzadeh, M. S. (2023). Theorising vloggers' approaches and practices in travel vlog production through grounded theory. *Journal of Hospitality Marketing & Management*, *32*(2), 196–223. doi:10.1080/19368623.2023.2164392

Giang Barrera, K., & Shah, D. (2023). Marketing in the Metaverse: Conceptual understanding, framework, and research agenda. *Journal of Business Research*, *155*, 113420. doi:10.1016/j.jbusres.2022.113420

Giglio, F. (2021). Fintech: A Literature Review. *European Research Studies Journal*, *24*(2b), 600–627. doi:10.5539/ibr.v15n1p80

Glenk, S. (2023, July 7). *The Metaverse: Dreamland or Dystopia?* SAP News Center. https://news.sap.com/2023/07/metaverse-art-exhibition/

Go, H., & Kang, M. (2023). Metaverse tourism for sustainable tourism development: Tourism agenda 2030. *Tourism Review*, *78*(2), 381–394. doi:10.1108/TR-02-2022-0102

Golob, U., Burghausen, M., Kernstock, J., & Davies, M. A. (2022). Brand management and sustainability: Exploring potential for the transformative power of brands. *Journal of Brand Management*, *29*(6), 1–7. doi:10.1057/s41262-022-00293-7

Golonka, E. M., Bowles, A. R., Frank, V. M., Richardson, D. L., & Freynik, S. (2014). Technologies for foreign language learning: A review of technology types and their effectiveness. *Computer Assisted Language Learning, 27*(1), 70–105. doi:10.1080/09588221.2012.700315

Gomber, P., Koch, J. A., & Siering, M. (2017). Digital Finance and FinTech: Current research and future research directions. *Journal of Business Economics, 87*, 537–580. doi:10.1007/s11573-017-0852-x

Gong, X., Wang, C., Yan, Y., Liu, M., & Ali, R. (2020). What drives sustainable brand awareness: Exploring the cognitive symmetry between brand strategy and consumer brand knowledge. *Symmetry, 12*(2), 198. doi:10.3390/sym12020198

Gretzel, U., Yoo, K. H., & Purifoy, M. (2007). *Online travel review study: Role and impact of online travel reviews.*

Gretzel, U. (2021). Conceptualizing the smart tourism mindset: Fostering utopian thinking in smart tourism development. *Journal of Smart Tourism, 1*(1), 3–8. doi:10.52255/smarttourism.2021.1.1.2

Gretzel, U., & Koo, C. (2021). Smart tourism cities: A duality of place where technology supports the convergence of touristic and residential experiences. *Asia Pacific Journal of Tourism Research, 26*(4), 352–364. doi:10.1080/10941665.2021.1897636

Grillon, H., Riquier, F., Herbelin, B., & Thalmann, D. (2006). Virtual reality as a therapeutic tool in the confines of social anxiety disorder treatment. *International Journal on Disability and Human Development : IJDHD, 5*(3), 243–250. doi:10.1515/IJDHD.2006.5.3.243

Grubor, A., & Milovanov, O. (2017). Brand strategies in the era of sustainability. *Interdisciplinary Description of Complex Systems: INDECS, 15*(1), 78–88. doi:10.7906/indecs.15.1.6

Guadamuz, A. (December, 2021). Non-Fungible Tokens (Nfts) And Copyright, *Wipo Magazine.* https://www.wipo.int/wipo_magazine/en/2021/04/article_0007.html

Guo, Y., & Liang, C. (2016). Blockchain application and outlook in the banking industry. *Financial Innovation, 2*(1), 24. doi:10.1186/s40854-016-0034-9

Gupta, B. B., Gaurav, A., Albeshri, A. A., & Alsalman, D. (2023). New paradigms of sustainable entrepreneurship in metaverse: A micro-level perspective. *The International Entrepreneurship and Management Journal, 19*(3), 1–17. doi:10.1007/s11365-023-00875-0

Gursoy, D., Malodia, S., & Dhir, A. (2022). The metaverse in the hospitality and tourism industry: An overview of current trends and future research directions. *Journal of Hospitality Marketing & Management, 22*(5), 1–8. doi:10.1080/19368623.2022.2072504

Hagendorff, T. (2020). The ethics of AI ethics: An evaluation of guidelines. *Minds and Machines, 30*(1), 99–120. doi:10.1007/s11023-020-09517-8

Hammi, B., Zeadally, S., & Perez, A. J. (2023). Non-fungible tokens: A review. *IEEE Internet of Things Magazine, 6*(1), 46–50. doi:10.1109/IOTM.001.2200244

Handoko, B. L., Lindawati, A. S. L., Sarjono, H., & Mustapha, M. (2023). Innovation Diffusion and Technology Acceptance Model in Predicting Auditor Acceptance of Metaverse Technology. *Journal of System and Management Sciences, 13*(5), 443–456.

Harris, J. G., Craig, E., & Light, D. A. (2011). Talent and analytics: New approaches, higher ROI. *The Journal of Business Strategy, 32*(6), 4–13. doi:10.1108/02756661111180087

Hasanova, H., Baek, U., Shin, M., Cho, K., & Kim, M.-S. (2019). A survey on blockchain cybersecurity vulnerabilities and possible countermeasures. *International Journal of Network Management, 29*(2), e2060. doi:10.1002/nem.2060

Hassani, H., Huang, X., & Silva, E. (2018). Banking with blockchain-ed big data. *Journal of Management Analytics, 5*(4), 256–275. doi:10.1080/23270012.2018.1528900

Hazan, S. (2010). *Musing the metaverse. Heritage in the Digital Era, Multi-Science Publishing, Brentwood.* Esse.

HCMI. (2022). Employee Engagement Analytics: How to Engage and Retain Talent. HCMI. https://www.hcmi.co/post/employee-engagement-analytics-how-to- engage-and-retain-talent.

He, J., Xu, D., & Chen, T. (2022). Travel vlogging practice and its impacts on tourist experiences. *Current Issues in Tourism, 25*(15), 2518–2533. doi:10.1080/13683500.2021.1971166

Hennig-Thurau, T., Gwinner, K. P., Walsh, G., & Gremler, D. D. (2004). Electronic word-of-mouth via consumer-opinion platforms: What motivates consumers to articulate themselves on the internet? *Journal of Interactive Marketing, 18*(1), 38–52. doi:10.1002/dir.10073

Hernandez-Ortega, B. (2019). Not so positive, please!: Effects of online consumer reviews on evaluations during the decision-making process. *Internet Research, 29*(4), 606–637. doi:10.1108/INTR-07-2017-0257

Heuvel, S., & Bondarouk, T. (2017). The rise (and fall?) of HR Analyticss: A study into the future application, value, structure, and system support. *Journal of organisational Effectiveness. People and Performance, 4*(2), 127–148.

Hom, P. W., Lee, T. W., Shaw, J. D., & Hausknecht, J. P. (2017). One hundred years of employee turnover theory and research. *The Journal of Applied Psychology, 102*(3), 530–545. doi:10.1037/apl0000103 PMID:28125259

Houser, D., & Wooders, J. (2006). Reputation in auctions: Theory, and evidence from eBay. *Journal of Economics & Management Strategy, 15*(2), 353–369. doi:10.1111/j.1530-9134.2006.00103.x

Huang, K.-T., Ball, C., Francis, J., Ratan, R., Boumis, J., & Fordham, J. (2019). Augmented versus virtual reality in education: An exploratory study examining science knowledge retention when using augmented reality/virtual reality mobile applications. *Cyberpsychology, Behavior, and Social Networking, 22*(2), 105–110. doi:10.1089/cyber.2018.0150 PMID:30657334

Huddleston, T., Jr. (2021). *This 29 year old book predicted the 'metaverse' and some of Facebook's plans are eerily similar.* CNBC. https://www.cnbc.com/2021/11/03/how-the-1992-sci-fi-novel-snow-crash-predicted-facebooks-metaverse.html

Huertas, A. (2018). How live videos and stories in social media influence tourist opinions and behaviour. *Information Technology & Tourism, 19*(1), 1–28. doi:10.1007/s40558-018-0112-0

Huselid, M. A. (2018). The science and practice of workforce analytics: Introduction to the HRM special issue. *Human Resource Management, 57*(3), 679–684. doi:10.1002/hrm.21916

Huseynov, F., & Dhahak, K. (2020). The Impact of Online Consumer Reviews (OCR) on Online Consumers Purchase Intention. *Journal of Business Research - Turk, 12*(2), 990–1005. doi:10.20491/isarder.2020.889

Huynh-The, T., Gadekallu, T. R., Wang, W., Yenduri, G., Ranaweera, P., Pham, Q. V., da Costa, D. B., & Liyanage, M. (2023). Blockchain for the metaverse: A Review. *Future Generation Computer Systems, 143*, 401–419. doi:10.1016/j.future.2023.02.008

Ibrahim, A. K. (2021). Evolution Of The Web: From Web 1.0 To 4.0. *Qubahan Academic Journal, 1*(3), doi: . doi:20-28

Ioannidis, S., & Kontis, A. P. (2023). Metaverse for tourists and tourism destinations. *Information Technology & Tourism, 25*(4), 483–506. doi:10.1007/s40558-023-00271-y

Ishaq, M. I., & Di Maria, E. (2020). Sustainability countenance in brand equity: A critical review and future research directions. *Journal of Brand Management, 27*(1), 15–34. doi:10.1057/s41262-019-00167-5

Ismail, L., & Materwala, H. (2019). A Review of Blockchain Architecture and Consensus Protocols: Use Cases, Challenges, and Solutions. *Symmetry, 11*(10), 10. doi:10.3390/sym11101198

Jacobides, M. G., Candelon, F., Krayer, L., Round, K., & Chen, W. (2023). Building synthetic worlds: Lessons from the excessive infatuation and oversold disillusionment with the metaverse. *Industry and Innovation*, 1–25.

Jahan, N., Naveed, S., Zeshan, M., & Tahir, M. A. (2016, November 4). (n.d.). How to Conduct a Systematic Review: A Narrative Literature Review. *Cureus, 8*(11), e864. doi:10.7759/cureus.864 PMID:27924252

Jaimini, U., Zhang, T., Brikis, G. O., & Sheth, A. (2022). iMetaverseKG: Industrial Metaverse Knowledge Graph to Promote Interoperability in Design and Engineering Applications. *IEEE Internet Computing, 26*(6), 59–67. doi:10.1109/MIC.2022.3212085

Jain, A., & Nagar, N. (2015). An Emerging Trend in Human Resource Management. *SS International Journal of Economics and Management, 5*(1), 1–10.

Jamader, A. R., Chowdhary, S., & Shankar Jha, S. (2023). A Road Map for Two Decades of Sustainable Tourism Development Framework. In Resilient and Sustainable Destinations After Disaster: Challenges and Strategies (pp. 9-18). Emerald Publishing Limited. doi:10.1108/978-1-80382-021-720231002

Jamader, A. R. (2022). A Brief Report Of The Upcoming & Present Economic Impact To Hospitality Industry In COVID19 Situations. *Journal of Pharmaceutical Negative Results*, 2289–2302.

Jamader A. R. (2023). The Sustainable Ecotourism Strategy: Participation & Combating. *Available at* SSRN 4399894.

Jamader, A. R., Chowdhary, S., Jha, S. S., & Roy, B. (2023). Application of Economic Models to Green Circumstance for Management of Littoral Area: A Sustainable Tourism Arrangement. *SMART Journal of Business Management Studies*, *19*(1), 70–84. doi:10.5958/2321-2012.2023.00008.8

Jamader, A. R., Immanuel, J. S., Ebenezer, V., Rakhi, R. A., Sagayam, K. M., & Das, P. (2023). Virtual Education, Training And Internships In Hospitality And Tourism During Covid-19 Situation. *Journal of Pharmaceutical Negative Results*, 286–290.

Jauhiainen, J. S., Krohn, C., & Junnila, J. (2022). Metaverse and Sustainability: Systematic Review of Scientific Publications until 2022 and Beyond. *Sustainability (Basel)*, *15*(1), 346. doi:10.3390/su15010346

Jefferson, R. N., & Arnold, L. W. (2009). Effects of virtual education on academic culture: Perceived advantages and disadvantages. *Online Submission*, *6*(3), 61–66.

Jeon, J. E. (2021). The effects of user experience-based design innovativeness on user-metaverse platform channel relationships in South Korea. *Journal of Distribution Science*, *19*(11), 81–90.

Jobin, A., Ienca, M., & Vayena, E. (2019). The global landscape of AI ethics guidelines. *Nature Machine Intelligence*, *1*(9), 389–399. doi:10.1038/s42256-019-0088-2

Jones, K. (2014). Conquering HR Analyticss: Do you need a rocket scientist or a crystal ball? *Workforce Solutions Review*, *5*(1), 43–44.

Jung, T., Cho, J., Han, D.-I. D., Ahn, S. J., Gupta, M., Das, G., Heo, C. Y., Loureiro, S. M. C., Sigala, M., Trunfio, M., Taylor, A., & tom Dieck, M. C. (2024). Metaverse for service industries: Future applications, opportunities, challenges and research directions. *Computers in Human Behavior*, *151*, 108039. doi:10.1016/j.chb.2023.108039

Kabát, M. (2016). Teaching Metaverse. What and how to (not) teach using the medium of virtual reality. *Edutainment, 1*(1).

Kale, G. Ö., & Öztürk, G. (2016). The importance of sustainability in luxury brand management. *Intermedia. International Journal (Toronto, Ont.)*, *3*(4), 106–126.

Kale, H., Aher, D., & Anute, A. (2022). HR Analytics and its Impact on organisations Performance. [IJRAR]. *International Journal of Research and Analytical Reviews*, *9*(3), 619–630.

Kamkankaew, P. (2021). A Stakeholder-Oriented Sustainability Brand Management: An Introductory Review. วารสาร วิชาการ การ ตลาด และ การ จัดการ มหาวิทยาลัย เทคโนโลยี ราช มงคล ธัญบุรี, *8*(1), 99-129.

Kandalaft, M. R., Didehbani, N., Krawczyk, D. C., Allen, T. T., & Chapman, S. B. (2013). Virtual reality social cognition training for young adults with high-functioning autism. *Journal of Autism and Developmental Disorders*, *43*(1), 34–44. doi:10.1007/s10803-012-1544-6 PMID:22570145

Kang, D., & Ki, E.-J. (2024). Relationship cultivation strategies in the metaverse. *Public Relations Review*, *50*(1), 102397. doi:10.1016/j.pubrev.2023.102397

Karaarslan, E., & Yazici Yilmaz, S. (2023). Metaverse and Decentralization. In F. S. Esen, H. Tinmaz, & M. Singh (Eds.), *Metaverse: Technologies, Opportunities and Threats* (pp. 31–44). Springer Nature., doi:10.1007/978-981-99-4641-9_3

Karlsson, L., & Shamoun, M. (2022). *Virtual Realities for Remote Working: Exploring employee's attitudes toward the use of Metaverse for remote working.*

Katz, E., Lazarsfeld, P. F., & Roper, E. (2017). Personal influence: The part played by people in the flow of mass communications. In *Personal Influence: The Part Played by People in the Flow of Mass Communications.* Routledge. doi:10.4324/9781315126234

Kaufmann, H., & Schmalstieg, D. (2002). Mathematics and geometry education with collaborative augmented reality. Paper *presented at the ACM SIGGRAPH 2002 conference abstracts and applications.* ACM. 10.1145/1242073.1242086

Kaufmann, H., Schmalstieg, D., & Wagner, M. (2000). Construct3D: A virtual reality application for mathematics and geometry education. *Education and Information Technologies*, *5*(4), 263–276. doi:10.1023/A:1012049406877

Kaur, N., Saha, S., Agarwal, V., & Gulati, S. (2023, February). Metaverse and Fintech: Pathway for Innovation and Development. In *2023 3rd International Conference on Innovative Practices in Technology and Management (ICIPTM)* (pp. 1-6). IEEE. doi: 10.1109/ICIPTM57143.2023.10117956

Kaya, B., Bayar, S. B., & Meydan Uygur, S. (2022). *Is Metaverse a comfortable parallel universe for the tourism industry or a nightmare full of fear?* University of South Florida (USF) M3 Publishing.

Kazim, E., & Koshiyama, A. S. (2021). A high-level overview of AI ethics. *Patterns (New York, N.Y.)*, *2*(9), 100314. doi:10.1016/j.patter.2021.100314 PMID:34553166

Kharitonova, Y. (2024). Tokenization of the Creative Industries: The Intersection Between Emerging Technologies and Sustainability. *Digital Technologies and Distributed Registries for Sustainable Development: Legal Challenges*, 59-75. doi:10.1007/978-3-031-51067-0_4

Khoshnevisan, B., & Le, N. (2018). Augmented reality in language education: A systematic literature review. *Adv. Glob. Educ. Res*, *2*, 57–71.

Kim, J. (2021). Advertising in the metaverse: Research agenda. *Journal of Interactive Advertising*, *21*(3), 141–144. doi:10.1080/15252019.2021.2001273

Kim, J., & Hwang, J. (2022). Who is an evangelist? Food tourists' positive and negative eWOM behavior. *International Journal of Contemporary Hospitality Management*, *34*(2), 555–577. doi:10.1108/IJCHM-06-2021-0707

Kiran, K. S., Sharma, N., & Brijmohan, D. R. (2018). HR analytics: Transactional to transformational HR approach. *International Journal of Advance & Innovative Research*, *5*(3), 1–11.

Kiran, P. V. S., Sujitha, S., Estherita, A. S., & Vasantha, S. (2023). Effect Of Hr Analytics, Human Capital Management on Organisational Performance. *Journal for Educators. Teachers and Trainers*, *14*(2), 117–129.

Kirtane, A. (2015). Corporate sustainable HR Analytical practices. *Journal of Management & Administration Tomorrow*, *4*(1), 33–40.

Klein, M., Neitzert, F., Hartmann-Wendels, T., & Kraus, S. (2019). Start-up financing in the digital age: A systematic review and comparison of new forms of financing. *The Journal of Entrepreneurial Finance (JEF)*, *21*(2), 46-98. http://hdl.handle.net/10419/264405

Knox, J. (2022). The metaverse, or the serious business of tech frontiers. *Postdigital Science and Education*, *4*(2), 207–215. doi:10.1007/s42438-022-00300-9

Kocyigit, O., & Ringle, C. M. (2011). The impact of brand confusion on sustainable brand satisfaction and private label proneness: A subtle decay of brand equity. *Journal of Brand Management*, *19*(3), 195–212. doi:10.1057/bm.2011.32

Koo, C., Kwon, J., Chung, N., & Kim, J. (2022). Metaverse tourism: Conceptual framework and research propositions. *Current Issues in Tourism*. doi:10.1080/13683500.2022.2122781

Koohang, A., Nord, J., Ooi, K., Tan, G., Al-Emran, M., Aw, E., Baabdullah, A., Buhalis, D., Cham, T., Dennis, C., Dutot, V., Dwivedi, Y., Hughes, L., Mogaji, E., Pandey, N., Phau, I., Raman, R., Sharma, A., Sigala, M., & Wong, L. (2023). Shaping the metaverse into reality: multidisciplinary perspectives on opportunities, challenges, and future research. *Journal of Computer Information Systems*, *63*. https://www.academia.edu/94457087/

Koohang, A., Nord, J. H., Ooi, K. B., Tan, G. W. H., Al-Emran, M., Aw, E. C. X., Baabdullah, A. M., Buhalis, D., Cham, T.-H., Dennis, C., Dutot, V., Dwivedi, Y. K., Hughes, L., Mogaji, E., Pandey, N., Phau, I., Raman, R., Sharma, A., Sigala, M., & Wong, L. W. (2023). Shaping the metaverse into reality: A holistic multidisciplinary understanding of opportunities, challenges, and avenues for future investigation. *Journal of Computer Information Systems*, *63*(3), 735–765. doi:10.1080/08874417.2023.2165197

Kouroupi, N., & Metaxas, T. (2023). Can the Metaverse and Its Associated Digital Tools and Technologies Provide an Opportunity for Destinations to Address the Vulnerability of Overtourism? *Tourism and Hospitality*, *4*(2), 355–373. doi:10.3390/tourhosp4020022

Kraiger, Kurt. (2002). Decision-based evaluation. *Improving Training Effectiveness in Work Organizations*, 291-322.

Kraus, S., Kanbach, D. K., Krysta, P. M., Steinhoff, M. M., & Tomini, N. (2022). Facebook and the creation of the metaverse: Radical business model innovation or incremental transformation? *International Journal of Entrepreneurial Behaviour & Research*, 28(9), 52–77. doi:10.1108/ IJEBR-12-2021-0984

Kudos. (2021). *What You Need to Know About HR Analytics and Engagement*. Kudos. https:// www.kudos.com/blog/hr-analytics-and-employee-enga gement-what-you-need-to-know.

Kulakova, O. S. (2022). Digital Art In The Light Of Nft: Market Role And Legal Uncertainty. *Digital Lj*, 3, 36. doi:10.38044/2686-9136-2022-3-2-36-50

Kumar, A., Shankar, A., Shaik, A. S., Jain, G., & Malibari, A. (2023). Risking it all in the metaverse ecosystem: Forecasting resistance towards the enterprise metaverse. *Information Technology & People*. doi:10.1108/ITP-04-2023-0374

Kumar, A., Shankar, A., & Nayal, P. (2024). Metaverse is not my cup of tea! An investigation into how personality traits shape metaverse usage intentions. *Journal of Retailing and Consumer Services*, 77, 103639. doi:10.1016/j.jretconser.2023.103639

Kumar, S., Sureka, R., Lucey, B. M., Dowling, M., Vigne, S., & Lim, W. M. (2023). MetaMoney: Exploring the intersection of financial systems and virtual worlds. *Research in International Business and Finance*, 102195. doi:10.1016/j.ribaf.2023.102195

Kye, B., Han, N., Kim, E., Park, Y., & Jo, S. (2021). Educational applications of metaverse: Possibilities and limitations. *Journal of Educational Evaluation for Health Professions*, 18, 18. doi:10.3352/jeehp.2021.18.32 PMID:34897242

Lalwani, P. (2021). *What Is HR Analytics? Definition, Importance, Key Metrics, Data Requirements, and Implementation*. Spice Works. https://www.spicew orks.com/hr/hr-analytics/articles/what-is-hr-analytics/

Landers, R. N., & Armstrong, M. B. (2017). Enhancing instructional outcomes with gamification: An empirical test of the Technology-Enhanced Training Effectiveness Model. *Computers in Human Behavior*, 71, 499–507. doi:10.1016/j.chb.2015.07.031

Landers, R. N., & Callan, R. C. (2012). Training evaluation in virtual worlds: Development of a model. *Journal of Virtual Worlds Research*, 5(3). doi:10.4101/jvwr.v5i3.6335

Landers, R. N., & Callan, R. C. (2017). An Experiment on Anonymity and Multi-User Virtual Environments: Manipulating Identity to Increase Learning. In *Transforming Gaming and Computer Simulation Technologies across Industries* (pp. 80–93). IGI Global. doi:10.4018/978-1-5225-1817-4.ch004

Lawler, E. E., Levenson, A., & Boudreau, J. W. (2004). HR Metrics and Analytics: Use and Impact. *Human Resource Planning*, 27, 27–35.

Lee, H., & Hwang, Y. (2022). Technology-enhanced education through VR-making and metaverse-linking to foster teacher readiness and sustainable learning. *Sustainability (Basel)*, *14*(8), 4786. doi:10.3390/su14084786

Lee, K. (2012). Augmented Reality in Education and Training. *TechTrends*, *56*(2), 13–21. doi:10.1007/s11528-012-0559-3

Lee, M., Kwon, W., & Back, K. J. (2021). Artificial intelligence for hospitality big data analytics: Developing a prediction model of restaurant review helpfulness for customer decision-making. *International Journal of Contemporary Hospitality Management*, *33*(6), 2117–2136. doi:10.1108/IJCHM-06-2020-0587

Lee, Y. K., & Park, J. W. (2016). Impact of a sustainable brand on improving business performance of airport enterprises: The case of Incheon International Airport. *Journal of Air Transport Management*, *53*, 46–53. doi:10.1016/j.jairtraman.2016.01.002

Le, L. H., & Hancer, M. (2021). Using social learning theory in examining YouTube viewers' desire to imitate travel vloggers. *Journal of Hospitality and Tourism Technology*, *12*(3), 512–532. doi:10.1108/JHTT-08-2020-0200

Levenson, A., & Fink, A. (2017). Human capital analytics: Too much data and analysis, not enough models and business insights. *J Organ Eff*, *4*(2), 145–156. doi:10.1108/JOEPP-03-2017-0029

Liang, A., & Gössling, S. (2020). *Exploring the Formation and Representation of Destination Images in Travel Vlogs on Social Media*. Lund University. https://lup.lub.lu.se/student-papers/record/9012220

Li, L., Lee, K. Y., & Yang, S. B. (2019). Exploring the effect of heuristic factors on the popularity of user-curated 'Best places to visit' recommendations in an online travel community. *Information Processing & Management*, *56*(4), 1391–1408. doi:10.1016/j.ipm.2018.03.009

Lin, X., Featherman, M., Brooks, S. L., & Hajli, N. (2018). Exploring Gender Differences in Online Consumer Purchase Decision Making: An Online Product Presentation Perspective. *Information Systems Frontiers*, *21*(5), 1187–1201. doi:10.1007/s10796-018-9831-1

Liu, S., Xie, J., & Wang, X. (2023). QoE enhancement of the industrial metaverse based on Mixed Reality application optimization. *Displays*, *79*, 102463. doi:10.1016/j.displa.2023.102463

Liyushiana, L., Rustanto, A. E., Ulfah, M., Akbar, R. A., & Imran, I. (2023). Digital Transformation in Tourism: Capturing the Perspective of a Travel Agency. *International Journal of Artificial Intelligence Research*, *6*(1.1).

Loftin, R. B., Engleberg, M., & Benedetti, R. (1993). Applying virtual reality in education: A prototypical virtual physics laboratory. *Paper presented at the Proceedings of 1993 IEEE Research Properties in Virtual Reality Symposium*. IEEE. 10.1109/VRAIS.1993.378261

Longo, F., Padovano, A., & Umbrello, S. (2020). Value-oriented and ethical technology engineering in industry 5.0: A human-centric perspective for the design of the factory of the future. *Applied Sciences (Basel, Switzerland)*, *10*(12), 4182. doi:10.3390/app10124182

Loureiro, S. M. C., Friedmann, E., Breazeale, M., & Middendorf, I. (2023). How can brands encourage consumers to donate data to a data-driven social partnership? An examination of hedonic vs. functional categories. *Journal of Business Research, 164*, 113958. doi:10.1016/j.jbusres.2023.113958

Lunardo, R., Oliver, M. A., & Shepherd, S. (2023). How believing in brand conspiracies shapes relationships with brands. *Journal of Business Research, 159*, 113729. doi:10.1016/j.jbusres.2023.113729

Lu, W. (2018). Blockchain Technology and Its Applications in FinTech. In I. Traore, I. Woungang, S. S. Ahmed, & Y. Malik (Eds.), *Intelligent, Secure, and Dependable Systems in Distributed and Cloud Environments* (pp. 118–124). Springer International Publishing. doi:10.1007/978-3-030-03712-3_10

Maggiore, G., lo Presti, L., Orlowski, M., & Morvillo, A. (2022). In the travel bloggers' wonderland: Mechanisms of the blogger – follower relationship in tourism and hospitality management – a systematic literature review. *International Journal of Contemporary Hospitality Management, 34*(7), 2747–2772. doi:10.1108/IJCHM-11-2021-1377

Maio, E. (2003). Managing brand in the new stakeholder environment. *Journal of Business Ethics, 44*(2), 235–246. doi:10.1023/A:1023364119516

Majerova, J., Sroka, W., Krizanova, A., Gajanova, L., Lazaroiu, G., & Nadanyiova, M. (2020). Sustainable brand management of alimentary goods. *Sustainability (Basel), 12*(2), 556. doi:10.3390/su12020556

Makridakis, S., & Christodoulou, K. (2019). Blockchain: Current challenges and future prospects/applications. *Future Internet, 11*(12), 258. doi:10.3390/fi11120258

Malloy, K. M., & Milling, L. S. (2010). The effectiveness of virtual reality distraction for pain reduction: A systematic review. *Clinical Psychology Review, 30*(8), 1011–1018. doi:10.1016/j.cpr.2010.07.001 PMID:20691523

Mandler, T., Bartsch, F., & Zeugner-Roth, K. P. (2023). Are brands re-evaluated when consumers learn about brand origin misperceptions? Outcomes, processes, and contingent effects. *Journal of Business Research, 164*, 113941. doi:10.1016/j.jbusres.2023.113941

Manser Payne, E. H., Dahl, A. J., & Peltier, J. (2021). Digital servitization value co-creation framework for AI services: A research agenda for digital transformation in financial service ecosystems. *Journal of Research in Interactive Marketing, 15*(2), 200–222. doi:10.1108/JRIM-12-2020-0252

Mantelero, A. (2022). Regulating AI. In *Beyond Data: Human Rights, Ethical and Social Impact Assessment in AI* (pp. 139–183). TMC Asser Press. doi:10.1007/978-94-6265-531-7_4

Maples-Keller, J. L., Bunnell, B. E., Kim, S.-J., & Rothbaum, B. O. (2017). The use of virtual reality technology in the treatment of anxiety and other psychiatric disorders. *Harvard Review of Psychiatry, 25*(3), 103–113. doi:10.1097/HRP.0000000000000138 PMID:28475502

Mariani, M., Ek Styven, M., & Ayeh, J. K. (2019). Using Facebook for travel decision-making: An international study of antecedents. *International Journal of Contemporary Hospitality Management, 31*(2), 1021–1044. doi:10.1108/IJCHM-02-2018-0158

Markowitz, D. M., & Bailenson, J. N. (2021). Virtual reality and the psychology of climate change. *Current Opinion in Psychology, 42,* 60–65. doi:10.1016/j.copsyc.2021.03.009 PMID:33930832

Marson, J. (2022). *6 ways people analytics can help HR improve retention.* Tech Target. https://www.techtarget.com/searchhrsoftware/tip/Ways-people- analytics-can-help- HR-improve-retention.

Martín-Gutiérrez, J., Mora, C. E., Añorbe-Díaz, B., & González-Marrero, A. (2017). Virtual technologies trends in education. *Eurasia Journal of Mathematics, Science and Technology Education, 13*(2), 469–486.

Martins, M. R., & da Costa, R. A. (2022). Backpackers' Sociodemographic Characteristics, Travel Organisation and the Impact of New Technologies. *The Backpacker Tourist: A Contemporary Perspective.* Emerald. doi:10.1108/978-1-80262-255-320221006

Mauri, A. G., & Minazzi, R. (2013). Web reviews influence on expectations and purchasing intentions of hotel potential customers. *International Journal of Hospitality Management, 34*(1), 99–107. doi:10.1016/j.ijhm.2013.02.012

Mavrodieva, A. V., & Shaw, R. (2020). Disaster and climate change issues in Japan's Society 5.0—A discussion. *Sustainability (Basel), 12*(5), 1893. doi:10.3390/su12051893

McIver, D., Lengnick-Hall, M. L., & Lengnick- Hall, C. A. (2018). A strategic approach to workforce analytics: integrating science and agility. *Bus Horiz, 61*(3), 397–407.

Metamandrill. (2023). *Metaverse Guide; Understanding The Basics Will Open Up a New World.* Meta Man Drill. https://metamandrill.com/metaverse/ (accessed 4 December 2023).

Metaverse in Banking: An Initiative for Banking Transformation from Emerging Country Prospective - ProQuest. (n.d.). Proquest. https://www.proquest.com/openview/ad29e7b2bfafe3 4b5a85d2f61ab652d3/1?pq-origsite=gscholar&cbl=38744

Mileva, G. (2022). *48 Metaverse Statistics.* Influencer Marketing Hub. https://influencermarketinghub.com/metaverse-stats/

Milian, E. Z., Spinola, M. D. M., & Carvalho, M. M. D. (2019). Fintechs: A literature review and research agenda. *Electronic Commerce Research and Applications, 34,* 100833. doi:10.1016/j.elerap.2019.100833

Minbaeva, D. (2018). Building credible human capital analytics for organisational competitive advantage. *Human Resource Management, 57*(3), 701–713. doi:10.1002/hrm.21848

Mishra, A. (n.d.). How is the Technology of Metaverse Transforming the Future of Banks. *The Times of India.* https://timesofindia.indiatimes.com/blogs/voices/how-is-the-technology-of-metaverse-transforming-the-future-of-banks/

Mitra, S. (2023). Metaverse: A Potential Virtual-Physical Ecosystem for Innovative Blended Education and Training. *Journal of Metaverse, 3*(1), 66–72. doi:10.57019/jmv.1168056

Mochram, R. A. A., Makawowor, C. T., Tanujaya, K. M., Moniaga, J. V., & Jabar, B. A. (2022, September). Systematic literature review: Blockchain security in nft ownership. In *2022 International Conference on Electrical and Information Technology (IEIT)* (pp. 302-306). IEEE. doi: 10.1109/IEIT56384.2022.9967897

Mohamed, A., & Faisal, R. (2024). Exploring metaverse-enabled innovation in banking: Leveraging NFTS, blockchain, and smart contracts for transformative business opportunities. *International Journal of Data and Network Science, 8*(1), 35–44. doi:10.5267/j.ijdns.2023.10.020

Mohanty, S., Pradhan, B. B., & Sahoo, D. (2022). A Study to Investigate Consumer's Resonance Experience Effect and Engagement Behaviour on Travel Vlogs. *NMIMS Management Review, 30*(02), 35–57. doi:10.53908/NMMR.300203

Monaco, S., & Sacchi, G. (2023). Travelling the metaverse: Potential benefits and main challenges for tourism sectors and research applications. *Sustainability (Basel), 15*(4), 3348. doi:10.3390/su15043348

Mondare, S., Douthitt, S., & Carson, M. (2011). Maximizing the impact and effectiveness of HR Analytics to drive business outcomes. *People Strategy, 34*, 20–27.

Moore, S. G., & Lafreniere, K. C. (2020). How online word-of-mouth impacts receivers. *Consumer Psychology Review, 3*(1), 34–59. doi:10.1002/arcp.1055

Mowat, J. (2017, May 21). *Why travel brands win with a video first marketing strategy*. Hurricane. https://www.hurricanemedia.co.uk/blog/news/travel-brands-lead-video-first-marketing-strategy/

Moy, C., & Gadgil, A. (2022). *Opportunities in the metaverse: How businesses can explore the metaverse and navigate the hype vs reality*. JPMorgan.

Mozumder, M. A. I., Armand, T. P. T., Imtiyaj Uddin, S. M., Athar, A., Sumon, R. I., Hussain, A., & Kim, H. C. (2023). Metaverse for Digital Anti-Aging Healthcare: An Overview of Potential Use Cases Based on Artificial Intelligence, Blockchain, IoT Technologies, Its Challenges, and Future Directions. *Applied Sciences (Basel, Switzerland), 13*(8), 5127. doi:10.3390/app13085127

Nagy, S., Molnár, L., & Papp, A. (2024). Customer Adoption of Neobank Services from a Technology Acceptance Perspective – Evidence from Hungary. *Decision Making: Applications in Management and Engineering, 7*(1), 1. doi:10.31181/dmame712024883

Nahavandi, S. (2019). Industry 5.0—A human-centric solution. *Sustainability (Basel), 11*(16), 4371. doi:10.3390/su11164371

Nair, V. M., & Menon, D. G. (2017). Fin Tech firms-A new challenge to Traditional Banks: A Review. *International Journal of Applied Business and Economic Research, 15*(Special Issue), 173–184.

Nedergaard, N., & Gyrd-Jones, R. (2013). Sustainable brand-based innovation: The role of corporate brands in driving sustainable innovation. *Journal of Brand Management*, *20*(9), 762–778. doi:10.1057/bm.2013.16

Nevmerzhitskaya, J. (2013). *Scenarios of the future work of business travel agencies*. [Master's thesis, Haaga-Helia University of Applied Sciences, Helsinki, Finland].

Ngarmwongnoi, C., Oliveira, J. S., AbedRabbo, M., & Mousavi, S. (2020). The implications of eWOM adoption on the customer journey. *Journal of Consumer Marketing*, *37*(7), 749–759. doi:10.1108/JCM-10-2019-3450

Nguyen, L.-T., Duc, D. T. V., Dang, T.-Q., & Nguyen, D. P. (2023). Metaverse Banking Service: Are We Ready to Adopt? A Deep Learning-Based Dual-Stage SEM-ANN Analysis. *Human Behavior and Emerging Technologies*, *2023*, e6617371. doi:10.1155/2023/6617371

Nilashi, M., & Asadi, S. (2021). Recommendation agents and information sharing through social media for coronavirus outbreak. *Telematics and Informatics*, *61*, 101597. doi:10.1016/j.tele.2021.101597 PMID:34887615

Ning, H., Wang, H., Lin, Y., Wang, W., Dhelim, S., Farha, F., & Daneshmand, M. (2023). A Survey on the Metaverse: The State-of-the-Art, Technologies, Applications, and Challenges. *IEEE Internet of Things Journal*.

Niranjanamurthy, M., Nithya, B. N., & Jagannatha, S. (2019). Analysis of Blockchain technology: Pros, cons and SWOT. *Cluster Computing*, *22*(6), 14743–14757. doi:10.1007/s10586-018-2387-5

Nishii, L. H., Lepak, D. P., & Schneider, B. (2008). Employee attributions of the "why" of HR practices: Their effects on employee attitudes and behaviors, and customer satisfaction. *Personnel Psychology*, *61*(3), 503–545. doi:10.1111/j.1744-6570.2008.00121.x

Nishijima, I. (2021). Ariana Grande x Fortnite Rift Tour: the apogee of pop culture or just the beginning? *Medium*. https://medium.com/headlineasia/ariana-grande-x-fortnite-rift-tour-the-apogee-of-pop-culture-or-just-the-beginning-5052584f8d63 (accessed 2 February 2024).

Oatley, G. C. (2022). Themes in data mining, big data, and crime analytics. *Wiley Interdisciplinary Reviews. Data Mining and Knowledge Discovery*, *12*(2), e1432. doi:10.1002/widm.1432

Oh, H. J., Kim, J., Chang, J. J., Park, N., & Lee, S. (2023). Social benefits of living in the metaverse: The relationships among social presence, supportive interaction, social selfefficacy, and feelings of loneliness. *Computers in Human Behavior*, *139*, 107498. https://doi.org/. 107498 doi:10.1016/j.chb.2022

Oliveira, T., Araujo, B., & Tam, C. (2020). Why do people share their travel experiences on social media? *Tourism Management*, *78*, 104041. doi:10.1016/j.tourman.2019.104041 PMID:32322615

Orth, M., & Volmer, J. (2017). Daily within-person effects of job autonomy and work engagement on innovative behaviour: The cross-level moderating role of creative self-efficacy. *European Journal of Work and Organizational Psychology*, *26*(4), 601–612. doi:10.1080/1359432X.2017.1332042

Osorio, M. L., Centeno, E., & Cambra-Fierro, J. (2023). An empirical examination of human brand authenticity as a driver of brand love. *Journal of Business Research*, *165*, 114059. doi:10.1016/j. jbusres.2023.114059

Özdemir Uçgun, G., & Şahin, S. Z. (2023). How does Metaverse affect the tourism industry? Current practices and future forecasts. *Current Issues in Tourism*, 1–15. doi:10.1080/1368350 0.2023.2238111

Özdemir, V., & Hekim, N. (2018). Birth of industry 5.0: Making sense of big data with artificial intelligence, "the internet of things" and next-generation technology policy. *OMICS: A Journal of Integrative Biology*, *22*(1), 65–76. doi:10.1089/omi.2017.0194 PMID:29293405

Özyalvaç, B. (2023). İzlemeniz Gereken En İyi Metaverse Temalı Film ve Diziler. *Oggusto*. https://www.oggusto.com/teknoloji/en-iyi-metaverse-filmleri

Pamucar, D., Deveci, M., Gokasar, I., Tavana, M., & Köppen, M. (2022). A metaverse assessment model for sustainable transportation using ordinal priority approach and Aczel-Alsina norms. *Technological Forecasting and Social Change*, *182*, 121778. doi:10.1016/j.techfore.2022.121778

Pang, J., & Capek, J. (2020). Factors Influencing Researcher Cooperation in Virtual Academic Communities Based on Principal Component Analysis. *Acta Informatica Pragensia*, *9*(1), 4–17. doi:10.18267/j.aip.128

Park, M. J., Kim, D. J., Lee, U., Na, E. J., & Jeon, H. J. (2019). A Literature Overview of Virtual Reality (VR) in Treatment of Psychiatric Disorders: Recent Advances and Limitations. *Frontiers in Psychiatry*, *10*, 505. doi:10.3389/fpsyt.2019.00505 PMID:31379623

Park, S., & Kim, S. (2022). Identifying world types to deliver gameful experiences for sustainable learning in the metaverse. *Sustainability (Basel)*, *14*(3), 1361. doi:10.3390/su14031361

Parsons, T. D., & Rizzo, A. A. (2008). Affective outcomes of virtual reality exposure therapy for anxiety and specific phobias: A meta-analysis. *Journal of Behavior Therapy and Experimental Psychiatry*, *39*(3), 250–261. doi:10.1016/j.jbtep.2007.07.007 PMID:17720136

Patil, R. (2021). *How HR Analytics Can Help Improve Employee Performance*. Spice Works. https://www.spiceworks.com/hr/hr-analytics/guest-article/how-hr- analytics-can-help-improve-employee-performance/

Pellegrino, A., Stasi, A., & Wang, R. (2023). Exploring the intersection of sustainable consumption and the Metaverse: A review of current literature and future research directions. *Heliyon*, *9*(9), e19190. doi:10.1016/j.heliyon.2023.e19190 PMID:37681133

Peralta, R. L. (2019). How vlogging promotes a destination image: A narrative analysis of popular travel vlogs about the Philippines. *Place Branding and Public Diplomacy*, *15*(4), 244–256. doi:10.1057/s41254-019-00134-6

Perelygina, M., Kucukusta, D., & Law, R. (2022). Digital business model configurations in the travel industry. *Tourism Management*, *88*, 104408. doi:10.1016/j.tourman.2021.104408

Phon, D. N. E., Ali, M. B., & Abd Halim, N. D. (2014). Collaborative augmented reality in education: A review. *Paper presented at the 2014 International Conference on Teaching and Learning in Computing and Engineering*. IEEE. 10.1109/LaTiCE.2014.23

Pinnington, A. H., & Ayoko, O. B. (2021). Managing physical and virtual work environments during the COVID-19 pandemic: Improving employee well-being and achieving mutual gains. *Journal of Management & Organization, 27*(6), 993–1002. doi:10.1017/jmo.2022.2

Podhorska, I., Sroka, W., & Majerova, J. (2021). *SUSTAINABLE BRAND MANAGEMENT. Sustainable Branding: Ethical*. Social, and Environmental Cases and Perspectives.

PortalCripto. (2022). *Ariva Wonderland NFT Metaverse: Oyun ve VR Deneyimi Nedir?* Portal Cripto. https://portalcripto.com.br/tr/ariva-harikalar-diyar%C4%B1-nft-metaverse-oyunu-ve-rv-deneyimi-nedir/

Powers, M. B., & Emmelkamp, P. M. (2008). Virtual reality exposure therapy for anxiety disorders: A meta-analysis. *Journal of Anxiety Disorders, 22*(3), 561–569. doi:10.1016/j.janxdis.2007.04.006 PMID:17544252

Procter, R., Glover, B., & Jones, E. (2020). *Research 4.0: Research in the Age of Automation.*

Qadir, A. M. A., & Fatah, A. O. (2023). Platformization and the metaverse: Opportunities and challenges for urban sustainability and economic development. *EAI Endorsed Transactions on Energy Web, 10*(1).

Quach, S., Thaichon, P., Martin, K. D., Weaven, S., & Palmatier, R. W. (2022). Digital technologies: Tensions in privacy and data. *Journal of the Academy of Marketing Science, 50*(6), 1299–1323. doi:10.1007/s11747-022-00845-y PMID:35281634

Qureshi, F. N., Bashir, S., Mahmood, A., Ahmad, S., Attiq, S., & Zeeshan, M. (2022). Impact of internal brand management on sustainable competitive advantage: An explanatory study based on the mediating roles of brand commitment and brand citizenship behavior. *PLoS One, 17*(3), e0264379. doi:10.1371/journal.pone.0264379 PMID:35275925

Radianti, J., Majchrzak, T. A., Fromm, J., & Wohlgenannt, I. (2020). A systematic review of immersive virtual reality applications for higher education: Design elements, lessons learned, and research agenda. *Computers & Education, 147*, 103778. doi:10.1016/j.compedu.2019.103778

Radoff, J. (2021). The Metaverse Value-Chain. *Medium*. https://medium.com/building-the-metaverse/the-metaverse-value-chain-afcf9e09e3a7.

Radziwill, N. (2018a). Blockchain Revolution: How the Technology Behind Bitcoin is Changing Money, Business, and the World. *The Quality Management Journal, 25*(1), 64–65. doi:10.108 0/10686967.2018.1404373

Radziwill, N. (2018b). Mapping Innovation: A Playbook for Navigating a Disruptive Age. *The Quality Management Journal, 25*(1), 64–64. doi:10.1080/10686967.2018.1404372

Rahimizhian, S., Ozturen, A., & Ilkan, M. (2020). Emerging realm of 360-degree technology to promote tourism destination. *Technology in Society*, *63*, 101411. doi:10.1016/j.techsoc.2020.101411

Ranieri, M., Luzzi, D., Cuomo, S., & Bruni, I. (2022). If and how do 360 videos fit into education settings? Results from a scoping review of empirical research. *Journal of Computer Assisted Learning*, *38*(5), 1199–1219. doi:10.1111/jcal.12683

Ranjan, R., & Basak, A. (2013). *Creating Value through Analytics in HR. Role of Third-party services*. Everest Global.

Rather, R. A. (2023). Metaverse marketing and consumer research: Theoretical framework and future research agenda in tourism and hospitality industry. *Tourism Recreation Research*, 1–9. Advance online publication. doi:10.1080/02508281.2023.2216525

Rather, R., Hollebeek, L. D., Loureiro, S. M. C., Khan, I., & Hasan, R. (2023). Exploring tourists' virtual reality-based brand engagement: A uses-and-gratifications perspective. *Journal of Travel Research*. doi:10.1177/00472875231166598

Rauschnabel, P. (2022). XR in tourism marketing. In D. Buhalis D (Ed.), Encyclopedia of tourism management and marketing. Edward Elgar Publishing. doi:10.4337/9781800377486.xr.in.tourism

Razi, Q., Devrani, A., Abhyankar, H., Chalapathi, G. S. S., Hassija, V., & Guizani, M. (2023). Non-fungible tokens (NFTs)-survey of current applications, evolution and future directions. *IEEE Open Journal of the Communications Society*.

Razi, Q., Devrani, A., Abhyankar, H., Chalapathi, G. S. S., Hassija, V., & Guizani, M. (2023). Non-Fungible Tokens (Nfts)-Survey Of Current Applications, Evolution And Future Directions. *IEEE Open Journal of the Communications Society*. doi:10.1109/OJCOMS.2023.3343926

Reddy, P. R., & Lakshmikeerthi, P. (2017). HR Analyticss' - An Effective Evidence Based HRM Tool. *International Journal of Business and Management Invention*, *6*(7), 23–34.

Reena, R., Ansari, M. M. K., & Jayakrishnan, S. S. (2019). Emerging trends in human resource analytics in upcoming decade. *International Journal of Engineering Applied Sciences and Technology*, *4*(8), 260–264. doi:10.33564/IJEAST.2019.v04i08.045

Rehman, W., Zainab, H., Imran, J., & Bawany, N. Z. (2021, December). NFTs: Applications and challenges. In *2021 22nd International Arab Conference on Information Technology (ACIT)* (pp. 1-7). IEEE. doi: 10.1109/ACIT53391.2021.9677260

Renduchintala, T., Alfauri, H., Yang, Z., Pietro, R. D., & Jain, R. (2022). A Survey of Blockchain Applications in the FinTech Sector. *Journal of Open Innovation*, *8*(4), 185. doi:10.3390/joitmc8040185

Rességuier, A., & Rodrigues, R. (2020). AI ethics should not remain toothless! A call to bring back the teeth of ethics. *Big Data & Society*, *7*(2), 2053951720942541. doi:10.1177/2053951720942541

Revfine. (2023a). *Metaverse Tourism: Overview, Benefits, Examples and More*. Revfine. https://www.revfine.com/metaverse-tourism/ (accessed 4 December 2023).

Revfine. (2023b). *Metaverse and the Hospitality Industry; The No. 1 Information Guide!* Revfine. https://www.revfine.com/metaverse-hospitality/

Richman, A. (2006). Everyone wants an engaged workforce how can you create it? *Workspan*, *49*, 36–39.

Riva, G. (2005). Virtual reality in psychotherapy. *Cyberpsychology & Behavior*, *8*(3), 220–230. doi:10.1089/cpb.2005.8.220 PMID:15971972

Rokhim, R., Mayasari, I., & Wulandari, P. (2021, March). Is brand management critical to SMEs' product sustainability? Qualitative analysis in the context of Indonesia small enterprise environment. []. IOP Publishing.]. *IOP Conference Series. Earth and Environmental Science*, *716*(1), 012109. doi:10.1088/1755-1315/716/1/012109

Rothbaum, B. O., Hodges, L. F., Ready, D., Graap, K., & Alarcon, R. D. (2001). Virtual reality exposure therapy for Vietnam veterans with posttraumatic stress disorder. *The Journal of Clinical Psychiatry*, *62*(8), 617–622. doi:10.4088/JCP.v62n0808 PMID:11561934

Sadler, R., & Thrasher, T. (2021). *Teaching languages with virtual reality: Things you may need to know.* CALICO Infobytes.

Saks, A. M. (2006). Antecedents and consequences of employee engagement. *Journal of Managerial Psychology*, *21*(7), 600–619. doi:10.1108/02683940610690169

Samaan, D. K. (2021). Job Scenarios 2030: How the World of Work Has Changed Around the Globe. *Managing Work in the Digital Economy: Challenges, Strategies and Practices for the Next Decade*, 47-71. Springer. doi:10.1007/978-3-030-65173-2_4

Sarkar, A. N., & Singh, J. (2005). New paradigm in evolving brand management strategy. *Journal of Management Research*, *5*(2), 80–90.

Sato, M., Yoshida, M., Doyle, J., & Choi, W. (2023). Consumer-brand identification and happiness in experiential consumption. *Psychology and Marketing*, *40*(8), 1579–1592. doi:10.1002/mar.21852

Savale, S. K., & Savale, V. K. (2016). Intellectual property rights (IPR). *World Journal of Pharmacy and Pharmaceutical Sciences*, *5*, 2559–2592. doi:10.20959/wjpps20166-7102

Schaufeli, W. B., Bakker, A. B., & Salanova, M. (2006). The measurement of work engagement with a short questionnaire: A cross-national study. *Educational and Psychological Measurement*, *66*(4), 701–716. doi:10.1177/0013164405282471

Schneider, C. (2006). The new human-capital metrics: A sophisticated crop of measurement tools could take the guesswork out of human resources management. *CFO Magazine*, 1-5.

Schuetz, S., & Venkatesh, V. (2020). Blockchain, adoption, and financial inclusion in India: Research opportunities. *International Journal of Information Management*, *52*, 101936. doi:10.1016/j.ijinfomgt.2019.04.009

Schultz, D. E., & Block, M. P. (2015). Beyond brand loyalty: Brand sustainability. *Journal of Marketing Communications, 21*(5), 340–355. doi:10.1080/13527266.2013.821227

Schumacher, P. (2022). The metaverse as opportunity for architecture and society: Design drivers, core competencies. *Architectural Intelligence, 1*(1), 11. PMID:35993030

Shaheer, I., Nayak, N., & Polus, R. (2022). Challenges and opportunities for sacred journeys: A media representation of the impact of COVID-19. *Tourism Recreation Research*, 1–7. doi:10.1 080/02508281.2022.2100195

Sharma, T. K. (2023). Hybrid Working: The Future of Organizations. In Reshaping the Business World Post-COVID-19 (pp. 41-68). Apple Academic Press.

Sharma, A., & Sharma, T. (2017). HR Analytics and Performance appraisal system: A Conceptual framework for employee performance improvement. *Management Research Review, 40*(6), 684–697. doi:10.1108/MRR-04-2016-0084

Shaw, K. (2005). An engagement strategy process for communicators. *Strategic Communication Management, 9*(3), 26–29.

Shi, F., Ning, H., Zhang, X., Li, R., Tian, Q., Zhang, S., Zheng, Y., Guo, Y., & Daneshmand, M. (2023). A new technology perspective of the Metaverse: Its essence, framework and challenges. *Digital Communications and Networks*. doi:10.1016/j.dcan.2023.02.017

Shin, H., & Kang, J. (2024). How does the metaverse travel experience influence virtual and actual travel behaviors? Focusing on the role of telepresence and avatar identification. *Journal of Hospitality and Tourism Management, 58*, 174–183. doi:10.1016/j.jhtm.2023.12.009

Siddiqui, M. S., Siddiqui, U. A., Khan, M. A., Alkandi, I. G., Saxena, A. K., & Siddiqui, J. H. (2021). Creating electronic word of mouth credibility through social networking sites and determining its impact on brand image and online purchase intentions in India. *Journal of Theoretical and Applied Electronic Commerce Research, 16*(4), 1008–1024. doi:10.3390/jtaer16040057

Singh, S., & Sisodia, H. (2023). Building Blocks for the Metaverse: Virtual Worlds, Marketplaces, and Tools. In Concepts, Technologies, Challenges, and the Future of Web 3 (pp. 198-221). IGI Global. doi:10.4018/978-1-6684-9919-1.ch011

Singh, A., Parizi, R. M., Zhang, Q., Choo, K. K. R., & Dehghantanha, A. (2020). Blockchain smart contracts formalization: Approaches and challenges to address vulnerabilities. *Computers & Security, 88*, 101654. doi:10.1016/j.cose.2019.101654

Singh, A., Singh, H., & Singh, A. (2022). People Analytics: Augmenting Horizon from Predictive Analytics to Prescriptive Analytics. In P. M. Jeyanthi, T. Choudhury, D. Hack-Polay, T. P. Singh, & S. Abujar (Eds.), *Decision Intelligence Analytics and the Implementation of Strategic Business Management. EAI/Springer Innovations in Communication and Computing*. Springer. doi:10.1007/978-3-030-82763-2_13

Singla, B., Bhattacharya, S., & Naik, N. (2023). Introduction to Metaverse and Consumer Behaviour Change: Adoption of Metaverse Among Consumers. In P. Keikhosrokiani (Ed.), (pp. 113–129). Advances in Marketing, Customer Relationship Management, and E-Services. IGI Global., doi:10.4018/978-1-6684-7029-9.ch006

Son, J., & Hwang, K. (2023). How to make vertical farming more attractive: Effects of vegetable growing conditions on consumer assessment. *Psychology and Marketing*, *40*(8), 1466–1483. doi:10.1002/mar.21823

Soumyasanto, S. (2016). *Caring about Analytics for HR*. Data Science Central. http://www.datasciencecentral.com/profiles/blogs/caring-about-analytics-for-hr

Sparkes, M. (2021). *What is a metaverse*. Research Gate.

Sriram, P. H. (2023). 3D avatars and blockchain integration: The future of virtual identity in metaverse—Digital Transformation News. *The Financial Express*. https://www.financialexpress.com/business/digital-transformation-3d-avatars-and-blockchain-integration-the-future-of-virtual-identity-in-metaverse-3265057/

Srivastava, S. (2023, February 9). Web3 and the Metaverse: Building a Stronger Digital Economy. *Appinventiv*. https://appinventiv.com/blog/web3-metaverse-for-digital-economy/

Stamatakis, D., Kogias, D. G., Papadopoulos, P., Karkazis, P. A., & Leligou, H. C. (2024). Blockchain-Powered Gaming: Bridging Entertainment With Serious Game Objectives. *Computers*, *13*(1), 14. doi:10.3390/computers13010014

Stephenson, N. (1992). *Snow crash*. Bantam Books.

Stoll, C., Gallersdörfer, U., & Klaaßen, L. (2022). Climate impacts of the metaverse. *Joule*, *6*(12), 2668–2673. doi:10.1016/j.joule.2022.10.013

Suanpang, P., Niamsorn, C., Pothipassa, P., Chunhapataragul, T., Netwong, T., & Jermsittiparsert, K. (2022). Extensible metaverse implication for a smart tourism city. *Sustainability (Basel)*, *14*(21), 14027. doi:10.3390/su142114027

Sulbaran, T., & Baker, N. C. (2000). Enhancing engineering education through distributed virtual reality. Paper presented at the *30th Annual Frontiers in Education Conference*. IEEE. 10.1109/FIE.2000.896621

Sweller, J. (1988). Cognitive load during problem solving: Effects on learning. *Cognitive Science*, *12*(2), 257–285. doi:10.1207/s15516709cog1202_4

Talwar, M., Talwar, S., Kaur, P., Islam, A. K. M. N., & Dhir, A. (2021). Positive and negative word of mouth (WOM) are not necessarily opposites: A reappraisal using the dual factor theory. *Journal of Retailing and Consumer Services*, *63*, 102396. doi:10.1016/j.jretconser.2020.102396

Tayfun, A., Silik, C. E., Şimşek, E., & Dülger, A. S. (2022). Metaverse: Turizm için bir fırsat mı? Yoksa bir tehdit mi? (Metaverse: An opportunity for tourism? Or is it a threat?). *Journal of Tourism and Gastronomy Studies*, *10*(2), 818–836. doi:10.21325/jotags.2022.1017

Taylor, P. J., Dargahi, T., Dehghantanha, A., Parizi, R. M., & Choo, K.-K. R. (2020). A systematic literature review of blockchain cyber security. *Digital Communications and Networks*, *6*(2), 147–156. doi:10.1016/j.dcan.2019.01.005

Thapa, P. (2023). Metaverse and tourism industry: A conceptual proposition. *In How the Metaverse Will Reshape Business and Sustainability* (pp. 131-137). Singapore: Springer. *Nature in Singapore*. doi:10.1007/978-981-99-5126-0_12

Thomas, F., & Capelli, S. (2023). Increasing purchase intention while limiting binge-eating: The role of repeating the same flavor-giving ingredient image on a front of package. *Psychology and Marketing*, *40*(8), 1539–1555. doi:10.1002/mar.21839

Tikhonov, A. I. (2020). Maim objectives of Russian companies, solved by HR-analytics. *Journal of Natural and Humanitarian Studies*, *28*(2), 262–266.

TikTok. (2020). The Weeknd experience, an innovative TikTok live stream, draws over 2 million unique viewers. *The Weeknd Experience*.

Timuçin, T., & Bıroğul, S. (2023). The Evolution Of Smart Contract Platforms: A Look At Current Trends And Future Directions. *Mugla Journal Of Science And Technology*, *9*(2), 46–55. doi:10.22531/muglajsci.1280985

Tomar, S., & Gaur, M. (2020). HR analytics in Business: Role, Opportunities, and Challenges of Using It. *Journal of Xi'an University of Architecture & Technology*, *xii*(vii), 1299–1306.

Tomić, N., Todorović, V., & Jakšić, M. (2023). Future Tendencies of Non-fungible Tokens. *Naše gospodarstvo/Our economy, 69*(2), 60-67. oi:10.2478/ngoe-2023-0012

Tran, G. A., & Strutton, D. (2020). Comparing email and SNS users: Investigating e-servicescape, customer reviews, trust, loyalty and E-WOM. *Journal of Retailing and Consumer Services*, *53*, 101782. doi:10.1016/j.jretconser.2019.03.009

Trinh, V. D., & Nguyen, D. Y. L. (2019). How to Change Perceived Destination Image Through Vlogging on Youtube. SSRN *Electronic Journal*. doi:10.2139/ssrn.3426968

Truong, V. T., Le, L., & Niyato, D. (2023). Blockchain Meets Metaverse and Digital Asset Management: A Comprehensive Survey. *IEEE Access : Practical Innovations, Open Solutions*, *11*, 26258–26288. doi:10.1109/ACCESS.2023.3257029

Tukur, M., Schneider, J., Househ, M., Dokoro, A. H., Ismail, U. I., Dawaki, M., & Agus, M. (2024). The metaverse digital environments: A scoping review of the techniques, technologies, and applications. *Journal of King Saud University. Computer and Information Sciences*, *101967*. doi:10.1016/j.jksuci.2024.101967

TURSAB. (2019). *Turizm Sektörü Dijitalleşme Yol Haritası Giriş*. TURSAB. https://www.tursab.org.tr/apps//Files/Content/ad5f3ddb-5a11-410f-9e3c-fe8b2dc4df8b.pdf

Tursunbayeva, A., Di Lauro, S., & Pagliari, C. (2018). People analytics—A scoping review of conceptual boundaries and value propositions. *International Journal of Information Management*, *43*, 224–247. doi:10.1016/j.ijinfomgt.2018.08.002

Uludag, K. (2022). 'Coronary Blindness: Desensitization after excessive exposure to coronavirus-related information '. *Health Policy and Technology*.

United Nations. (2021). *Interagency report for second Global Sustainable Transport Conference*. UN. https://sdgs.un.org/publications/interagency-report-second-global-sustainable-transport-conference

Vahlen, F. V. (2016). *Work Rules!: Wie Google die Art und Weise, wie wir leben und arbeiten.* Verändert.

Valeonti, F., Bikakis, A., Terras, M., Speed, C., Hudson-Smith, A., & Chalkias, K. (2021). Crypto collectibles, museum funding and OpenGLAM: Challenges, opportunities and the potential of Non-Fungible Tokens (NFTs). *Applied Sciences (Basel, Switzerland)*, *11*(21), 9931. doi:10.3390/app11219931

Vergura, D. T., Luceri, B., & Zerbini, C. (2021). The Effect of Social EWOM on Consumers' Behaviour Patterns in the Fashion Sector. In *The Art of Digital Marketing for Fashion and Luxury Brands* (pp. 221–242). Springer International Publishing. doi:10.1007/978-3-030-70324-0_10

Vernaza, A., Armuelles, V. I., & Ruiz, I. (2012). Towards to an open and interoperable virtual learning enviroment using Metaverse at University of Panama. Paper presented at the *2012 Technologies Applied to Electronics Teaching (TAEE)*. IEEE. 10.1109/TAEE.2012.6235458

Vettehen, P. H., Wiltink, D., Huiskamp, M., Schaap, G., & Ketelaar, P. (2019). Taking the full view: How viewers respond to 360-degree video news. *Computers in Human Behavior*, *91*, 24–32. doi:10.1016/j.chb.2018.09.018

Vidal-Tomás, D. (2022). The New Crypto Niche: Nfts, Play-To-Earn, And Metaverse Tokens. *Finance Research Letters*, *47*, 102742. doi:10.1016/j.frl.2022.102742

Vilhelmson, B., & Thulin, E. (2016). Who and where are the flexible workers? Exploring the current diffusion of telework in Sweden. *New Technology, Work and Employment*, *31*(1), 77–96. doi:10.1111/ntwe.12060

Vlăduțescu, Ș., & Stănescu, G. C. (2023). Environmental Sustainability of Metaverse: Perspectives from Romanian Developers. *Sustainability (Basel)*, *15*(15), 11704. doi:10.3390/su151511704

Volchek, K., & Brysch, A. (2023, January). Metaverse and tourism: From a new niche to a transformation. In *ENTER22 e-Tourism Conference* (pp. 300–311). Springer Nature Switzerland. doi:10.1007/978-3-031-25752-0_32

Volles, B. K., Van Kerckhove, A., & Geuens, M. (2023). Triggering brand switching in online stores: The effectiveness of recommendations for private labels versus national brands. *Journal of Business Research*, *164*, 114020. doi:10.1016/j.jbusres.2023.114020

Wang, X., & Chang, B. (2020). The Impact of the Audience's Continuance Intention Towards the Vlog: Focusing on Intimacy, Media Synchronicity and Authenticity. *International Journal of Contents*, *16*(2), 65–77. doi:10.5392/IJOC.2020.16.2.065

Wang, Y., Su, Z., Zhang, N., Xing, R., Liu, D., Luan, T. H., & Shen, X. (2022). A survey on metaverse: Fundamentals, security, and privacy. *IEEE Communications Surveys and Tutorials*.

Wang, Y., Su, Z., Zhang, N., Xing, R., Liu, D., Luan, T. H., & Shen, X. (2023). A Survey on Metaverse: Fundamentals, Security, and Privacy. *IEEE Communications Surveys and Tutorials*, *25*(1), 319–352. doi:10.1109/COMST.2022.3202047

WEF. (2020, July). *Digital Transformation: Powering the Great Reset Switzerland*. Davos Forum. http://www3.weforum.org/docs/ _Great_Reset_2020.pdf.

Wei, W. (2023). A buzzword, a phase or the next chapter for the Internet? The status and possibilities of the metaverse for tourism. *Journal of Hospitality and Tourism Insights*. doi:10.1108/JHTI-11-2022-0568

Weiss, P. L., & Jessel, A. S. (1998). Virtual reality applications to work. *Work (Reading, Mass.)*, *11*(3), 277–293. doi:10.3233/WOR-1998-11305 PMID:24441599

Weking, J., Desouza, K. C., Fielt, E., & Kowalkiewicz, M. (2023). Metaverse-enabled entrepreneurship. *Journal of Business Venturing Insights*, *19*, e00375. doi:10.1016/j.jbvi.2023.e00375

Woldemichael, H. T. (2019). Emerging Cyber Security Threats in Organization. *International Journal of Scientific Research in Network Security and Communication*, *7*(6), 7–10.

Wu, C. H., Liu, C. Y., & Weng, T. S. (2023). Critical Factors and Trends in NFT Technology Innovations. *Sustainability (Basel)*, *15*(9), 7573. doi:10.3390/su15097573

Wu, D., Yang, Z., Zhang, P., Wang, R., Yang, B., & Ma, X. (2023). Virtual-Reality Inter-Promotion Technology for Metaverse: A Survey. *IEEE Internet of Things Journal*, *10*(18), 15788–15809. doi:10.1109/JIOT.2023.3265848

Wu, H.-K., Lee, S. W.-Y., Chang, H.-Y., & Liang, J.-C. (2013). Current status, opportunities and challenges of augmented reality in education. *Computers & Education*, *62*, 41–49. doi:10.1016/j.compedu.2012.10.024

Wu, M.-Y., & Pearce, P. L. (2016). Tourism Blogging Motivations. *Journal of Travel Research*, *55*(4), 537–549. doi:10.1177/0047287514553057

Xrtoday. (2021). Unpacking meta: where did the word Metaverse come from? *XR Today*. https://www.xrtoday.com/virtual-reality/unpacking-meta-where-did-the-word-metaverse-come-from/ (accessed 4 December 2023).

Xu, D., Chen, T., Pearce, J., Mohammadi, Z., & Pearce, P. L. (2021). Reaching audiences through travel vlogs: The perspective of involvement. *Tourism Management*, *86*, 104326. doi:10.1016/j.tourman.2021.104326

Xu, W., & Zhang, X. (2021). Online expression as Well-be(com)ing: A study of travel blogs on Nepal by Chinese female tourists. *Tourism Management*, *83*, 104224. doi:10.1016/j.tourman.2020.104224

Xu, X., Lu, Y., Vogel-Heuser, B., & Wang, L. (2021). Industry 4.0 and Industry 5.0—Inception, conception and perception. *Journal of Manufacturing Systems*, *61*, 530–535. doi:10.1016/j.jmsy.2021.10.006

Yaqoob, I., Salah, K., Jayaraman, R., & Omar, M. (2023). Metaverse applications in smart cities: Enabling technologies, opportunities, challenges, and future directions. *Internet of Things : Engineering Cyber Physical Human Systems*, *23*, 100884. doi:10.1016/j.iot.2023.100884

Yemenici, A. D. (2022). Entrepreneurship in the world of metaverse: Virtual or real? *Journal of Metaverse*, *2*(2), 71–82. doi:10.57019/jmv.1126135

Yilmaz, E. S. (2020). The Effects on Consumer Behavior of Hotel Related Comments on the TripAdvisor Website: An Istanbul Case. [AHTR]. *Advances in Hospitality and Tourism Research*, *8*(1), 1–29. doi:10.30519/ahtr.536303

YouTube. (2024a). *Life inside the Metaverse.* [Video]. Youtube. https://www.youtube.com/watch?v=ZptPoWfH2nA

YouTube. (2024b). *Ariva Wonderland Teaser #3.* [Video]. Youtube. https://www.youtube.com/watch?v=APa3Ka_3gTs

Zadeh, G., Sadegh, M., Chapuis, J.-M., & Lehu, J.-M. (2021). Tourism netnography: How travel bloggers influence destination image. *Tourism Recreation Research*, 1–17. doi:10.1080/02508281.2021.1911274

Zainurin, M. Z. L., Haji Masri, M., Besar, M. H. A., & Anshari, M. (2023). Towards an understanding of metaverse banking: A conceptual paper. *Journal of Financial Reporting and Accounting*, *21*(1), 178–190. doi:10.1108/JFRA-12-2021-0487

Zaniboni, S., Fraccaroli, F., Truxillo, D. M., Bertolino, M., & Bauer, T. N. (2011). Training valence, instrumentality, and expectancy scale (T-VIES-it) Factor structure and nomological network in an Italian sample. *Journal of Workplace Learning*, *23*(2), 133–151. doi:10.1108/13665621111108792

Zengin, Y., Naktiyok, S., Kaygın, E., Kavak, O., & Topçuoğlu, E. (2021). An investigation upon industry 4.0 and society 5.0 within the context of sustainable development goals. *Sustainability (Basel)*, *13*(5), 2682. doi:10.3390/su13052682

Zhang, S., Peng, M. Y. P., Peng, Y., Zhang, Y., Ren, G., & Chen, C. C. (2020). Expressive brand relationship, brand love, and brand loyalty for tablet pcs: Building a sustainable brand. *Frontiers in psychology, 11,* 231.

Zhang, G. Q., Zhang, G. Q., Yang, Q. F., Cheng, S. Q., & Zhou, T. (2008). Evolution Of The Internet And Its Cores. *New Journal of Physics*, *10*(12), 123027. doi:10.1088/1367-2630/10/12/123027

Zhang, L., Kuo, P.-J., & McCall, M. (2019). Microcelebrity: The Impact of Information Source, Hotel Type, and Misleading Photos on Consumers' Responses. *Cornell Hospitality Quarterly*, *60*(4), 285–297. doi:10.1177/1938965519851461

Zhou, J., Chen, F., Berry, A., Reed, M., Zhang, S., & Savage, S. (2020, December). A survey on ethical principles of AI and implementations. In *2020 IEEE Symposium Series on Computational Intelligence (SSCI)* (pp. 3010-3017). IEEE. 10.1109/SSCI47803.2020.9308437

Zhu, L., Lin, Y., & Cheng, M. (2020). Sentiment and guest satisfaction with peer-to-peer accommodation: When are online ratings more trustworthy? *International Journal of Hospitality Management*, *86*, 102369. doi:10.1016/j.ijhm.2019.102369

Zhumadilova, A. (2016). The impact of TV shows and video blogs on tourists' destination choice. *Tourism Today (Nicosia)*, *166*, 148–168.

About the Contributors

Manpreet Arora, a Senior Assistant Professor of Management at the Central University of Himachal Pradesh, Dharamshala, India, brings over twenty-two years of rich teaching experience. She holds academic accolades including a Ph.D. in International Trade, an M.Phil, a gold medalist and several other academic distinctions from Himachal Pradesh University, Shimla. Dr. Arora's diverse research interests encompass Accounting, Finance, Strategic Management, Entrepreneurship, Qualitative Research and Microfinance. She works on Mixed methods research. Noteworthy for guiding doctoral research and delving into Microfinance, Entrepreneurship, Behavioral Finance and Corporate reporting, she has presented at numerous seminars, delivering talks on various academic subjects across multiple universities and colleges. An accomplished academic, she has an impressive publication record, having authored over 30 papers in esteemed national and international journals listed in Scopus, WOS and Category journals, alongside contributing to Sixty book chapters in publications by reputed publishers like IGI, Emerald, Routledge, CABI, Springer Nature, AAP, Wiley and more. Her commitment to management research is evident through the editing of four edited books. Presently she is working in the area of Metaverse and is Editing books from renowned publishers like IGI and Emerald. Her impactful contributions showcase a multifaceted professional excelling in academia, research, and social advocacy.

***

Esra Anış is a PhD student of Tourism Management at Aydın Adnan Menderes University, Turkey. She completed her undergraduate education at Yaşar University, Department of Tourism Management (50% scholarship, 100% English language of instruction) in 2012. Between 2010 and 2022, she worked as a front desk receptionist, Spa receptionist, service member in the F&B department and both full time and part time cashier and team member in international fast food businesses. In 2021, she completed his master's degree in Aydın Adnan Menderes University, Institute of Social Sciences, Department of Tourism Management, by completing his thesis on " The Effect of Brand Personality on Purchasing Motivations (Motives) in Restaurant Businesses: An Application in Franchise Operation". She has been studying for a doctorate in the same university and department since 2021. Study Subjects: Food and Beverage and Hospitality Management, Franchising, Marketing, Brand Management, Consumer Behaviors, Experiences, Attitudes and Perceptions, Purchasing Behaviors and Motivations, Destination Promotion, Cittaslow, Destination Marketing, Virtual Reality (VR), Metaverse and Organizational Cynicism.

Hassan Badawy has more than twenty years of industry and academic experience in the field of tourism, He held a number of positions in different professional, and academic entities including the Egyptian Ministry of Tourism, the British University in Egypt (BUE), The Faculty of Tourism and Hotels at Luxor University in Egypt, and a number of internationally funded tourism development projects. Graduated with a Bachelor's degree in tourism guidance, he then got a master and Ph.D. degrees in tourism, and then he got a Master degree in cultural heritage management from Sorbonne University where he specialized in cultural tourism marketing. As an acknowledgment of his contribution and effort in academia and community development, he was awarded the Fulbright Scholarship in 2022 in tourism and Heritage studies. He also won different scholarships from different international organizations where he attended a number of tourism training programs. Invited as a keynote speaker at a number of international scientific Conferences and Seminars centered around different topics especially sustainable development, cultural heritage management, Entrepreneurship, and heritage Tourism Marketing. Worked as a consultant and trainer for a number of international development projects funded by international organizations including USAID, UNDP, and UNWFP where he was responsible for developing a number of work plans to enhance employability in the tourism sector, he was also responsible for identifying training needs, developing training materials, and the delivery of the training. Supervised and evaluated a number of scientific researches in areas and topics related to tourism marketing and sustainable development. Active in community services such as working as a voluntary Start-ups Mentor with German development cooperation (GIZ), he also delivered different training programs on women's empowerment.

Saurabh Bhattacharya is a Management graduate with an M.Com and an MBA from BIMTECH. He has spent over 15 years in the domain of Banking Technology. He is based out of Pune and is an Analyst at a Global Bank

Ülker Çolakoğlu is currently an Associate Professor in the Faculty of Tourism, University of Aydın Adnan Menderes, Aydın, Turkey. Her doctorate is in Tourism Management from the University of Dokuz Eylül, İzmir, Turkey. She completed her dissertation research on "Communication strategies between managers and employers in accommodation establishments." She focuses on the management in tourism businesses. She has many publications in her fields both national and international. She has been the thesis advisor of many students at master of science and doctoral levels.

Saumendra Das presently working as an Associate Professor at the School of Management Studies, GIET University, Gunupur, Odisha. He has more than 20 years of teaching, research, and industry experience. He has published more than 57 articles in national and international journals, conference proceedings, and book chapters. He also authored and edited six books. Dr Das has participated and presented many papers in seminars, conferences, and workshops in India and abroad. He has organized many FDPs and workshops in his career. He is an academician, author, and editor. He has also published two patents. He is an active member of various professional bodies such as ICA, ISTE and RFI. In the year 2023, he was awarded as the best teacher by Research Foundation India.

Vaishali Dhiman is an esteemed research scholar associated with HPKVBS, School of Commerce and Management Studies, Central University of Himachal Pradesh, India. Her research endeavors revolve around the domains of entrepreneurship, incubation, skill development, and tourism. With a keen interest in fostering innovation and economic growth, Vaishali delves into understanding the intricacies of entrepreneurial ecosystems, exploring strategies for effective incubation, and identifying avenues for skill enhancement in the context of emerging industries. Her profound insights and dedication to advancing knowledge in these fields position her as a valuable asset to the academic community, poised to contribute significantly to the promotion of entrepreneurship and sustainable tourism development in both regional and global contexts.

Siti Rahayu Hussin is working as a senior lecturer in the School of Business and Economics, Universiti Putra Malaysia, Malaysia. She completed her Masters of Business Administration (MBA) from Roosevelt University, Illinois, USA. She completed her Bachelor of Business Administration (BBA) from International Islamic University, Malaysia. Siti Rahayu Hussin has acted as the academic advisor and supervisor of several graduate and post-graduate students. She has served as a reviewer and editorial board member in several international journals. Siti Rahayu Hussin has published several research articles in many international journals and presented the findings of her research at various national and international conferences. Her area of research interest includes marketing, entrepreneurship, and tourism.

Tariqul Islam, a Ph.D. candidate in Hospitality and Tourism at Taylor's University, Malaysia. He holds a Master of Science (by research) in Tourism from Universiti Putra Malaysia, Malaysia. He graduated with distinction in Airlines, Tourism, and Hospitality from Lovely Professional University, India. Tariqul has published several research articles in ABDC- listed and Scopus-indexed journals and presented the findings of his research at various national and international conferences. His area of research includes consumer behaviour and technology adoption.

Asik Rahaman Jamader is working as an Assistant Professor in the department of Hospitality & Hotel Administration at Pailan College of Management & Technology, Kolkata, India, also he is the Corporate Advisory Board Member of the Smart Journal of Business Management Studies indexed by Emerging Sources Citation Index (ESCI) - Web of Science (Clarivate Analytics) with 5.748 Impact factor. His research interest is in Hospitality and innovative Technique implemented in Hospitality Industry. He is a scientist by having 23 numbers of International granted patents & 12 numbers of registered and published national & International patents also have a good number of authored Book/Book Chapters publications, including some SCOPUS/SCIE/ESCI/WOS publications. Recently he joined as an Ad Hoc reviewer of the International Journal of Business Intelligence Research (IJBIR), IGI Global publishing indexed by WOS and Scopus.

Manjit Kour is a PhD in management from Punjab Technical University. Presently she is working as Professor in University school of management, Chandigarh University, Punjab. Her specialization is finance and marketing. Her areas of research interests include Business Ethics, Online marketing, Metaverse, Corporate finance and Fintech. She has authored two books and have published 43 research papers in quality journals including Web of Science, ABDC, Scopus, UGC care list. She has presented numerous research papers in various national and international conferences. She is innovation ambassador with Ministry of Education, India and has delivered more than 30 expert talks in various seminars and workshops, she is on editorial board of Journal of Commerce and Accounting (ABDC indexed journal). She is active reviewer in various web of Science and Scopus indexed journals as well.

Kritika is a post graduate (Master of Technology(M.Tech)) in computer science and engineering and awarded with Young Researcher Award 2023 and holds accolades from Government of India for obtaining distinction during high school and senior school. The author is serving as Lifetime Member of International Association of Engineers(IAENG), Member of Women In Cybersecurity(WiCys) India Affiliate and also holds the position of an independent researcher and peer reviewer of reputed journals indexed in SCOPUS, Web of Science, Elsevier. The author has obtained certifications in cyber security and a Gold Medal recipient in International Olympiad of Mathematics and top scorer in examinations like NTSE(India). The areas of research include cybersecurity, digital forensics, neuroscience, and e-governance.

Praveen Kumar, Assistant Professor at the University School of Business in Chandigarh University, with 5.5 years of experience in teaching and Research. He has cleared the Junior Research Fellowship (UGC-JRF) which is conducted by University Grant Commission (UGC). He has awarded his Ph.D. in Management with the research topic "Consumers Perception and Purchase Intention towards Organic Food Products". He has attended many international and national conferences, workshops, seminars, and faculty development programs. He has published many Scopus-indexed research papers and book chapters in reputed Journals in the field of Marketing, Finance, and Human Resource Management. He has also written many book chapters in different areas of Management and published national and International Patents in various fields. He has practical experience and knowledge of Statistical software viz. SPSS, AMOS- SEM, PLS. He has been invited as a keynote speaker in various workshops, and seminars related to Research methodology at different colleges and Universities.

Sridhar Manohar currently working In Doctoral Research Center, Chitkara University, completed his doctorate in the area of Services Marketing from VIT Business School, VIT University. He has a Bachelor of Technology and Dual Masters in Business Administration and Organization Psychology. Dr. Sridhar further certified with FDP at IIM-A. He is expertise in Service Marketing, Innovation and Entrepreneurship, Scale Development Process and Multivariate Analytics and interests in teaching Business Analytics, Innovation and Entrepreneurship, Research Methodology and Marketing Management. He has published around 20 research papers that includes Scopus listed and ABDC ranked International Journals like – Society and Business Review, Benchmarking-An International Journal, Electronics Market, Corporate Reputation Review, International Journal of Services and Operations Management, International journal of Business Excellence and presented papers and ideas in numerous international conferences.

Tapaswini Panda is presently working as Guest Faculty at Model Degree College, Rayagada, Odisha. She has completed Master of Business Administration from GIET University, Gunupur, India. Her research interest is on Work Life Balance, Quality of Work Life and Human Resource Information System. She has published three patents in India and abroad. She is a passionate researcher and a true academician teaches the subject such as Principles of Management, Human Resource Management, Organizational Development and Change. She has published one paper in National Journal and two book chapters.

Udaya Sankar Patro is presently working as a Lecturer at Rayagada Autonomous College, Rayagada, Odisha. He has completed a Master of Business Administration from GIET University, Gunupur, India. His research interest is on Workplace Spirituality, Work life Integrity and Human Resource Management. He has published three patents in India and abroad. He is a passionate researcher and a true academician who teaches the subjects such as Management and Theory Practices, Managerial Economics, and Human Resource Management. He has published one paper in National Journal and two book chapters.

Kavita Rani is a PhD in Human Resources management. She is working as Associate Professor at University School of Business, Chandigarh University. her research interests are Metaverse, HR analytics and Marketing Analytics.

Soni Rathi is presently a Research scholar at the University School of Business in Chandigarh University, Punjab. Her current research interests include work life balance, job stress, work life conflict, job satisfaction, HR Analytics, Metaverse, human resource management, employees' creativity and generational differences. She has attended many international and national conferences, workshops, and faculty development programs. She has many Scopus-indexed and Web of Science research papers and a Scopus-indexed book chapter published in reputed Journals in the field of Business management and Human Resource Management. She has also reviewed many research papers & book chapters in different areas of Management. She has practical experience and knowledge of Statistical software viz. Smart PLS 3 & 4, SPSS v.25, Vos viewer.

Sunena Rathore is a dedicated research scholar affiliated with HPKVBS, School of Commerce and Management Studies, Central University of Himachal Pradesh, India. Her research interests lie at the intersection of corporate reporting, sustainability reporting, and general management. With a passion for advancing knowledge in these areas, Sunena focuses on exploring the dynamics of corporate disclosure practices, examining their impact on organizational performance and stakeholder relations. Her commitment to academic excellence and her innovative approach to research make her a valuable contributor to the scholarly community, with the potential to drive positive change in both academia and industry.

Nayan Deep S Kanwal is an experienced senior Executive Editor, Editor-in-Chief, Author, Reviewer and a Professor, with a demonstrated history of working in the publishing industry. Skilled in Academic Publishing, Publications, Creative Writing, and Text Editing. Strong media and communication professional with substantial experience in Communications, Media, Print Design with a strong scholarly journal publishing background. He has written on a wide range of subjects beyond his area of study, agriculture. He has published articles in different publications as well as book chapters in his long academic and professional career. He has also authored and co-authored several research and development books. The subjects he has written on range from management and administration of research to information technology. Nayan is described as a man with conviction and commitment, responsible for the education of countless postgraduate students from all over the world. He is a brilliant and intelligent communicator who has devoted himself for the promotion of academic publications not only for Malaysia, but also for the developing world and for the entire humanity. There must be some method to his madness that single-handed he has created this mammoth publishing impact. He is full of surprises and his level of energy is very high and contagious". Professor Nayan Kanwal has authored and co-authored numerous academic books and journals, served as a reviewer to many SCOPUS-indexed journals. He has also served as an external examiner/ evaluator for PHD thesis with several universities around the globe. He has delivered countless lecturers, invited by universities in Malaysia, Thailand and Indonesia; attended copious Seminars/Workshops/Courses and has been invited as a Special Guest at more than a hundred Plenary/ Keynote/ Invited Talks. In addition, he has also been involved in research consultancies in Indonesia, Thailand, Vietnam and Malaysia. He is a Fellow of the Royal Society of Arts (FRSA), United Kingdom, a Life Member of the British Institute of Management (BIM), United Kingdom, an Associate Member of the Marketing Institute of Singapore (AMIS) and an Associate Member of the Australian Institute of Agricultural Science and Technology (AIAST).

Saibabu Neyyila is an Assistant Professor Department of Management Studies at Aditya Institute of Technology and Management, Tekkali, Andhra Pradesh. He holds a post-graduate degree in M. Com, MBA from Andhra University, PGDIM from Pondicherry University and PhD from Acharya Nagarjuna University, Andhra Pradesh. He has published more than 12 articles in reputed national and international journals. He has participated and presented many papers in national and international conferences. He has taught post-graduate and undergraduate subjects such as Accounting, Finance, Economics and Marketing. Additionally, he had qualified the Andhra Pradesh State Eligibility Test (APSET) in the both disciplines of Management and Commerce.

Babita Singla is a professor at Chitkara Business School, Chitkara University, Punjab, India. She has a Ph.D. in management and is UGC-NET qualified. She has over 13 years of experience in teaching, research, and administration. Her areas of expertise are marketing, e-commerce, omnichannel, and retail. In her career, she has been involved in important academic and research assignments such as being the guest editor of reputed journal, organizing and conducting international and national-level conferences, faculty development programs, and providing guidance for research projects along the way. She has research publications in reputable international and national journals such as Scopus, SCI, etc., and has presented research papers at various national and international conferences. In the short span of 13 years of her career in academia and administration, she has authored and edited several books on retailing, supply chain management, branding, customer relationship management, and product management, covering the course content of various universities across the nation. She has successfully delivered guest sessions at international and national universities

Muhammad Usman Tariq has more than 16+ year's experience in industry and academia. He has been working as a consultant and trainer for industries representing six sigma, quality, health and safety, environmental systems, project management, and information security standards. His work has encompassed sectors in aviation, manufacturing, food, hospitality, education, finance, research, software and transportation. He has diverse and significant experience working with accreditation agencies of ABET, ACBSP, AACSB, WASC, CAA, EFQM and NCEAC. Additionally, Dr. Tariq has operational experience in incubators, research labs, government research projects, private sector startups, program creation and management at various industrial and academic levels. He is Certified Higher Education Teacher from Harvard University, USA, Certified Online Educator from HMBSU, Certified Six Sigma Master Black Belt, Lead Auditor ISO 9001 Certified, ISO 14001, IOSH MS, OSHA 30, and OSHA 48. He is member of Harvard Business Review Advisory Council.

Kadir Uludag, Ph.D., is an accomplished researcher in the field of Applied Psychology, with expertise in areas such as schizophrenia research, drug addiction, machine learning, and educational psychology. He completed his Ph.D. at the Chinese Academy of Sciences and is currently engaged in a postdoctoral research position at Shanghai Jiao Tong University. In addition to his academic pursuits, Kadir is actively involved in knowledge dissemination and community engagement through his website (ifx0.com/), where he facilitates the sharing and discussion of peer-reviewed articles.

Wong Foong Yee is working as a senior lecturer in the School of Business and Economics, Universiti Putra Malaysia, Malaysia. She completed her Masters of Business Administration (MBA) from Universiti Putra Malaysia, Malaysia. Her research interests are marketing, business management, hospitality and tourism. Ms. Wong has acted as the supervisor of several undergraduate and post-graduate students. She has served as a reviewer in several international and local journals. Ms. Wong is also the project leader in numerous government-funded projects. Ms. Wong has published her research articles, as well as case studies in many international journals, and presented the findings of her research at various national and international conferences. Ms. Wong also published books in local publisher and international publishers.

Index

 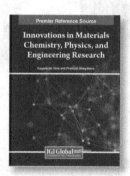 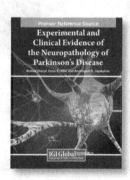 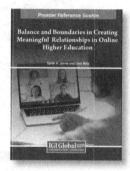

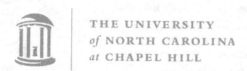